AF806580

Studies in National Governance and Emerging Technologies

Series Editors
Edward Abbott-Halpin, Leeds Beckett University, Leeds, UK
Carolina Aguerre, Victoria, Argentina
Alberto Asquer, School of Finance, University of London, SOAS, London, UK
Malcolm Campbell-Verduyn, International Relations, University of Groningen, Groningen, The Netherlands
Maria João Maia, Institute for Technology Assessment, Karlsruhe Institute of Technology, Karlsruhe, Germany

From genome editing to deep learning, and from blockchain to quantum computing, the rise of emerging technologies poses a number of opportunities, threats and risks to society. Emerging technologies provide affordances to innovative products and services that can potentially revolutionize fields like medicine, transport and finance. They may also result, however, in unwelcome side-effects, unintended consequences and deliberate harms to particular groups and individuals, as well as entire systems and the environment. Questions about whether emerging technologies should be regulated at the national level, and how precisely governments should encourage and respond to them, are controversial. Precautionary approaches may discourage investment and make countries lose ground with respect to other economies. Permissive regimes may put consumers and natural environments at risk. Governments, business firms and the civil society are expected to play a role in (re-)designing how emerging technologies will be regulated, re-regulated and steered.

This series invites contributions on the intersection between technological development and the processes of promoting, steering and regulating the development and applications of emerging technologies. Books will address theoretical issues, such as what drives the development of new technologies, how new technologies reconfigure governance systems, and the effects of new technologies on democracy, accountability, efficiency, economic growth, justice, power, legitimacy, sustainability and inclusion. Empirically, the series welcomes contributions that address any area of emerging technologies, including Artificial Intelligence, control of sensor networks and Internet-of-Things, robotics, cryptocurrencies, renewable energy sources, nano-technologies, genetic therapies, smart cities, and the significance of space and technology to future development.

Tafsir Matin Johansson ·
Jonatan Echebarria Fernández ·
Dimitrios Dalaklis · Aspasia Pastra ·
Jon A. Skinner
Editors

Autonomous Vessels in Maritime Affairs

Law and Governance Implications

palgrave
macmillan

Editors
Tafsir Matin Johansson
World Maritime University-Sasakawa
Global Ocean Institute
Malmö, Sweden

Jonatan Echebarria Fernández
The City Law School, City
University of London
London, UK

Dimitrios Dalaklis
World Maritime University
Malmö, Sweden

Aspasia Pastra
World Maritime University-Sasakawa
Global Ocean Institute
Malmö, Sweden

Jon A. Skinner
MatSu College
University of Alaska Anchorage
Palmer, AK, USA

Global College of PME
Air University
Montgomery, Alabama, USA

ISSN 2524-6291 ISSN 2524-6305 (electronic)
Studies in National Governance and Emerging Technologies
ISBN 978-3-031-24739-2 ISBN 978-3-031-24740-8 (eBook)
https://doi.org/10.1007/978-3-031-24740-8

© The Editor(s) (if applicable) and The Author(s), under exclusive license to Springer Nature Switzerland AG 2023
Chapter 11 and Chapter 18 are licensed under the terms of the Creative Commons Attribution 4.0 International License (http://creativecommons.org/licenses/by/4.0/). For further details see license information in the chapters.
This work is subject to copyright. All rights are solely and exclusively licensed by the Publisher, whether the whole or part of the material is concerned, specifically the rights of translation, reprinting, reuse of illustrations, recitation, broadcasting, reproduction on microfilms or in any other physical way, and transmission or information storage and retrieval, electronic adaptation, computer software, or by similar or dissimilar methodology now known or hereafter developed.
The use of general descriptive names, registered names, trademarks, service marks, etc. in this publication does not imply, even in the absence of a specific statement, that such names are exempt from the relevant protective laws and regulations and therefore free for general use.
The publisher, the authors, and the editors are safe to assume that the advice and information in this book are believed to be true and accurate at the date of publication. Neither the publisher nor the authors or the editors give a warranty, expressed or implied, with respect to the material contained herein or for any errors or omissions that may have been made. The publisher remains neutral with regard to jurisdictional claims in published maps and institutional affiliations.

Cover credit: arild lillebø/Alamy Stock Photo

This Palgrave Macmillan imprint is published by the registered company Springer Nature Switzerland AG
The registered company address is: Gewerbestrasse 11, 6330 Cham, Switzerland

Acknowledgments

The editors of this volume acknowledge the contributions of many individuals and organizations. First and foremost, the editors owe an extraordinary debt to all the authors and co-authors that have published in this peer-reviewed volume. A warm note of thanks to Mitchell Lennan, Lecturer (Assistant Professor) in Energy & Environment Law at the University of Aberdeen, Scotland, for providing additional editorial assistance. The co-editors are extremely indebted to external reviewers: Paul Myburgh, Associate Professor and Deputy Director, Centre for Maritime Law, Faculty of Law, National University of Singapore; Jos Leijten, Retired Innovation Strategist, previously in Joint Institute for innovation Policy (Brussels) and TNO (Netherlands); Chang Hee Lee, Professor, College of Maritime Science, Korea Maritime & Ocean University; Tae-eun Kim; Associate Professor of Maritime Safety Management, Department of Technology and Safety, Faculty of Science and Technology, University of Tromsø (UiT)—The Arctic University of Norway; and Kivilcim Ceren Buken; PhD Candidate, Hacettepe University, as well as others that were a part of the blinded review. A special thanks to our contributors Matti Eronen, Mikis Tsimplis, and Vibe Ulfbeck, and external contributors Yoss LeClerc; President and CEO, Logistro Consulting International, Vancouver BC; Former President, International Harbour Masters Association, London UK; and Mikael Hilden, owner of AMH Maritime Consultancy for playing an important role in the triple peer-review process.

The editors would also like to extend sincere appreciation to the Nippon Foundation, the World Maritime University and the World Maritime University-Sasakawa Global Ocean Institute, the City Law School, and the University of Alaska for their generous support.

Sweden
November 2022

Tafsir Matin Johansson
Jonatan Echebarria Fernández
Dimitrios Dalaklis
Aspasia Pastra
Jon A. Skinner

Contents

Notes on Contributors

Vera Alexandropoulou has worked for the Harvard Business School, FHM—a major shipping law firm in New York, and Norton Rose, was legal counsel at the Piraeus Port Authority (2005–2018) and is Vice President of Thalassa Foundation since 2013. She established the Alexandropoulou Law Firm in 2005. Vera has acquired significant experience in sectors including commercial and corporate law, shipping, energy, banking and finance, and real estate. She is involved as legal consultant with various institutions and associations, mainly in the field of energy business and fund structures, and is the author of codification of Greek renewable energy and natural gas legislation, having published articles on Greek ship finance, Greek listed funds, environmental issues, sustainable shipping, and ports. Being a member of the BUGWRIGHT2 Senior Advisory Group for WMU-GOI H2020 Project, she has co-authored the article on "Maritime remote inspection technology in hull survey & inspection: A synopsis of liability issues from a European Union context", *Journal of International Maritime Safety, Environmental Affairs, and Shipping* Volume 5, 2021, Issue 4. She speaks fluently English, French, German, and Spanish, while she understands Chinese.

Aslı Arda is a Postdoctoral Researcher at the University of Copenhagen, Faculty of Law, Center for Private Governance (CEPRI) and a qualified lawyer admitted to Bar of Ankara, Turkey. Aslı holds a Ph.D. in Law from the University of Exeter, UK. She has a background in contract law, shipping, reinsurance, and arbitration. Her current research mainly concerns the liability and management aspects of the implementation of remotely controlled and autonomous ships and she is particularly interested in digitalization in shipping and green shipping. She is also a member of the Shipping and Ocean Law Group (SHOC) at the University of Copenhagen.

Annie Brett is an Assistant Professor of Law at the University of Florida Levin College of Law, where she teaches and writes in the areas of environmental law, ocean and coastal law, and the intersection of law and science. Her scholarship focuses on how emerging technologies are impacting environmental and maritime law. In addition to legal venues, Professor Brett has published in leading scientific outlets, presented in national and international policy forums, and served on several US National Academy of Sciences, Engineering and Medicine committees dealing with issues around maritime law and emerging technologies. Prior to joining the University of Florida, Annie worked on international ocean policy for Stanford University and the World Economic Forum. She is an accomplished mariner, spending years as a sailing vessel captain in the Pacific and continues to participate in scientific and legal expeditions globally.

Dimitrios Dalaklis joined the World Maritime University (WMU) in 2014, upon completion of a twenty-six years distinguished career with the Hellenic Navy, and currently holds a Professorial position. His expertise revolves around the interrelated maritime safety and security domains. He is an Associate Fellow of the Nautical Institute (NI) and a Member of the International Association of Maritime Economists (IAME). With a Bachelor's from the Hellenic Naval Academy, his postgraduate studies took place in the Naval Postgraduate School of the United States (M.Sc. in Information Technology Management, with distinction & M.Sc. in Defense Analysis). He then conducted his Ph.D. research at the University of the Aegean, Department of Shipping, Trade and Transport. He is the author/co-author of many peer-reviewed articles, books, and studies in both the Greek and English languages, with a strong research focus on issues related to the implementation of the SOLAS Convention and especially electronic equipment/systems supporting the safety of navigation.

Jonatan Echebarria Fernández is an Honorary Lecturer at The City Law School (City, University of London) and a Spanish qualified lawyer. He holds a Ph.D. in Law from the Copenhagen Business School (CBS) and he is a member of a variety of associations related to his main teaching and research interests, spanning from Maritime & Commercial Law to Public & Private International Law, as well as Environmental Law. Dr. Echebarria has served as an Associate Professor of Law in 2021 and 2022 at BI Norwegian Business School. His previous professional experience includes working at Copenhagen Business School, the Permanent Representation of Spain to the EU, the European Investment Bank, the Spanish Embassy in Brussels, the Luxembourg Maritime Administration, and the Bilbao Port Authority.

Mr. Matti K. Eronen has an LL.M. degree in maritime law from the Turku University in 1988. He also has run Oslo University Nordic Maritime Institute in 1986. He did court training in 1990–1991 and Helsinki University EU-expert training in 1994. He published research on EU Market Protection Mechanisms at Finnish Lawyers' Association, 1994. He did national expert professional training (NEPT) at EMSA in 2012. Since 2015 he has been a Turku University post graduate doctoral student on subject "VTS liability issues". He is specialized to transport and maritime legislation and has in-depth experience in handling international administrative matters for more than 30 years. His employment history includes working at private shipping companies as forwarding agent, P&I- and H&M insurance specialist, and maritime lawyer. Since 1989 he has worked at the administration, Finnish Maritime Administration as Secretary for international affairs, Deputy director and Chief of legal department. Since 2010 he has worked as legal counsel at the Finnish Transport Infrastructure Agency. He has represented Finland at committees and subcommittees of IMO since 1989. He regularly represents Finland at the Legal Advisory Panel (LaP) of IALA.

Johanna Hjalmarsson is the Informa Associate Professor in Maritime and Commercial Law at the University of Southampton and a member of the Institute of Maritime Law. She is an editor of *Lloyd's Law Reports* and *Lloyd's Law Reporter*. She also co-edits *Lloyd's Shipping & Trade Law* and *The Ratification of Maritime Conventions*. Johanna's research covers maritime and commercial law, insurance law, and dispute resolution with recent publications in *Lloyd's Maritime and Commercial Law Quarterly*, *Journal of International Maritime Law*, and *Civil Justice Quarterly* and has edited and contributed to a number of books. At Southampton, she teaches shipping and insurance-related subjects.

Even Ambros Holte is currently working as a Research Scientist for the research institute SINTEF Ocean. Holding a Master's degree in Logistics Management from the University of Sydney (Institute of Transport Studies), he has been performing research, development, and research-based advisory services within the marine and maritime sectors since 2006. With a particular interest for developing sustainable transport solutions and innovative practices for the maritime industry, he has been heavily engaged in the development of autonomous transport solutions for the past 3–4 years. He has also been involved in several reports focusing on industry analysis. Living in Trondheim, Norway, Even has considerable experience as a project manager, and has authored and co-authored several publications.

Tafsir Matin Johansson is an Assistant Professor at the World Maritime University-Sasakawa Global Ocean Institute (GOI) in Malmö, Sweden. Tafsir is a techno-policy analyst with a Ph.D. in Maritime Affairs from the World Maritime University, and an LL.M. in Maritime Law from the University of Lund, Sweden. His duties at the GOI include ocean governance and policy research, teaching, and developing innovative policy models to better assess drivers and indicators relevant to ocean research agenda. Tafsir has published extensively on maritime and ocean issues including techno-regulatory dynamic governance, Arctic governance, vessels of concern, corporate social responsibility, marine pollution, climate change, conflict management and trust ecosystem, and Brexit and fisheries. Tafsir has worked on or led a number of multidisciplinary projects, including regulatory development projects funded by Transport Canada (Government of Canada) since 2014, as well as those funded under the Canadian Government's Oceans Protection Plan covering numerous topics critical to the maritime and ocean domain. Currently Tafsir serves as a CO-PI in a European Union Horizon 2020 Programme funded project titled "Overcoming Regulatory Barriers for Service Robotics in an Ocean Industry Context".

Stig O. Johnsen is a Senior Researcher at SINTEF in Norway. He has a Ph.D. from NTNU in Norway with a focus on resilience in complex socio-technical systems and has a Master's in Technology Management from MIT/NTNU. He is chairing the Human Factors in Control network (HFC) in Norway to strengthen the Human Factors focus during development and implementation of safety critical technology. His research interest has been meaningful human control to support safety and resilience during automation and digitalization. Chair of Accident and Incident Modelling—European Safety and Reliability Association (ESRA).

Maria Katsivela joined the common law program in French at the University of Ottawa in 2010. She is currently teaching maritime law (in French and English) and common law torts-civil law extra-contractual liability at the Programme de Droit Canadien (bijural program) of the University of Ottawa. Her research lies in the areas of transportation law (Ph.D. thesis topic), comparative maritime law, and comparative tort law. Pr. Katsivela has published articles in comparative tort law and comparative maritime law. She is currently working on regulatory and ethical issues present with respect to unmanned vessels. Throughout the years she has received different grants to support her research interests and publications. Pr. Katsivela worked as an attorney in New York for three years before pursuing an academic career. She is a member of the bars of New York, Greece (Piraeus), and Ontario (Canada). Before joining the University of Ottawa Pr. Katsivela taught at the College of the Bahamas Department of Law in Nassau (Bahamas) for four years.

Klimanthia Kontaxaki is a lawyer, a graduate of the Faculty of Law at the University of Athens. Having a particular interest in the fields of the Law of the Sea and International Shipping Law, she is a holder of an LL.M. degree in International Public Law from the University of Athens with thesis on Maritime Spatial Planning and an LL.M. degree in International Shipping Law from the Queen Mary University of London with a thesis on Marine Insurance Law, under a scholarship awarded by the Centre of Commercial Law Studies (CCLS) at Queen Mary University of London. She also holds a Certificate in "Ocean Management and Maritime Law" from the Tulane University, New Orleans, USA, having successfully attended the latter's summer courses program under a full scholarship awarded by the Aegean Institute of the Law of the Sea & Maritime Law. Her legal practice mainly engages in shipping, contract, business, and corporate law. She has contributed as co-author in published articles and book chapters mainly related to the environmental sustainability issue in shipping and ports, with most relevant to the theme of the present book the article on "Maritime remote inspection technology in hull survey & inspection: A synopsis of liability issues from a European Union context", *Journal of International Maritime Safety, Environmental*

Affairs, and Shipping Volume 5, 2021—Issue 4. She speaks fluently English, German, Spanish, French, and elementary Italian.

Proshanto Kumar Mukherjee is Professor of Law and Foreign Expert at Dalian Maritime University and Emeritus Professor of Maritime Law and Policy at World Maritime University (WMU). He was previously Vice President (Research) and Director, Doctoral Programmes at WMU; Director of LL.M. and Ph.D. Programmes in Maritime Law, Lund University; IMO Legal Adviser for the Caribbean Region; Senior Adviser, Maritime Policy and International Affairs, Canadian Hydrographic Service, Senior Deputy Director and Professor of Maritime Law, IMO International Maritime Law Institute, Malta. He is a member of the Canadian Maritime Law Association and the CMI Working Group on Fair Treatment of Seafarers. He is author of *Maritime Legislation* and *Mukherjee on Maritime Legislation*, lead author of *Farthing on International Shipping*, Fourth Edition, Lead Editor of *Maritime Law in Motion*, and Editor of *Maritime Law Perspectives Old and New* Volume I (under publication). He has numerous other publications to his credit on virtually every aspect of maritime affairs and maritime law.

Thor Myklebust is a Senior Researcher at SINTEF Digital, Norway (Cand. Scient. Physics and). He attended a two and a half years course at university level in Economy, Innovation, Psychology, Statistics, and Artificial intelligence. He has experience in certification of products and systems since 1987. Myklebust has participated in several international committees since 1988. Member of safety (IEC 65), IEC 61508 committee, and railway (CENELEC/TC 9). He was Vice-chairman and Chairman of NB-rail October 2013–October 2015. Myklebust is involved in large industry-oriented research and development projects addressing the implementation and effect of agile methods for developing safety systems that will undergo certification according to functional safety standards (IEC61508, EN5012X, ISO 26262, UL4600) and relevant security standards (IEC 62443, ISO/SAE 21434, ETSI 303 645, EN TS 50701). He is co-founder of SafeScrum. In addition, he has co-authored three Springer books.

Dag Atle Nesheim is a Research Scientist at SINTEF Ocean, Norway. He received a Master's degree in Information Systems from the University of Agder in 2003. Prior to joining SINTEF Ocean, Dag Atle worked as a business analyst at LogIT Systems, focusing on implementation of software solutions related to multimodal transport chain management. At SINTEF Ocean, Dag Atle works within a wide field of research related to HSEQ performance management, standardization, cyber security and in the later years, maritime digitalization and autonomous shipping. Dag Atle's latest publications include "Validation methodology for assessment of new eNav services"; "The Need for Collaborative Business Models in Autonomous Vessel Ecosystems"; "Autonomous ship concept evaluation—Quantification of competitiveness and societal impact"; and "Assessing cyber threats for storyless systems". Dag Atle has been a member of the Baltic and International Maritime Council's Shipping KPI Expert Group since 2015.

Anil Ozturk is a recent Ph.D. graduate at Maynooth University School of Law and Criminology. He has completed his undergraduate education in law at Bilkent University (Turkey), graduating with a B.A. in 2016, where his interests stemmed from the evolving nature of legal theory. Then, Anil has received an LL.M. degree in International and Comparative Law from Trinity College Dublin in 2017. His Master's thesis explored how pre-contractual liability is conceptualized in different legal systems and how it is addressed under European Private International Law. His current research focuses on intersection of law and robotics, including autonomous driving, robotics and privacy, and liability for personal robots.

Aspasia Pastra has been appointed as a Post-Doc Fellow and Maritime Policy Analyst at the World Maritime University-Sasakawa Global Ocean Institute (GOI) in Malmö, Sweden. To date, she has been involved in a number of State-of-the-Art Regulatory Projects in maritime policy, ocean technology, environmental protection, port governance, and gender diversity in the maritime sector. Dr. Pastra has published extensively in the field of maritime policy and governance, maritime robotics & techno-regulatory advancements, global environmental change, team dynamics, and leadership. She has been a lecturer in UK institutions in the field of business and maritime administration. She has extensive experience in shipping as she worked for many years in large shipping companies. She has also participated in the Marine Environment Protection Committee (MEPC) and Maritime Safety Committee (MSC) of the International Maritime Organisation (IMO), as a member of the Greek Delegation. Dr. Pastra holds a BSc degree in Public Administration from Panteion University of Social and Political Sciences in Greece, an M.B.A. from Cardiff

University in the UK, and an M.Sc. in Maritime Administration from the World Maritime University. She was awarded her Ph.D. in the area of corporate governance from Brunel University in London.

Raul Pedrozo (Captain, USN, Ret.) is the Howard S. Levie Professor on the Law of Armed Conflict, US Naval War College, Stockton Center for International Law. Prior to his retirement from active duty after 34 years of service, he served in numerous positions advising senior military and civilian Defense officials, including as Special Assistant to the Under Secretary of Defense for Policy and senior legal advisor to Commander, US Pacific Command. He also served as the Director of the Navy's International and Operational Law Department in the Pentagon. Professor Pedrozo has lectured extensively at military and civilian academic institutions, has written extensively on maritime security, naval warfare, and South China Sea issues, and has authored three books. He has an LL.M. (International & Comparative Law), Georgetown University Law Center and JD (Law), The Ohio State University College of Law.

Anna Petrig holds the Chair of International Law and Public Law at the University of Basel in Switzerland. She has a Ph.D. in the field of the law of the sea and human rights law and an LL.M. from Harvard Law School. Anna is a member of the Bar of the Canton of Berne (Switzerland) and the New York State Bar (USA). Her broad legal experience includes work in private practice, the courts, and the Legal Division of the International Committee of the Red Cross (ICRC). She has provided expert advice and legal counsel on maritime-related matters to the Swiss Government, NGOs, and international organizations and is involved in the International Maritime Organization's efforts to regulate autonomous ships. Anna has served as Judge ad hoc for Switzerland on the International Tribunal for the Law of the Sea in Cases 27 and 29.

Andrei Polejack (he/his) is a senior advisor for the Brazilian Ministry of Science, Technology and Innovation, with a Ph.D. in Maritime Affairs from the WMU-Sasakawa Global Ocean Institute of the World Maritime University. In Brazil, he used to coordinate the national ocean and polar research programs, providing technical advice to governance, formulating and implementing public policies, and negotiating international agreements, among many other duties. As a transdisciplinary researcher, Andrei is interested in Ocean Science Diplomacy as a field of study, seeking to understand the role of science and scientists in international ocean affairs, along with the political sphere of power dynamics and interests in the marine realm. Theoretically passionate about post- and de-colonial reasoning applied to international relations and its many ways of linking with ocean science. A Latino soul, proud father of three of the best humans, and a lover of dogs, cats, sea puffins, beer, and fikas.

Sean T. Pribyl, Esq. is a business attorney in Holland & Knight's Washington, DC, office. He focuses his practice on regulatory compliance, marine casualties, international trade, autonomous transportation, sanctions, and white collar criminal law. He has decades of experience in the transportation sector as a former deck officer, US Coast Guard lawyer, and international protection and indemnity (P&I) club lawyer. Mr. Pribyl is a Member of the National Academy of Sciences Marine Board and serves as a Senior Advisor to the World Maritime University Overcoming Regulatory Barriers for Service Robotics in an Ocean Industry Context (BUGWRIGHT2). He is a Proctor in Admiralty with the US Maritime Law Association. Mr. Pribyl holds an M.A. from the US Naval War College, a JD from Washburn University School of Law, and a BS from the US Merchant Marine Academy. He is pursuing his LL.M. in International Business and Economic Law from Georgetown Law.

Marilia Ramos is a Research Scientist at the B. John Garrick Institute for the Risk Sciences at the University of California Los Angeles (GIRS-UCLA), where she manages and conducts research projects on complex systems modeling, risk assessment, and human reliability. Before her current position, she was a Post-Doctoral Research Fellow at the Norwegian University of Science and Technology (NTNU), Norway, where she conducted research on autonomous vessels risk assessment and human-system interaction modeling. She holds a Ph.D. (2017) in Chemical Engineering from the Federal University of Pernambuco (UFPE), Brazil. Her research interests lie in risk assessment and human-system interaction on highly automated and autonomous systems.

Agathe Rialland is a Researcher from SINTEF Ocean, department of Energy and Transport. Graduated from EM Lyon Business School, France (2002) and BI Norwegian Business School, Norway (2006), she has 15 years of experience in applied research for the maritime industry, dedicated to energy efficiency and emission reductions from ships and shipping operations. Her work includes techno-economic feasibility studies, development of decision-support systems, and contribution to policy development. She has co-authored several publications on measures and pathways towards shipping decarbonization in a.o. Transportation Research Part D, Ocean Engineering, SNAME Maritime Convention.

Ørnulf Jan Rødseth has an M.Sc. in cybernetics and electronic engineering from the Norwegian Institute of Technology (now NTNU) in 1983. He is a well-known researcher in maritime information and communication technology and has worked in the area for more than 25 years. This has mostly been in research institutes, but he has also four years' experience from maritime electronics industry. Since 2011, he has worked mainly with autonomous ship technology, but is still active in digitalization onboard the ships, and in communication between ships and shore. He is a senior scientist at SINTEF Ocean, a not-for-profit and independent research institute in Trondheim, Norway. He is also general manager in Norwegian Forum for Autonomous Ships (NFAS) and is coordinator for the International Network for Autonomous Ships (INAS). He spends significant time on standardization and is a member of ISO TC8 and IEC TC80. He regularly meets at IMO as observer for ISO.

Jon A. Skinner is a retired Commander, US Navy, and a long time Alaskan resident. His PhD from the University of Alaska Fairbanks is Interdisciplinary—Polar Geography and Strategic Studies. His dissertation explored scenario futures for Russian capacity as a Great State by assessing its ability to succeed and expand its frontier energy sector—Russian Capacity to Develop Its Offshore Hydrocarbons in the Kara Sea: Arctic and Global Implications. He also holds an M.S. (Intelligence) and an M.A. (Strategic Planning) from the Naval Postgraduate School, Monterey California. He currently serves as an Adjunct with MatSu College, University of Alaska Anchorage and as a Course Instructor with the Global College of PME, Air University. His research focuses on the Polar regions from an energy and maritime perspective with the belief that the Arctic can be envisioned as a "geographic" laboratory with less actors and therefore less variables to account for.

Øyvind Smogeli received his Ph.D. in Marine Technology from the Norwegian University of Science and Technology (NTNU) in 2006. He has spent his career working on modeling, simulation, testing and verification, complex cyber-physical systems, maritime autonomy, mobility, and assurance of digital technologies. He has previously held positions as CTO, COO, and CEO of Marine Cybernetics, Head of Department within Offshore Classification and Maritime Advisory in DNV Maritime, and Program Director for Digital Assurance within DNV Group Technology and Research. Øyvind is now the CTO and co-founder of Zeabuz, where he is leading the development of the autonomy platform, the simulator technology, the assurance processes, and the autonomy service business model. From 2021 Øyvind has also held an Adjunct Professorship at the Department of Marine Technology at NTNU, where teaches a course on Maritime Autonomous Systems to graduate students.

Christoph Thieme holds a Ph.D. in Marine Technology from the Norwegian University of Science and Technology (NTNU). He has specialized in risk analysis and modeling of autonomous marine systems. Currently, he is a research scientist in SINTEF Digital where he works in various projects related to risk assessment of digital and complex systems. He is the co-initiator of the International Workshop for Autonomous Systems Safety (IWASS). Previously Christoph has been a post postdoctoral research fellow at NTNU in the UNLOCK project, working on risk assessment methods development and applications on autonomous control systems. In addition, he holds an M.Sc. in Marine Technology from NTNU and a B.Sc. within Maritime Technology focusing on renewable marine energies and sensor systems.

Paul Topping is the Director of Regulatory and Environmental Affairs at the Chamber of Marine Commerce located in Canada's capital, Ottawa, and works with Canadian domestic shipowners on various issues from reducing air emissions, to protecting waters, to COVID response. Prior to joining the Chamber in 2017, he worked for 28 years in marine-related positions in the Canadian government. Paul has experience managing regulatory programs on water pollution, air emissions, ballast water, ocean noise, marine protected areas, and other issues at both Environment Canada and Transport Canada. He has represented Canada at the International Maritime Organization on Canada's delegation to the Marine Environment Protection Committee and at other international fora. As well, he has chaired the Standing Committee on the Environment at the national Canadian Marine Advisory Council. Paul holds an Honours

Bachelor of Science Degree in biology from the University of Waterloo and lives in Ottawa valley region.

Michael Tsimplis is a Professor at the School of Law of City University of Hong Kong since 2018. He studied Physics at the National University of Athens (Greece) and obtained Ph.D. in Physical Oceanography at the University of Southampton and an LL.M. Maritime Law from the same university. He worked for the Natural Environment Research Council as a Higher Scientific Officer and then for the University of Southampton in various roles between 1995 and 2018. He was the Director of the Southampton Institute of Maritime Law between 2014 and 2017 and the Deputy Director of the Southampton Marine and Maritime Institute (an interdisciplinary institution for the period 2017–2018). He has written extensively in maritime law, oceanography, and sea level rise and has served in various positions (see https://www.cityu.edu.hk/slw/people/people_michael_tsimplis.html). He has recently published the book Environmental Norms in Maritime Law. A detailed list of publications can be found at https://scholars.cityu.edu.hk/en/persons/mikis-tsimplis(8418e5ab-a28f-49c6-8cb0-bd62443992e6)/publications.html?page=0.

Henrik Tunfors is a senior maritime advisor and currently the Focal point for autonomous shipping and smart ships at the Swedish Transport Agency, where he has held several positions over 20 years in the service of shipping, including legal advisor, international liaison, and various management positions. Henrik has been a regular at the International Maritime Organization (IMO) over the past decade both as a delegate, Head of Delegation, and for different Chairing assignments. His most recent assignments are as Chair of the Working Group on Maritime Autonomous Surface Ships (MASS) at the Maritime Safety Committee and the Facilitation Committee as well as the Joint MSC-LEG-FAL Working Group on MASS. Henrik has a Master's in Law, from Lund University, Sweden, specializing in maritime and competition law, his Master's thesis was a comparative study of different exemption regimes in shipping, Liner Conferences, and he has completed the International and Comparative Law Programme at Katholeike Universiteit Brabant (Tilburg University), The Netherlands.

Vibe Ulfbeck is a Professor of private law with a special focus on maritime and transport law at the Faculty of Law, University of Copenhagen. Here, she is the director of the Centre for Private Governance and also head of the research group on Shipping and Ocean Law (SHOC). For several years, she has also been affiliated with the Scandinavian Institute for Maritime Law, Oslo University and she is a member of the board for the Danish Maritime Law Association (CMI). She has written extensively in the field of maritime law, in particular from contract law and tort law perspectives. Most recently, her research has focused on the maritime value chain from a liability perspective, digitalization and automation from a product liability perspective and the green transition in shipping.

Manuel Varela Chouciño is a Spanish maritime lawyer. He obtained an LLM in Maritime Law from the University of Southampton (United Kingdom) and an M.Sc. in Maritime Law and Port Management from University of A Coruña (Spain). As a maritime lawyer he has worked in a Spanish top tier law firm, Uría Menéndez. He is currently working as business development manager in maritime business for Mapfre Insurance Company, in the Spanish region. He also worked as a marine underwriter in the Spanish market. Manuel Varela has obtained experience as business manager in the fishing industry in the LATAM and European region.

Mika Viljanen works as an Associate Professor of private law at the University of Turku. With a background in studying tort law and financial regulation, Dr. Viljanen has been working on AI- and MASS-related topics since 2018, contributing to several research projects (AAWA, AALAW, ETAIROS, AIGA). He has written on MASS insurance provision problems, existing regulatory AI regulatory frameworks, harm dynamics in AI contexts, and AI governance frameworks.

List of Figures

Chapter 2

Chapter 9

Chapter 10

Chapter 11

Chapter 18

List of Tables

Chapter 17

Chapter 18

CHAPTER 1

Introduction to Autonomous Vessels in Maritime Affairs: Law & Governance Implications

Tafsir Matin Johansson, Jon A. Skinner, Jonatan Echebarria Fernández, Aspasia Pastra, and Dimitrios Dalaklis

Technological innovation under the auspices of the fourth industrial revolution has catalysed the evolutionary growth of autonomous artefacts (Johansson, 2022). Cascade of transformations in science and technology

T. M. Johansson (✉) · A. Pastra
World Maritime University-Sasakawa Global Ocean Institute, World Maritime University, Malmö, Sweden
e-mail: tm@wmu.se

A. Pastra
e-mail: asp@wmu.se

J. A. Skinner
MatSu College, University of Alaska Anchorage, Palmer, Alaska, USA

© The Author(s), under exclusive license to Springer Nature Switzerland AG 2023

T. M. Johansson et al. (eds.), *Autonomous Vessels in Maritime Affairs*, Studies in National Governance and Emerging Technologies,
https://doi.org/10.1007/978-3-031-24740-8_1

has indeed positively influenced the transportation sector. We are turning to autonomous modes, i.e., increased reliance on artificial intelligence—a mere reflection of our intention to reach the plateau of accessibility, independence and dissipation of human error.

It is the presumption of the editors of this volume that all actors and stakeholders in the maritime and ocean domain are, to some extent or another, acquainted with the term "autonomous vessels". As such, the term itself needs no re-introduction. What needs emphasis however is how we define the term. During the initial literature review the editors delved into carving out a definition for "autonomous vessels". This review took into account both primary and secondary sources on law and governance, as well as legal doctrines (perceived as *scientia juris* or a "scientific discipline" during the Middle Ages, as in those times "authoritative interpretation", not empirical research, was the main criterion for the scientific status of a discipline). The word "vessel" was detached from "autonomous" and studied separately.

To develop an overarching definition of "vessel", heavy reliance was made on the United Nations Convention on the Law of the Sea, 1982 (UNCLOS), that applies to vessels or ships, as well as international instruments including International Regulations for Preventing Collisions at Sea, 1972, and International Convention on Salvage, 1989. The review emphasized the recurring discrepancies between definitions found in two or more international instruments. It is also observed that in the absence of a basic definition, authorities have proceeded to define the term "ship" or "vessel" in domestic legislation or policy. Ergo, without submitting to complex discussions on ship/vessel classification based on size and type, we therefore decided to keep the definition of "vessel" open-ended so

e-mail: jskinne6@alaska.edu

Global College of PME, Air University, Montgomery, Alabama, USA

J. E. Fernández
The City Law School, University of London, London, United Kingdom
e-mail: jexebez@gmail.com

D. Dalaklis
World Maritime University, Malmö, Sweden
e-mail: dd@wmu.se

as to allow authors to define or refer to appropriate sources, and align discussions of respective chapters with definitions as deemed fit.

Much can be said about "autonomy". We agree that it is a *prima facie* quintessential basis of legal, technical and ethical debates in this era of emerging technology, and its maturing applications. Specific to transport, especially maritime, "autonomy" is a prevalent topic that is discussed by international organizations, industry, manufacturers, academics as well as end users. "Autonomous" takes from the Greek word "autos" meaning "self", and "nomos" meaning "rule/regulation". Scholarly publications produced to-date generally only hint at the fact that autonomous vessels or autonomous ships, uncrewed vessels and unmanned ships as generic broad terms that refer to a watercraft piloted by self-regulating artificial intelligence. In common parlance, any object with the capacity of self-regulation is capable of interacting with the environment on its own and able to make decisions and steer itself through movements in any given environment. Whether or not "human-in-the-loop" or "human-on-the-loop" preserves or coexists with "autonomy" (the ability of self-governance)—is a matter subject to further debates and discussions, ideally, with reference to the four degrees of autonomy as found in the work of the International Maritime Organization's (IMO) Maritime Autonomous Surface Ships' (MASS) working group.

When observing numbers crunched by the United Nations Conference on Trade and Development (UNCTAD), we note that around 100,000 ships of more than 100 tonnes constitute the so-called global maritime shipping industry (UNCTAD, 2021). Execution of all operations in a just-in-time-fashion with optimum safety and environmental performance is the principal driver that drives the industry. Today, trial and error revolve around the objective of delivering to the global shipping industry autonomous vessels. In maritime, the notion of "autonomy" is said to revolutionize the industry and help reach that desired level of efficiency, while providing environment-friendly solutions.

Undoubtedly, autonomous vessels are the face of future shipping and ocean commerce. Machine-learning-based self-regulating control systems using sensor technology are maturing as we write. Parallel initiatives include regulating those areas through the development of governance schemes, standards and codes that will not only enable market growth, but also foster future innovation. The above initiatives have, in tandem, paved the way for academics to delve into research work to explore the legal and governance implications pertaining to vessel autonomy. As "automation" (derived from predetermined heuristics) in the maritime domain slowly progresses towards "autonomy" realized through design and concepts associated with MASS, there is a vital need to capture the grey areas of governance challenges and regulatory considerations. In other words, a study on MASS requires international actors to thoroughly revisit governance and policy implications with a state-of-the-art focus. This is because, at the heart of the transition-phase lies the need to ensure that ships continue to complete tasks while maintaining the tenets and international provisions critical to maritime safety, security and environmental protection. For a holistic insight into MASS—all important niche strands and key insights from multitude angles need to be extracted and critically assessed.

Key insights in this volume are spread across a number of chapters under six specific parts: setting the scene; naval warfare and security; safety, seaworthiness and techno-regulatory assessments; global environmental change; autonomous passenger transportation; liability and insurance; selected national and regional developments; and tying the threads.

Two papers authored by senior figures in the field of techno-regulatory governance open this volume on autonomous vessels. The second chapter, by Andrei Polejack provides new insights into the role of maritime technological innovation in a global context. By introducing the concept of "innovation diplomacy" to the maritime sector, that is, the intersection of technology development with international relations, the author presents timely examples of how a balance between cooperation and competition, as well as between national and global interests, can shape the decisions of the global maritime community with regards to trends in maritime technology (Polejack, 2023). By advocating that most of the technological innovation belongs to the Global North—the author presents new perspectives rooted in the disruptions that maritime technologies could have in the Global South (Polejack, 2023).

The Chapter 3, authored by Henrik Tunfors, is a detailed insight into the state-of-play concerning the endeavour to develop international legislation for MASS (Tunfors, 2023). It is difficult to perceive a book on "autonomous vessels" without a first-hand comprehension of the evolving landscape of MASS over the years. Stages of discussions are wrapped around the work conducted at various sessions (at IMO) starting in 2018 with MSC 99 (Tunfors, 2023). An important foundation to this volume, this chapter highlights key outputs and achievements, joint efforts and correspondences as well as a first-hand appreciation of what lies ahead (Tunfors, 2023).

After setting the scene, Part II picks up on a timely topic concerned with naval warfare and security. In Chapter 4, Raul Pedrozo discusses the rules applicable to the missions and tasks of autonomous and unmanned systems during both peace and war. The author confirms that unmanned surface vessels and unmanned underwater vehicles will operate in an autonomous or semi-autonomous mode and will transform maritime operations as we know them today (Pedrozo, 2023). These systems, according to the author, provide an ideal alternative to manned platforms for dull, dirty, and dangerous missions, all at a reduced cost and less risk to human life (Pedrozo, 2023). Therefore, their enhanced survivability and ability to remain on station in high threat environments will free up manned platforms for more vital missions (Pedrozo, 2023).

In Chapter 5, Anna Petrig considers unmanned ships as a game changer for the commission of crimes at sea due to the fact that they open new avenues to compromise maritime security while lowering the perpetrator's risk of being killed, injured, arrested, or even detected. According to the author, the use of unmanned ships for the commission of crimes at sea amounts to a watershed moment for maritime security law as its rules are firmly based on the assumption that perpetrators act from on board the offender ship, and that a human–human encounter between enforcers and suspects at sea takes place, with the possibility for direct interaction and communication as well as an exchange of physical documentation (Petrig, 2023). Against this backdrop, it is unsurprising that the absence of a crew on board offender ships queries the continued applicability and relevance of many—if not most—rules designed for the suppression of crime at sea (Petrig, 2023). The author submits that the need for regulatory steps is evident, formal amendment of relevant treaties—such as the UNCLOS, the United Nations Convention against Illicit Traffic in Narcotic Drugs and Psychotropic Substances, 1988, and the Convention for the Suppression of Unlawful Acts Against the Safety of Maritime Navigation, 1988 and 2005 respectively—seems out of sight (Petrig, 2023). In the author's opinion, rather than through an update of formal law, the turn to unmanned ships will more likely be accommodated through informal law—at least for the time being (Petrig, 2023).

Three distinct strands of discussions comprise Part III. This part covers three chapters on "safety and seaworthiness" authored by eminent scholars and practitioners. Chapter 6, by Mikis Tsimplis notes that an autonomous ship must be able to call for salvage assistance and deviate from the planned route in appropriate situations. The author observes that cargo interests are likely to object to contributing to a salvage reward if the need for assistance is created by a loss of communication with the autonomous ship instead of an actual danger (Tsimplis, 2023). States have a legal obligation to protect life that is at risk at sea. This duty is discharged by imposing a duty on the master of the ship to assist in collision cases as well as in general situations where human life is at risk (Tsimplis, 2023). The development of autonomous ships, according to the author, would necessitate transferring this obligation to its owner or operator or through the broadening of the legal definition of the master (Tsimplis, 2023). Agreeing on the exact requirements an autonomous ship should satisfy in order to be of use in search and rescue operations and to assist in a collision will facilitate the quick development of compliant autonomous ships (Tsimplis, 2023).

In Chapter 7, Vera Alexandropoulou and co-author Klimanthia Kontaxaki refer to "seaworthiness" as a variable and evolving concept, emanating from IMO instruments and generally accepted industry standards and practices at the relevant time. Authors note the safety concerns and seaworthiness challenges in relation to MASS in the shipping and port sector, and stress on the current calls for the design of a comprehensive safety regulatory framework and a safety management system (Alexandropoulou & Kontaxaki, 2023). Authors are of the opinion that such a novel system, if developed, should potentially integrate automation and digitalization in a befitting manner while relying on a holistic and risk-based approach that reflects all the "interoperation" and "interrelation" aspects and addresses major issues and concerns of the stakeholders involved in the maritime sector (Alexandropoulou & Kontaxaki, 2023).

Chapter 8, by Mika Viljanen asserts that MASS autonomous navigation systems are key drivers of MASS safety, and therefore, autonomous navigation systems should be targets for future regulatory interventions (Viljanen, 2023). The author holds the position that the technological nature of autonomous navigations systems will likely force regulators to adopt performance-regulation as their primary regulatory strategy (Viljanen, 2023). Simulation-based testing will likely be the only feasible approach to verifying MASS navigational safety (Viljanen, 2023). As such, the author projects that the future regulatory framework will be layered, consisting of navigational performance standards verified by simulations and real-world tests and limited technical standards for select equipment (Viljanen, 2023).

Part IV titled "global environmental change" contains a chapter of paramount importance considering complex human interactions and interferences within the global ecosystem. Chapter 9 authored by Sean Pribyl details and assesses autonomous vessels from a "global environmental change" standpoint. As Sean Pribyl demonstrates, the regulatory landscape governing marine autonomy remains unsettled and environmental compliance in the maritime space is becoming more complex (Pribyl, 2023). Financial institutions and shipowners continue to closely monitor emerging sustainability initiatives and seek incentives to meet decarbonization goals at the international and domestic levels. Consequently, according to the author, the maritime industry is experiencing a sea change in innovation as early movers and new entrants offer novel solutions to emerging operational, crewing and environmental risks (Pribyl, 2023). While the full reach of smart autonomy in marine operations is yet to be realized, new solutions and reliable legal frameworks are still evolving although proponents of autonomy support the position that autonomous shipping has clear environmental benefits as vessel owners and operators are seeking available technologies to meet goal-based measures on which to base their investments (Pribyl, 2023). To this end, the author draws reference to the United States (US) that offers several use cases that are spurring development in several important emerging areas that can support greater efficiency in marine operations as well as reductions in greenhouse gas emission monitoring (Pribyl, 2023).

As the title suggests, the two chapters contained in Part V delve into the extraordinarily complex domain of "autonomous passenger transportation". The author of Chapter 10, Øyvind Smogeli, proffers an incisive examination into regulatory dimensions designed to ensure safety as well as societal trustworthiness of new autonomous mobility modes. The author emphasizes that both European and international private and governmental entities have identified the need to transition to cleaner, smarter and eventually unmanned forms of transportation in inland waterways (Smogeli, 2023). The author highlights that despite recent regulatory developments at the international, regional and national levels—there remains no readily available path towards autonomous and unmanned operations (Smogeli, 2023). The author is of the view that projects with this ambition will, therefore, need to carve out the necessary measures to close any gaps through equivalent safety principles in close cooperation with regulators (Smogeli, 2023). To this end, a compelling commencing point (containing both commercial and regulatory threads) could be a network of small, electric urban passenger ferries operated at a given city centre with operations overseen by a safety operator in close proximity. The author also notes that building trust in such a system will require a fit-for-purpose assurance process focusing on the needs of an extended set of stakeholders and the construction of a systematic assurance case—providing evidence in support of technical safety, perceived safety, societal trustworthiness and sustainability (Smogeli, 2023).

Christoph Thieme, has co-authored Chapter 11 together with Marilia Ramos, Even Holte, Stig Johnsen, Thor Myklebust and Øyvind Smogeli. This pioneering piece presents findings from two major projects: Automated safety solutions for passenger ferries (AutoSafe) and Meaningful Human Control in autonomy/digitalization of safety critical systems (MAS). In this very chapter, authors grapple with regulatory challenges emanating from the design and operational aspects pertaining to remotely supervised and autonomous passenger ferries (Thieme et al., 2023). The authors present a high-quality academic paper based on the results of a "gap analysis" that assesses the planned design and operation against the current rules and regulations (Thieme et al., 2023). Based on this assessment, the authors outline procedural aspects that could potentially address those identified gaps. A relevant use-case (under development) for developing emergency procedures is presented and subsequently, analysed through a Concurrent Task Analysis (Thieme et al., 2023). The procedures above help to highlight information-needs and decision-points, which, according to the authors, must be made available in a meaningful manner for efficient supervisors on land (Thieme et al., 2023).

The next five chapters under Part VI cover erudite discussions on two interrelated topics, namely liability and insurance. The first of the five, i.e., Chapter 12, by Matti Eronen, focuses on coastal States' administrative concerns in a hypothetical new situation where automatization increases and the share of human labour consequently, decreases. Increased automation and the declining human factor, in the author's view, poses a number of challenges for coastal States (Eronen, 2023). Here, the author also underscores an existing drawback: indemnity questions have been studied in several presentations and articles whereby examinations only illuminate the shipowners' context with little to no focus on coastal authorities' liability (Eronen, 2023). Administrations can execute "control" and "safeguard" responsibilities when ships operate within merchant fairways—that is a given (Eronen, 2023). In light of the given, the author holds that as digitalization increases and ships shift towards autonomy, the legal thoughts surrounding those two responsibilities need re-examination (Eronen, 2023). To this end, the author brings to light specific coastal State concerns by highlighting the significant areas where efforts should be focused (Eronen, 2023).

In Chapter 13, i.e., the second chapter under the thematic strand of liability and insurance, Vibe Ulfbeck and Aslı Arda, examine vicarious liability for remotely controlled vessels. This examination is conducted from a twofold context: Scandinavian law and English law (Ulfbeck & Arda, 2023). The authors note that currently, the exact legal status of a shore-based controller (SBC) of a remotely controlled ship remains uncertain. Notwithstanding, the assessment of this status will have a significant bearing on the allocation of liability that may arise from the remotely controlled operation of a ship (Ulfbeck & Arda, 2023). Authors pose questions: will SBCs be considered employees or independent contractors? Or perhaps neither of the above? Through this intellectual piece, the authors propound that English and Scandinavian laws provide different approaches concerning the vicarious liability that may be imposed on the shipowners, and accordingly, the evaluation of the new legal status of the SBCs necessitates the comparison of the liability regimes adopted in these legal systems (Ulfbeck & Arda, 2023).

Proshanto Mukherjee explores the precarious legal position of SBC in Chapter 14. Here, the author focuses on the liability of the SBC and puts forward the view that in the event of a collision, the controller should be at the receiving end of sanctions, penal or civil, in no less a way than an on-board master would, in traditional shipping (Mukherjee, 2023). Maritime Safety Committee (MSC) and Legal Committee (LEG) documents indicate that the current international maritime legal regime will have to undergo significant changes to accommodate MASS and the position of the remote-control operator (Mukherjee, 2023). In the opinion of the author, regardless of how advanced MASS technology is, or is poised to be, traditional mariners and seafarers will suffer tremendously (Mukherjee, 2023). Only stakeholders in the wealthy world will be able to afford it (Mukherjee, 2023). The author is obviously concerned that what becomes of the majority of seafarers who hail from the developing world is a question mark (Mukherjee, 2023). Moreover, the author posits that SBC's will all become "techies" is an absurd proposition, and that the liability regime of MASS is as yet underdeveloped and therefore it is unlikely to become a universal practical reality anytime soon (Mukherjee, 2023).

Chapter 15 is the fourth chapter under this important strand that analyses civil liability for MASS through the prism of Bertolini's risk-based management approach. Anil Ozturk argues that existing legal mechanisms offered by private law systems cannot adequately address questions regarding civil liability for undesirable outcomes arising from independent activities of autonomous vessels (Ozturk, 2023). On the assumption that the primary function of existing legal mechanisms offered by private law systems is to resolve the conflicts between legally recognized interests of legal persons, the author suggests that these mechanisms were not developed with autonomous artificial agents (including MASS) in mind (Ozturk, 2023). These mechanisms, according to the author, cannot balance legally recognized interests in the manner intended since they do not recognize that autonomous artificial agents can make and execute decisions independently but have no individual interests to drive these independent decisions (Ozturk, 2023). There are some proposals advanced by various scholars, as well as some lawmaking bodies, to allow the law to accommodate the distinctive characteristics of autonomous artificial agents, including suggestions regarding new types of legal personhood and expansions to existing no-fault liability regimes (Ozturk, 2023). However, the author's evaluation leads to the proposition that even though these proposals give effect to the distinctive characteristics of autonomous artificial agents, and therefore MASS, most do not pay enough attention to maintaining the balance of interests foreseen by existing legal mechanisms (Ozturk, 2023). Ozturk shows that the exception to that general trend is the risk-management approach that suggests distributing civil liability for undesirable outcomes arising from autonomous artificial agents' independent activities based on who is best placed to manage the risk of such outcomes (Ozturk, 2023).

The final chapter under Part VI is authored by Manuel Varela Chouciño, Jonatan Echebarria Fernández and Johanna Hjalmarsson. Authors of Chapter 16 provide an intriguing detail of risk allocation, seaworthiness and technological challenges from the perspective of an underwriter (Chouciño et al., 2023). Authors stress that the "evolution" introduced by MASS in the shipping sector is not alien to existing marine insurance practices (Chouciño et al., 2023). As such, if developments in operational technology confirm the reduction of crew on board for MASS, the implied warranty of seaworthiness in respect of crewmembers may require an update (Chouciño et al., 2023). Authors stress that cyber risk management must be considered by marine underwriters as material information in relation to MASS insurance contracts (Chouciño et al., 2023). According to the authors, marine underwriters could rely on traditional insurance clauses to provide insurance cover for MASS; however, marine cyber-related events represent a new frontier which still requires further analysis by the market (Chouciño et al., 2023). In that continuum, the exercise of due diligence in respect of cyber security will be a crucial factor to consider in relation to marine insurance (Chouciño et al., 2023).

The chapters in Part VII of this volume are presented under the heading "Selected National and Regional Developments". In Chapter 17 Maria Katsivela offers a comparative overview of selected industry issues from a Canadian backdrop (Katsivela, 2023). At the outset, the author views MASS as an emerging reality in Canada and other major maritime nations (Katsivela, 2023). The author explains that frequently recurring issues constraining the development of MASS include: the need to further MASS through regulation, the absence of widespread use of these vessels by the domestic marine industry, and the need to develop supporting mechanisms/services in anticipation of their increased use in the future (Katsivela, 2023). Intensifying collective efforts in the process of developing and deploying MASS, strategizing through implementation of overarching regulations and policies, developing smart ports and other support mechanisms/services/platforms before MASS become an everyday reality are proposed ways forward according to the author (Katsivela, 2023).

In Chapter 18, Ørnulf Rødseth and distinguished co-authors Dag Atle Nesheim, Agathe Rialland and Even Holte touch upon societal impacts of MASS drawing reference to best practices and lessons learned from Norway while bearing in mind the critical global effects. In this chapter, authors take into account both qualitative and quantitative data when assessing the desired impacts. Authors argue that the concept of autonomous ships for most practical purposes can be bound by a clearer definition: "an uncrewed ship with advanced but limited automation and supervision and assistance from a remote control center" (Rødseth et al., 2023). The main societal impacts identified by the authors include, inter alia, improved working conditions and creation of new types of jobs, yet fewer jobs in most areas; reduced burden on society's infrastructure with less terminal space required, less truck transport; contributions to more resilient sea transport systems, improved mobility and more flexible sea transport; contributions to lower energy consumption, decarbonization and less harmful emissions; confirmed higher-level of safety at sea and better regulated shipping (Rødseth et al., 2023). The identified societal effects, according to the authors, are linked to the main attributes of autonomous ships as well as to the 2030 United Nations Sustainable Development Goals (Rødseth et al., 2023). According to the editors, exploring the above link through a visual is a unique contribution to academia that could serve as an important reference for both policy makers and academics. Another noteworthy contribution comes with reference to examples of key performance indicators (KPI) that have the potential to quantitatively measure some of the effects in the selected area (Rødseth et al., 2023).

Chapter 19, by Annie Brett provides an overview of the US regulatory perspectives on maritime autonomy. According to the author, autonomous vessels are being widely used in the US by a variety of different actors, from commercial maritime industries to scientists to the US military (Brett, 2023). The author notes that the US has begun scoping for the initial regulation of commercial autonomous vessels, a process that will take several years before final rules are in place (Brett, 2023). Regulation of other types of autonomy in the US, for instance the Federal Aviation Administration's rules for aerial drones, in the view of the author, could provide important lessons for the Coast Guard's regulation of autonomous vessels (Brett, 2023). Relevantly, the author highlights that most regulatory attention in the US has been focused on how autonomous vessel use can be harmonized with existing maritime regulations, a process that will require amending existing laws, particularly in safety areas (Brett, 2023). Squarely, the author suggests that the Coast Guard and other regulators should also ensure that broader impacts of autonomous vessels, including novel and non-commercial uses, workplace changes and environmental consequences, are also included in future regulatory frameworks for autonomous vessels (Brett, 2023).

Finally, Paul Topping ties in Chapter 20 of Part VIII all important threads discussed by authors of this volume. In other words, this final chapter brings together the many pieces that need to be in place, including technology, technological progress, societal trust and law (Topping, 2023). Through a careful assessment Paul Topping illuminates a range of strategic approaches while weighing both sides of the coin (Topping, 2023). Among Paul Topping's multifaceted expert insights remains his recognition for considering the cost and economic side of things (Topping, 2023). We concur that without a concrete proposal demonstrating how MASS will help generate a reasonable return on investment within the short-term period—there is indeed a possibility that ship owners will remain discouraged from investing in autonomous ships (Topping, 2023). One final observation made by the author that captures the main essence of this volume: "As we move forward in time, one wonders if people in the later future may see some of today's industry and regulatory responses as either prudent approaches or another kind of rule to carry a red flag". Self-explanatory from the sub-title of this book, authors have made an endeavour to shed light on that very aspect by navigating through the complex landscape of "law and governance implications".

References

Alexandropoulou, V., & Kontaxaki, K. (2023). Safety and Seaworthiness Challenges of MASS in the Shipping and Port Sector. In T. M. Johansson, J. E. Fernandez, D. Dalaklis, A. Pastra, & J. Skinner (Eds.), *Autonomous Vessel Maritime Affairs: Law & Governance Implications*. Palgrave Macmillan.

Brett, A. (2023). US Perspectives on Regulating Maritime Autonomy. In T. M. Johansson, J. E. Fernandez, D. Dalaklis, A. Pastra, & J. Skinner (Eds.), *Autonomous Vessel in Maritime Affairs: Law & Governance Implications*. Palgrave Macmillan.

Chouciño, M. V., Fernández, J. E., & Hjalmarsson, J. (2023). Insurance of Marine Autonomous Surface Ships: Risk Allocation, Seaworthiness and Technological Challenges from an Underwriter Perspective. In T. M. Johansson, J. E. Fernandez, D. Dalaklis, A. Pastra, & J. Skinner (Eds.), *Autonomous Vessel Maritime Affairs: Law & Governance Implications*. Palgrave Macmillan.

Eronen, M. (2023). Autonomy, Autonomous Shipping & Coastal Authorities' Concerns. In T. M. Johansson, J. E. Fernandez, D. Dalaklis, A. Pastra, & J. Skinner (Eds.), *Autonomous Vessel Maritime Affairs: Law & Governance Implications*. Palgrave Macmillan.

Johansson, T. (2022). International Standards for Hull Inspection and Maintenance of Robotics and Autonomous Systems. In J. Kraska & Y. Park (Eds.), *Emerging Technology and the Law of the Sea*. Cambridge University Press.

Katsivela, M. (2023). Selected Industry Issues Regarding Autonomous Vessels: The Canadian Perspective. In T. M. Johansson, J. E. Fernandez, D. Dalaklis, A. Pastra, & J. Skinner (Eds.), *Autonomous Vessel Maritime Affairs: Law & Governance Implications*. Palgrave Macmillan.

Mukherjee, P. M. (2023). Maritime Autonomous Surface Ships (MASS): Precarious Legal Position of the Shore-Based Remote Controller. In T. M.

Johansson, J. E. Fernandez, D. Dalaklis, A. Pastra, & J. Skinner (Eds.), *Autonomous Vessel in Maritime Affairs: Law & Governance Implications*. Palgrave Macmillan.

Ozturk, A. (2023). Navigating the Turbulent Waters of Liability: Making the Case for the Application of Risk-Management Based Liability Approach to Autonomous Vessels. In T. M. Johansson, J. E. Fernandez, D. Dalaklis, A. Pastra, & J. Skinner (Eds.), *Autonomous Vessel in Maritime Affairs: Law & Governance Implications*. Palgrave Macmillan.

Pedrozo, R. (2023). Advent of a New Era in Naval Warfare: Autonomous and Unmanned Systems. In T. M. Johansson, J. E. Fernandez, D. Dalaklis, A. Pastra, & J. Skinner (Eds.), *Autonomous Vessel in Maritime Affairs: Law & Governance Implications*. Palgrave Macmillan.

Petrig, A. (2023). Maritime Security in the Age of Autonomous Ships. In T. M. Johansson, J. E. Fernandez, D. Dalaklis, A. Pastra, & J. Skinner (Eds.), *Autonomous Vessel in Maritime Affairs: Law & Governance Implications*. Palgrave Macmillan.

Polejack A. (2023). Innovate or Fade—Introducing Ocean Innovation Diplomacy to the Maritime Sector. In T. M. Johansson, J. E. Fernandez, D. Dalaklis, A. Pastra, & J. Skinner (Eds.), *Autonomous Vessel in Maritime Affairs: Law & Governance Implications*. Palgrave Macmillan.

Pribyl, S. (2023). Autonomous Vessels in the Era of Global Environmental Change. In T. M. Johansson, J. E. Fernandez, D. Dalaklis, A. Pastra, & J. Skinner (Eds.), *Autonomous Vessel in Maritime Affairs: Law & Governance Implications*. Palgrave Macmillan.

Rødseth, Ø. J., Nesheim, D. A., Rialland, A., & Holte, E. A. (2023). The Societal Impacts of Autonomous Ships: The Norwegian Perspective. In T. M. Johansson, J. E. Fernandez, D. Dalaklis, A. Pastra, & J. Skinner (Eds.), *Autonomous Vessel in Maritime Affairs: Law & Governance Implications*. Palgrave Macmillan.

Smogeli, Ø. (2023). Autonomous Urban Passenger Ferries—A New Mobility Mode in Need of Appropriate Regulation. In T. M. Johansson, J. E. Fernandez, D. Dalaklis, A. Pastra, & J. Skinner (Eds.), *Autonomous Vessel in Maritime Affairs: Law & Governance Implications*. Palgrave Macmillan.

Thieme, C. A., Ramos, M. A., Holte, E. A., Johnsen, S. O., Thor Myklebust, T., & Smogeli, Ø. (2023). New Design Solutions and Procedures for Ensuring Meaningful Human Control and Interaction with Autonomy: Automated Ferries in Profile. In T. M. Johansson, J. E. Fernandez, D. Dalaklis, A. Pastra, & J. Skinner (Eds.), *Autonomous Vessel in Maritime Affairs: Law & Governance Implications*. Palgrave Macmillan.

Topping, P. (2023). Autonomous ships: Where is it Going From Here? In T. M. Johansson, J. E. Fernandez, D. Dalaklis, A. Pastra, & J. Skinner (Eds.), *Autonomous Vessel in Maritime Affairs: Law & Governance Implications*. Palgrave Macmillan.

Tsimplis, M. (2023). Designing Norms for Autonomous Ships: The Obligation to Call for Help and the Duty to Save Life in Danger at Sea. In T. M. Johansson, J. E. Fernandez, D. Dalaklis, A. Pastra, & J. Skinner (Eds.), *Autonomous Vessel in Maritime Affairs: Law & Governance Implications*. Palgrave Macmillan.

Tunfors, H. (2023). Evolution of IMO's MASS: Through the Prism of the Chair. In T. M. Johansson, J. E. Fernandez, D. Dalaklis, A. Pastra, & J. Skinner (Eds.), *Autonomous Vessel in Maritime Affairs: Law & Governance Implications*. Palgrave Macmillan.

Ulfbeck, V., & Arda, A. (2023). Remote Control and Remote Risk of Liability?—Vicarious Liability for Remotely Controlled Vessels in Scandinavian and English Law. In T. M. Johansson, J. E. Fernandez, D. Dalaklis, A. Pastra, & J. Skinner (Eds.), *Autonomous Vessel in Maritime Affairs: Law & Governance Implications*. Palgrave Macmillan.

UNCTAD. (2021). Review of Maritime Transport, United Nations, 2021, Geneva.

Viljanen, M. (2023). How to Ensure Safe Navigation: Navigation Safety Regulation in MASS. In T. M. Johansson, J. E. Fernandez, D. Dalaklis, A. Pastra, & J. Skinner (Eds.), *Autonomous Vessel in Maritime Affairs: Law & Governance Implications*. Palgrave Macmillan.

PART I

Setting the Scene

CHAPTER 2

Innovate or Fade—Introducing Ocean Innovation Diplomacy to the Maritime Sector

Andrei Polejack

1 Introduction

How does innovation diplomacy relate with marine technological innovation? Why is this relevant to the maritime industry? Altogether, at the very outset, one might wonder what "innovation diplomacy" truly embodies. In fact, opening this volume with a concept still at a very nascent stage is a challenge, but necessary. Ocean innovation diplomacy is a social phenomenon underlying international collaborative marine technological processes in modern society. It refers to how international cooperation

A. Polejack (✉)
WMU-Sasakawa Global Ocean Institute,
World Maritime University, Malmö, Sweden
e-mail: andrei.polejack@gmail.com

Ministry of Science, Technology and Innovation, Brasilia, Brazil

© The Author(s), under exclusive license to Springer Nature Switzerland AG 2023

T. M. Johansson et al. (eds.), *Autonomous Vessels in Maritime Affairs*, Studies in National Governance and Emerging Technologies,
https://doi.org/10.1007/978-3-031-24740-8_2

in technology development impacts and subsequently, influences international relations, ranging from laboratories cooperating in basic deductive research to foreign market trade and commercialization (Griset, 2020).

The concept of "innovation diplomacy" derives from the umbrella term *science diplomacy*. Science diplomacy in ocean-related matters refers to the interactive dynamics between marine research and international relations where issues such as evidence provision, international decision making, balance between national and international interests and even the power dynamics between countries are subject matters of research (Polejack, 2021). It can be said, innovation diplomacy is more focus-oriented than science diplomacy whereby the interests of the private sector, including economic benefits and social responsibility, are at the core of the relationship between governments, scientists and society.

The ocean is certainly an area where innovation diplomacy should be applied. Most of the global trade is carried over the waves. The ocean regulates our climate and weather, supporting life as we know it. Marine natural resources feed, comfort and medicate us. Preserving the ocean's ecosystem services serves all of our best interests, which makes it a global concern. Over the years, the ocean has been exposed to many environmental threats, including pollution, acidification and overexploitation of biodiversity, and that is why there is an observed dire need to coordinate international efforts and innovate towards sustainability. The need for viable solutions to dissipate those threats places technological innovation as the inevitable central tool that could be used to promote ocean sustainability and societal wellbeing. It is through science diplomacy processes that these technological advancements and scientific evidence inform the global community on how and when to act. As diplomacy needs to account for both the demands of society as well as the market push, science and innovation diplomacy have become important processes for assessment and comprehension.

In general, science diplomacy has been publicized into the policy world as a tool for peace-building. It caters to promoting dialogue and discussions among communities and countries all the while remaining grounded on the assumption that science is guided by principles such as cooperation, neutrality and internationalization (Berkman, 2019). This perspective of science is, however, challenged in science diplomacy research. Despite the attention to ethics, science can be used as a form of soft power to promote national values and assets abroad, and influence multilateral decisions for the benefit of a few (Flink, 2021). Science can also be used as a soft power allowing for the maintenance of the world's discrepancies in terms of scientific capabilities: an elite holding the majority of the ocean sciences' infrastructure and human capital while other parts of the world struggle to develop their own marine scientific research (Nye, 2017). This status quo seems to be beneficial for promoting the notion that privileged countries are the holders of scientific truths and facts, attracting others to their national values and ultimately inspiring other countries to form alliances in search of those scientific capabilities that could also bring them to the alluded truth. This, fortunately or unfortunately, has been the case for research in general and is explicitly visible in marine technological development and deployment.

2 Ocean Innovation Diplomacy, What Is It?

Marine technologies motivated countries to adopt distinct positions when negotiating the United Nations Convention on the Law of the Sea, 1982 (UNCLOS), influencing its adoption and implementation (Robinson, 2020). The historical and critical importance of marine technologies in the international ocean regime exemplifies how necessary it is to understand the processes that fall under the auspices of ocean innovation diplomacy. As it is, ocean innovation diplomacy underlines a critical process with the help of which communities can profit from developing technologies, to solving common problems, such as ocean observing platforms. Communities can also foster inequalities by granting access to technologies to only a few privileged groups so as to produce knowledge that is impactful in international negotiations. For example, most countries are unable to satisfy the technological requirements for facilitating the *transition to a greener (or bluer)* shipping. Notwithstanding, the scientific evidence behind those endorsements was very influential in fostering binding guidelines adopted by the International Maritime Organization (IMO).

Diplomatic delegates to IMO are aware that only a handful of industries in the world have the capacity to supplement the necessary technologies to replace on-board ship systems and reinvent shipbuilding. Those industries are located in the developed part of the world (Pascali, 2017). The scientific evidence presented at the IMO, along with available technological innovations, support negotiations on how we should move forward to lessen the carbon footprint of ships. Thus, technological innovation becomes a country's "commodity". Technological innovation not only opens foreign markets for domestic companies, but can also influence other countries to make decisions that ultimately favour those companies. Companies' interests are, of course, defended by their national diplomats as a part of their countries' foreign policy which dictates their position in intergovernmental diplomatic setups. Public and private investments in the development of new technological solutions to global problems are significant. It is only natural for these companies (and countries) to expect profit in return. This is where ocean innovation diplomacy questions how the existence of a few privileged innovation ecosystems around the world influences the choice of pathways to sustainability that are not available equally to all.

3 Is Ocean Diplomacy for All?

Undoubtedly, there is a need to innovate to find better technological solutions against challenges faced in the Anthropocene—a period during which human influence on climate and environment is viewed as being determinant. With solutions, we also need to acknowledge that current innovation processes in the maritime sector are usually led by a few companies that lack adequate understanding of the potential disruptions that technology may have on communities that are technologically less privileged. This perception was a decisive factor in the negotiation and adoption of Part XIV of UNCLOS, which requires state parties to implement mechanisms to foster the transfer of marine technology, and develop globally balanced scientific capacities for all to benefit from better informed decision making and the enhanced application of technology for sustainability. The provisions under Part XIV were well designed but proved to be difficult to implement (Polejack & Coelho, 2021). One possible reason for the underachieved implementation of Part XIV is that the private sector is not a part of UNCLOS, and therefore, not bound by its provisions. Private companies rely on profit and are held accountable by shareholders to find better lucrative deals. At the same time, society increasingly pressures companies to support *corporate social responsibility* through which the private sector can prove itself promoting a better future for the planet. Therefore, the relationship between the private sector and the global community is a balance between cooperation and competition, or bluntly speaking, *co-opetition* (Brandenburger & Nalebuff, 1996).

It is acknowledged that the processes that comprise ocean innovation diplomacy towards a blue and green future are not simple. All shades of blue permeate the forces pushing companies to either cooperate or compete. In light of the above, and to better grapple with the concept of ocean innovation diplomacy in a real-life context, the intention of this chapter is to present some aspects of this complexity while navigating through the innovation process. Guided by the TRL, this chapter will identify the relationship between "diplomacy" and "technology innovation" in context so it becomes easier to sight the importance of ocean innovation diplomacy.

4 Technology Innovation Readiness Level (TRL)

The TRL were developed by the National Aeronautic Space Administration (NASA) to situate the promptness of a given technology to be deployed in space research. It embodies nine-scaled stages to which any given technology innovation is subject to. The scales range from basic lab research to technology test and deployment, as shown in Table 1.

Despite the fact that the original usage of TRL sought to position technologies based on applicability, the industry has nevertheless pushed these TRL towards commercialization (Mankins, 2009). Ergo, today, the TRL are generally perceived as a scale centred on the economic value of innovation. TRL, in the context of this chapter, are applied to maintaining the above position. Notably, academia tends to focus on TRL 1 to 4 whereas industry prefers to work with TRL 7 to 9 avoiding TRL 5 to 6. This means that governments, responsible for budgeting universities

Table 1 The nine technology readiness levels

1	Basic principles observed
2	Technology concept formulated
3	Experimental proof of concept
4	Technology validated in a lab
5	Technology validated in a relevant environment
6	Technology demonstrated in a relevant environment
7	System prototype demonstrated in an operational environment
8	System complete and qualified
9	System deployed in an operational environment

Source Adapted from Mankins (2009)

and research centres, usually limit their investments to basic and applied research (TRL 1 to 4, with lesser funding available for TRL 5 and 6). From a public finance perspective, governments are responsible for maintaining a country's scientific capability targeted at intellectual discovery and knowledge development. Industry, on the other hand, is focused on investing in those technologies that are best suited to the market needs, thus, adding a nuance to the TRL that govern the commercial side.

For example, government-led research that develops new autonomous vehicles for data collection seeking to lessen dependency on research vessels lowers the operational cost of oceanographic cruises. Industry would certainly be interested in such a vehicle should it successfully also satisfy all the criteria of a commercially viable product. What is noteworthy is that the industry tends to invest in technologies with low-risk of investment (between TRL 7 and 9). In this scenario, TRL 5 to 6 represent a gap between academic research and industrial commercialization. This gap, in common parlance, is noted as the technological "valley of death" emphasizing that many new technologies reach TRL 4 to 6 but eventually, fade away. Figure 1 provides a schematic overview of the TRL in the face of required investments highlighting the location of this so-called "valley of death".

Bluntly speaking, an idea or a concept is delineated in labs through traditional research practices. The next step is the experimental testing of that idea, which is also largely conducted through classic scientific endeavours. The results are aimed at publication whereby cooperation among researchers is natural, cherished and expected. Once the concept finds a way to survive the "valley of death", an industry-based shift tends to occur. In this new environment, scientific cooperation faces new institutional realities that usually encompass sensible issues such as intellectual property rights, confidential contractual clauses and industrial espionage. Here, we see a transition from academic classic research, mostly funded by the public sector and stimulated to be a cooperative action, to a competitive setup where innovation is disclosed and debated within a select audience that primarily deals with the legal and regulatory burdens associated with commercialization.

It may be more natural to connect diplomacy to the classical government-led practice where it is expected to facilitate the gathering of international research teams to co-develop a given technology. However,

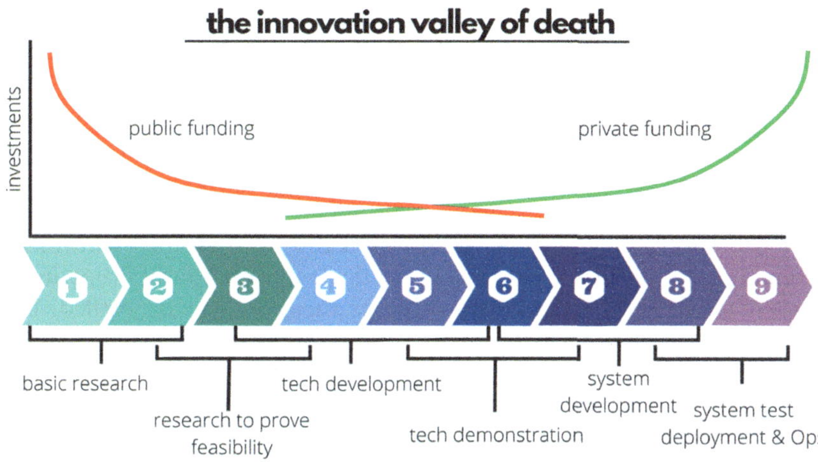

Fig. 1 Schematic representation of the nine TRL (*Source* Adapted from Mankins [2009]. *Note* The nine TRL are represented as coloured arrows and grouped by functionalities that go from basic research to technology deployment, shown right below the arrows. On the top, a fictitious graphic representation of funding investments by the public [red curve] and private [green curve] sectors. The "valley of death" is illustrated where investments are lowest by both public and private sectors)

when industry enters the playing field, diplomacy tends to defend industrial interests and focuses on the opening of markets for new technology. That is where ocean innovation diplomacy comes into play to closely examine this *schizophrenic relationship*—sometimes acting as fair and just, and at other times harsh and aggressive.

5 Ocean Innovation Diplomacy: The Reality

Let us cite an example from the current international maritime agenda: make ship operations safer and cheaper through autonomous systems. Interested researchers and tech-companies identify technologies that will allow autonomous and unmanned ships to depart and call to port remotely, without the need of on-board operators. Presently, challenges are many since ports need to be equipped with sensors, high-speed internet, updated information on the state of the environment, including real-time data on wind, current, tide, weather, the seabed map, etc. Therefore, what looks like a straight-forward task, i.e., enabling ships to call to port without human intervention, is actually much more complex due to the presence of an assortment of layers and intelligent systems that function using algorithms. The systems are built using components manufactured by several companies from different countries. Thus, it takes significant cooperation between multiple agents to develop, calibrate and maintain, for example, a single sensor so it can be combined with other technologies to ultimately allow ships to dock autonomously maintaining utmost safety. Researchers and companies therefore can be baffled, but nonetheless continue to forge ahead.

Clearly, this technological revolution has an embedded private interest, i.e., diminishing the high costs of ship operations. Then again, there is an environmental interest as autonomous vessels could potentially dissipate maritime incidents that are detrimental to life below water. It goes without saying therefore that major maritime nations are competitors in this technological race. They intend to profit from exporting domestic technology to global markets. In the end, one comes across many stakeholders residing in the midst of this revolutionary landscape. Thus, intergovernmental organizations, such as the IMO are in the process of assessing the relevant issues to find suitable ways to regulate and guide industries, both cutting edge and the less tech-savvy.

TRL 1 to 3. With this dilemma in mind, let us revert back to the basic research aspect of this paper's thesis. Researchers are generally used to working in collaboration with their peers. They find the necessary tools to develop the right idea or concept regardless of their geographical origins. Under these initial TRL, they are free to find and work together with foreign partners through public funding that is most likely to be available through calls for proposals. The higher the level of international cooperation—the higher their proposal is likely to be scored. In this case, innovation diplomacy is observed to facilitate the matchmaking between research groups because it is only through international cooperation enshrined with innovation diplomacy, they are able to further develop and implement their ideas. In this scenario, innovation diplomacy holds humankind's interest in the highest esteem. Bi and multilateral agreements are signed, co-funding schemes are created with intergovernmental organizations welcoming such endeavours.

Further in the pipeline, more applied research is being developed. This stage is not only about combining the physics of light dispersion with computational modelling, but more about focusing on the end process, the sensor in itself. At this late stage, collaboration with peers coupled with diplomacy does not negatively impact the process. Therefore, basic and applied research can be distinctly viewed from TRL 1 to 3.

TRL 4 to 6. Once a conceptual sensor has demonstrated the required feasibility for the autonomous docking of ships, the new technology must be subject to testing and experimentation. At this stage, prototypes are tested where "design" is critical. The challenge is to find a suitable and appealing design that works well in specific circumstances. Many unforeseen problems appear and need to be dealt with, e.g., durable, water resistant, biofouling-free, etc. It is noteworthy that this is the stage that can no longer be classified as applied research and is thus ineligible for public funding. There is also a high-risk that this new technology may not match the needs of the market. It is here, between TRL 4 and 6 that many good ideas fall short of funding. Also, here, intellectual property rights and secrecy/confidentiality become relevant. It is also at this stage that research-inventors start to search for private partners to sell their ideas. If a good prototype is developed, only then will industry be interested. Diplomacy turns to support international business whereby collaborators are requested to keep innovation behind closed doors.

At this stage, there is little that diplomacy can achieve. Technology developers seek investors from their countries and abroad, and since the technology is still in testing, it is a matter of risk-taking. Diplomacy can facilitate this process by promoting the exchange between start-up programmes and investors, mostly perceived as a peer-to-peer cooperation rather than a matter of foreign policy.

TRL 7 to 9. Assuming an innovative technology reaches this far through support from government and industry, its potential as a possible candidate for becoming a "product" is high. As a product, this technology is no longer subject to discovery and development, but subject to contracts, deals and business practices. Researchers become less involved and the market dictates actions. Diplomacy at this stage facilitates the closing of international deals and proceeds to defend the industry's interests. Unfortunately, this stage does not accommodate peer-to-peer scientific cooperation. At these final TRL, i.e., between 7 and 9, commercialization is the main driver as opportunities are sought to increase the technology market share. It is also at these final stages that we see diplomacy promoting new technologies—which is perceived as the appropriate norm for achieving global solutions to autonomous shipping. The focus,

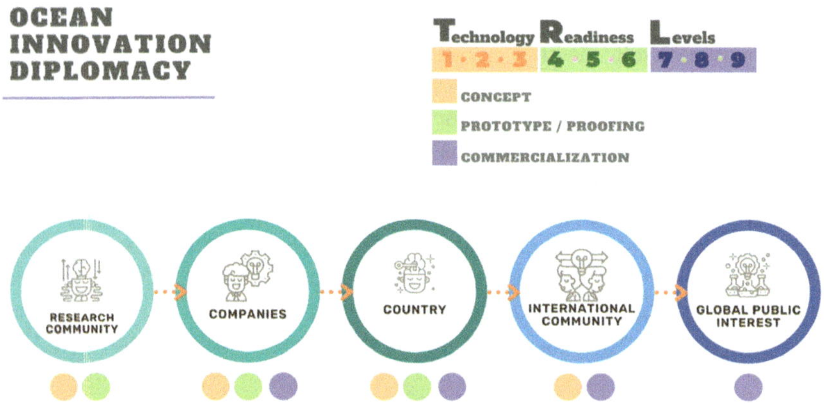

Fig. 2 Schematic representation of the potential relationships between the TRL at different stages (*Source* Author. *Note* TRL 1 to 3 represent the concept stage [basic and applied research] [shown in orange colour]. TRL 4 to 6 represent the proofing of a new technology, testing and finally the prototype design [shown in green colour]. TRL 7 to 9, where the new technology is ready for commercialization and attracts more attention from industry [shown in purple colour]. Below the representation of each stakeholder's interests is a colour palette referring to potentially the most influential TRL that comprise those interests)

apparently, has changed. Intergovernmental organizations, case-in-point the IMO, note that all countries should apply such technology. Debates revolving around regulating practices are initiated multilaterally. Here, national diplomats promote their domestic product as the panacea to the needs of the world at large. As a consequence, the above action raises the margin of profit in respective national industries. The reality described thus far has been captured in Fig. 2.

6 Is Innovation Diplomacy the Same Throughout the World?

Until this point, attention has been drawn only to geographical areas where there is a capacity to develop research, existence of heavy private investments for innovation and a high number of diplomatic corps that are spread across the world. To take but one example, Norway has assigned foreign commerce experts to embassies around the world. They are chartered with the task to conduct bilateral matchmaking of commercial interest grounded in innovation. Norway has a state-owned company mandated to carry out the above task with many employees stationed at embassies throughout the globe. In fact, many countries in the developed world also have dedicated staff looking for innovative business opportunities abroad, mainly placed in their diplomatic houses. Among these countries, we can at least identify the United Kingdom (UK), Sweden, the United States of America (US) and Canada, among many others. This begs the question: what happens in other parts of the world?

Firstly, the innovation scenario is global and is difficult to explain through regional models. However, some aspects can be easily identified when it comes to observing the status of the Global South in this international technological race. First, research teams in the less privileged countries tend to depend on research facilities located in the North. In addition, in the realm of science, it is very common that Southern scientists are trained in the North, and because of that, they tend to build long-lasting networks that nurture future international collaboration. Consequently, it is very common that scientists in the South initiate interesting ideas and concepts that are then developed cooperatively with scientists in the North, and this is in fact very welcomed and rewarded in academia. Diplomacy, in this case, will do all in its power to establish cooperative frameworks under which these scientists can work together through agreements and meaningful participation. A good example can be drawn from biotechnology research. Scientists that belong to the South have access to a more rich marine biodiversity, with historical indigenous applications, and therefore are generally more triggered by curiosity to identify the molecular compounds that generate medicinal benefits. However, these scientists usually cooperate with their Northern peers to access analytical equipment and then proceed to applied research. If any newly discovered compound proves of commercial value, such a scenario ends to change considerably since almost all of the pharmaceutical industries most likely to invest in this research are located in the North. In the end, we see that typically a natural organism from the South is studied by a global consortium whose products resulting from this research are endorsed by Northern companies.

Secondly, though there is a rising trend of start-up programmes and university incubators in the South, technical expertise tends to be restricted only to research. Therefore, the institutional setup in the South usually lacks expertise in governance and regulation, placing those bureaucratic burdens on the scientists that conduct the research. In the end, scientists need to deal with patent processes, tax registries, contracts and other administrative work that their peers in the North usually hand over to specific departments in their institutions (Polejack & Coelho, 2021). In a sense, innovation in the case of the South remains a one-man show.

Thirdly, it is not very unusual for successful marine technological companies in the South to be eventually acquired by multinational corporations. This occurs when companies become prominent innovators with added market value. Multinational corporations are frequently invisible in innovation diplomacy. Despite their power to influence diplomacy in many broad aspects, such as providing scientific evidence that their teams have produced to orchestrating collaboration between international staff of researchers with their own domestic decision makers to influence foreign policy, their presence remains nonetheless obscure (Bernstein & Cashore, 2007).

The above three points are selected aspects of the issue at hand. Each national innovation system has its own peculiarities and complexities that drive international partnerships differently. The overall aim is to argue that ocean innovation diplomacy may appear to differ depending on the context in which it operates. Any further attempt to establish a taxonomy to describe it concretely should be done in a careful and prudent manner considering the differentiated realities.

However, there are possible solutions that could level the playing field for technology innovation throughout the world. In a chapter written for the second volume of this series, this paper advocates that countries in the South could map and assess internal market and innovation ecosystems (identify strengths, weaknesses, set priorities) defend interests multilaterally and act bi-trilaterally, establish public–private partnerships and multi-stakeholder engagement and explore new possibilities and learn from experience (Polejack & Machado, 2023). The debate has been in the open for many years in traditional diplomacy, in particular with regard to the ocean international regime, but change will most likely be prompted only when less privileged countries unveil the inequalities that lie dormant behind innovation diplomacy (Polejack & Coelho, 2021).

7 Conclusions

This chapter aimed at providing insights on the importance of innovation diplomacy processes to marine technologies applied to the maritime industry. Innovation diplomacy, as it appears, broadly derives from science diplomacy, which is used to examine the nexus between research and international affairs. Ocean innovation diplomacy deals with issues pertaining to international technology development partnerships—that changes once a new technology is ready for commercialization. Therefore, the goal was to use the TRL as a guiding principle. This has led to the following conclusions:

1. TRL 1 to 3: connected to basic and applied research and international scientific cooperation, and mainly funded by public investments with scale of reward contingent on the level of international cooperation. As we move towards proofs and tests, technologies become more appealing to the market, but investment wise—they remain on the "high-risk" scale and threatened by the innovation "valley of death";
2. TRL 4 to 6: there are many uncertainties in relation to the application viability and value of technology. As such, they generally stay outside the scope of diplomatic negotiations; and
3. TRL 7 to 9: after surviving the "valley of death" and moving into the core business part of the process, technologies become a market-share, and consequently, an industrial interest that has the potential to influence diplomatic negotiations towards fullfilling national interests in face of global regulations.

The above conceptualization is not a one-size-fit-for-all. National innovation ecosystems, the lack of proper research and technical capabilities and domestic regulatory frameworks must be considered as they restrict innovators in the Global South to experience ocean innovation diplomacy in the same way as their Northern peers. Therefore, caution is in order when regarding ocean innovation diplomacy as a single process in the maritime "autonomy" sector. As power relations and inequality seem to fuel most of the ocean innovation diplomacy processes, particularly between North and South, a strategic way forward must be devised in consultation with all stakeholders so that maritime robotic and autonomous systems can continue to thrive in the era of the fourth industrial revolution.

References

Berkman, P. A. (2019). Evolution of Science Diplomacy and Its Local-Global Applications. *European Foreign Affairs Review*, *24*(Special issue), 63–80.

Bernstein, S., & Cashore, B. (2007). Can Non-State Global Governance be Legitimate? *An Analytical Framework. Regulation & Governance, 1*(4), 347–371.

Brandenburger, A. M., & Nalebuff, B. J. (1996). In A. M. Brandenburger & B. J. Nalebuff (Eds.), *Co-opetition*. Currency Doubleday.

Flink, T. (2021). Taking the Pulse of Science Diplomacy and Developing Practices of Valuation. *Science and Public Policy*, 1–10.

Griset, P. (2020). Innovation Diplomacy: A New Concept for Ancient Practices? *The Hague Journal of Diplomacy, 15*(3), 383–397.

Mankins, J. C. (2009). Technology Readiness Assessments: A Retrospective. *Acta Astronautica, 65*(9–10), 1216–1223.

Nye, J. S. (2017). Soft Power: The Origins and Political Progress of a Concept. *Palgrave Communications*, *3*(1), 17008. https://doi.org/10.1057/palcomms.2017.8

Pascali, L. (2017). The Wind of Change: Maritime Technology, Trade, and Economic Development. *American Economic Review*, *107*(9), 2821–2854. https://doi.org/10.1257/aer.20140832

Polejack, A. (2021). The Importance of Ocean Science Diplomacy for Ocean Affairs, Global Sustainability, and the UN Decade of Ocean Science. *Frontiers in Marine Science*, 8.

Polejack, A., & Coelho, L. F. (2021). Ocean Science Diplomacy can Be a Game Changer to Promote the Access to Marine Technology in Latin America and the Caribbean. *Frontiers in Research Metrics and Analytics, 6*, 34–36.

Polejack, A., & Machado, L. F. C. da S. (2023). The Possibilities of Ocean Innovation Diplomacy to Promote Transnational Innovation Ecosystems for the Maritime Sector. In T. Johansson, J. Echebarria Fernández, D. Dalaklis, A. Pastra, & M. Lennan (Eds.), *Smart Ports & Robotic Systems: Navigating the Waves of Techno-regulation & Governance* (Vol. 2). Palgrave Macmillan.

Robinson, S. (2020). Early Twentieth-Century Ocean Science Diplomacy. *Historical Studies in the Natural Sciences, 50*(4), 384–410.

CHAPTER 3

Evolution of IMO's MASS: Through the Prism of the Chair

Henrik Tunfors

1 Introduction

The world is already years into its endeavor of creating legally sound operations for maritime autonomous surface ships (MASS), and yet it seems as if the work has only just begun. At the time of writing (spring of 2022), delegates are preparing to commence the work planned thus far at the 105th session of the International Maritime Organization's (IMO)

The views and opinions expressed in this chapter are those of the authors and do not reflect the position of any department, agency, institution or organization whether national or international.

H. Tunfors (✉)
Maritime and Civil Aviation Department, Swedish Transport Agency, Norrköping, Sweden
e-mail: henrik.tunfors@transportstyrelsen.se

© The Author(s), under exclusive license to Springer Nature Switzerland AG 2023

T. M. Johansson et al. (eds.), *Autonomous Vessels in Maritime Affairs*, Studies in National Governance and Emerging Technologies, https://doi.org/10.1007/978-3-031-24740-8_3

Maritime Safety Committee (MSC). One can safely assert that the excitement has not worn off—MASS is still a popular and prevalent concept in the world of shipping. The industry continues its engagement with projects, research, innovation and development work, which continues to challenge the current legal framework, while the regulator, on the other hand, is mindful of the industry's wants and needs.

The IMO consists of 175 Member States (MS) and a large number of other stakeholders, inter-governmental organizations, non-governmental organizations and observers, inter alia. Meetings covering this topic, where the ultimate goal is to create a mandatory instrument for MASS operations will perhaps be blessed with new ideas, good ideas, irrelevant ideas and ideas that are re-introduced into the conversation. Examples of the latter can be found annexed to the final report of the MASS Regulatory Scoping Exercise (RSE). Notably, the RSE was only a little hitch in the long road toward establishing a concrete global, harmonized, regulatory framework for MASS operations. Through the finalizations of the RSEs, all of the active IMO Committees, the Facilitation Committee (FAL), the Legal Committee (LEG) and MSC have carved out a few of the most invaluable conclusions. Those will assist in the making of a MASS regulatory governance instrument considering gaps and themes that are common to all RSEs. To date, the most challenging issue of all is the *role and responsibility of the master and crew*.

Before observing the future trajectory, the author would like to take the liberty to detail a summary of the activities and corresponding results of IMO's MASS Working Groups, coupled with a partially biased account of discussions that took place at the IMO between 2018 and 2022. A hybrid observation is in order to provide the readers with a holistic overview. At its 98th session in 2017, the MSC agreed to an output—an RSE for the use of MASS. It was around the same time that the FAL and the LEG also started their respective RSEs. While the FAL had only one instrument to scope, i.e. the Facilitation convention, the scope of LEG's exercise spanned over nineteen (19) instruments, e.g. insurance, civil liability, limitation of liability limitation and suppression of unlawful acts. The scope of MSC's exercise was comprised of thirty-one (31) instruments whereby the convention central to maritime safety, i.e. the International Convention for the Safety of Life at Sea of 1974 (SOLAS 74), had to be divided into several parts resulting in forty (40) scoping activities.

2 Setting the Scene: Assembling the MASS Working Group

Denmark et al. spurred the original initiative in 2017 through document MSC 98/20/2 (Maritime Autonomous Surface Ships—Proposal for a regulatory scoping exercise) with support from Estonia, Finland, Japan, the Netherlands, Norway, the Republic of Korea, the United Kingdom and the United States of America (US). The above submission was supplemented by MSC 98/INF.13—a pre-investigation report on autonomous ships that Denmark had already commissioned in 2016 encompassing a variety of perspectives including safety and legal issues (Blanke, 2016). Probably fuelled by the (in)famous Rolls Royce Video, Denmark announced in 2016 its plans to introduce a step-by-step approach starting with reduced manning, then remotely piloted systems (manned and unmanned) and finally, the promise to deliver a fully autonomous ship by 2035.

The coalition was deemed strong as it had the support of the maritime industry given that autonomous ships were in the process of coming into the early parts of the hype curve. Despite early oppositions, as well as many oral interventions from the International Transport Workers' Federation (ITF), noted in the document issued pursuant to MSC 98/20/13, the output (as IMO agenda items are called) was nevertheless installed in the agenda of MSC with a number of foci including, most importantly, the need to take into consideration the human element (MSC 98/23, para. 20.2).

The first session of the Working Group on maritime autonomous surface ships (MASS) (MASS WG) took place a year later in May 2018 at MSC 99. At this meeting, a great number of high-octane documents attempting to set the scene were tabled. The IMO Secretariat, of course, laid the foundation of MSC 99/5. The Secretariat proposed a number of actions for consideration by the Committee to guide future work: the establishment of a framework for the exercise, the development of a work plan and expected deliverables, a coordinated mechanism with other Committees of the Organization, intersessional arrangements and the establishment of a cross-divisional MASS taskforce under the general coordination of the Maritime Safety Division to assist with developments related to MASS. All others followed suit and the Working Group was established with the following Terms of Reference:

1. Develop a framework for the regulatory scoping exercise, including aims, objectives, methodology, instruments, type and size of ships, provisional definitions and different types and concepts of autonomy, automation, operation and manning to be considered;
2. Develop a plan of work for the regulatory scoping exercise, including timelines, deliverables and priorities, involvement of other committees and intersessional arrangements;
3. Consider the need to establish a mechanism for sharing information and lessons learned and liaison with other international organizations to share up-to-date information on MASS, and advise, as appropriate; and
4. Consider the need for a Correspondence Group and develop draft terms of reference, as appropriate (MSC 99/22, 2018, para. 5.25).

3 State-of-Play: Stages of Discussion

After being assembled under MSC, the MASS WG convened on five different occasions between May 2018 and May 2021: four times during Committee sessions (MSC 99 thru MSC 103) and once at an intersession. The only Committee meeting that convened without a MASS WG during this period was at MSC 102 due to the Covid-19 pandemic.

3.1 The 99th Session of the Maritime Safety Committee (MSC 99) (MSC 99/WP.9)

MSC 99 met in May 2018 to develop a framework for the regulatory scoping exercise. The framework included the development of aims and objectives, methodology, instruments, type and size of ships, provisional definitions and different types and concepts of autonomy, automation, operations and manning-critical considerations, as well as strategic plans composed of timelines, deliverables and priorities, areas of involvement for other committees and intersessional arrangements (MSC 99, para. 4). The group was also instructed to consider the need to establish a mechanism for sharing information and lessons learned, liaise with other international organizations for sharing up-to-date information on MASS, and the feasibility of establishing the need for a correspondence group. In short, mammoth tasks were undertaken under the auspices of MSC 99. As mentioned earlier, the MASS WG started with a carte blanche. Notwithstanding, a plethora of proposals and ideas were submitted to the session from various IMO member states (MS) and relevant stakeholders.

Markedly, the MASS WG (at MSC 99) successfully established a framework for the regulatory scoping exercise guided by appropriate methods and principles. The Framework laid down the fundamentals for the RSE including aim and objective, a glossary of commonly used definitions of MASS and four relevant degrees (developed only for the RSE), and most importantly, the scope for the exercise that revolved around instruments under the purview of MSC. The WG also agreed that the exercise should be organized following two steps: firstly, the identification of relevant provisions in IMO instruments with regard to the applicability to MASS, and secondly, an analysis to determine the most appropriate way of addressing MASS operations, taking into account, the human element, technology and operational factors, inter alia.

In an attempt to further explore the human element aspects and influences on the execution of duties and functions on board a ship, the WG discussed the possibilities of including additional questions to be addressed as a part of the methodology (to aid the work during the above two steps). This entailed answering questions as to whether physical human interaction is required to execute a certain regulation; whether the regulation is intended to safeguard a human/person? Other questions posed were aimed at understanding if the regulatory goals could be achieved through alternative means of interaction, or via alternative levels of human intervention, or through ensuring the safety of people on board a ship. Notably, the human element was deemed sufficiently addressed partly through the actual content of the provisions to be scoped. Since this work had not been completed before at the IMO level, the WG felt it prudent to, through correspondence, test the framework with a specific focus on the methodology pertaining to the regulatory scoping exercise. The results, comprised of only three individual regulations, clearly showed that this was indeed a daunting task that required clear instructions.

3.2 *The 100th Session of the Maritime Safety Committee (MSC 100) (MSC 100/WP.8)*

The MASS WG convened again in December 2018 (para. 4) to finalize the framework for the regulatory scoping exercise. The focus of the WG was on the template, the plan and the methodology, and, if time permitted, the WG would consider the development of interim guidelines for MASS trials. Subsequently, the group managed to finalize the framework for the RSE, as well as the reporting template. In the process, it was important to shed light on the framework since it was a pathway to ensuring a consistent and harmonized approach for all RSEs conducted at the IMO since both FAL and LEG opted for it. The 100th session also agreed on the following list of instruments to be part of the RSE:

- COLREG 1972—International Regulations for Preventing Collisions at Sea, 1972;
- CSC 1972—International Convention for Safe Containers (CSC), 1972, as amended;
- LL 1966—International Convention on Load Lines 1966 and the LL PROT 1988—Protocol of 1988 relating to the International Convention on Load Lines 1966;
- SAR 1979—International Convention on Maritime Search and Rescue, 1979;
- SOLAS 1974—International Convention for the Safety of Life at Sea, 1974, as amended;
- STCW 1978—International Convention on Standards of Training, Certification and Watchkeeping for Seafarers, 1978, as amended;
- STCW-F 1995—International Convention on Standards of Training, Certification and Watchkeeping for Fishing Vessel Personnel, 1995; and
- TONNAGE 1969—International Convention on Tonnage Measurement of Ships, 1969.

In the context of the RSE, it is important to be cognizant of the fact that not all instruments under the purview of the MSC were scoped. The following instruments were left outside of the scope:

- SOLAS AGR 1996—Agreement concerning specific stability requirements for ro-ro passenger ships;
- SOLAS PROT 1978—Protocol of 1978 relating to the International Convention for the Safety of Life at Sea, 1974;
- SOLAS PROT 1988—Protocol of 1988 relating to the International Convention for the Safety of Life at Sea, 1974;

- SPACE STP 1973—Protocol on Space Requirements for Special Trade Passenger Ships; and
- 1973 STP 1971—Special Trade Passenger Ships Agreement, 1971

Due to the (projected) limited scope for MASS operations for SOLAS AGR 96, STPS 1971, SPACE STP 1973 and SOLAS PROT 1978, coupled with the presumption that it was already reviewed for SOLAS PROT 1988—the WG agreed that, to avoid delaying the RSE, it was not necessary to consider the above instruments during the current RSE discussions. In order to meet the 2020 deadline, and to facilitate progress between sessions, it was also agreed that IMO MS would voluntarily conduct work, in groups, if necessary, to carry out the first step of the RSE for all instruments, aptly known as the *initial review*. It was in this first stage that the RSE identified provisions from IMO instruments which, as currently drafted:

A. Apply to MASS and prevent MASS operations; or
B. Apply to MASS and do not prevent MASS operations and require no actions; or
C. Apply to MASS and do not prevent MASS operations but may need to be amended or clarified, and/or may contain gaps; or
D. Have no application to MASS operations (MSC 100/WP.8, 2018, para. 10)

3.3 The 101st Session of the Maritime Safety Committee (MSC 101) (MSC 101/WP.8)

MSC 101 was held in June 2019. The principal mandate of the session was to consider and mark the progress of the RSE; finalize the interim guidelines for MASS trials, and prepare the terms of reference for an Intersessional MASS WG (MSC 101/WP 8, 2019, para. 4).

3.3.1 The Regulatory Scoping Exercise

The first step of the RSE contained a "commenting stage" where all IMO MS could provide input through a global integrated shipping information system (GISIS) Module that was created to alleviate the administrative burden for all involved in the regulatory scoping exercise. These discussions were still ongoing during MSC 101. Since the results of the first step were to be considered at an intersessional meeting held between MSC 101 and MSC 102—the WG at this session (acknowledging that the groups had already used different approaches) utilized the time to share experiences to further tighten the reporting formats with a view to enhancing the chances of drawing robust conclusions and extrapolating from the RSE final results.

3.3.2 Interim Guidelines for MASS Trials[1]

There was also a noteworthy desire to establish guidance for IMO MS and industry for MASS tests and trials. Although the issue had been discussed at earlier sessions, there were no concrete proposals for consideration. Consequently, the WG managed to agree on a high-level, generic and goal-based Interim Guidelines for testing equipment, systems and procedures from a MASS standpoint. Important to note that the Interim Guidelines for MASS Trials were developed to assist relevant authorities and relevant stakeholders to conduct MASS-related system and infrastructure trials with utmost safety and security, and with due regard to the protection of the marine environment. In other words, trials under the Guidelines should be conducted in a manner that provides at least the same degree of safety and security for humans and protection of the marine environment as stipulated in relevant IMO instruments (MSC 101/WP.8, 2019, para. 2). One of the central principles of the Interim Guidelines is compliance with mandatory instruments (MSC 101/WP.8, 2019, para. 2.2.1). Seemingly, risk management is also a pillar critical to the Interim Guidelines (MSC 101/WP.8, 2019, para. 2.1). Before trials, all relevant safety risks should be identified and reduced to the extent possible and practicable with emergency plans established based on the risk assessment to mitigate the impact of identified risks. Trial safety should be continuously evaluated, and suspended or stopped where safety parameters are exceeded.

Other principles to be observed and adhered to included: minimum manning requirements (MSC 101/WP.8, 2019, para. 2.3), the human element (MSC 101/WP.8, 2019, para. 2.4), proper infrastructure

[1] All references in this section are to the Draft MSC Circular Interim Guidelines for MASS Trials, Annex 3, MSC 101/WP.8 (2019). Report of the Working Group on a Regulatory Scoping Exercise for the use of Maritime Autonomous Surface Ships (MASS), subsequently published as MSC.1/Circ.1604, Interim Guidelines for MASS Trials.

(MSC 101/WP.8, 2019, para. 2.5), trial awareness (MSC 101/WP.8, 2019, para. 2.6), communication and data exchange (MSC 101/WP.8, 2019, para. 2.7), reporting and information sharing (MSC 101/WP.8, 2019, para. 2.8), establishing the scope for each individual trial (MSC 101/WP.8, 2019, para. 2.9) and the assurance of sufficient cyber risk management and infrastructure when conducting MASS trial (MSC 101/WP.8, 2019, para. 2.10).

3.4 Intersessional Working Group on Maritime Autonomous Surface Ships (ISWG/MASS 1/6)

The intersessional working group (ISWG) met in September 2019 to consider the results of the first step of the RSE, take necessary actions for commencing the second step, and consider how the outcome of the second step should be reported to MSC 102. Furthermore, based on a high-level discussion on the gaps, themes and/or relevant findings identified during the first step, the group was ordained with the task to provide guidance to MS for use in the second step (MSC 101/24, 2019, para. 5.20).

The ISWG proceeded to consider the extensive input given through the 21 submissions provided by individual IMO MS that volunteered to conduct the first step, and agreed to the commencement of the second step for all ongoing parts of the RSE. In essence, this meeting would bolster support to commence the second step. The second step, the *analysis*, was based on the results gathered from the first step, and would determine the most appropriate ways of addressing MASS operations through:

I. Equivalence as provided for by the instruments or developing interpretations; and/or
II. Amending existing instruments; and/or
III. Developing new instruments; or
IV. None of the above as a result of the analysis.

Throughout the process, due consideration was given to the human element, technology and operational factors. In order to simplify the process, and present and communicate the results through easy-reference and concise manner, the analysis would be carried out from an instrument level, or in the case of SOLAS 74, at a chapter level.

3.5 The 103rd Session of the Maritime Safety Committee (MSC 103) (MSC 103/WP.8)

The initial plan was to finalize the RSE in 2020 and establish the WG at MSC 102. Unfortunately, this plan failed to materialize due to the Covid-19 pandemic. Therefore, it was decided that the MASS WG would be established at MSC 103 to finalize the RSE for MASS from the safety and security context.

The terms of reference of the MASS WG was not brief owing to the fact that it was instructed to consider the results of the second step of the RSE (MSC 102/5/3, MSC 102/5/4, MSC 102/5/5, MSC 102/5/6, MSC 102/5/8, MSC 102/5/9, MSC 102/5/10, MSC 102/5/11, MSC 102/5/12, MSC 102/5/13, MSC 102/5/15, MSC 102/5/17, MSC 102/5/19, MSC 102/5/20, MSC 102/5/21, MSC 102/5/22, MSC 102/5/23, MSC 102/5/24, MSC 102/5/25 and MSC 102/5/26), while taking into account document MSC 102/5/1 and the relevant parts of MSC 103/5/4, and prepare the outcome of the RSE. Ergo, the outcome of the RSE contained as a minimum:

1. Information for all degrees of autonomy for every instrument under the purview of the Maritime Safety Committee expected to be affected by MASS operations;
2. The most appropriate way(s) of addressing MASS operations in those instruments, as appropriate;
3. Identification of common themes and/or potential gaps that require addressing, taking into account documents MSC 102/5/7, MSC 102/5/30, MSC 103/5, MSC 103/5/1 and MSC 103/5/2;
4. Identification of possible links between instruments; and
5. Identification of priorities for further work, including terminology and the order in which instruments could be addressed taking into account common themes and potential gaps, and documents MSC 102/5/27, MSC 102/5/32, MSC 103/5, MSC 103/5/2, MSC 103/5/3, MSC 103/5/4, MSC 103/5/6, MSC 103/5/11 and MSC 103/5/12.

Fortunately, however, the group had a base/foundation document to work with, without which it could be presumed that RSE-work would remain ongoing. Finalization encompasses the result of the RSE at the instrument level (as presented in MSC/Circ.1368). This also involves common potential gaps, themes and links between and among instruments, which are crucial to establishing nexus with other ongoing RSEs undertaken by FAL and LEG. This would, in turn, facilitate the continuation of IMO's efforts as certain gaps and themes require attention from all committees concerned.

An important issue which has not received adequate attention is the potential gap in chapter VIII of the STCW Convention and the STCW Code. During the above-mentioned deliberations, it was noted that no analysis had been conducted with respect to chapter VIII (watchkeeping) of the STCW Convention and Code (and STCW-F Convention), in particular the issue surrounding the bridge watchkeeper, as this might be perceived as creating a potential issue for MASS operations. The WG agreed that this issue might require further consideration. The general consensus was that the STCW Convention and Code would be among the latter instruments that addressed MASS operations and that the focus for the RSE on STCW had been on the training and certification parts of the Convention and Code. However, it was agreed that watchkeeping would require an additional analysis to address MASS operations in the future. This, according to the author, is a potentially major barrier and threat to realizing MASS operations.

4 The Mandate: Striking a Balance

Striking a balance is of vital importance as we move towards drafting and agreeing on new rules and regulations for MASS. This notion has been somewhat abstract despite RSE's mindfulness of IMO's commitment to keeping the human element (safety and security of humans on board and elsewhere) pillar intact and visible alongside other important pillars, such as protection of the marine environment, facilitation and efficiency of global shipping. This is evident from the MSC 104 report and the carefully delineated road map for MASS anticipated there—all of which were discussed at the subsequent MSC session (MSC 105) where deliberations on the plan for developing a MASS Code were agreed upon (MSC 105/18, 2021, para. 15.9; MSC 105/20, 2022, para. 7.24). The main avenue for addressing MASS operations is the development of a goal-based MASS Code, which could help align the existing instruments with MASS provisions and simultaneously minimize the risk of inconsistencies. For more human-centric instruments, such as COLREGs and STCW), it was concluded that barriers could be treated through interpretations and equivalence, i.e., avenues already present in existing regulations. With regard to COLREGs, the prevalent opinion was that MASS should adhere to the same principles for navigation and collision avoidance in a fashion similar to conventional vessels.

As mentioned briefly above, an important part of the RSE is finalization with a sharp focus on potential common gaps and themes, i.e., terms, and other issues in the regulations that cut across several instruments (or SOLAS chapters), which renders them as being pivotal in the process (MSC.1/Circ.1638, para. 5.2). The word "pivotal" is used in the sense that they hold the keys to unlock many central issues horizontally across the IMO legal framework. That is why the following potential common gaps and themes were highly prioritized as efforts continued:

- Meaning of master and other personnel;
- Remote Control Station; and
- Remote Control Operator as a seafarer (MSC.1/Circ.1638, para. 5.4–5.7).

The report also indicates the high priority issues that could optimally guide and prioritize the future work on MASS operations (MSC.1/Circ.1638, sections 5 and 6 [in particular Table 6]). Those include:

- Development of a goal-based MASS Code
- Overseeing the MASS definition and supporting terminology for MASS operations, and
- Consideration of the development of a non-mandatory MASS instrument.

5 What Has Been Achieved?

5.1 Finalization

Evidently, three IMO Committees have conducted and finalized regulatory scoping exercises for MASS purposes: FAL, LEG and MSC.

5.1.1 Maritime Safety Committee (MSC)

The Maritime Safety Committee (MSC) was the first Committee to agree on an output for an RSE and the first Committee to finalize the output at MSC 103 in May 2021. The report has been disseminated through MSC.1/Circ.1638 (MSC 1/Circ. 1638, 2021).

The report contains proposals and recommendations in relation to how the IMO should address the barriers and grey areas for MASS operations in some "thirty plus" international conventions and codes, most notably SOLAS, International Convention on Load Lines, 1966 (LL), STCW, and Convention on the International Regulations for Preventing Collisions at Sea, 1972 (COLREGs).

Of particular interest are those deemed as being of high priority (see Table 1). A labeling system has been created mainly due to the frequent occurrence of potential common gaps and themes. They, therefore, need to be addressed in parallel with others in order to address those common potential gaps and/or themes (MSC.1/Circ.1638, para. 6.7.1 and Table 3; MSC.1/Circ.1638, para. 6.7.3).

The main avenue for addressing MASS operations is the development of a goal-based MASS Code, which could help align the existing instruments with MASS provisions and simultaneously minimize the risk of inconsistencies.

For more human-centric instruments, such as COLREGs and STCW, it was concluded that barriers could be treated through interpretations and equivalence, i.e., avenues already present in existing regulations. With regard to COLREGs, the prevalent opinion was that MASS should adhere to the same principles for navigation and collision avoidance in a fashion similar to conventional vessels.

The potential common gaps and themes, i.e., terms, and other issues in the regulations that cut across several instruments (or SOLAS chapters) were identified early in the process, and they will remain pivotal as we move forward in the process to regulate MASS. Here, again, the word "pivotal" is used in the sense that they hold the keys to unlock many central issues horizontally across the IMO legal framework. That is why the following potential common gaps and themes were highly prioritized as efforts continued:

- Meaning of master and other personnel;
- Remote Control Station; and
- Remote Control Operator as a seafarer (MSC.1/Circ.1638, para. 5.4; v).

Table 1 IMO list of high-priority instruments

SOLAS II-1: Degree of Autonomy (The most appropriate way(s) of addressing MASS operations)			
1 (IV)	2 (II)	3 (II–III)	4 (II–III)
SOLAS II-2: Degree of Autonomy (The most appropriate way(s) of addressing MASS operations)			
1 (IV)	2 (II–III)	3 (II–III)	4 (II–III)
SOLAS III: Degree of Autonomy (The most appropriate way(s) of addressing MASS operations)			
1 (IV)	2 (II–III)	3 (III)	4 (III)
SOLAS IV: Degree of Autonomy (The most appropriate way(s) of addressing MASS operations)			
1 (II)	2 (II–III)	3 (III)	4 (III)
SOLAS V: Degree of Autonomy (The most appropriate way(s) of addressing MASS operations)			
1 (II)	2 (II–III)	3 (III)	4 (III)
SOLAS VI: Degree of Autonomy (The most appropriate way(s) of addressing MASS operations)			
1 (IV)	2 (II–III)	3 (II–III)	4 (II–III)
SOLAS VII: Degree of Autonomy (The most appropriate way(s) of addressing MASS operations)			
1 (IV)	2 (II–III)	3 (II–III)	4 (II–III)
SOLAS IX: Degree of Autonomy (The most appropriate way(s) of addressing MASS operations)			
1 (IV)	2 (III)	3 (III)	4 (III)
SOLAS XI-1: Degree of Autonomy (The most appropriate way(s) of addressing MASS operations)			
1 (IV)	2 (III)	3 (I–III)	4 (I–III)
SOLAS XI-2: Degree of Autonomy (The most appropriate way(s) of addressing MASS operations)			
1 (I–II)	2 (II–III)	3 (II–III)	4 (II–III)
COLREG: Degree of Autonomy (The most appropriate way(s) of addressing MASS operations)			
1 (I)	2 (I–II)	3 (I–II)	4 (II)
STCW: Degree of Autonomy (The most appropriate way(s) of addressing MASS operations)			
1 (I–II)	2 (I–II–III)	3 (I–II–III)	4 (IV)
STCW-F: Degree of Autonomy (The most appropriate way(s) of addressing MASS operations)			
1 (I–II)	2 (I–II–III)	3 (I–II–III)	4 (IV)

(continued)

Table 1 (continued)

LL 1966 + 1988 Protocol: Degree of Autonomy (The most appropriate way(s) of addressing MASS operations)			
1 (IV)	2 (II)	3 (II)	4 (II)
SAR 1979: Degree of Autonomy (The most appropriate way(s) of addressing MASS operations)			
1 (IV)	2 (II)	3 (II)	4 (II)
TONNAGE 1969: Degree of Autonomy (The most appropriate way(s) of addressing MASS operations)			
1 (IV)	2 (I)	3 (I)	4 (I)
IMDG Code: Degree of Autonomy (The most appropriate way(s) of addressing MASS operations)			
1 (IV)	2 (II–III)	3 (II–III)	4 (II–III)
IMSBC Code: Degree of Autonomy (The most appropriate way(s) of addressing MASS operations)			
1 (IV)	2 (II–III)	3 (II–III)	4 (II–III)
FSS Code: Degree of Autonomy (The most appropriate way(s) of addressing MASS operations)			
1 (IV)	2 (II–III)	3 (II–III)	4 (II–III)
IBC Code: Degree of Autonomy (The most appropriate way(s) of addressing MASS operations)			
1 (IV)	2 (II–III)	3 (II–III)	4 (II–III)
IGC Code: Degree of Autonomy (The most appropriate way(s) of addressing MASS operations)			
1 (IV)	2 (II–III)	3 (II–III)	4 (II–III)

Source Adapted from IMO; MSC.1/Circ.1638, 3 June 2021, p. 13

The report also indicates the high priority issues that could optimally guide and prioritize the future work on MASS operations (MSC.1/Circ.1638, sections 5 and 6 [in particular Table 6]). Those include:

- The provisions that make MASS operations possible should be developed holistically, i.e., in a MASS Code, and be goal-based (MSC.1/Circular.1394/Rev.1—Generic Guidelines for Developing IMO Goal-Based Standards); and
- To consider the possibility of first developing non-mandatory provisions, which can supplement mandatory provisions. Here one needs to be heedful that MSC 104 subsequently decided that the ultimate goal would be the preparation of a mandatory instrument to address MASS operations (MSC 104/18, para. 15.9.4). In this

regard, IMO has used this sequence before, where non-mandatory precedes mandatory provisions—one of the examples being the IGF Code (International Code of Safety for Ship Using Gases or Other Low-flashpoint Fuels [IGF Code]) (International Code of Safety for Ship Using Gases or Other Low-flashpoint Fuels [IGF Code], 2015).

5.1.2 The Legal Committee

The RSEs of the LEG and FAL Committees were also finalized in 2021, however, the formal finalization of the FAL RSE was approved at FAL 46 in May 2022 (FAL.5/Circ.49, 2022). As anticipated, RSE concluded that addressing MASS operations do not necessarily trigger the need for a new instrument, but rather interpretations, minor editorial corrections or the odd amendment of a regulation. Of the two Committees, LEG had the most extensive RSE comprising 19 instruments (see Table 2, list of instruments and the appropriate way of addressing MASS operations). The full account of the LEG RSE can be found in LEG.1/Circ.11 (LEG.1/Circ.11, 2021).

It is relevant to note that, the most appropriate ways of addressing MASS operations (I-IV) bear the following meaning (LEG.1/Circ.11, 2021, para. 3.13):

I. Equivalence as provided for by the instruments or developing interpretations; and/or
II. Amending existing instruments; and/or
III. Developing new instruments; or
IV. None of the above as a result of the analysis.

Finally, with regard to MSC, the LEG identified the following common potential gaps and themes, which cut across several instruments:

1. The role and responsibility of the master;
2. The role and responsibility of the remote operator;
3. Questions of liability;
4. Definitions/terminology of MASS; and
5. Certificates (LEG.1/Circ.11, 2021, para. 5.1).

Table 2 Overview of the most appropriate way of addressing MASS operations

BUNKERS 2001: Degree of Autonomy (Most appropriate way of addressing MASS operations)			
1 (IV)	2 (IV)	3 (I, III)	4 (I, III)
CLC 1969: Degree of Autonomy (Most appropriate way of addressing MASS operations)			
1 (I, II, III)	2 (I, II, III)	3 (I, II, III)	4 (I, II, III)
CLC PROT 1976: Degree of Autonomy (Most appropriate way of addressing MASS operations)			
1 (IV)	2 (IV)	3 (IV)	4 (IV)
CLC 1992 (unofficial consolidated text): Degree of Autonomy (Most appropriate way of addressing MASS operations)			
1 (I, II, III)	2 (I, II, III)	3 (I, II, III)	4 (I, II, III)
FUND 1992 (unofficial consolidated text): Degree of Autonomy (Most appropriate way of addressing MASS operations)			
1 (IV)	2 (IV)	3 (IV)	4 (IV)
FUND PROT 2003: Degree of Autonomy (Most appropriate way of addressing MASS operations)			
1 (IV)	2 (IV)	3 (IV)	4 (IV)
NUCLEAR 1971: Degree of Autonomy (Most appropriate way of addressing MASS operations)			
1 (IV)	2 (IV)	3 (IV)	4 (I, II)
PAL 1974: Degree of Autonomy (Most appropriate way of addressing MASS operations)			
1 (I)	2 (I)	3 (I, II)	4 (I, II)
PAL 2002 (certified consolidated text): Degree of Autonomy (Most appropriate way of addressing MASS operations)			
1 (I)	2 (I)	3 (I, II)	4 (I, II)
PAL PROT 1976: Degree of Autonomy (Most appropriate way of addressing MASS operations)			
1 (IV)	2 (IV)	3 (IV)	4 (IV)
LLMC 1976: Degree of Autonomy (Most appropriate way of addressing MASS operations)			
1 (IV)	2 (II)	3 (II)	4 (II)
LLM PROT 1996 (unofficial consolidated text): Degree of Autonomy (Most appropriate way of addressing MASS operations)			
1 (IV)	2 (II)	3 (II)	4 (II)
HNS 2010 (unofficial consolidated text): Degree of Autonomy (Most appropriate way of addressing MASS operations)			
1 (IV)	2 (I)	3 (I, II)	4 (I, II)
SALVAGE 1989: Degree of Autonomy (Most appropriate way of addressing MASS operations)			
1 (IV)	2 (IV)	3 (I)	4 (I)

(continued)

Table 2 (continued)

NAIROBI WRC 2007: Degree of Autonomy (Most appropriate way of addressing MASS operations)			
1 (IV)	2 (I)	3 (I, II)	4 (I, II)
SUA 1988: Degree of Autonomy (Most appropriate way of addressing MASS operations)			
1 (IV)	2 (IV)	3 (IV)	4 (IV)
SUA 2005 (certified consolidated text): Degree of Autonomy (Most appropriate way of addressing MASS operations)			
1 (IV)	2 (IV)	3 (IV)	4 (IV)
SUA PROT: Degree of Autonomy (Most appropriate way of addressing MASS operations)			
1 (IV)	2 (IV)	3 (IV)	4 (IV)
SUA PROT 2005 (certified consolidated text): Degree of Autonomy (Most appropriate way of addressing MASS operations)			
1 (IV)	2 (IV)	3 (IV)	4 (IV)

Source Adapted from LEG.1/Circ.1, 15 December 2021

LEG also recognized that not all common potential gaps and/or themes possess the same traits. Some of those contain critical and fundamental issues that may shape the course of addressing MASS operations, while others concern more technical aspects (LEG.1/Circ.11, 2021, para. 5.10). Again, while some of these common potential gaps and/or themes are high priority issues that serve as core pathways to the introduction of safe and effective MASS operations into the regulatory framework, they may nevertheless, require a policy decision before addressing individual instruments. These include, for instance:

1. Meaning of the terms master, crew or responsible person;
2. Remote control station/center; and
3. Remote operator designated as seafarer (LEG.1/Circ.11, 2021, para. 5.11).

5.1.3 *The Facilitation Committee*

The regulatory scoping exercise of the FAL Committee comprised the FAL Convention and its supplementary guidelines. In summary, the FAL RSE concluded that the FAL Convention is capable of addressing MASS operations into the instrument without major amendments. The results of the RSE mainly demonstrate that sections 1, 2, and 4 of the FAL

Convention require a review or interpretation to accommodate MASS operations. Most requirements in section 3 of the FAL Convention have no application to MASS. That being said, some provisions may require amendments. Sections 5, 6, and 7 do not affect MASS and are applicable in their current forms (FAL.5/Circ.49, para. 4.2).

As for the MSC and LEG instruments, FAL identified common potential gaps and/or themes that may require clarifications to accommodate MASS within the existing regulatory framework. These include:

1. The role and responsibility of the master and crew;
2. The role and responsibility of the remote operator;
3. Persons rescued at sea, stowaways and refugees;
4. Sharing of information;
5. Definitions and terminology; and
6. Certificates and other documents (FAL.5/Circ.49, para. 5.1).

Since FAL was the last to finalize its RSE, the Committee was in a position to establish potential links with other Committee instruments. In this respect, FAL not only identified possible links with MSC and LEG instruments, but also identified, through a cross examination, all results, gaps and themes common across MSC, LEG and FAL instruments (FAL 46/14, annex, para. 5.12; FAL 46/14, annex, para. 5.18). These included:

1. The role and responsibility of the master and crew;
2. The role and responsibility of the remote operator;
3. Definitions/terminology of MASS; and
4. Certificates and other documents (FAL.5/Circ.49, para. 5.21).

Admittedly, the three to four basic issues identified on a whim at the early stages of the scoping exercise headed by the role and responsibility of the master and crew are likely the fundamental barriers that need to be addressed across the IMO universe. The question is: were four years misspent? The author's response to this would be "no". On the contrary, according to the author, it was very satisfying to be able to confirm the initial perception.

5.2 *Life After Finalization*

Given that the output for the safety and security instruments of the IMO was finalized in May 2021 at MSC 103, the inherent barriers to unreasonable hasty progress led to the need for a new output (agenda item) for MASS work to continue (MSC 103/21, 2021, para. 5.45 and 5.49). This concerned all areas under the purview of the three Committees. Hence, in October 2021 at MSC 104, a new output was agreed upon titled "Development of a goal-based instrument for maritime autonomous surface ships (MASS)" with 2025 as the target year of completion (MSC 104/18, para. 15.9.1). Subsequently, the Legal Committee and the FAL Committee have taken similar decisions (LEG 109/16/1, para. 13.9, 2022; FAL 46/24/1, para. 14.11, 2022).

5.2.1 *Mapping out the Beginning*

To structure this gargantuan task, MSC 104 decided that the Chair of MASS and key stakeholders would prepare a road map consisting of scope, steps and timelines, as well as undertake coordination work with other IMO bodies taking into account the documents submitted with the outcome of the RSE for detailed consideration at MSC 105 (MSC.1/Circ.1638; MSC 104/18, para. 15.9.1). Another key agreement was that the ultimate goal would be the preparation of a mandatory instrument to address MASS operations (MSC 104/18, para. 15.9.4). However, this agreement would be eventually slightly modified followed by a decision taken in April 2022 at MSC 105 that a non-mandatory goal-based Code should be developed as the first step before proceeding to the development of a mandatory Code. In addition, it was decided that the non-mandatory Code should initially cover cargo ships while also assessing the application to passenger ships with a view to considering detailed provisions for such ships at a later stage. All relevant issues pertaining to the development of the MASS code, predominantly those of high priority, were part of the Road map for developing a goal-based Code for MASS approved at MSC 105 (MSC 105/20, para. 7.24).

5.2.2 *Joint Efforts*

A part of the joint endeavor to address MASS operations is the establishment of a joint MSC–LEG–FAL joint working group (JWG) on MASS—a matter which all concerned Committees jointly agreed to on separate occasions (MSC 105/20, para. 7.25). The rationale behind establishing JWG is, as reflected in its terms of reference, to:

1. Develop a work plan, taking into account the road maps developed and updated by the three committees;
2. Address the common issues identified by the three committees based on MSC.1/Circ.1638, LEG.1/Circ.11 and the FAL RSE, to be finalized by FAL 46; and
3. Provide advice to the committees after every meeting (based on MSC.1/Circ.1638, LEG.1/Circ.11 and the FAL RSE, to be finalized by FAL 46).

It is noted that the JWG has the potential to bridge not only the common gaps and themes identified during the RSEs conducted by the three committees, but also those that initiate potential divergence of views between the committees given the inherent differences in the subject matters of the instruments under purview. It was underlined that the intention was not to have the JWG oversee, monitor or supervise the MASS work of the Organization. Rather, it is merely a subsidiary body to the three committees, and functions based on instructions received. At the time of writing this particular part of the chapter, in September 2022, the Joint Working Group on MASS has just finalized its first session, thus constituting itself and also creating a structure for its considerations and a template to document its results.

5.2.3 MASS Through Correspondence

Another robust measure agreed at MSC 105 was to establish an intersessional correspondence group, known as MSC MASS CG, based on MSC.1/Circ.1638, LEG.1/Circ.11 and the FAL RSE. The MSC MASS CG would work until May 2023 (MSC 107). Considering the steep IMO submission deadlines, this form of arrangement (where it does not report to MSC 106) is convenient as it gives MSC MASS CG several extra months for deliberating on essential and instrumental issues at MSC and therefore, at IMO altogether.

The instructions deferred to MSC MASS CG are similarly steep in its terms of reference that comprise both consideration of key principles and common understanding of the MASS Code's purpose and objectives, and the commencement of developing a non-mandatory provision (based on MSC.1/Circ.1638, LEG.1/Circ.11 and the FAL RSE, to be finalized by FAL 46). The above takes into account the potential gaps and themes identified, the scope and framework of the non-mandatory Code and the common potential gaps and/or themes identified during the RSE while focusing on the high priority items as well as the various relevant submissions to MSC 105/7/2, MSC 105/7/3, MSC 105/7/6, MSC 105/7/7, MSC 105/7/8 and MSC 105/7/9.

Should time permit, the MSC MASS CG would develop MSC MASS positions on the following points with the intention that these are submitted to a Joint MSC/LEG/FAL MASS WG, which include but not limited to:

1. Consideration, together with relevant documents, whether to amend the definition for MASS and degrees of autonomy (including the respective definition);
2. Meaning of the terms master, crew or responsible person;
3. Remote control station/center; and
4. Determination of the remote operator as a seafarer.

As indicated earlier, the deadline for the MASS output, i.e., the development of a goal-based instrument MASS is 2025. The author submits that the importance of this correspondence group cannot be underestimated. In the short term, the group will hopefully deliver texts on the high priority issues/common gaps and themes as well as texts on developing a non-mandatory Code.

6 Concluding Remarks

Establishing a trajectory is one that is far from easy. Although there were many mobile parts, we have successfully agreed on: a final RSE that was presented in MSC.1Circ. 1638 (and the corresponding finalizations of the other Committees engaged in this work at this stage); and a number of bearing principles that will serve as the plinth for future work.

As presented in the preceding sections, the finalization of the RSE contains several indicators as to what can be expected as IMO continues efforts to regulate MASS. A new instrument will be developed covering IMO's safety and security provisions. While non-mandatory in the interim, they will inevitably be mandatory. As can be foreseen, the instrument will be goal-based—referring to the fact that the provisions will be universally applicable and easy to communicate. Be that as it may, it will present a challenge for administrations, recognized organizations (RO) and the industry when determining (during certification and other approval processes) whether a MASS ship or system will have at least the same level of safety as a conventional ship.

Regarding the inventory of problems, issues, gaps and themes identified during the RSE, we did not encounter that many surprises. It would be fair to say that the shipping community, flag State administrations, academia and the industry at large had a fairly good knowledge over what needed to be addressed, including matters related to the possible designation of a "remote operator" as "seafarer"—a theme that was a potential common gap in several instruments. Furthermore, and this is an apparent elephant in the room, the degrees of autonomy need to be re-evaluated taking into account the lessons learned during the RSE. New definitions were proposed in several places both as a part of the RSE and in submissions to MSC sessions. Those are well in for further consideration (MSC.1/Circ.1638, paras. 5.4–5.8). Not many surprises were revealed. All matters and issues are now well documented.

Looking to the future, we need to decide to what degree and extent will MASS be a goal-based code (GBS). Are we satisfied with a "goal-based light code" in the Polar Code (MEPC 68/21/Add.1) mold or are we going to fully tilt GBS in the mold of SOLAS Chapter II-1 ship construction standards for bulk and tank ships of at least 150 meters in length? The latter would pose an extreme challenge for the IMO whereas the former could be considered as painting an incomplete picture.

When it comes to the entry into force mechanisms and the scope of the code, one needs to consider whether the code should be a complementary (add-on) code or a stand-alone instrument. This also begs the question: should consider developing provisions for all relevant IMO instruments under MSC remit or only a few, e.g., SOLAS 74? Here one needs to consider the massive implications if we were to choose a stand-alone instrument, e.g., MASS SOLAS, which would imply the development of a completely new goal-based SOLAS—something that would take several decades to achieve, if at all. This is why the more moderate, but still very comprehensive, option is a complementary (add-on) code containing provisions to address the new risks identified vis-à-vis MASS operations.

Regarding entry into force of the code, when mandatory, instigates the question whether the code should focus on the subject matter of one or a few instruments, e.g., SOLAS, COLREGs, STCW, or if MASS operations should be considered holistically where all those high priority instruments identified in the RSE should be addressed all at once. Considering only the SOLAS chapters, which cover several areas including design, construction, stability, machinery, fire protection, life-saving, communication, navigation, would be quite challenging. This has the potential to give the code a natural habitat within the ambit of SOLAS, and help bring the code into force through its own chapter. However, this would render the code of not having the expected holistic features pursuant to the RSE, but it would make it possible for the code to enter into force in a more expeditious manner compared to the option of linking it to several instruments. As a deterrent, one could revisit the complicated process through which the IMO Member State Audit Scheme (IMSAS) became a treaty obligation in January 2016 through nine instruments including COLREGs, Load Lines, MARPOL and SOLAS. To conclude, this remains inconclusive.

Now if I were to put my money on one option: add-on or stand-alone—I would opt for add-on, especially, if we consider developing a MASS Code in the Polar Code mold. And if I allow myself to look ahead, in order not to repeat or create provisions in areas where there are no existing problems or heightened risks vis-à-vis MASS operations, a MASS (ship or system) could seamlessly apply all applicable provisions (of SOLAS and other mandatory instruments) which are "non-problematic." This may extend to 95 percent of (ship) approval-related matters, or even more. In which case the MASS Code would address only those areas where there is observed heightened risk when the ship/system is remotely controlled or in an autonomous operation.

Against my option, the critics could argue, and with good intent, that we already have a system in place. Administrations and ROs (that are recognized by flag State Administrations to perform flag State inspections and surveys required by IMO instruments) could use the third-party approval procedure in MSC.1/Circ.1455(MSC. 1/Circ. 1455, 2013). They could then notify the IMO and its MS of their approval to provide the ship access to international trade without the risk of sanctions. The flaw of this reasoning is that the "1455 process" is heavy and complex and since there is no harmonized international instrument or standards to apply, lack of predictability and transparency would probably hamper development and industry investment. Presumably, MASS will not operate without IMO provisions, guidelines or regulations in place.

As my primal task concentrated on safety and security instruments of the IMO, other areas of mandatory rules and regulations have been outside the scope of my focus. When considering the above, one cannot ignore the United Nations Convention on the Law of the Sea, 1982 (UNCLOS)—the constitution that establishes a legal framework for all marine and maritime activities.

In particular, the flag State obligations are of interest, e.g., that the flag State should "take such measures...as are necessary to ensure safety at sea with regard, inter alia, to ... the manning of ships, labor conditions and the training of crews, taking into account the applicable international instruments" (UNCLOS, Article 94[3][b]). This provision further stipulates that this includes measures necessary to ensure: "... that each ship is in the charge of a master and officers who possess appropriate qualifications, in particular in seamanship, navigation, communications and marine engineering, and that the crew is appropriate in qualification and numbers for the type, size, machinery and equipment of the ship" (UNCLOS, Article 94[4][b]). However, the IMO through the rule of reference requires each flag State "to conform to generally accepted international regulations, procedures and practices and to take any steps which may be necessary to secure their observance" when adopting prescribed measures (UNCLOS, Article 94[5]). As alluded to above, UNCLOS can, and should, be understood as a constitution, setting the scene for more detailed provisions on safe, secure and sustainable shipping.

Here the IMO is not the only provider of international provisions. For Swedish ships that adhere to the International Convention for the Unification of Certain Rules of Law relating to Bills of Lading (1924)/First Protocol (1968)/Second Protocol (1979), some of the implementing provisions have resulted in being problematic, in particular, chapter 6 of the Swedish Maritime Code (1994:1004), when it comes to the positioning of the Master during navigation and other conditions. The same applies to other Nordic countries. Also, these potential ("non-IMO") legal barriers need the attention of legislator both international and domestic.

Recent events at IMO concluded with the note that predictability is instrumental for flag State Administrations and industry. Before wrapping up with these closing remarks, one needs to dwell on the most important aspect of this disruption of the transport sector (paradigm shift)—and that is public opinion and how to gain the people's trust in MASS. Here tests and trials are vital as well as transparency of results and other data. If the public, and their representatives, are in doubt regarding the safety and security of MASS, then MASS will not change the shape of transport. Instead, the paradigm shift will make a U-turn. That is why the human element must guide this work—as well as everything else that IMO does—because humans are designing the systems, humans are testing the systems; therefore, humans need to understand the systems and how they function, and how they connect with other systems, whether MASS and conventional ships. Humans are at the receiving end of MASS operations, whether as buyers of transport services or as passengers (or their relatives), and it is therefore, my firm belief that the role of the human element will remain constant, if not increase, in parallel with the increased use of technology.

References

Blanke, M. (2016). En Foranalyse Om Autonome Skibe.

COLREGs. (1972). Convention on International Regulations for Preventing Collisions at Sea, Oct. 20, 1972, 28 U.S.T. 3459, T.I.A.S. 8587CSC (1972).

IGF Code. (2015). International Code of Safety for Ship Using Gases or Other Low-flashpoint Fuels adopted in 2015 Through Resolution MSC.391 (95).

IMO Doc. MSC.1/Circ. 1455. (2013). Guidelines for the Approval of Alternatives and Equivalents as Provided for in Various IMO Instruments (24 June, 2013).

IMO Doc. MSC 98/23. (2017). Report of the Maritime Safety Committee on Its Ninety-Eighth Session (28 June, 2017).

IMO Doc. MSC 98/INF.13. (2017). A Pre-analysis on Autonomous Ships, Submitted by Denmark (4 April, 2017).

IMO Doc MSC 99/22. (2018). Report of the Maritime Safety Committee on Its Ninety-Ninth Session.

IMO Doc MSC 100/WP.8. (2018). Report of the Working Group on a Regulatory Scoping Exercise for the use of Maritime Autonomous Surface Ships (MASS).

IMO Doc. MSC 101/WP.8. (2019a). Report of the Working Group on a Regulatory Scoping Exercise for the use of Maritime Autonomous Surface Ships (MASS).

IMO Doc. MSC 101/WP.8 (2019b), Regulatory Scoping Exercise for the Use of Maritime Autonomous Surface Ships (MASS) (June 12, 2019) (subsequently published as MSC.1/Circ.1604, Interim Guidelines for MASS Trials.

IMO Doc. MSC 99/22. (2018). Report of the Maritime Safety Committee on Its Ninety-Ninth Session (June 5, 2018).
IMO Doc. MSC 101/24. (2019). Report of the Maritime Safety Committee on Its 101st Session (July 12, 2019).
IMO Doc. MSC 103/WP.11. (2021a). Regulatory Scoping Exercise for the Use of Maritime Autonomous Surface Ships (MASS) (April 29, 2021).
IMO Doc. MSC 103/21. (2021b). Report of the Maritime Safety Committee on Its 103rd Session (May 25, 2021).
IMO Doc MSC 103/WP.11. (2021). Draft Outcome of the Regulatory Scoping Exercise for the Use of MASS.
MSC.1/Circ.1455. (2013). Guidelines for the Approval of Alternatives and Equivalents as Provided for in Various IMO Instruments.
IMO Doc. MSC.1/Circ.1638. (2021). Outcome of the Regulatory Scoping Exercise for the Use of Maritime Autonomous Surface Ships (MASS) (June 3, 2021).
IMO Doc. MSC 104/18. (2021). Report of the Maritime Safety Committee on Its 104th Session (October 19, 2021).
IMO Doc MSC 104. (2021). Maritime Safety Committee (MSC), 104th Session (October 4–8, 2021).
IMO Doc MSC 104/18. (2021). Report of the Maritime Safety Committee on Its 104th Session (October 19, 2021).
IMO Doc MSC 105/20. (2022). Report of the Maritime Safety Committee on Its 105th Session (May 19, 2022).
IMO Doc. LEG.1/Circ.11. (2021). Outcome of the Regulatory Scoping Exercise and Gap Analysis of Conventions emanating from the Legal Committee with Respect to Maritime Autonomous Surface Ships (MASS) (December 15, 2021).
IMO Doc. LEG 109/16/1. (2022). Report of the Legal Committee on the Work of Its 109th Session (April 7, 2022).
IMO Doc FAL.5/Circ.49. (2022). Outcome of the Regulatory Scoping Exercise and Gap Analysis of the FAL Convention with Respect to Maritime Autonomous Surface Ships (MASS).
IMO Doc. FAL 46/14. (2021). Regulatory Scoping Exercise for the Use of Maritime Autonomous Surface Ships (MASS) (November 3, 2021).
IMO Doc. FAL 46/24. (2022). Report of the Facilitation Committee on Its Forty-Sixth Session (May 25, 2022).
IMO FAL 46/24/1. (2022). The Report of the Forty-Sixth Session of the Facilitation Committee.
International Maritime Organization. (IMO). International Convention on Maritime Search and Rescue, 27 April 1979, 1403 UNTS.

Load Line. (1966). International Convention on Load Lines as Amended by the Protocol of 1988, April 5, 1966, International Maritime Organization, 640 UNTS.

MSC 104. (2021). Maritime Safety Committee (MSC), 104th Session (October 4–8, 2021).

SOLAS. (1974). International Convention for the Safety of Life at Sea, Nov. 1, 1974, 32 U.S.T. 47, T.I.A.S. 9700.

Special Trade Passenger Ships Agreement. (1971, October 6). United Nations—Treaty Series.

STCW. (1978). International Convention on Standards of Training, Certification and Watchkeeping, 1361 *UNTS 2* as amended in 1995 and 2010 (Manila Amendments). 1361 *UNTS* 190.

STCW-F. (1995). International Convention on Standards of Training, Certification and Watchkeeping for Fishing Vessel Personnel, 7 July 1995, International Maritime Organization.

TONNAGE. (1969). International Convention on Tonnage Measurement of Ships, 23 June 1969, International Maritime Organization, 1291 UNTS.

United Nations Convention on the Law of the Sea, adopted 10 December 1982, UNTS 1833 (Entered into Force 16 November 1994) (UNCLOS).

PART II

Naval Warfare & Security

CHAPTER 4

Advent of a New Era in Naval Warfare: Autonomous and Unmanned Systems

Raul Pedrozo

1 Introduction

The survival of the free and open global commons that has brought peace and prosperity to much of the world for over seven decades is at an inflection point. The re-emergence of great power competition with China and Russia, and increased threats from rogue states like Iran and North Korea, are eroding the rules-based international order. Coupled with unparalleled technological advances in artificial intelligence (AI), autonomy,

The views expressed in this chapter are those of the author and do not reflect the views of the U.S. Government, U.S. Department of Defense, or the U.S. Naval War College.

R. Pedrozo (✉)
Stockton Center for International Law, US Naval War College, Newport, RI, USA
e-mail: Raul.Pedrozo@usnwc.edu

© The Author(s), under exclusive license to Springer Nature Switzerland AG 2023

T. M. Johansson et al. (eds.), *Autonomous Vessels in Maritime Affairs*, Studies in National Governance and Emerging Technologies,
https://doi.org/10.1007/978-3-031-24740-8_4

and unmanned systems (UxS), great power rivalries have created a more complex and volatile security environment than any experienced in recent times. To meet these new threats, the United States is building a more lethal and distributed hybrid naval force across all domains to deter and defeat future adversaries. The advanced technologies and autonomous systems that support this hybrid manned-unmanned force "stands to be the greatest transformation in modern warfare since the gunpowder revolution" (Engelhardt, 2021). Thus, the question is no longer whether the United States of America (US) Navy will leverage unmanned platforms and systems across all domains to provide additional warfighting capability and capacity to augment the traditional force structure, but how quickly and efficiently it will be able to do so to meet future security challenges. Chief of Naval Operations Admiral Mike Gilday has indicated that his number two priority for the fleet is the integration of unmanned and manned systems (Eckstein, 2021).

Over the past two years, the US Navy has conducted a series of successful tests designed to further enhance autonomous systems, demonstrate their reliability in the maritime environment, and develop new operational concepts to integrate manned and unmanned platforms more rapidly. Between September 18 and November 5, 2020, an Overload large unmanned surface vessel (USV)—*Ranger*—made an autonomous voyage from Mobile, Alabama, to Port Hueneme, California, stopping along the way to conduct operations in the Gulf of Mexico before transiting the Panama Canal. The 59-meter USV—equipped with autonomous navigation and engineering systems—is part of the Navy's "Ghost Fleet" program, which stood up in 2018 in partnership with the DoD Strategic Capabilities Office (SCO). The highly successful six-week voyage covered over 4700 nautical miles, 97 percent of which was in the autonomous mode. Except for the transit of the Panama Canal, command and control of the USV was accomplished remotely from a San Diego-based command center by sailors assigned to Surface Development Squadron One (SURFDEVRON ONE). After arriving in California, *Ranger* participated in Exercise Dawn Blitz, where it demonstrated its ability to interact with manned platforms, comply with the International Regulations for Preventing Collisions at Sea (COLREGs), and engage in station keeping, loiter, and transit missions. During the exercise, *Ranger* operated autonomously for over 130 hours and traveled over 950 nautical miles—98 percent of its underway time (Lopez, 2021).

A second successful Ghost Fleet Overload test was conducted by USV *Nomad* in May 2021. Like her sister ship, *Nomad* traveled 4421 nautical miles from Mobile, Alabama, to Point Loma, California. The USV operated under manned control only when it transited the Panama Canal. The rest of the voyage (98 percent) was remotely controlled from the San Diego-based Unmanned Operations Center (UOC). The command-and-control system was programmed with a scheme of maneuver that allowed the system to calculate course and speed to complete the mission. The system is programmed to react to contacts along the way so it can replan and reprioritize how to accomplish its mission (LaGrone, 2021).

The UOC is manned 24/7 by surface warfare-qualified officers and enlisted personnel with appropriate rates trained in COLREGs and ship-handling. The UOC is also responsible for supervising the development of code for the supervisory control system of the vessel to ensure precise and reliable command and control of the USV (Eckstein, 2020). These two milestone tests provided the Navy with an opportunity to evaluate the USV's endurance, autonomous operations capabilities, and command-and-control system, as well as the endurance of the USV's hull, mechanical, and engineering systems. The results of these tests clearly demonstrate the ability of USVs to integrate with manned platforms safely and effectively.

The integration of UxS to create a hybrid fleet of manned and unmanned platforms will fundamentally shift the way the Navy conducts naval operations. The development of new operational concepts to support this integration potentially raises numerous issues under international and domestic law (Kraska, 1995, 2010). Can a government-owned or operated unmanned maritime system (UMS) be a ship under international and domestic law? Do UxS enjoy the same navigational rights and duties in and over the ocean as manned ships and aircraft? Can UxS comply with existing international rules regarding safety of navigation and civil aviation? Can a UMS engage in offensive belligerent acts during an armed conflict at sea consistent with the law of naval warfare? This chapter will analyze these and other related questions by examining state practice, relevant international instruments, and the laws of naval warfare.

2 Why Unmanned Systems?

Since their inception, UxS, have been the preferred alternative to manned systems for dull, dirty, and dangerous missions because they reduce risk to human life. The use of UAVs during the US wars in Iraq and Afghanistan has demonstrated that dull missions, like persistent, long-duration intelligence, surveillance, and reconnaissance (ISR) operations, are better suited for UxS. Similarly, UxS are superior to manned systems in conducting dirty work, like detection, of chemical, biological, nuclear, or radiological material because they significantly reduce exposing humans to hazardous conditions. UxS are also fearless and are therefore superior at performing inherently dangerous missions, such as mine clearance operations and deactivating improvised explosive devices (DoD Integrated Roadmap, 2014).

Integrating unmanned and autonomous systems and AI capabilities into the fleet offers the Navy numerous advantages, such as reduced personnel and manpower requirements; reduced risk to personnel; lower operating costs; greater persistence and range; enhanced speed and accuracy of data processing; greater access to denied areas; and enable a faster decision cycle. When integrated into the fleet, combined manned-unmanned capabilities will far exceed the effectiveness of manned platforms or humans alone (Navy Strategic Roadmap, 2021).

Apart from their many advantages, UxS are also financially attractive. The USVs *Sea Hunter* and *Sea Hawk* cost about $20 million and $35.5 million, respectively, compared to the estimated cost of $1.2 billion for the Navy's new guided missile frigate (FFG[X]) (Naval CBO, 2020; Technology, 2018). Operating costs for the USVs are also much lower—$15–20,000 per day compared with a manned destroyer's operating costs of about $700,000 per day (Macias, 2018). Similarly, the Navy's new extra-large unmanned underwater vehicle (XLUUV) *Orca* costs about $54.88 million, compared to $3.4 billion for a Virginia-class attack submarine (Naval Howard, 2021; Roblin, 2019; Technology, 2019). Thus, in addition to the many operational advantages the integration of UxS offer to the fleet, these cost advantages will allow the Navy to create a more effective force architecture by reducing the number of expensive manned combatants and significantly increasing the number of relatively inexpensive UMSs of various sizes and capabilities that will enhance the fleet's warfighting capacity across all domains throughout the spectrum of conflict.

A more distributed, hybrid fleet architecture allows the Navy to spread sensors and weapon systems among a greater number of platforms, thus complicating the enemy's targeting capability by increasing the number of units to detect, identify, track, and engage. A hybrid fleet comprised of manned and unmanned platforms with similar capabilities also reduces the effects of the loss of an individual high-value platform. Moreover, increasing the number of UxSs deployed with the fleet facilitates the execution of missions in denied or contested areas that would be too risky for manned platforms (CRS R45757, 2021).

3 Unmanned Maritime Systems Mission Sets

The US Navy is currently operating and developing a variety of UMSs—both autonomous or remotely operated USVs and UUVs—that will augment manned platforms to conduct a variety of missions in support of fleet operations in times of peace or war. These systems can be launched from aircraft, submarines, or surface ships to perform a wide range of high-priority missions with minimal risk to personnel and with greater persistence, range, accuracy, and speed. Anticipated UMS mission sets include: inshore port and harbor defense; mine countermeasures (MCM) in contested waters; ISR in denied ocean spaces; offensive mining of enemy ports or strategic chokepoints; anti-submarine warfare (ASW) and anti-surface warfare (ASuW); ocean mapping and tracking; special operations support; payload delivery; Communication/Navigation Network Nodes (CN3); electronic warfare (EW); information operations (IO); inspection and identification; facilitating maritime interdiction operations (MIO) in peacetime and the belligerent right of visit and search in wartime; and precision/Time Critical Strikes (TCS) (Navy UUV Master Plan, 2004, 2007).

To effectively conduct these missions at sea in peacetime and wartime, some UMSs will need to be designated "ships" or "warships" in order to lawfully engage in belligerent rights and exercise navigation and overflight rights and freedoms, and other internationally lawful uses of the seas, on, under, and over the world's oceans. The Convention on International Civil Aviation (Chicago Convention) and instruments adopted by the International Civil Aviation Organization (ICAO) clearly define the legal status of UAVs as aircraft (Chicago Convention, 1944; DoDI 4540.01, 2015; DoD Law of War Manual, 2016; ICAO Cir. 328, 2011). State practice, as reflected in military manuals of numerous states, also treats

UAVs as military aircraft. International law does not, however, provide a similar bright-line test for whether UMSs qualify as "ships" or "vessels." UMSs are not specifically addressed in instruments adopted by the International Maritime Organization (IMO).

4 Status of Unmanned Maritime Systems

Not all UMSs will qualify as a ship or warship. Clearly, an unmanned autonomous ocean glider, equipped with advanced sensors to monitor temperature, salinity, current, and other ocean conditions, is uniquely suited to collect data in remote locations, safely and at a reduced cost. These systems travel through the oceans over great distances and over long periods of time without human intervention. They are not considered ships, but if government-owned or operated, they are entitled to sovereign immunity as state property, whether launched from a sovereign immune ship or aircraft or deployed from shore (NWP 1-14M, 2017). The question is whether larger UMSs, like USV *Sea Hunter/Sea Hawk*, USV *Ranger/Nomad*, and XLUUV *Orca* can be designated ships or warships by the flag state consistent with domestic and international law. As states shift toward commercial and military use of UMSs, the legal status of these systems is becoming a more pressing issue.

4.1 Definition of Ship or Vessel

Regulation V/2 of International Convention for the Safety of Life at Sea 1974 (SOLAS) defines "ships" as "any ship, vessel or craft irrespective of type and purpose" (IMO Res. MSC. 99[73], 2000; SOLAS, 1974). "Ship" is more precisely defined in article 2 of the Convention for the Prevention of Pollution from Ships (MARPOL) as "a vessel of any type whatsoever operating in the marine environment and includes hydrofoil boats, air-cushion vehicles, submersibles, floating craft and fixed or floating platforms" (MARPOL, 1973/1978). Rule 3 of COLREGs similarly provides a more expanded definition of the term "vessel" to include "every description of watercraft, including non-displacement craft, WIG (wing-in-ground) craft and seaplanes, used or capable of being used as a means of transportation on water" (COLREGs, 1972). Article 1 of the London Dumping Convention also contains a fairly broad definition of "vessel" to include "waterborne...craft of any type whatsoever...[and] includes air-cushioned craft and floating craft, whether self-propelled or not" (LDC, 1972) Finally, article 1 of the Convention on the Suppression of Unlawful Acts against the Safety of Maritime Navigation (SUA) defines a "ship" as "a vessel of any type whatsoever not permanently attached to the sea-bed, including dynamically supported craft, submersibles, or any other floating craft" (SUA, 2005).

In evaluating whether a UMS can qualify as a ship or vessel, the Comité Maritime International (CMI) noted that:

> existing international conventions that define the term 'ship' do not include references to crewing and at national level...[and] the definition of a ship is usually disconnected from the question of whether or not the ship is manned. It would...seem unjustified that two ships, one manned and the other unmanned, doing similar tasks involving similar dangers would not be subject to the same rules that have been designed to address those dangers. (CMI, 2018)

Thus, whether a platform is manned or unmanned or under human or autonomous control are not essential characteristics of what constitutes a "ship" or "vessel." Therefore, lacking a definitive statement to the contrary in an international instrument, most UMSs can be characterized as a "ship" or "vessel" under domestic and international law.

Although "ship" and "vessel" are not defined in the 1982 United Nations Convention on the Law of the Sea (UNCLOS), it envisions the use of UMSs in the marine environment. Article 19 provides that ships engaged in innocent passage may not launch, land, or take on board any military device, which would presumably include military UAVs and UMSs. Similarly, Article 20 requires submarines and "underwater vehicles" to navigate on the surface and show their flag when transiting the territorial sea in innocent passage. The term "underwater vehicles" includes UUVs.

Nonetheless, UNCLOS Article 94 indicates that ships should be manned by a crew and under the control of a master. Flag States are required to take necessary measures to ensure safety at sea regarding their flag vessels, to include the "manning of ships...and the training of crews, taking into account the applicable international instruments." Such measures include those necessary to ensure, *inter alia*:

- that each ship is in the charge of a master and officers who possess appropriate qualifications in seamanship, navigation, communications, and marine engineering, and a qualified crew sufficient in numbers for the type, size, machinery, and equipment of the ship; and
- that the master, officers, and the crew (if appropriate) are fully conversant with and can observe the applicable international regulations reflected in SOLAS (including radio communications), COLREGs, and MARPOL.

In taking these measures, Article 94 requires that the flag State shall conform and observe generally accepted international regulations, procedures, and practices adopted by the IMO. UNCLOS does not, however, specifically require that the master or crew be physically present on board the ship. In this regard, CMI has concluded that the requirements of article 94 can "arguably be met in the case of remotely operated ships" (CMI, 2018). Moreover, international law makes clear that the flag State alone has the authority to fix the conditions for the grant of its nationality to ships, for the registration of ships in its territory, and for the right to fly its flag (The Muscat Dhows, 1916; UNCLOS, 1982).

Thus, like remotely piloted UAVs that have been used over the past three decades to conduct counter-terrorism operations in the Middle East and Africa, it is conceivable that UMSs could similarly be remotely manned and operated by a crew and under the charge of a master that is shore-based, far-removed from the area of operation, or embarked on a warship or naval auxiliary in the vicinity of the UMS. The only requirement is that the flag State must ensure that the master, officers, and crew that are remotely manning and operating the UMS are fully conversant with, and required to observe, the applicable international regulations reflected in IMO instruments, and that the system can comply with these regulations.

4.2 *IMO and Maritime Autonomous Surface Ships*

Since 2017, the IMO Maritime Safety Committee (MSC) has been discussing the relationship between maritime autonomous surface ships (MASS) and IMO instruments (IMO Doc. MSC 98/20/2, 2017). In December 2018, MSC adopted a framework for a regulatory scoping exercise for MASS operations. For purposes of the scoping exercise, MASS is defined as "a ship which, to a varying degree, can operate independently of human interaction." The varying degrees of autonomy considered by the Committee during the exercise included:

- *Ship with automated processes and decision support*: Seafarers are on board to operate and control shipboard systems and functions. Some operations may be automated.
- *Remotely controlled ship with seafarers on board*: The ship is controlled and operated from another location, but seafarers are on board to take control if necessary.
- *Remotely controlled ship without seafarers on board*: The ship is controlled and operated from another location. There are no seafarers on board.
- *Fully autonomous ship*: The operating system of the ship can make decisions and determine actions by itself (IMO Doc. MSC 100/20/Add.1, 2018).

The scoping exercise was completed in May 2021 with the MSC's approval of the *Outcome of the Regulatory Scoping Exercise for the use of Maritime Autonomous Surface Ships (MASS)*. The report provides an assessment of the degree to which existing IMO treaties and instruments under the purview of the MSC might be affected by MASS operations. In general, the MSC concluded that, depending on the degree of autonomy, many IMO instruments could apply to unmanned vessels through "equivalences" or interpretation, while others would require amendment of the instruments or development of a new instrument altogether IMO Doc. MSC.99/WP.9, 2018; IMO Doc. MSC/99/22; IMO Doc. MSC.1/Circ. 1638 (2021). MSC additionally approved Interim Guidelines for Maritime Autonomous Surface Ships (MASS) trials (IMO Doc. MSC.1/Circ. 1604, 2019).

In support of the IMO's scoping exercise, the CMI Executive Council established a working group to examine the current international legal framework and consider what amendments, adaptions, or clarifications are required in relation to UMSs to ensure the use and operation of such vessels is consistent with international law. To this end, CMI developed a questionnaire for the IMO that asked nations whether UMSs could be considered "ships" under their national laws. Ninety percent of the nations that responded to the questionnaire indicated that UMSs could constitute a ship under their domestic laws and regulations (IMO Doc. MSC 99/20, 2018).

4.3 *Definition of Warship*

If a government-owned or operated UMS can qualify as a "ship," can the flag State designate it as a "warship" as that term is defined in international law? Such a designation is important for the flag State since only warships can exercise belligerent rights—offensive attacks or the right of visit and search of neutral ships—during an international armed conflict under the law of naval warfare (Hague VII, 1907; NWP 1-14M, 2017; Oxford Manual, 1913; Paris Declaration, 1856).

"Warship" is defined in UNCLOS Article 29 as "a ship belonging to the armed forces of a State bearing the external marks distinguishing such ships of its nationality, under the command of an officer duly commissioned by the government of the State and whose name appears in the appropriate service list or its equivalent and manned by a crew which is under regular armed forces discipline." This definition dates to the Paris Declaration of 1856 when privateering was abolished as a method of warfare and was codified during the negotiations of the 1907 Hague VII Convention concerning the conversion of merchant ships into warships. This definition is recognized as customary international law by most states, including the United States (Colombos, 1967; DoD Law of War Manual, 2016; NWP 1-14M, 2017). The warship does not have to be armed, but it must be under the command of a duly commissioned officer and manned by a qualified crew subject to armed forces discipline.

A UMS can obviously be owned or operated by the armed forces of a state and can bear external markings regarding its nationality. However, can a UMS be remotely or autonomously "under the command" of a commissioned officer and "manned" by a crew subject to armed forces discipline?

Articles 1–4 of the 1907 Hague VII Convention, which governs the conversion of merchant ships to warships, requires that the converted merchant ship: (1) be "placed under the direct authority, immediate control, and responsibility of the Power whose flag it flies;" (2) "bear the external marks which distinguish the warships of their nationality;" (3) be under the command of a duly commissioned officer in the service of the State whose "name must figure on the list of the officers of the fighting fleet;" and (4) be manned by a crew "subject to military discipline." The drafters of Hague VII could not have envisioned the advent of UMSs. Such systems are already in operation and will profoundly shape armed conflict at sea. Consequently, the definition of "warship" should be re-interpreted considering these current and emerging technologies.

Like the IMO instruments applicable to civilian vessels, there is nothing in UNCLOS or any other international instrument that requires the commanding officer and crew to be physically on board the warship. Like remotely piloted UAVs, the flag State can determine that a UMS can be remotely manned by a crew and under the command of a commissioned officer that is not physically present on the ship and therefore qualify as a "warship" under domestic and international law. As is the case with civilian ships, the flag State decides under what conditions a UMS can be designated a "warship" under its domestic laws and regulations (The Muscat Dhows, 1916).

In the United States, the Chief of Naval Operations (CNO) is authorized to register, classify, and designate naval waterborne craft as "warships" (Navy Regs, 1990; 10 U.S.C. § 6011, 2018). Any ship built or armed for naval combat that the CNO places on the Naval Vessel Register can be classified as a "warship." These ships are entered into the battle force ship inventory and commissioned United States Ship (USS) warships capable of conducting offensive belligerent rights during an armed conflict (SECNAVINST 5030.8C, 2016). Neither US Navy Regulations nor Secretary of the Navy Instructions distinguishes between manned and unmanned platforms. Therefore, the CNO may legally designate a UMS as a warship if he or she determines that the UMS can be remotely or autonomously commanded and operated safely and can comply with applicable international regulations.

That is not to say that all UMSs should be designated "warships." Those that are not so designated can still be classified as naval auxiliaries. These auxiliary UMSs may defend themselves against attack but may not conduct offensive attacks during an international armed conflict. However, as UMSs are increasingly integrated into the fleet and their mission sets expand to include offensive operations like ASW, ASuW, offensive mining, and TCS, states will need to readjust their policies concerning the status of UMSs as "warships" consistent with their international legal obligations (Navy UUV Master Plan).

5 Sovereign Immunity

As a matter of customary international law, as reflected in UNCLOS Articles 32, 95, and 96, all manned and unmanned vessels and aircraft owned or operated by a state, and used, for the time being, only on government noncommercial service are entitled to sovereign immunity. The characterization of a UxS, however, will determine if it enjoys sovereign immunity as a distinct sovereign immune platform or whether it enjoys sovereign immunity as government property or an appendage or extension of a manned platform that is entitled to sovereign immunity. Nonetheless, regardless of whether a UMS is considered a warship, naval auxiliary, or simply a device, it is entitled to all the rights, privileges, and immunities enjoyed by such vessels and devices under international law. If designated a ship or vessel, the immunity of the UMS is not derived from the launch platform, but rather is inherent in the UMS (NWP 1-14M, 2017). Thus, government UxSs, wherever located, are subject to the exclusive jurisdiction of the flag State and are immune from arrest, search, inspection, and foreign taxation (NWP 1-14M, 2017).

6 Navigational Rights and Freedom

The legal character of a UMS also determines the extent to which it enjoys navigational rights and freedoms in and under the world's oceans. CMI suggests that UMSs that qualify as ships or vessels within the meaning of UNCLOS enjoy the same navigational rights and freedoms that apply to manned ships and cannot be denied access to coastal State waters simply because they are not manned (CMI Position Paper, 2018). The flag State, however, has an obligation to ensure UMSs that fly its flag comply with the same international rules that apply to manned vessels. Seventy percent of States responding to a CMI questionnaire replied that UMSs enjoy the same rights and duties as manned ships under UNCLOS (IMO Doc. MSC 99/INF.8, 2018). The US Maritime Law Association takes a similar position, indicating that under US law "ship" is defined without regard to manning and that UMSs are subject to the same rights and obligations of manned ships under the law of the sea (IMO Doc. MSC 99/INF.8, 2018).

UMSs may therefore exercise the right of innocent passage in foreign territorial seas and archipelagic waters. It is also permissible for another military platform to launch a USV while engaged in innocent passage if the USV's employment is not prejudicial to the peace, good order, or security of the coastal State (NWP 1-14M, 2017).

UxSs likewise enjoy the right of unimpeded transit passage, in the normal mode, through straits used for international navigation between one part of the high seas or an exclusive economic zone (EEZ) and another part of the high seas or an EEZ and their approaches. UxSs may similarly exercise the right of archipelagic sea lanes passage (ASLP), in the normal mode, while transiting through, under, or over archipelagic sea lanes, which include all routes normally used for international navigation and overflight, whether designated or not by the archipelagic State. Finally, beyond foreign territorial seas, UxSs retain the full range of high seas freedoms of navigation and overflight, and other internationally lawful uses of the sea, guaranteed to manned ships and aircraft by international law (DoDI 4540.01, 2015; NWP 1-14M, 2017).

When exercising these navigational rights and freedoms, UxSs incur corresponding duties and obligations. When exercising the right of innocent passage, UMSs may not engage in activities that are prejudicial to the peace, good order, or security of the coastal State, including:

- Using force (or threatening the use of force) against the sovereignty, territorial integrity, or political independence of the coastal State, or in any other manner in violation of the principles of international law embodied in the UN Charter;
- Exercising or practicing with weapons of any kind;
- Collecting information to the prejudice of the defense or security of the coastal State;
- Engaging in acts of propaganda aimed at affecting the defense or security of the coastal State;
- Launching, landing, or taking on board of any aircraft or military device;
- Carrying out of marine scientific research or hydrographic survey activities; and
- Conducting acts aimed at interfering with any systems of communication or any other facilities or installations of the coastal State (UNCLOS, 1982).

UUVs engaged in innocent passage must also navigate on the surface and show their flag. If a UMS engages in prohibited conduct in the territorial sea and disregards a request for compliance with applicable coastal State laws and regulations, the coastal State may require the UMS to leave the territorial sea immediately. This may prove difficult for the coastal State given that the UMS is unmanned and may not respond to a demand or order to leave the territorial sea. Nonetheless, the flag State bears international responsibility for any loss or damage to the coastal State resulting from the non-compliance by a sovereign immune vessel, including UMSs, with coastal State laws and regulations concerning innocent passage, the provisions of UNCLOS, or other rules of international law.

Coastal States may designate traffic separation schemes (TSS) and sea lanes in their territorial sea or international straits to regulate shipping if such measures are necessary to ensure safety of navigation (SOLAS, 1974; UNCLOS, 1982). Warships, naval auxiliaries, and other government noncommercial ships, including UMSs, however, are legally exempt from complying with such sea lanes or TSSs (SOLAS, 1974). When navigating in TSSs and designated sea lanes, sovereign immune vessels (including UMSs) shall exercise due regard for the safety of navigation. A similar due regard standard applies in the EEZ—when exercising high seas freedoms of navigation and overflight, and other internationally lawful uses of the sea, in and over the EEZ, UxSs must do so with due regard to the resource rights of the coastal State (UNCLOS, 1982).

7 Conclusions

Unmanned and autonomous systems are fundamentally changing the way States conduct military operations. New technologies, including greater stealth, increased persistence, full autonomy, machine learning, and improved durability, are on the horizon that will significantly reduce operational risk and markedly exceed the current capabilities and limitations of manned ships and aircraft. As these technologies come online, mission sets normally reserved for manned platforms will be increasingly assigned to unmanned and autonomous systems. This is particularly true during an armed conflict at sea where targeting is platform-based. Where concerns over incidental injury to civilians and collateral damage to civilian objects may be warranted in an urban environment, these concerns are much less relevant in a maritime context. Today's electronic technologies, which will only improve over time, are already capable of distinguishing between an enemy warship and a protected neutral merchant vessel. Moreover, the possibility of collateral damage is virtually non-existent as neutral shipping and civil aviation will steer clear of an area of naval operations for reasons of safety of navigation and overflight. The nature of naval warfare will allow belligerents to program fully autonomous weapons systems to only attack lawful military objectives and thus allow full compliance with the principles military necessity, distinction, proportionality, and precautions in attack.

References

CBO (2020, October). *The Cost of the Navy's New Frigate*, Congressional Budget Office. https://www.cbo.gov/publication/56675. Accessed 28 May 2022.

Chicago Convention. (1944). Convention on International Civil Aviation, art. 8, annex 1 § 1.1, Dec. 7, 1944, 61 Stat. 1180, T.I.A.S. No. 1591, 15 U.N.T.S. 295.

CMI Position Paper. (2018). Comité Maritime International, CMI International Working Group Position Paper on Unmanned Ships and the International Regulatory Framework 3 (2018).

Colombos, C. (1967). International Law of the Sea § 270 (6th ed.).

COLREGs. (1972). Convention on International Regulations for Preventing Collisions at Sea, Oct. 20, 1972, 28 U.S.T. 3459, T.I.A.S. 8587.

CRS R45757. (2021, July 15). Congressional Research Service, Pub. No. R45757, Navy Large Unmanned Surface and Undersea Vehicles: Background and Issues for Congress 4.

DoD Integrated Roadmap. (2014). U.S. Department of Defense, Pub. No. 14-S-0553, Unmanned Systems Integrated Roadmap: FY2013–2038 (p. 20).

DoD Law of War Manual. (2016). Office of General Counsel, U.S. Department of Defense, Law of War Manual.

DoDI 4540.01. (2015). U.S. Department of Defense, Pub. No. 4540.01, Instruction: Use of International Airspace by U.S. Military Aircraft and for Missile and Projectile Firings 11.

Eckstein, M. (2020, November 10). Pentagon 'Ghost Fleet' Ship Makes Record-Breaking Trip from Mobile to California. *USNI News*. https://news.usni.org/2020/11/10/pentagon-ghost-fleet-ship-makes-record-breaking-trip-from-mobile-to-california. Accessed 14 May 2022.

Eckstein, M. (2021, September 8). Gilday: New task force will help US Navy speed up unmanned system integration. *Defense News*. https://www.defensenews.com/naval/2021/09/08/gilday-new-task-force-will-help-us-navy-speed-unmanned-system-integration/. Accessed 15 May 2022.

Engelhardt, D. (2021, Winter). Transformational warfare—The "Why" of unmanned, a personal perspective. The Disruptor (Issue #1).

Hague VII. (1907). Convention No. VII relating to the conversion of Merchant Ships into Warships, Oct. 18, 1907, 205 Consol. T.S. 319.

Howard, B. (2021, June 4). *Quiet, deadly and expensive: The Navy's costly plan to upgrade aging submarines*. CNBC. https://www.cnbc.com/2021/06/04/quiet-deadly-and-expensive-the-navys-costly-plan-to-upgrade-aging-submarines.html. Accessed 21 May 2022.

ICAO Cir 328. (2011). International Civil Aviation Organization [ICAO], Cir. No. 328 (AN/190), Unmanned Aircraft Systems (UAS).

IMO Doc. MSC.1/Circ.1604. (2019, June 14). IMO Doc. MSC.1/Circ.1604, Interim Guidelines for MASS Trials.

IMO Doc. MSC 98/20/2. (2017, February 27). IMO Doc. MSC 98/20/2, Maritime Autonomous Surface Ships: Proposal for a regulatory scoping exercise (MASS RSE), Submitted by Denmark, Estonia, Finland, Japan, the Netherlands, Norway, the Republic of Korea, the United Kingdom, and the United States.

IMO Doc. MSC.99/WP.9. (2018, May 23). IMO Doc. MSC.99/WP.9, Regulatory scoping exercise for the use of Maritime Autonomous Surface Ships (MASS), Report of the Working Group.

IMO Doc. MSC 99/INF.8. (2018a, February 13). IMO Doc. MSC 99/INF.8, Work conducted by the CMI International Working Group on Unmanned Ships, annex 1.

IMO Doc. MSC 99/20. (2018b, February 13). IMO Doc. MSC 99/20, Report of the Maritime Safety Committee on its Ninety-Ninth Session, at annex 1.

IMO Doc. MSC/99/22. (2018, June 5). IMO Doc. MSC/99/22, Report of the Maritime Safety Committee on its Ninety-Ninth Session.

IMO Doc. MSC.1/Circ.1638. (2021, June 3). Outcome of the regulatory scoping exercise for the use of Maritime Autonomous Surface Ships (MASS).

IMO Doc. MSC 100/20/Add.1. (2018, December 7). IMO Doc. MSC 100/20/Add.1, Report of the Maritime Safety Committee on its One Hundredth Session, at annex 2, 1.

IMO Res. MSC. 99(73). (2000, December 5). Adoption of Amendments to the International Convention for the Safety of Life at Sea, as amended.

Kraska, J. (1995). Autonomous and Expendable Marine Instruments in U.S. and International Law. *Ocean Development & International Law, 26*, 311–355.

Kraska, J. (2010). Unmanned Naval Systems and International Law. 5 *Journal Ocean Technology, 5*, 44–68.

LaGrone, S. (2021). Two More 'Ghost Fleet' Unmanned Test Ships to Join Fleet Next Year. *USNI News*. https://news.usni.org/2021/07/13/two-more-ghost-fleet-unmanned-test-ships-to-join-fleet-next-year. Accessed 4 May 2022.

LDC. (1972). Convention on the Prevention of Marine Pollution by Dumping of Wastes and Other Matter, Dec. 29, 1972, 26 U.S.T. 2403, 1046 U.N.T.S. 120.

Lopez, T. (2021, January 13). DoD's Autonomous Vessel Sails Through Transit Test, Participates in Exercise Dawn Blitz. Dep't. of Defense, Defense News. https://www.defense.gov/Explore/News/Article/Article/2471165/dods-autonomous-vessel-sails-through-transit-test-participates-in-exercise-dawn/. Accessed 11 May 2022.

Macias, A. (2018, April 25). *The first drone warship just joined the Navy and now nearly every element of it is classified*. CNBC. https://www.cnbc.com/2018/04/25/first-drone-warship-joins-us-navy-nearly-every-element-classified.html

MARPOL. (1973/1978). International Convention for the Prevention of Pollution from Ships, art. 2, Nov. 2, 1973, 12 I.L.M. 1319; Protocol of 1978 Relating to the International Convention for the Prevention of Pollution from Ships, Feb. 17, 1978, 17 I.L.M. 546.

Naval Technology. (2018, May 3). *Sea Hunter: Inside the US Navy's autonomous submarine tracking vessel*. Naval Technology. https://www.naval-technology.com/features/sea-hunter-inside-us-navys-autonomous-submarine-tracking-vessel/. Accessed 8 May 2022.

Naval Technology. (2019, July 1). *Orca XLUUV: Boeing's whale of an unmanned sub*. Naval Technology. https://www.naval-technology.com/features/boeing-orca-xluuv-unmanned-submarine/

Navy Regs. (1990). U.S. Department of the Navy, United States Navy Regulations art. 0406 (1990).

Navy Strategic Roadmap. (2021). U.S. Department of the Navy, *Strategic Roadmap for Unmanned Systems* (Short Version).

Navy USV Master Plan. (2007). U.S. Department of the Navy, The Navy Unmanned Surface Vehicle (USV) Master Plan xi, 1–3.

Navy UUV Master Plan. (2004). U.S. Department of the Navy, The Navy Unmanned Undersea Vehicle (UUV) Master Plan xvi, xx–xxii (2004).

NWP 1-14M. (2017). U.S. Navy, Pub. No. NWP 1-14M, The Commander's Handbook on the Law of Naval Operations.

Oxford Manual. (1913). International Institute of International Law, Manual of the Laws of Naval War art. 12.

Paris Declaration. (1856, April 16), Paris Declaration Respecting Maritime Law, *reprinted in* 46 British & Foreign State Papers, 26–27 (1865).

Roblin, S. (2019, October 20). The U.S. Navy has Orca Robot submarines on the way that could transform Naval warfare. The National Interest. https://nationalinterest.org/blog/buzz/us-navy-has-orca-robot-submarines-way-could-transform-naval-warfare-89721. Accessed 15 June 2022.

SECNAVINST 5030.8C. (2016). U.S. Department of the Navy, Secretary of the Navy Instruction 5030.8C, General Guidance for the Classification of Naval Vessels and Battle Force Ship County Procedures.
SOLAS. (1974). International Convention for the Safety of Life at Sea, Nov. 1, 1974, 32 U.S.T. 47, T.I.A.S. 9700.
SUA. (2005, November 1). IMO Doc. LEG/CONF. 15/21, Adoption of the Final Act and Any Instruments, Recommendations and Resolutions Resulting from the Work of the Conference, Protocol of 2005 to the Convention for the Suppression of Unlawful Acts against the Safety of Maritime Navigation.
The Muscat Dhows. (1916). The Muscat Dhows Case (Fr. v. Gr. Brit.), Hague Ct Rep. (Scott) 93, 96 (Perm. Ct. Arb. 1916).
UNCLOS. (1982). United Nations Convention on the Law of the Sea, Dec. 10, 1982, 1833 U.N.T.S. 397.
U.S.C. § 6011. (2018).

CHAPTER 5

Maritime Security in the Age of Autonomous Ships

Anna Petrig

1 A Game Changer for the Commission of Crimes at Sea

From the vantage point of maritime security, the advent of autonomous ships is a double-edged sword. Autonomous ships have great potential to reduce lawlessness at sea by augmenting the capabilities, effectiveness and reach of maritime law enforcement operations while squeezing their costs. At the same time, however, this novel type of vessel provides criminals with a cutting edge as it opens new avenues to the commission of crimes at sea while lowering the perpetrator's risk of being killed, injured, arrested or even detected (Petrig, 2020). Criminals are usually quick to embrace new technologies (Goodmann, 2015), which is no different for autonomous ships: offenders have already started relying on this new technology to commit crimes at sea.

A. Petrig (✉)
Faculty of Law, University of Basel, Basel, Switzerland
e-mail: anna.petrig@unibas.ch

© The Author(s), under exclusive license to Springer Nature Switzerland AG 2023

T. M. Johansson et al. (eds.), *Autonomous Vessels in Maritime Affairs*, Studies in National Governance and Emerging Technologies,
https://doi.org/10.1007/978-3-031-24740-8_5

Among the most widely reported incidents are the attacks by Houthi rebels with remote-controlled boats rigged with explosives against merchant ships, warships and installations in the Red Sea, which started in 2017 and are ongoing (Haugstvedt, 2021). Although the technology deployed is rudimentary and features a do-it-yourself touch, its potential to cause harm is immense. An example in this respect is a foiled attack against an oil tanker, which could have produced a large secondary explosion resulting in major (environmental) harm (Reuters, 2020). With autonomous technology becoming increasingly potent, cheaper and user-friendly, the "gap between attack capabilities and defense capabilities" is expected to widen further (Brundage et al., 2018).

Moreover, as drug cartels have adapted their criminal strategies continuously in the past to lower risks, raise profits and evade enforcement action (Coito, 2021), autonomous technology is very likely to become a hallmark of drug trafficking in the not-too-distant future. Reports that Spanish and Italian authorities have detected unmanned crafts built and even used to smuggle drugs evidence the turn to autonomous ships for trafficking purposes (Sands, 2022; Sutton, 2019). With the introduction of large unmanned commercial ships looming on the horizon (Bates Ramirez, 2022), enforcers must also prepare for the scenario where illicit cargo—such as narcotics (McLaughlin & Klein, 2021) or other prohibited items, including illegally traded weapons or goods falling under a sanction regime—is transported alongside lawful cargo.

Autonomous ships are thus already a game changer for the commission of crimes at sea—and even more so with technologies used for their construction and operation moving through further innovation stages and maturing.

2 A Watershed Moment for Maritime Security Law

The introduction of autonomous ships also amounts to a watershed moment for the law. It is true that the world of shipping has experienced tremendous change in the past century and norms governing it "proved flexible enough to accommodate technological developments, from sail to steam to containerisation" (Carey, 2017). Yet, past technological innovations have all aligned with the premise on which rules of the law of the sea and maritime law rest: that ships carry an onboard crew responsible for their navigation, task and mission (IMO Doc MASS-JWG 1/2, 2022).

With the appearance of autonomous ships, this age-old certainty—not to say truism—ended abruptly. In the maritime security context specifically, a series of assumptions underpinning relevant rules no longer necessarily apply: that perpetrators act from on board the offender ship; that enforcer crafts have law enforcement officials embarked; and that a human–human encounter between enforcers and suspects "in theater" takes place, with the possibility for direct interaction and communication as well as an exchange of physical documentation. The absence of an onboard crew calls into question the continued applicability and relevance of many rules designed to suppress crime at sea as the assumption on which they are built is no longer met. After a remark on terminology, a selection of them is discussed.

2.1 Terminology

At the present juncture, both the concept of "autonomy" and the various "levels of autonomy" remain elusive against the backdrop of differing interpretations and understandings proposed in practice and doctrine. In this chapter, the term "autonomous ship" is used in a generic way to denote crafts "which, to a varying degree, can operate independent of human interaction" (IMO Doc LEG 106/WP.5, 2019). Thereby, the focus is on one specific feature that ship automation may bring about: that vessels no longer carry an onboard crew; they are "unmanned". In International Maritime Organization (IMO) parlance, these are ships featuring autonomy degrees three or four (remotely controlled or fully autonomous ships without onboard crew), as ships of degrees one and two (ships with automated processes and decision support or remotely controlled ships having seafarers on board) still feature an onboard crew (IMO Doc LEG 106/WP.5, 2019).

To be sure, unmanned ships do not entail the complete absence of human involvement—even if the term may feed this perception. However, the persons' manner, level, place and time of involvement in the operation and mission of unmanned ships differs from traditional vessels (Petrig, 2020). This may even hold true for vessels still having an onboard crew, which, however, is starkly reduced with key functions carried out elsewhere, notably on shore (IMO Doc LEG 107/8/17, 2020). These changes regarding human involvement are sufficient to challenge the application of maritime security rules and may even disturb the entire mechanics of the legal framework aimed at suppressing crimes at sea—as will be demonstrated hereunder.

2.2 The Notion of Ship

When considering the criminal use of unmanned crafts, the first issue to clarify is arguably whether they amount to "ships" or "vessels". It is because many maritime security provisions—be it, for instance, offense definitions, authorizations to enforce the law or provisions on cooperation to suppress crime at sea—comprise a reference to either one of these terms. Yet, to seek a generally valid answer to this question seems a futile exercise.

Firstly, this is due to the broad range of ship automation technology already in use and still in development. The large vehicle-carrying *Soleil*, for example, cannot be distinguished from a conventional car ferry from the outside (Coxworth, 2022). By contrast, the "underwater drones" recently seized by the Spanish police in a counter-drug operation—each capable of transporting around 200 kilograms of narcotics—have a closer resemblance to a long-drawn metal waste container than what one deems to be a ship (Sands, 2022). Not only the appearance of unmanned waterborne crafts but also their capabilities differ greatly. In addition, the same type of craft may be used for various tasks and missions.

The second reason why the question of whether unmanned watercrafts are ships defies a clear "yes or no" answer is to be found in the law. There is simply no single, generally valid definition of the term "ship". Instead, treaties comprise differing definitions—each crafted with a view to best serve the respective treaty's object and purpose. The drafters of the SUA Convention (1988), for example, opted for an expansive definition of "ship", one that—together with the definition of "fixed platform" in the Fixed Platforms Protocol (1988)–covers as many targets at sea as possible (IMO Doc SUA/CONF/CW/WP.18, 1988). As per Article 1, a ship "means a vessel of any type whatsoever not permanently attached to the sea-bed, including dynamically supported craft, submersibles, or any other floating craft". Given the inclusive wording ("of any type whatsoever" and no explicit mention of an onboard crew), the purpose of the treaty and its drafting history, unmanned offender crafts are likely to fall under this definition, which is identical in the SUA Convention (2005) (Petrig, 2021). The United Nations Convention on the Law of the Sea, 1982 (UNCLOS), in turn, despite relying heavily on the notions of "ship" and "vessel," does not define them—for good reason. As the definition of "ship" depends on the subject matter and context of the rules in which it appears and given that UNCLOS aspires to regulate "all issues relating to the law of the sea" (UNCLOS, preamble), a single definition would be neither possible nor helpful (Noyes, 2012). What amounts to a "ship" or "vessel" must thus be discerned with regard to a specific provision.

In sum, a meaningful answer as to whether an unmanned waterborne craft is a "ship" in the legal sense can only be obtained through a case-by-case assessment that considers both the technology and the law at stake (Allen, 2018).

2.3 *Offense Definitions*

The use of autonomous ships for malicious purposes further raises the question of whether a specific offense definition can be fulfilled if offenders rely on unmanned rather than manned crafts. This is crucial not only for the ultimate prosecution of suspects but also for taking enforcement measures at sea as this is generally predicated on the existence of reasonable grounds for suspecting that a vessel engages in a specific offense. The question again eludes a simple answer as much depends on the relevant provision's wording and interpretation. Broadly speaking, three different drafting techniques can be identified to define offenses—depending on which one is used, it is easier or more challenging to argue that the crime in question can be committed using an unmanned ship.

On one end of the spectrum, various provisions refer to ships—rather than persons—engaging in the prohibited conduct. By way of example, Article 111(1) UNCLOS authorizes hot pursuit if there is "good reason to believe that the ship has violated the laws or regulations" of the coastal state. In a similar fashion, Articles 17(2) and 17(3) of the United Nations Convention against Illicit Traffic in Narcotic Drugs and Psychotropic Substances, 1988 (Vienna Convention) (1988) refer to a "vessel ... engaged in illicit traffic". This drafting technique seems startling as, after all, the commission of crimes is intrinsically linked with human conduct. However, it is precisely because of the assumption that ships are manned—underlying the entire law of the sea—that the drafters did not deem it necessary to always distinguish carefully between the ship and persons on board. In the present context, this odd wording makes it easier to support the idea that the offense in question can be committed by both manned and unmanned vessels.

On the spectrum's other end, there are offense definitions that not only refer to a ship but also to a specific category of persons—such as the master or crew—whom the drafters assumed to be on board. The paradigmatic example is piracy: Article 101(a) UNCLOS requires that the harmful act is "committed … by the crew or the passengers of a private ship". While a "passenger" has, perforce, to be on board the ship, the term "crew" could be interpreted as covering a remote crew—at least if perpetrators use remote-controlled crafts, thus exercising contemporaneous control over the device used to engage in crime at sea. Such interpretation is more challenging if the offender launches an "intelligent" craft capable of making decisions and determining actions en route without human intervention, for example, based on sensor data. Compared with remote-controlled vessels, the link between the perpetrator and the ship is much looser, and it may be more challenging to argue that persons simply launching a system belong to the "crew … of a private ship" (Petrig, 2020).

The third type of offense definition mentions neither a ship nor a category of persons traditionally assumed to be on board a ship undertaking the prohibited activity; rather, it is worded in a neutral fashion and simply refers to a "person" engaging in the relevant conduct. Such drafting technique has, for example, been used in the context of the Convention for the Suppression of Unlawful Acts Against the Safety of Maritime Navigation, and Protocol for the Suppression of Unlawful Acts Against the Safety of Fixed Platforms Located on the Continental Shelf (SUA Conventions) (1988, 2005). This is no coincidence as the possibility of contributions from dry land has been envisaged—albeit not by persons controlling unmanned ships from on shore, but by corporations (Petrig, 2021). Despite this rather accommodating wording, doubts have been expressed whether remote operators of unmanned ships or persons deploying an "intelligent" craft are covered by the offense definitions (IMO Doc LEG 107/8/5, 2020).

In sum, regardless of an explicit mention in the respective offense definition, the assumption has always been that ships used to engage in crime at sea carry an onboard crew. A common understanding of whether these offenses can be committed using unmanned ships is yet to be developed.

2.4 Communication and Interaction

During a law enforcement response, communication between the enforcers and suspects is key. In cases where offender ships do not carry an onboard crew, the question ensues with whom and how law enforcement officials interact. The response differs depending on the type of craft on which criminals rely. The spectrum is huge, ranging from waterborne "metal containers" with GPS technology construed for smuggling drugs with which communication is hardly possible (Sands, 2022) to 300 TEU unmanned commercial ships—akin to the one that recently went into operation in China (The Maritime Executive, 2022)—equipped with the latest communication technology. The focus of the following is on ships with which enforcers are, in principle, able to interact.

The first step in a gradual law enforcement response usually consists of conveying the suspect ship a signal to stop. The relevant rules in place not only reflect the assumption that human beings on board are supposed to be the recipient of the signal but, at times, also the then-prevailing technology. In this vein, Article 111(4) UNCLOS refers to "a visual or auditory signal to stop". Yet today, even manned ships are no longer hailed by waving flags or using megaphones but rather through more modern means, such as VHF messages. In the *Arctic Sunrise* Arbitration, the tribunal confirmed that the respective rules "must be interpreted in the light of their object and purpose, having regard to the modern use of technology" (para. 259). However, for unmanned offender ships, it is not simply about using new technology or, more generally speaking, how to communicate with the suspect ship. Rather, this new type of vessel involves a new allocation of tasks, which also affects the question with whom enforcers interact.

In a traditional setting, it is quite plain who the primary interlocutor of enforcers is: the master, who is the person "in charge" on board the vessel, including for queries from officials and authorities. However, with unmanned ships, new actors such as remote operators enter the scene, triggering a series of principled questions: Who will perform the role and functions traditionally incumbent on the master if the vessel is without an onboard crew? Will functions traditionally allocated to one single person be distributed among different types of actors? Could a legal rather than a natural person bear the ultimate responsibility for carrying out specific functions? Suppose there is still a residual crew on board the offender ship; in that case, other intricate questions arise: Can a residual crew on whom tasks are incumbent, which historically were carried out by the "black gang" rather than the master, be the interlocutor of enforcement officials at sea? Or can a residual crew only be the interlocutor if they have—next to shore-based actors—a major actual or potential (for example, in case of system failure) role in the vessel's operation?

The determination of the meaning of terms denoting actors involved in the operation of unmanned ships, such as master, crew and remote operator, is among the high-priority issues to be considered in the context of the envisaged IMO MASS Code (IMO Doc MASS-JWG 1/2, 2022). The clarification of who is responsible for what with regard to an unmanned ship is essential knowledge to design procedures at the interface between the operation of unmanned ships and law enforcement activities at sea, such as those relating to communication and interaction.

2.5 *Boarding, Verification of Nationality and Search*

The drafters of boarding provisions assumed that both the determination of nationality and any further examination of the suspect ship, such as a search of the cargo, take place on board. Moreover, they presumed that facts are established through human–human interaction and the exchange of physical documents, such as the certificate of registry or the bill of lading. Not consistently, but sometimes, this assumption explicitly accrues from the provision's wording. Article 110(2) UNCLOS, for instance, mentions the option of sending a boat under the command of an officer to the suspect vessel to determine its nationality. Moreover, it stipulates that "further examination" takes place "on board the ship".

The physical boarding of a suspect unmanned vessel, however, raises a spate of operational questions. They include "how to conduct a boarding when there is no master or crew to answer questions regarding the craft's nationality, to maneuver the craft to accommodate the boarding, or to present the necessary documents once the boarding team is on board" (Allen, 2018). Moreover, "if you put a boarding team on board an uncrewed vessel, what is to stop it [from] sailing off again" with "the boarding team suddenly disappearing off and being taken hostage?" (Tuckett, 2021). Given the practical challenges of an unmanned ship's physical boarding, it is worth considering whether a remote or even virtual exercise of the right to visit to establish nationality and obtain information about potentially unlawful activities and the ship's cargo is legally permissible under Article 110 UNCLOS and similar provisions.

A remote determination of nationality is notably possible by sighting the markings and numbers on the ship's hull, which unmanned ships of a certain size and function are likely to be obliged to display. This should be considered lawful as it is the usual flag verification method when exercising the right of approach and does not interfere with the freedom of navigation of the suspect ship if—as usual these days—exercised from a distance (Lewis, 2015). The more delicate question is whether a virtual determination of nationality using cyber means is legally permissible. The Tallinn Manual 2.0 (Schmitt, 2017) is one of the few sources discussing this, yet views—expressed in the context of traditional ships—are diametrically opposed. Some experts argue that a virtual visit would be a reasonable way of exercising this enforcement power and less intrusive than a physical one; moreover, the respective provisions would not in any way restrict the means for conducting a visit. Other experts opine that a virtual visit does not comport with the underlying assumption of the provision, which is an onboard visit; moreover, it could be more intrusive compared to a document check on board as more information may be obtained than is necessary to verify nationality. Importantly, these views were collected specifically regarding the "use [of] cyber means to verify the nationality of the vessel concerned by monitoring its communications or inspect its cyber infrastructure remotely" (Schmitt, 2017). The latter scenario seems to imply that enforcers penetrate the operational and/or information technology systems of suspect ships, which may entail certain risks to the safety of the ship, cargo and crew.

An utterly different scenario, which is not contemplated in the Tallinn Manual 2.0 (Schmitt, 2017), is the virtual inspection of e-certificates that, for example, entail information about the ship's nationality. While the many documents that a ship must carry are traditionally all in paper format, the trend goes—also for conventional ships—towards e-certificates. One of the biggest flag states, Liberia, has been treating e-certificates of registry that can be verified online for their genuineness and status in real time as "original" and "authentic" since 2006 (Watt, 2019). Responding to this trend, the IMO issued "Guidelines for the Use of Electronic Certificates" to ensure a consistent and secure practice (IMO Doc FAL.5/Circ.39/Rev.2, Annex, 2016). The use of e-certificates by unmanned ships, notably the format they could take and how they could be requested and produced absent seafarers on board, will be considered in the context of a future IMO Maritime Autonomous

Surface Ships (MASS) Code (IMO Doc MASS-JWG 1/2, 2022). Clarification on these aspects will allow for a more elaborate discussion of the permissibility and limits of virtually determining the nationality of unmanned ships as part of a maritime law enforcement response.

If suspicion remains after documents have been checked, the right of visit authorizes "further examination on board" as per Article 110(2) UNCLOS. In the context of ships without an onboard crew, this notably entails the question of whether a remote or virtual search of the cargo is feasible and lawful. The deployment of modern—and specifically autonomous—technology by enforcers already allows for some types of remote searches to be conducted. For instance, autonomous underwater systems can search for "oddities such as trapdoors, moon pools, or hidden cargo compartments" in the suspect ship's hull. Further, they can identify "unusual phenomena", such as traces of chemical, biological, nuclear, radiological or explosive material, or the presence of human beings in "cargo" holds (US Navy USV Master Plan, 2007). Autonomous aerial systems, in turn, could not only provide footage of illicit cargo from a bird's perspective but also identify certain substances. The European Maritime Safety Agency is, for example, relying on the so-called "sniffer", a device attached to an unmanned aerial vehicle that can track down ships using prohibited fuel (EMSA, 2022). A virtual visit, on its part, is possible for those unmanned ships, which will carry digital certificates containing information about their cargo, such as an e-bill of lading. Remote and virtual visits may also prove useful in the context of a traditional, manned ship as a search of cargo on the open sea is, at least for ships transporting their cargo in containers, generally not a feasible option (Haines, 2016).

The permissibility of a remote or virtual exercise of the right of visit will ultimately also depend on whether safeguards, such as those stipulated in Article 8*bis* SUA Convention (2005), can be respected. The provision notably comprises a series of requirements aimed at ensuring that only authorized law enforcement vessels and officials take enforcement action and that the master and crew of the suspect are put in a position to verify this. Specifically, only warships or state crafts clearly marked and identifiable as being on government service and sanctioned to enforce the law are authorized to take enforcement measures; officials on board must be "uniformed or otherwise clearly identifiable members of law enforcement"; and they must "provide appropriate government-issued identification documents for examination by the master of the ship upon boarding". Yet, if offenders rely on unmanned ships, there is simply no person on board who could see and check markings, uniforms and IDs. What, in such a case, could and should amount to functional equivalents—for example, a sort of e-authentication of authorities—has yet to be analyzed.

While the master and crew are obviously aware of being subjected to enforcement measures in cases of physical boarding, a remote or virtual exercise of the right of visit may go unnoticed. Yet, such knowledge seems crucial if the suspicion proves unfounded and the ship has not itself set the cause for the intervention by enforcers, giving rise to a right of compensation (Article 110(3) UNCLOS). Without being aware of the remote or virtual visit, conduct cannot be attributed, and responsibility is thus not established. But even if it can, it is not readily obvious what the loss and damage of the ship in question is in cases of a remote or virtual visit. Unlike physical boarding, they will often not cause any delay, which is the primordial ground for compensation. Yet, if enforcers access a ship's operational or information technology systems, it is conceivable that the ship's operation is affected. In the case of accessing e-certificates, more information may be retrieved than allowed under the respective authorization, which may potentially amount to a violation of a commercial secret.

Overall, the operational feasibility and legal permissibility of a remote or virtual exercise of the right of visit needs further consideration. The clarification on the use of e-certificates during the debates concerning a potential IMO MASS Code is essential to further design an appropriate law enforcement response to unmanned ships engaged in crime at sea—at least for those vessels that are required to carry such certificates.

2.6 Arrest and Prosecution of Suspects

With offenders relying on unmanned ships to commit crimes at sea, states conducting maritime law enforcement operations are stripped of one of the most compelling enforcement measures: the arrest of suspects at sea to subject them to criminal prosecution (CMI Position Paper, 2018). In the likely case that the offender acts from shore, the suppression of crime at sea will heavily depend on enforcement action on dry land. Moreover, it may well be that the offender sits in a state different from the one in whose waters the crime was committed or the one that interdicted the vessel in international waters. Hence, it will only be possible to arrest the suspect and to bring him or her to justice through a cooperative effort between the interdicting state (inter alia, possessing important evidence) and the state where the suspect happens to be. This, in turn, hinges upon both the willingness and ability of the latter state to take steps leading towards the arrest of the suspect and his or her prosecution or extradition.

Not all states may be willing to take such steps; it is conceivable that states shield persons using their territory to commit crimes through unmanned ships or at least tolerate such behavior. Further, states may practically not be able to arrest persons because the commission of crimes using autonomous technology will often allow offenders to act in anonymity or to cloak their identity (Brundage et al., 2018). Challenges of this nature may, for instance, arise in the context of attacks akin those carried out by Houthi rebels described earlier in this chapter.

As regards commercial unmanned ships that can, for instance, be used for smuggling purposes, it is essential for maritime security to ensure that they possess nationality and that the flag state is able to arrest persons involved in the operation of the ship. As enforcement jurisdiction is generally limited to a state's own territory, a flag state can only arrest remote operators located in its territory. If the flag state is solely the place of incorporation of a shell company and the actual operations are carried out from another state, the flag state has little means to enforce the law against persons committing crimes involving unmanned ships flying its flag. In such a situation, a serious enforcement gap would arise as the interdicting state cannot arrest suspects because they are not on board the offender ship, while the flag state cannot do so because they are not in its territory. The future IMO MASS Code offers an opportunity to define the link that a remote operation center and remote operator must feature with the flag state. If the link is defined too loosely, the flag of convenience problem will be accentuated in the case of unmanned ships (Van Hooydonk, 2014). The bottom line should thus be that a remote operation center has its seat, real operations and personnel in the flag state.

3 The Regulatory Way Ahead

This overview has demonstrated that the introduction of unmanned ships queries the continued applicability and relevance of many—if not most—rules designed for the suppression of crime at sea. The need for regulatory steps is thus evident. Yet, maritime law enforcement is governed by a complex web of rules, which not only stem from the international and domestic levels but also pertain to various fields of law, such as the law of the sea, transnational criminal law and international human rights law. While the means and procedures to adapt the law to new realities differ greatly between these different sets of rules, a general observation regarding the regulatory way ahead is still possible.

For the time being, formal amendment of relevant treaties seems out of sight. UNCLOS, which is the centerpiece of regulation for all activities at sea, including maritime security, is very unlikely to be subjected to formal amendment for both legal and political reasons. Further, within the UNODC, there seems currently no initiative underway to even discuss the impact of the advent of autonomous ships on treaties adopted under its auspices and relevant for the suppression of crime at sea, such as the Vienna Convention (1988). As regards the four SUA treaties, which belong to the more than 50 treaties for which the IMO is responsible, there is little appetite to formally amend them. Rather than through an update of formal law, the turn to autonomous ships will more likely be accommodated through informal law—at least for the time being. Indeed, the characteristics ascribed to informal law make it a particularly suitable tool to regulate autonomous ships, the construction and operation of which involves several emerging technologies, each of which is complex, inchoate and developing at an unprecedented pace. First of all, informal law is a tool that can get the normative ball rolling as it usually allows for common ground to be found in a previously unregulated field more easily as compared to treaty negotiations. Further, an informal instrument allows us to bridge the time until a firmer commitment is possible. Moreover, it permits the initial collection of regulatory experience that can be integrated later into a formal instrument; and it can be updated rather effortlessly as compared with treaties if the technology further develops. Finally, it is also conceivable that formal law only sets out the broad principles, while detailed regulation is left to the more adaptable informal law in the long run (Petrig, 2022).

Against this backdrop, it is of little surprise that the IMO envisages, in a first move, the adoption of a non-binding IMO MASS Code (IMO Doc MASS-JWG 1/2, 2022). While the planned Code does not directly address maritime security, this chapter has demonstrated that the transversal issues which it is likely to cover are highly relevant for the suppression of crimes at sea committed by unmanned ships. The Code is thus an important first step on the long regulatory path ahead to accommodate autonomous ships in the maritime security legal framework.

References

Allen, C. H. (2018). Determining the legal status of unmanned maritime vehicles: Formalism vs functionalism. *Journal of Maritime Law & Commerce, 49*(4), 477–514.

Arctic Sunrise Arbitration (The Netherlands v. Russian Federation). PCA-2014-02. Award on the Merits, 14 August 2015.

Bates Ramirez, V. (2022). Japan wants to make half its cargo ships autonomous by 2040. *Singularity Hub*. Available at: https://singularityhub.com/2022/02/23/japan-wants-to-make-half-its-cargo-ships-autonomous-by-2040/. Accessed 24 April 2022.

Brundage, M., et al. (2018). *The malicious use of artificial intelligence: Forecasting, prevention, and mitigation*. University of Oxford.

Carey, L. (2017). All hands off deck? The legal barriers to autonomous ships. *Journal of International Maritime Law, 23*(3), 202–219.

CMI Position Paper. (2018). *Comité Maritime International*. CMI international working group position paper on unmanned ships and the international regulatory framework 3.

Coito, J. (2021). Maritime autonomous surface ships: New possibilities—and challenges—in ocean law and policy. *International Law Studies, 97*, 259–306.

Coxworth, B. (2022). Large vehicle-carrying ferry makes first-ever autonomous run in Japan. *New Atlas*. Available at: https://newatlas.com/marine/smart-coastal-autonomous-ferry. Accessed 3 April 2022.

EMSA. (2022). *EMSA sniffer drone monitoring sulphur and nitrogen emissions from ships operating in the channel*. Available at: www.emsa.europa.eu/newsroom/press-releases/item/4740-emsa-sniffer-drone-monitoring-sulphur-and-nitrogen-emissions-from-ships-operating-in-the-channel.html. Accessed 3 May 2022.

Fixed Platforms Protocol. (1988). Protocol to the Convention of 10 March 1988 for the Suppression of Unlawful Acts Against the Safety of Fixed Platforms Located on the Continental Shelf, Mar. 10, 1988, 1678 U.N.T.S. 201.

Goodmann, M. (2015). *Future crimes: Inside the digital underground and the battle for our connected world*. Corgi Books.

Haines, S. (2016). War at sea: Nineteenth-century laws for twenty-first-century wars? *International Review of the Red Cross, 98*(2), 419–447.

Haugstvedt, H. (2021). Red Sea drones: How to counter Houthi maritime tactics. War on the Rocks. Available at: https://warontherocks.com/2021/09/red-sea-drones-how-to-counter-houthi-maritime-tactics. Accessed 7 April 2022.

IMO Doc SUA/CONF/CW/WP.18. (1988). Report and interpretation following informal consultation on Article 1 of the convention and on the protocol.

IMO Doc FAL.5/Circ.39/Rev.2, Annex. (2016). Guidelines for the use of electronic certificates.
IMO Doc LEG 106/WP.5. (2019). Report of the LEG working group on MASS.
IMO Doc LEG 107/8/5. (2020). Summary of results of the LEG regulatory scoping exercise for the Convention for the Suppression of Unlawful Acts against the Safety of Maritime Navigation, 1988.
IMO Doc LEG 107/8/17. (2020). Summary of main gaps and common themes in instruments under the purview of the Legal Committee.
IMO Doc MASS-JWG ½. (2022). Consideration of the common issues identified in the RSE of the three committees and how to best address them.
Lewis, A. (2015). Flag verification on the high seas: Understanding requirements for masters and commanders. *The International Journal of Marine and Coastal Law, 30*, 335–360.
McLaughlin, R., & Klein, N. (2021). Maritime autonomous vehicles and drug trafficking by sea: Some legal issues. *The International Journal of Marine and Coastal Law, 36*, 389–418.
Noyes, J. E. (2012). Interpreting the 1982 Law of the Sea Convention and defining its terms. In G. K. Walker (Ed.), *Definitions for the law of the sea: Terms not defined by the 1982 Convention* (pp. 45–83). Martinus Nijhoff.
Petrig, A. (2020). The commission of maritime crimes with unmanned systems: An interpretive challenge for the United Nations Convention on the Law of the Sea. In M. D. Evans & S. Galani (Eds.), *Maritime security and the law of the sea: Help or hindrance?* (pp. 123–130). Edward Elgar Publishing.
Petrig, A. (2021). Autonomous offender ships and international maritime security law. In H. Ringbom, E. Røsæg, & T. Solvang (Eds.), *Autonomous ships and the law* (pp. 23–55). Routledge.
Petrig, A. (2022). Unconventional Law for unconventional ships? The role of informal law in the International Maritime Organization's quest to regulate maritime autonomous surface ships. In N. Klein (Ed.), *Unconventional lawmaking in the law of the sea* (pp. 112–136). Oxford University Press.
Reuters. (2020). *Saudi-led coalition says it foiled attack on oil tanker off Yemen*. Available at: www.reuters.com/article/yemen-security-tanker-idUKL8N2AX4OE. Accessed 19 May 2022.
Sands, L. (2022). Drug smuggling: Underwater drones seized by Spanish police. *BBC News*. Available at: www.bbc.com/news/world-europe-62040790. Accessed 12 April 2022.
Sutton, H. I. (2019). *First narco-USV*. Available at: www.hisutton.com/Otranto_unmanned-drug-vessel.html. Accessed 12 June 2022.
SUA Convention. (1988). Convention for the Suppression of Unlawful Acts Against the Safety of Maritime Navigation, Mar. 10, 1988, 1678 U.N.T.S. 221.

SUA Convention. (2005). Protocol of 2005 to the Convention for the Suppression of Unlawful Acts Against the Safety of Maritime Navigation, Oct. 14, 2005. IMO Doc. LEG/CONF.15/21.

Schmitt, M. N. (ed.). (2017). *Tallinn Manual 2.0 on the International law applicable to cyber operations*. Cambridge University Press.

The Maritime Executive. (2022). *China launches its first autonomous container ship service*. Available at: https://maritime-executive.com/article/china-reports-first-autonomous-containership-entered-service. Accessed 27 May 2022.

Tuckett, C. (2021). UK House of Lords, International Relations and Defence Committee. Corrected oral evidence. UNCLOS: Fit for purpose in the 21st Century? Witness: Commander Caroline Tuckett, lead legal adviser, international law, Royal Navy. Available at: https://committees.parliament.uk/oralevidence/3000/pdf/. Accessed 14 May 2022.

UNCLOS. (1982). United Nations Convention on the Law of the Sea, Dec. 10, 1982, 1833 U.N.T.S. 397.

US Navy USV Master Plan. (2007). The Navy unmanned surface vehicle (USV) master plan.

Van Hooydonk, E. (2014). The law of unmanned merchant shipping: An exploration. *The Journal of International Maritime Law, 20*, 403–423.

Vienna Convention. (1988). United Nations Convention against Illicit Traffic in Narcotic Drugs and Psychotropic Substances, Dec. 20 , 1988, 1582 U.N.T.S. 95.

Watt, E. (2019). *Ship registration: Law and practice* (3rd ed.). Informa Law.

PART III

Safety & Seaworthiness

CHAPTER 6

Designing Norms for Autonomous Ships: The Obligation to Call for Help and the Duty to Save Life in Danger at Sea

Michael Tsimplis

1 Introduction

The technological evolution of conventional ships under the command of a master towards ships remotely or autonomously navigated, with or without a caretaker crew, has been accompanied by several legal studies (van Hooydonk, 2014; Veal & Tsimplis, 2017; Ringbom & Veal, 2017; Veal et al., 2019) and more technical studies (Dreyer & Oltedal, 2019; Wróbel et al., 2020). These studies consider the difficulties in operating autonomous ships primarily from a regulatory point of view. The

I am grateful to Paul Myburgh for his comments on the first draft of this paper.

M. Tsimplis (✉)
School of Law, City University of Hong Kong, Hong Kong (SAR), China
e-mail: m.tsimplis@cityu.edu.hk

© The Author(s), under exclusive license to Springer Nature Switzerland AG 2023

T. M. Johansson et al. (eds.), *Autonomous Vessels in Maritime Affairs*, Studies in National Governance and Emerging Technologies,
https://doi.org/10.1007/978-3-031-24740-8_6

published research demonstrates compartmentalisation of the approach, as there is little cross-referencing between them. This is unfortunate for two reasons. First, the regulatory system is not inflexible and can be tuned to support innovation. Second, understanding the legal norms can help the development of engineering options more likely to satisfy them.

The development of autonomous ships should be based, it is submitted, on the premise that they should be at least as safe as conventional ships. The safety requirement includes three components: risks posed to other users of the sea, cargo risks and risks to the marine environment. For conventional ships, the risk to the other users of the sea and the environment is a matter of public policy expressed in civil liability regimes. By contrast, the risk to the cargo is primarily a contractual allocation between cargo and carrier interests and their respective insurers. Where transferable shipping documents like bills of lading are issued, it is also a matter of public policy imposing minimum obligations on the carriers (Tsimplis, 2020).

Preserving human life, property and the environment depend on timely assistance. The ability to seek help and render assistance are characteristics of conventional ships facilitated and supported by the existing legal framework. This paper assesses whether autonomous ships are subject to similar legal duties which, unless removed, demand specific technical and operational capabilities to be developed.

The following section considers whether there is a legal requirement that any system, conventional or autonomous, must be capable of seeking assistance when in danger. The question of whether there is a legal duty to render assistance to people at risk at sea is discussed in the third section. The final part provides the conclusions of this chapter.

In the following discussion, autonomy is defined as navigation independent of human intervention while being performed. The possibility of developing self-learning computer systems onboard ships is not considered here. Autonomy can co-exist with a caretaking crew or be used on board an uncrewed ship. Remotely controlled ships with or without crew provide two additional scenarios. The most challenging design concerns an autonomous and uncrewed ship. Where a crew is posted on board, the possibility of switching to a conventional mode of navigation and intervening in cases where dangerous situations are developing remains available.

2 The Legal Obligation to Call for Help

An autonomous or remotely controlled ship with or without a crew should be able to seek salvage assistance. This capability is argued here as a legal obligation which is part of the duty to care for the cargo under the contract of carriage and corresponding bailment obligations. It could also be argued as part of the duty in marine insurance to mitigate losses (Clarke, 2003), a duty to protect the lives of passengers and a duty to avoid marine pollution following accidents (Tsimplis, 2021). Of course, the argued positive obligation to seek assistance is owed to a different entity in each of the aforementioned scenarios. Thus, regarding the carriage of goods, this obligation is based on bailment and contractual arrangements. In marine insurance, the obligation would be based on the insurance contract and, perhaps, on the role of insurance as a distributor of the risk of the maritime adventure. In the latter context, the obligation would be owed to all insured under the same pool. Regarding the marine environment, the obligation could be argued as one imposed by states in general, specifically by the flag state, to discharge their obligation to protect the marine environment. The obligation to protect human life, passengers and crew would have contractual and public obligations characteristics.

Here the term obligation is used to characterise the norm of calling for assistance and the term duty to characterise the norm of saving life at sea. Linguistically the terms are, in some contexts, used interchangeably and sometimes distinctly (Brandt, 1964). Here we distinguish between the obligation to call for help, which is, in most scenarios suggested above, based on the voluntary assumption of a contractual or bailment obligation and the duty to render assistance, which is imposed by states. Such a distinction is adequate to distinguish between the obligation to call for help, which, if breached, sounds in damages, and the duty to render assistance which, if breached, may lead to criminal liability. This broad distinction is not, however, entirely accurate. For example, the breach of the duty of care in negligence would not be consistent with a duty giving rise to criminal liability.

However, irrespective of the characterisation adopted, if there is an obligation to call for help, the autonomous ship must comply with it, or a persuasive argument must be developed to constrain this obligation to conventional ships only. The latter option will increase the cost of transporting goods and the incidents of marine pollution; thus, such an argument is, it is submitted, unlikely to succeed. It is also arguable that the liability imposed where the obligation to call for help is not satisfied is more efficient than any criminal law provision which would depend for its enforcement on the flag state's willingness to prosecute.

2.1 *Is the Obligation to Call for Help a Duty?*

The obligation to call for help can also be argued as a duty. The following points are relevant in this respect. First, the Salvage Convention (1989) does not include a general duty to call for help. Second, Art. 19 of the International Convention on Salvage, 1989 (Salvage Convention, 1989) provides that "Services rendered notwithstanding the express and reasonable prohibition of the owner or master of the vessel or the owner of any property in danger which is not and has not been on board the vessel shall not give rise to payment under this Convention". These two points support the argument that there is no general duty to seek salvage assistance. However, there are also strong counterarguments. First, it must be noted that the application of Art. 19 of the Salvage Convention (1989) depends upon the meaning of "reasonable prohibition". The term "reasonable" is not defined in the Convention; thus, the position before the Salvage Convention (1989) needs to be examined, especially as the Salvage Convention (1910) had a similar provision. English courts have awarded salvage despite the refusal of the salvage services by the master (Reeder, 2011; Rose, 2021) even where there was a possibility of self-help (*The* Flore, 1929) and where they were not required, as a matter of fact (*The Auguste Legembre*, 1902).

Thus, the reasonable refusal of salvage services under Art. 19, is not a liberty to let the ship and cargo be lost to the sea but, arguably, an option for property owners to decline services from incompetent salvors. This interpretation is also supported by comments in the *travaux préparatoires* of the 1989 Salvage Convention (CMI, 2003). Second, where the stricken ship poses an environmental risk or where the casualty may result in a wreck posing an environmental or navigational hazard, the coastal state has the powers to intervene and dictate the engagement of salvage services. In the UK, the Secretary of State's Representative (SOSREP) exercises such powers while the Wreck Removal Convention, 2007. Third, in salvage cases, there is a duty imposed under Art. 8 of the Salvage Convention (1989) on the salvor and the owners of property to exercise due care to prevent or minimise environmental damage. It would be surprising if such a duty of care only exists where salvage services are engaged but can be denied where the shipowner simply refuses to engage salvors.

Thus, it is submitted that the lack of an express duty to seek salvage assistance does not imply that there is no obligation to call for help when the ship or the cargo is in danger. The provision simply recognises that assistance in other forms may be available. The Salvage Convention (1989) was developed to support professional salvors and facilitate the use of salvage services to reduce losses or property to the sea and prevent pollution. Furthermore, the right in rem in support of salvage claims and the in rem priority given to salvage claims indicate a broader underlying public interest supporting the argued obligation, which may also be argued as a duty.

2.2 Bailment

Under English law, a contract for the carriage of goods by sea is a bailment arrangement for reward on terms (Tsimplis, 2020; *Volcafe Ltd v Cia Sud Americana de Vapores*, 2018). The terms are found in the contract of carriage, which could be the charter party or a contract evidenced by a bill of lading or another shipping document. In the absence of specific contractual terms, bailment imposes on the bailee an obligation to take reasonable care of the goods and to account to the bailor for any damage or loss to the goods (*Volcafe Ltd v Cia Sud Americana de Vapores*, 2018). The bailee only escapes liability if it has exercised reasonable care in looking after the goods, or by proving that the lack of care was not causative of the damage suffered. The bailee has the burden of proving that reasonable care has been exercised or that any breach of the duty did not cause damage to the goods (Palmer, 2011).

Where the bailed property becomes endangered, the bailee has the additional duty to take reasonable measures to protect the bailed property. Two cases can be provided in support of this proposition. The first is Cargo ex Argos (1873), a case which concerned a cargo loaded in London and destined for France. The French port authority did not permit the discharge of the cargo. Following delays and failed efforts by the master to arrange the discharge, including efforts to discharge in nearby ports, the cargo was carried back to England. The shipowner claimed against the shipper for the contractual freight, payable on discharge, for freight back to England, and demurrage concerning the delays incurred. In approving the shipowner's claim, the Privy Council stated: ".... a duty is cast on the master in many cases of accident and emergency to act for the safety of the cargo, in such manner as may be best under the circumstances in which it may be placed; and that, as a correlative right, he is entitled to charge its owner with the expenses properly incurred in so doing" (Cargo ex Argos, 1873, p. 1073).

A second case concerns the duty to mitigate the damage to cargo arising from accidents. In Notara v Henderson (1872) a cargo of beans became wet due to a collision. The liability for the collision was itself an exempted peril. The owners of the beans and claimant shippers asked for the beans to be discharged at the port reached after the collision so that they could be dried before being reshipped and carried to the destination. The master refused. The Court of Appeal confirmed that: "There is a duty on the master of a ship, as representing the shipowner, to take reasonable care of the goods, intrusted to him, not merely in doing what is necessary to preserve them on board the ship during the ordinary incidents of the voyage, but also in taking active measures, where reasonably practicable under all the circumstances, to check and arrest the loss or deterioration resulting from accidents, for the necessary and immediate consequences of-which the shipowner is not liable by reason of exceptions in the bill of lading. And for neglect of this duty by the master, the shipowner is responsible to the shipper" (Notara v Henderson, 1872, p. 235).

These two cases define the legal duty to protect and preserve the cargo carried by sea as one extending beyond the normal carriage operations and in cases where there is a risk of damage or loss of the cargo. Both expressly mention the duties of the master of the ship. However, the bailment is, arguably, with the master's employer; thus, such obligations are imposed on the shipowner or the demise charterer in case the ship is so chartered. Therefore, the bailee is obliged to seek assistance in the form of salvage or towage or take other reasonable actions to preserve the goods. Failing to do so would result in having to pay damages. This obligation is vital for cargo owners and underwriters because it reduces cargo losses and insurance costs. Where a caretaking crew brings the autonomous ship in and out of port, the bailment relationship would depend on whether this caretaking crew will be considered independent contractors or employees of the shipowner.

2.3 Application to Autonomous and Remotely Controlled Ships

When a crew is posted on board an autonomous or remotely operated ship, satisfying the legal duty to call for assistance would be easier. However, suppose there is no crew present. In that case, the need for external assistance is expected to be more frequent because it would be necessary even for minor problems that could have been resolved by crew intervention (Tsimplis, 2020). Thus the presence of crew can be considered as providing the equivalent standards to conventional ships with respect to the risk of cargo damage.

Where the ship is remotely controlled but uncrewed, it can be expected that there will be at least some awareness of the situation by the controller. Either instruments or sensors would indicate a problem on board, or if the communication with the ship has been lost, this will mean that the property is not under control and thus may be at risk.

Confirming that risk is developing would be much more complicated if the ship is autonomous and uncrewed. Whether communication with the ship's systems can be established and whether any signals and images obtained from the sensors onboard can be transmitted to the shore would be essential in identifying the degree of danger.

Thus uncrewed ships should develop systems dealing with the following issues. First, the system should be able to monitor the ship's and the cargo's condition continuously in time. Second, the system should be able to identify changes in the cargo's or the ship's conditions and differentiate between regular changes and changes indicating that risk is developing. Third, the system should be capable of sending alerts or distress signals to the shipowner or any controller involved. Fourth, the system should be able to send alerts and distress signals to salvors and coastal authorities. In addition, uncrewed ships should be designed so that salvors and their tugs can get access to them. Otherwise, calling them on location may not be efficient. The facilitation of access may increase the ship's vulnerability to acts of piracy and illegal access. These are beyond the scope of this chapter but also represent cargo risks and may create liability for the carrier.

The shipowner of an uncrewed ship will have difficulty distinguishing between a false alarm and a real danger, especially where the loss of communication between the ship and the shore is part of the problem. Arguably a reasonable bailee would prefer to seek assistance than risk the loss of the cargo. This precautionary approach raises the possibility of false alarms and could, in turn, lead to disputes with whoever attempts to assist. In situations where salvage assistance is required, the cargo owners would become liable to pay their share in proportion to the cargo's respective salved value. For false alarms and for simple problems which can be quickly resolved, the awards would be small, but disputes with the cargo interests are likely to occur because they will also be liable for salvage (Tsimplis, 2020).

If a crew is on board, it can call for assistance, and if the ship is remotely controlled, the controller will have to judge when to call for such assistance. However, for autonomous uncrewed ships, the capability of seeking assistance should be built into the controlling software. In the absence of direct monitoring of the situation on board the ship and the absence of a possibility for self-help, waiting for confirmation of the problem by finding the ship and landing a crew on board could, if late, be argued as a breach of the reasonable care of the cargo requirement. Redundancy in the safety systems could provide the self-help function if the problem is constrained to machinery breakdown.

2.4 The Associated Obligation to Deviate to Protect the Cargo

2.4.1 Is the Obligation Exempted Under the Carriage of Goods by Sea Conventions?

Carriage of goods under transferable shipping documents, for example, bills of lading, are controlled by a number of international conventions, which ensure minimum standards for the carrier's performance are put in place. The standards of cargo care imposed by the Hague Rules (1924), the Hamburg Rules (1978) and the Hague–Visby Rules (1968) are similar to those of bailment but with differences with respect to the available, to the carrier, exceptions of liability. Cargo interests would expect standards of care board autonomous or remotely controlled ships to be at least as high as those for conventional ships. A caretaking crew would arguably be able to provide similar standards in most aspects. When, however, diversion of the ship is required, for example, for re-stowing the cargo, either the option to override the autonomous navigation should be available, or for remotely controlled ships, the operator should be able to force such a diversion. The diversion to an appropriate port of refuge would need to be built into the system for an autonomous, uncrewed ship. This would require linking the continuous monitoring of the cargo spaces, including the cargo conditions and the ship's performance, with the navigational decision. Even if such systems are developed for autonomous ships, the lack of a crew would mean that some emergency measures to contain a developing risk will not be available. Whether such lowering of the standard of care for the cargo is permissible requires an examination of the usual contractual arrangements in contracts of carriage.

2.4.2 The Hamburg Rules

Article 4.1 of the Hamburg Rules provides that the carrier is liable for any damage to the goods during the whole period the goods are in its charge unless the carrier proves that it and its servants or agents took all reasonable measures to avoid the cause and the consequences of the damage (Art. 5.1). Thus, where the carrier can prove that it and its servants and agents have not been negligent in looking after the goods and have responded appropriately when a danger to the goods has arisen, there would be no liability on the carrier. There are additional exemptions under the Hamburg Rules. These include special rules for damage caused by fire (Art. 5.4), damage to a cargo of live animals (Art. 5.5), damage to unauthorised deck cargo (Art. 9.3), and situations where saving life or property in danger are the cause of the cargo damage (Art. 5.6).

Where the ship and the cargo are endangered, failure to seek assistance or failure to take the immediately necessary measures to avoid the damage will arguably disable the carrier from proving a lack of negligence and therefore make him liable. This is supported by the collision case The Fritz Thyssen (1967), where the failure to seek assistance was held to be a new intervening act that caused the loss of the ship instead of the collision that caused its original damage.

2.4.3 The Hague and Hague–Visby Rules

Under the Hague and Hague–Visby Rules, the protection of the cargo interests is based on a duty to ensure, before and at the beginning of the voyage, that the shipowner has exercised due diligence to make the ship seaworthy (Art III r.1). In addition, with respect to the care of the cargo Art III, r. 2 sets the duty as follows: "Subject to the provisions of Article IV, the carrier shall properly and carefully load, handle, stow, carry, keep, care for, and discharge the goods carried". The carrier's liability is exempted when one of the seventeen exceptions under Article IV operates. The difference with the Hamburg Rules is primarily in the broader set of exceptions available.

The first and broader exception of liability concerns faults or omissions in the navigation or the management of the ship by the "master, mariner, pilot or servants" (Art IV r 2(a)). The wording is wide enough to cover the liability of a person remotely controlling the ship. However, the wording would not be able to cover navigational mistakes caused by the software of an autonomous ship, except perhaps where these can be attributed to failure by the servant of the carrier who provided the specific voyage instructions to the navigational system. If such faulty instructions have been provided at the beginning of the voyage, a breach of the due diligence obligation under Art III, r. 1 could also be argued (Tsimplis, 2020).

There are two points to note in this respect. First, this exception will not be applicable if there is no master or crew to look after the ship. Therefore, the situations under which the carrier will be liable for cargo damage shipped on board an autonomous ship and caused by faults of navigation will increase in number. However, the exception will remain available for remotely controlled ships and arguably cover the operator's negligence. More complicated questions are likely to arise where a crew is on board the autonomous ship. The navigational error may arise from (a) an error in the software or the hardware of the navigational equipment attributable to a failure in the maintenance or the misuse of such equipment by the caretaker crew or (b) a failure by the crew to intervene when it becomes evident that there is a fault in the navigational system. A literal interpretation of the exception would, arguably, consider the first incident as an act, neglect or default in the management of the ship. In the second example, however, the failure to intervene will arguably be covered by the navigational error exception.

The second point concerns a failure to call for salvage assistance and whether negligence in performing this duty can be exempted under Art. IV r. 2(a). A fault in the system controlling an autonomous uncrewed ship will not be covered by such an exception as no relevant person could be identified. For remotely controlled and autonomous crewed ships, a failure to seek assistance would not relate to the ship's navigation. It could, however, be argued as one related to the management of the ship. For such an outcome, the term "management" would need to be given a broad meaning involving external to the ship's operations. For example, arranging for a conventional ship, a ship-to-ship transfer of bunkers may be characterised as an operation falling within the scope of the management of the ship. Whether seeking salvage assistance also falls under this type of activity is yet to be determined. The better view is that it cannot be classified as such because the call for assistance is an admission that the ship cannot be safely managed without assistance. Thus, a failure to seek salvage assistance while being part of the duty to care for the cargo is unlikely to fall under the exception of Art. IV r.2(a), and thus the carrier will be liable for cargo damages arising as a result of this breach of the contract.

The liability of the carrier may also be exempted under Art. IV r. 2(q), which requires the carrier to prove that there was no fault on its behalf or on behalf of its agents or servants. For autonomous, uncrewed ships, this could be relevant as a failure of the system to call for assistance would not be attributable to any person in particular. Arguably then, the carrier would be able to exempt its liability in this respect. However, such a failure may also reflect a breach of the due diligence obligation under Art. III r.1. Thus, the way the shipowner confirmed that the installed system was fit for purpose with respect to its capability of seeking salvage assistance would be relevant. Only if the system was capable of performing the task and any deficiency is a latent defect liability could be avoided.

International conventions, namely Hague-Visby Rules Art. IV r. 4 and Hamburg Rules r. 5.6 exclude the carrier's liability when there is a deviation to save life or property. However, whether this would be relevant for autonomous or remotely controlled ships would depend on whether there is a duty to save life at risk at sea and whether the option to contribute to saving property is available to autonomous ships too.

3 The Duty to Render Assistance

The second issue concerns the safety of life at sea and, in particular, the consequences for seafarers, migrants and refugees if conventional ships are replaced by autonomous ships. The issue is recognised in the literature but not resolved (Dreyer & Oltedal, 2019).

3.1 The Duty to Render Assistance Under International Law

There is little doubt that there is a moral duty to assist people in difficulty at sea. No published study disputes the existence of such a moral duty. However, the question is whether this is a legal duty too and whether it extends to any other entity apart from the master. The academic literature suggests that the duty to rescue people in distress is currently one of the best-established principles of several branches of international law, including international law of the sea, maritime law and humanitarian law (Barnes, 2004; Papanicolopulu, 2016). It is also argued as a part of customary international law codified in the more recent conventions (Pedrozo, 2018). Perhaps more to the point is the suggestion that customary international law imposes a duty to the master of the ship to render assistance (Attard, 2021). Notably, the examination of literature prior to 1910 suggests differently. First, it appears there was no legal obligation to save people at risk at sea, and there was no reward for salvaging a human being unless this person in danger was a slave. In The Mulhouse (1859), it was said, "Compensation for saving life, except the life of a slave unconnected with the saving of property, is left by the law to the voluntary bounty of individuals". This made the saving of lives secondary with respect to saving property (Smith, 1971). Second, early twentieth-century-research on the general issue of rendering assistance to others found that in the absence of statutory provisions or some special relationship, no legal duty to render assistance existed under common law in general (Lake, 1996).

One analysis found that there was probably a duty for a shipowner to collect a seafarer who fell off the ship (Bohlen, 1908) but no more general duty to render assistance. Third, there has been little evidence of enforcement on masters of ships for whom a legal duty and criminal sanctions are imposed (Severance, 2006; Smith, 1971). These three observations raise doubts about whether a legal duty existed before 1910. Perhaps a non-legal principle based on moral grounds existed before 1910. Common law systems supported this duty through the promise of a salvage reward for property salved, which attracted passing vessels to the place of the casualty, thus enabling the saving of life instead of an express legal duty. The situation has, however, changed radically since 1910. The historical origin of today's duty to render assistance supports the argument that the reason the legal duty is imposed solely on the master of the ship is the method chosen for discharging the corresponding duty of states under international law. It is submitted that a view that suggests that the removal of the master in autonomous ships will render such ships beyond any legal obligation to render assistance is misleading.

3.2 The Legal Duty to Render Assistance After 1910

States undertook the obligation to impose a legal duty to render assistance to the master of a ship under Art. 11 of the Salvage Convention (1910) (Friedell, 1979). States undertook the obligation to introduce a corresponding specific duty for the master to render assistance after a collision in the Collision Convention (1910). Presently, several international legal instruments implemented in national laws ensure that the master of every ship is under a duty to render assistance where life is at risk (Pugash, 1977). Thousands of lives are saved each year by merchant ships complying with this duty (Special Report, 2015) at the expense of the commercial interests of shipowners.

Naval ships and ships in governmental service are excluded from this duty under Art. 14 of the Salvage Convention (1910) and under Art. 4 of the Salvage Convention (1989). These exclusions suggest that the legal duty is not a direct transformation of the moral duty because the moral duty would be applicable to all ships.

The general and the specific obligations to render assistance are conditioned upon the safety of the ship, crew and passengers of the vessel which renders assistance. In addition, non-compliance with either the general or the specific legal duty does not create civil liability for the shipowner (Warshauer v. Lloyd, Maltzman & Ehrenreich, 2015; Sabaudo, 1934).

It is submitted that the legal duties imposed on the master are best understood as a practical approach adopted by states to protect human life by using reasonably, and without creating additional risks, all resources available in the vicinity of a shipping accident. This is further supported by the way this obligation is coupled with the development by coastal states of search and rescue operations. Art. 98(1) of the 1982 LOSC combines the general and the collision duty to render assistance requiring states to provide for such legal obligations on ship masters. The duty for general assistance is stronger under Art. 98(1) than under the Salvage Convention, 1910 because it requires that the master proceeds with "all possible speed". Art. 98(2) imposes an obligation on states to develop "adequate and effective" search and rescue services independently or in collaboration with nearby states. Regulation 33 of Chapter V of the International Convention for the Safety of Life at Sea, 1974 demonstrates how closely linked the two duties are. In situations where the master decides not to render assistance, the reason must be entered in the ship's logbook, and thus it becomes accessible to port and flag state control. Furthermore, the duty to render assistance under this provision includes the possibility of the ship becoming requisitioned by the master of the ship in distress or the search and rescue centre. In other words, the duty imposed on the master is part of the mechanism through which the search and rescue network is extended to resources capable of providing assistance irrespective of their flag or destination and without compensation for the time lost. Notably, the obligation to render assistance is not always properly enacted in national laws (Barnes, 2004), and even where it is enacted does not seem to be enforced against shipmasters (Severance, 2006). However, the large number of refugees collected by merchant ships demonstrates that most masters do comply with their legal duty despite the difficulties they may then have to face (Davies, 2003).

3.3 *Should There Be a Legal Duty to Render Assistance When There Is No Master on Board?*

The replacement of the master of the ship by either an operator located remotely or a fully computerised system in the case of autonomous ships will have profound effects on the safety of life at sea and search and rescue operations. Without a master, the legal duty to render assistance will become inoperative as a matter of literal interpretation. This could mean that autonomous or remotely controlled ships will have no duty to support search and rescue operations or even stand by and render assistance in collision cases. Such a result would be absurd because it would legitimise "hit and run" behaviour for autonomous ships, violating the obligations of states to ensure safety at sea. In addition, it would remove one of the two pillars of the search and rescue framework, thus requiring a general reconsideration of how states will discharge their obligation under international law. Having fewer ships available to assist in search and rescue operations may increase the need for state-funded search and rescue systems. Even if it is presumed that autonomous ships operate separately from conventional ships, for example, in dedicated traffic lanes, thus reducing the possibility of "hit and run" incidents, the effect in the search and rescue framework would still be an important one.

It is submitted that the legal duty of the master to render assistance must be viewed as an expression of the underlying norm of rendering assistance at sea, which has significantly evolved and developed in the twentieth century. The choice made by states in 1910 to impose this duty on the master alone cannot mean that the removal of the master or altering its role can remove the duty altogether. While the master is the person on which the legal system was designed, the policy objective was and still is to make nearby ships of every state, places of refuge for shipwrecked and stranded people. This policy still provides the quickest and most efficient way to save lives at risk at sea. Even if the adoption of uncrewed ships significantly reduces the number of seafarers, the sea may still endanger the lives of migrants, passengers, fisherfolk and amateur sailors.

The analysis suggests that the legal duty to render assistance after a collision or in general is how states discharge their respective obligations. For conventional ships, this hinges upon the master. For autonomous or remotely controlled ships, the duty will have to be modified to ensure that hit and run collisions between autonomous and conventional ships will not occur and that the search and rescue operations will have access to all suitable platforms. The design of autonomous and remotely controlled ships must include the capability to render assistance after a collision with a crewed ship and assist in search and rescue operations.

Regulatory changes will be needed to reformulate this duty. These should be outlined as early as possible to provide certainty for designers, builders, operators and investors regarding the kind of tasks expected to be performed by such ships and the way liability will be imposed where a master is not present.

One option would be to impose this duty on the shipowner. In 1910 the shipowner had little capability to communicate with the ship, could not be expected in an emergency to assess the risks involved in rendering assistance and could only create confusion and delay if it decided differently from the master. The situation has now changed. Communication with the ship is possible in most parts of the world, and conventional ships are almost continuously supervised. The development of autonomous or remotely controlled ships presumes that the owner has either a continuous or a predetermined say in what the ship will do and does not rely on the master to decide what the ship should do. It follows that the corresponding responsibility and duty should follow increased control. Thus imposing an express duty on the shipowner is reasonable and appropriate. The threat of civil liability claims in cases of non-compliance by the master was dealt with by expressly excluding such liability for the shipowner in 1910, and this does not need to be affected by an extension of this duty. The shipowner of a ship rendering assistance may lose significant amounts of money because of the delays involved. Imposing civil liability would make this financially costly operation riskier and would increase tendencies to avoid involvement with search and rescue operations.

Another option to deal with the necessary amendments would be to broaden the definition of the master so as to include the operator of a remotely controlled or the supervisor of an autonomous ship. A third option would be to impose at registration the requirement that autonomous ships could automatically go under the control of search and rescue centres when an emergency arises.

There is also the option to exclude autonomous ships from such duties. This would be a morally and legally unacceptable solution where there has been a collision with a crewed ship. Even if such exclusion may appear attractive to prospective shipowners of autonomous ships, it is bound to increase the loss of human life and the costs of providing adequate and effective search and rescue services for coastal states. This could be counteracted with respect to the additional costs by forcing the owners of autonomous ships to support search and rescue services directly. However, the financial balancing of the scales would not provide the answer to an incident where people may drown while an autonomous ship sails close by.

Compliance with the duty to render assistance and participate in search and rescue operations is essential in making autonomous shipping socially acceptable. The rescue of migrants by commercial ships, despite the inherent commercial risks posed by governmental actions, provides a charitable side of the shipping industry with humanitarian actions extending beyond its workforce, outside state borders and political conflict and, most importantly, beyond the capability of most coastal states.

3.4 *Would New Ships Be Able to Render Assistance?*

There is little doubt that an autonomous or remotely controlled ship with a crew on board will be able to render assistance and should therefore be bound by these obligations. Whoever is in charge of the crew could be considered the master even if it is not in charge of the ship's navigation. Similarly, for a remotely controlled ship, the controller or whoever is in charge of the controller could be considered the master and make the necessary assessment on when and how the ship can assist, receive requests and orders and participate in the search and rescue operations.

For autonomous and uncrewed ships, the possibility of rendering assistance would be a matter of design to identify people in distress and enable them to obtain access on board. To the extent that such a ship can identify a swimmer or a boat for collision avoidance, it should also have the technical capability of identifying a shipwrecked person and a group of refugees. The assistance an uncrewed ship could provide could range from standing by, releasing life-saving equipment, notifying authorities of the location, and providing access to a part of the autonomous ship for protection from the sea.

Making a ship travel on its own worldwide while avoiding collisions is a major technological achievement. Requiring that it should also have simple capabilities for assisting people at risk by lowering boats, releasing life-saving equipment or lowering a rope ladder is, it is submitted, much easier. Furthermore, because of the absence of the crew, the risk to such ships would be smaller, and therefore they could render assistance in riskier and more situations than conventional ships could.

4 Conclusions

Commercial shipping is efficient and profitable because standards for protecting the cargo are in place. Such standards include the capability to seek assistance when risks arise. It has been argued that this legal obligation sets a design standard for new types of ships. Crewed ships, whether autonomous or remotely controlled, would be capable of assessing the level of risk involved when something endangering the cargo happens. The crew should be able to call for help or take over and deviate to a port of refuge if the onboard safety arrangements are inadequate to deal with the risk. Uncrewed autonomous or remotely controlled ships provide more complex challenges. In order to discharge the obligation to call for help, such ships will need coupling between the monitoring systems on the ship and its navigational command and would require a decision-making system capable of seeking assistance.

Thus, an important aspect of developing commercially viable autonomous ships is their ability to deal with situations requiring diversion to a port of refuge or salvage assistance.

The development of a fleet of uncrewed ships poses risks for the operational framework of search and rescue because the current legal obligations are exclusively imposed on the master of the ship. Enabling autonomous ships to escape the obligation to render assistance may provide a commercial advantage over conventional ships. However, the current arrangement reflects the optimal way for states to discharge their duty, under international law, to render assistance with respect to conventional ships. The policy objective was and still is to ensure ships are available as platforms on which people could find rescue. The legal obligation imposed on the master is simply the means to achieve this.

It is argued that a corresponding duty will have to be imposed for new ship designs, which will have to render assistance both after a collision and with respect to refugees or other people stranded at sea when they are the most proximate platforms on which people could find safety. Resolving the way states will achieve this requires early action so that the duty to render assistance is reformulated and the developers of ships of new technology are aware of the duties and can design systems which can discharge them.

References

Attard, F. G. (2021). *The Duty of the Shipmaster to Render Assistance at Sea Under International Law*. Leiden, Brill.

Barnes, R. (2004). Refugee Law At Sea. *International and Comparative Law Quarterly, 53*(1), 47–77.

Bohlen F. H. (1908). The Moral Duty To Aid Others as a Basis of Tort Liability, 56 U. PA. L. REV. 217 (1908).

Brandt, R. B. (1964). The Concepts of Obligation and Duty. *Mind, 73*, 374–393.

Cargo ex Argos. (1873). LR 5 PC; Brown (App) v Gaudet (Resp.); Cargo ex Argos, [1861–73] All ER Rep. Ext 1057.

Clarke, M. (2003). Wisdom after the Event: The Duty to Mitigate Insured Loss. *Lloyd's Maritime & Commercial Law Quarterly, 4*, 525.

CMI. (2003). The Travaux Préparatoires of the Convention on Salvage 1989, 444–459. Available at: https://comitemaritime.org/wp-content/uploads/2018/05/Travaux-Preparatoires-of-the-Convention-on-Salvage-1989.pdf. Accessed 13 June 2022.

Davies, M. (2003). Obligations and Implications for Ships Encountering Persons in Need of Assistance at Sea. *Pac. Rim l. & Pol'y J., 12*, 109.
Dreyer, L. O., & Oltedal, H. A. (2019). Safety Challenges for Maritime Autonomous Surface Ships: A Systematic Review. In *The Third Conference on Maritime Human Factors*. Haugesund.
Friedell, S. F. (1979). Compensation and Reward for Saving Life at Sea. *Michigan Law Review, 77*(5), 1218–1240.
Hague Rules. (1924). International Convention for the Unification of Certain Rules of Law Relating to Bills of Lading (Brussels, 25 August 1924).
Hague-Visby Rules. (1968). The Hague Rules amended by the Protocol to Amend the International Convention for the Unification of Certain Rules of Law Relating to Bills of Lading (Brussels, 23 February 1968).
Hamburg Rules. (1978). United Nations Convention on the Carriage of Goods by Sea (Hamburg, 31 March 1978).
Lake, P. F. (1996). Recognizing the Importance of Remoteness to the Duty to Rescue. *DePaul l. Rev., 46*, 315.
Maltzman, J., & Ehrenreich, M. (2015). The Seafarer's Ancient Duty to Rescue and Modern Attempts to Regulate and Criminalise the Good Samaritan. *Tulane Law Review, 89*, 1267.
Notara v Henderson. (1872). LR 7 QB 225 (Ex Ch).
Palmer, N. (2011). The Case of the Vanishing Lovers: Bailment and Burden of Proof. *Art Antiquity & l., 16*, 85.
Papanicolopulu, I. (2016). The Duty to Rescue at Sea, in Peacetime and in War: A General Overview. *International Review of the Red Cross, 98*(902), 491–514.
Pedrozo, R. P. (2018). Duty to Render Assistance to Mariners in Distress During Armed Conflict at Sea: A US Perspective. *International Law Studies, 94*(1), 4, 126.
Pugash, J. Z. (1977). The Dilemma of the Sea Refugee: Rescue Without Refuge. *Harvard International Law Journal, 18*(3), 577–604.
Reeder, J. (2011). *Brice on Maritime Law of Salvage*. Sweet & Maxwell (Reeder J., ed).
Ringbom, H. M., & Veal, R. (2017). Unmanned ships and the international regulatory framework. *Journal of International Maritime Law, 23*(2), 100–118.
Rose, F. (2021). *Kennedy and Rose: Law of Salvage*. Wildy & Sons Ltd.
Salvage Convention. (1910). Convention for the Unification of Certain Rules with Respect to Assistance and Salvage at Sea, 23 September, 19ro, 37 Stat. x658, TS. No. 576, 1 BEVANS 780 (1968).
Salvage Convention. (1989). International Convention on Salvage, 1989. Adopted in London, 28/04/1989, entry into force on 14 July 1996, UNTS 1953.

Severance, A. (2006). The Duty to Render Assistance in the Satellite Age. *California Western International Law Journal, 36*(2), 377–400.
Smith, W. (1971). The Duty to Render Assistance at Sea: Is It Effective or Adrift. *California Western International Law Journal, 2*, 146–163.
Special Report. (2015). Commercial Ships Scoop Up Desperate Human Cargo, Which Puts This Number at More Than 65,000 in 2014–2015 Alone. Available at: https://www.reuters.com/article/europe-migrants-ship-special-report-pix-idUKL4N11L3U920150921. Accessed 1 June 2022.
The Auguste Legembre. (1902), 123.
The Flore. (1929). Ll. L. Rep. 172.
The Fritz Thyssen. (1967). 2 Lloyd's Rep. 199.
The Mulhouse, 17 F. Cas. 962, 967 (No. 9910) (SD Fla. 1859).
Tsimplis, M. (2020). On the Carriage of Goods on Autonomous, Remotely Controlled, Crewed and Uncrewed Ships. In S. Girvin, and V. Ulfbeck (Eds.), *Maritime Organisation, Management and Liability: A Legal Analysis of New Challenges in the Maritime Industry* (pp. 283–306). Oxford, Hart Publishing.
Tsimplis, M. (2021). *Environmental Norms in Maritime Law*. Edward Elgar Publishing.
Van Hooydonk, E. (2014). The Law of Unmanned Merchant Shipping—An Exploration. *The Journal of International Maritime Law, 20*(3), 403–423.
Veal, R., & Tsimplis, M. (2017). The Integration of Unmanned Ships into the Lex Maritima. *Lloyd's Maritime & Commercial Law Quarterly*, 303–335.
Veal, R., Tsimplis, M., & Serdy, A. (2019). The Legal Status and Operation of Unmanned Maritime Vehicles. *Ocean Development & International Law, 50*(1), 23–48.
Volcafe Ltd v Cia Sud Americana de Vapores (Trading as CSAV) [2018] UKSC 61, [2019] AC 358.
Warshauer v. Lloyd Sabaudo, S.A., 71 F.2d 146, 147 (2d Cir. 1934), cert. denied, 293 U.S. 610 (1934).
Wróbel, K., Gil, M., and Montewka, J. (2020). Identifying Research Directions of a Remotely-Controlled Merchant Ship by Revisiting Her System-Theoretic Safety Control Structure. *Safety Science, 129*, 104797, ISSN 0925-7535.
Wreck Removal Convention. (2007). The Nairobi International Convention on the Removal of Wrecks. Adopted 18 May 2007, entry into force on 14 May 2015. UNTS 55565.

CHAPTER 7

Safety and Seaworthiness Challenges of MASS in the Shipping and Port Sector

Klimanthia Kontaxaki and Vera Alexandropoulou

1 Introduction

Unmanned, remotely operated, and fully autonomous vessels are on the verge of fundamentally transforming the maritime transportation industry. The Maritime Safety Committee (MSC) of the International Maritime Organization (IMO) defines maritime autonomous surface ships (MASS) as a ship which, to a varying degree, can operate independently of human interaction (MSC 100, 2018). At its 103rd session (May 2021), the MSC completed a regulatory scoping exercise, having analyzed relevant safety

K. Kontaxaki · V. Alexandropoulou (✉)
VA Law Firm, Piraeus, Greece
e-mail: vera.alexandropoulou@alexandropouloulaw.com

K. Kontaxaki
e-mail: viniakontaxaki@yahoo.com; viniakontaxaki.valaw@gmail.com

V. Alexandropoulou
Thalassa Foundation, Geneva, Switzerland

© The Author(s), under exclusive license to Springer Nature Switzerland AG 2023

T. M. Johansson et al. (eds.), *Autonomous Vessels in Maritime Affairs*, Studies in National Governance and Emerging Technologies,
https://doi.org/10.1007/978-3-031-24740-8_7

shipping conventions to determine how safe, secure, and environmentally sound MASS operations might be addressed in IMO instruments, with the aim to assess how MASS could be regulated (MSC.1-Circ.1638). At the scoping exercise, varying degrees of autonomy were considered (see Chapter 2 in this book). The present analysis engages with autonomy degrees three and four, remotely controlled ships without seafarers on board and fully autonomous ships.

Research studies have assessed the safety risks and prevention of accidents in the context of autonomous vessels' operation, contending that unmanned ships may be assumed to be safer than conventional ships in terms of the usual human-related maritime navigational accidents, such as collisions and grounding, although other causes of accidents, even newly emerging ones, can be expected to increase (Porathe et al., 2018; Rødseth & Burmeister, 2015; Wróbel et al., 2017). Accordingly, legal analyses present the regulatory challenges in the legitimate implementation of autonomous shipping (Hogg & Ghosh, 2016; Ringbom, 2019; Tsimplis, 2021a, 2021b; Van Hooydonk, 2014; Veal et al., 2019) and the complexity of determining a safety regulatory framework which would cover all aspects and functions of the autonomous maritime system.

MASS will be, in any event, subject to at least the same safety requirements for manned ships in terms of safety of navigation and Port State Control. That has already been established in chapter 3 of this volume. The problem, now, is to define the acceptance criteria and to a lesser degree to test compliance (Rødseth & Burmeister, 2015, p. 359). It would also seem unjustified that manned and unmanned ships' operation, entailing similar dangers, are not subject to the same rules that have been designed to address those dangers (Ringbom & Veal, 2017, p. 103). In its 101 session (June 2019), the MEPC approved Interim guidelines for MASS trials, (MSC.1-Circ.1604) which, inter alia, state that trials should be conducted in a manner that provides at least the same degree of safety, security, and protection of the environment as required by the relevant IMO legal instruments. Similarly, remote operators of MASS should be appropriately qualified and experienced to safely conduct MASS trials while appropriate steps should also be taken to ensure sufficient cyber risk management of the systems and infrastructure used when conducting MASS trials.

The outstanding challenge in respect of unmanned MASS' operation, being highly dependent on connectivity with remote centers and satellites, is safeguarding the communication and facilitating the exchange of information between vessels with other maritime stakeholders interacting in a common maritime environment such as vessel traffic services system (VTS) operators and Pilots.

Ports will also be required to adapt to MASS accordingly. Ensuring safe maneuvering through densely trafficked ports will be paramount for the IMO and national regulators. Security issues also constitute a great concern associated with the high reliance on software and connectivity, for both the shipping sector with cybersecurity risk emerging as a matter of remote control and management of unmanned ships, and for the port sector as a rising threat against port security. Since autonomous ships depend heavily on information technology systems onboard and onshore, cyber-attacks are far more likely than conventional vessels. Automation in ports has facilitated so far, the efficient control of traffic and trade flows and the port operations to run more smoothly, signifying the optimization of every process for the least time consumption and resources, thereby enhancing port capacity and efficiency. It is contended that the regulatory framework of the port sector is more adaptable to technological advances, in specific towards the 'smart port', even in its absolute version (the 'Botport' with calls of autonomous ships, automation of port operations, digitalization of port related processes and handling of data) than that for maritime shipping (Van Hooydonk, 2020, p. 104).

The advent of unmanned MASS makes digitalization of shipping a prerequisite. Increased data collection, processing, and interconnectivity capabilities enable automated systems to be controlled remotely or through artificial intelligence. The latter will only be achieved with greater levels of collaboration between States, a focus on capacity building and increased cooperation between shipping, ports, and logistics. In this regard, IMO has advocated for the harmonized and standardized digitalization in shipping, through the development of standards for the electronic exchange of maritime-related information (IMO Compendium on Facilitation and Electronic Business linked to the Facilitation [FAL] Convention) and e-Navigation systems.

The design and deployment of a systemic safety regulatory framework and safety management is required for ensuring the safe and efficient operation of unmanned MASS, taking into consideration the increased interaction among all the involved stakeholders in the system, such as the marine equipment manufacturers, designers and shipbuilders, port operators, financers, and underwriters, Maritime Authorities, Pilots, VTS services and Classification societies. In this regard, the management of safety needs to be better coordinated and more efficiently implemented, resulting in a more proactive and transparent safety management approach among the different stakeholders of the autonomous vessel (Valdez Banda et al., 2018).

Respectively, regulations and standards have to be adopted, efficiently and uniformly implemented for the operations of autonomous vessels, integrating the participation and interaction of other critical stakeholders in the autonomous system. Consequently, the regulatory framework should follow a holistic approach providing for the construction, equipment, operations, the initial design of the services linked to the functioning of the vessel, taking into consideration the remote monitoring by an operator at a control center even in a state other than the flag State, sensors systems, and satellite services.

In order to highlight the safety and seaworthiness challenges of the unmanned MASS, this analysis will start from a brief outline of the International Regulatory Framework, the 1982 United Nations Convention on the Law of the Sea, 1982 (UNCLOS, 1982) and the key IMO instrument for the safety at sea, the International Convention for the Safety of Life at Sea, 1974 (SOLAS, 1974), followed by the International Regulations for Preventing Collisions at Sea, 1972 (COLREGs, 1972) and conclude with the concept of seaworthiness in the relevant case law which advocates in favor of the feasibility of the unmanned MASS' seaworthiness.

2 International Regulatory Framework of Safety and Seaworthiness

2.1 *Flag State*

In International Law of the Sea as crystallized in the United Nations Convention on the Law of the Sea, 1982 (UNCLOS) the rights of a state enshrined in its capacity as flag State are counterweighed with its duties to effectively exercise jurisdiction and control in administrative, technical, and social matters over ships flying its flag (UNCLOS, 1982, Article 94(1)). In particular, the flag State shall maintain a register of ships and assume jurisdiction under its internal law over each ship flying its flag and its master, officers, and crew in respect of administrative, technical, and social matters concerning the ship (UNCLOS, 1982, Article 94(2)). The requirement of the genuine link between the flag State and the ship (UNCLOS, 1982, Article 91) is thusly ascertained through its functionality. Under several UNCLOS provisions, the flag State is called upon to discharge certain duties, thereby ensuring the compliance of ships flying its flag in the context of safety and security at sea, efficiency of navigation, prevention, and control of marine pollution from ships, with generally accepted international rules and standards established through the competent international organization (UNCLOS, 1982, Article 217) and national laws and regulations adopted in accordance with UNCLOS.

In terms of safety at sea, the flag State's duties are designated in Article 94 (of UNCLOS, 1982) in taking such measures for ships flying its flag as are necessary to ensure safety at sea with regard, inter alia, to: (a) the construction, equipment and seaworthiness of ships; (b) the manning of ships, labor conditions and the training of crews, taking into account the applicable international instruments; (c) the use of signals, the maintenance of communications and the prevention of collisions (94(3)). Such measures shall include those necessary to ensure: (a) that each ship, before registration and thereafter at appropriate intervals, is surveyed by a qualified surveyor of ships, and has on board such charts, nautical publications, and navigational equipment and instruments as are appropriate for the safe navigation of the ship; (b) that each ship is in the charge of a master and officers who possess appropriate qualifications, in particular in seamanship, navigation, communications, and marine engineering, and that the crew is appropriate in qualification and numbers for the type, size, machinery, and equipment of the ship; and (c) that the master, officers and, to the extent appropriate, the crew are fully conversant with and required to observe the applicable international regulations concerning the safety of life at sea, the prevention of collisions, the prevention, reduction, and control of marine pollution, and the maintenance of communications by radio (94(4)). In taking the measures called for, the flag State is required to conform to generally accepted international regulations, procedures and practices and to take any steps which may be necessary to secure their observance (94(5)).

By virtue of its mandate, IMO is the specialized agency of the United Nations and the global standard-setting authority for the creation of a regulatory framework universally adopted and implemented in the context of safety, security, and environmental performance of international shipping (Article 1(a) of the IMO Convention). IMO's regulatory role is pinpointed in an implicit manner through rules of reference in several UNCLOS provisions (Chircop, 2019, p. 24).

In this respect, SOLAS, 1974, including its Chapters IX and XI-2, the International Safety Management (ISM) Code and the International Ship and Port Facility Security (ISPS) Code respectively, the latter covering the issue of safety and seaworthiness through security, the International Convention on Load Lines (CLL) and the International Convention on Standards of Training, Certification and Watchkeeping, 1978 (STCW, 1978), are regarded as the key IMO instruments reflecting shipping industry standards that are directly related to the concept of safety and seaworthiness of a ship. Since MASS at the 3rd and 4th autonomy level are unmanned, STCW, 1978 is presumed to not be prima facie applicable to unmanned MASS as it concerns seafarers onboard (STCW, 1978, Article 1). Plausibly, a respective standardized regulatory framework is needed to be introduced, providing for the certification and qualifications of the remote shore-based operator of an unmanned ship or programmer of AI systems for the fully autonomous ship, in order to enhance harmonization between flag States by a coherent regulatory framework as to the professional requirements.

The objective of SOLAS, 1974 (as amended) is to promote safety of life at sea by establishing rules which govern the safe construction of ships, the safety equipment with which ships are required to be fitted and the standards to which they should be operated in order to avoid maritime accidents. Regulation 14 of Chapter V of SOLAS, 1974 on ships' manning, similar to Art. 94(4b) UNCLOS leaves to the discretion of the flag State to establish appropriate minimum safe manning levels by following a transparent procedure, taking into account the guidance adopted by IMO (Assembly resolution A.1047(27) on Principles of minimum safe manning) thereby ensuring that from the point of view of safety of life at sea that all ships are 'sufficiently and efficiently manned' and issue an appropriate minimum safe manning document or equivalent as evidence of the minimum safe manning considered necessary. Since there is no requirement of minimum number of crew to be on board, as long as the safety requirement is satisfied, unmanned vessels may be regarded as technically efficient and compliant with SOLAS, 1974 when operated and monitored by shore-based support (Veal et al., 2019, p. 14) or by automated IT-systems on the fully autonomous ship. The 'efficiency' requirement under Regulation 14 of Chapter V of SOLAS, 1974 may be covered by hi-tech systems, various sensors, etc. (Komianos, 2018, p. 341).

The flag State must ensure that the ships registered under its flag are surveyed when they are first registered, in compliance with SOLAS, 1974 (SOLAS, 1974, Article I). Thereafter ships are periodically surveyed at stipulated intervals by the flag State, which also issues certificates prescribed by the Convention. Flag States are permitted to delegate these responsibilities to nominated surveyors or Recognized Organizations such as a classification society (SOLAS, 1974 Regulation 6). As to safety construction and operation standards of unmanned MASS, they are under ongoing processing and development; Industry Codes of Practice have been published, such as the Maritime Autonomous Surface Ships UK Code of Practice (last update Version 5, 2021) and Classification societies have already proceeded with issuing guidelines on autonomous shipping (indicatively, Bureau Veritas' NI 641 Guidelines for Autonomous Shipping (2017), Det Norske Veritas Germanisher Lloyd-Class Guideline-0264 (2018), American Bureau of Shipping Guide for Autonomous and Remote-Control Technologies [2021]). The prevailing role of Classification Societies, both statutory and private, in the enhancement of a safety culture and proliferation of safety standards is unquestionable. In order to avoid fragmentation in the safety framework by different Classification Societies, harmonization and uniformity in application of regulations and standards are essential.

The International Management Code for the Safe Operation of Ships and for Pollution Prevention (The ISM Code), incorporated as Chapter IX in the SOLAS, 1974 Convention, sets outs as its objectives (in Art.1.2.1) 'to ensure safety at sea, prevention of human injury or loss of life, and avoidance of damage to the environment, in particular to the marine environment and to property' thereby requiring the ship operators (owners or managers) to adopt a Safety Management System, appoint a designated person with responsibility to monitor its implementation and thereby be the link and improve communication between the ship and the ship operator at the shore, establish procedures for all operations and maintenance tasks while ensuring good safe practices afloat and ashore, establish emergency procedures and pursue an internal audit system. The ISM Code represents the internationally recognized standard of a vessel's efficient safety management; hence, compliance with the requirements and procedures of the ISM Code produces affirmative evidence in terms of the vessel's seaworthiness in litigation proceedings (Lorenzon, 2016, pp. 343–344) and failure to comply with its principles, could be argued to render the vessel unseaworthy or at least negatively affect the carrier's ability to provide evidence of having exercised due diligence at the relevant time (Lorenzon, 2020, p. 379).

Accordingly, under SOLAS, 1974, Chapter XI-2, the International Ship and Port Facility Security Code, 2004 (ISPS Code) has served as a basis for a comprehensive mandatory security regime for international shipping. The main objectives of the ISPS Code include the establishment of an international framework that fosters cooperation between the state parties, government agencies, local administrations, and the shipping and port industries, in assessing and detecting potential security threats to ships or port facilities used for international trade, so as to implement preventive security measures against such threats and ensuring the early and efficient collation and exchange of maritime security-related information, at national, regional, and international levels (ISPS Code, Part A, s 1.2.). In this respect, it provides a methodology for ship and port security assessments, which facilitates the development of ship, company, and port facility security plans and procedures in order to respond to ships' or ports' varying security levels while determining the respective roles and responsibilities of all parties concerned. Under the ISPS Code, appropriate security officers and personnel on each ship (ISPS Code Part A, s. 12), port facility (PFSOs), and shipping company (CSO, ISPS Code, Part A, s.11) are charged with the duties of assessing, as well as preparing and implementing effective security plans that are able to manage any potential security threat. Contracting states have responsibility for security levels on ships and port facilities approving ship security plans, verifying the compliance of and issuing security certificates to ships under its flag and overseeing the obligations of port facilities (ISPS Code, Part A, s 7., s.14, s.5). Non-compliance with the ISPS Code on the part of the operator (shipowner, carrier, assured) may entail similar consequences, as mentioned above, in the case of failure to comply with the ISM Code (Lorenzon, 2020, p. 385).

The 'genuine link' between the unmanned ship and the flag State and the potential by the latter to effectively exercise 'its jurisdiction on the unmanned ship is questioned, raising substandard shipping concerns, if her owner is established or the shore-based operator who controls her are in a different state, or she is controlled by a software created in another state and operating 'in the cloud'' (Van Hooydonk, 2014, p. 410). It is still to be determined who or whether the remote shore-based operator will assume the role of the designated person or the security officer in respect of the unmanned ship in the context of the safety management system of the ISM Code as well as in the preparation and implementation of security plans according to the ISPS Code respectively, and the involvement and what powers and duties, the remote shore-based operator might undertake in his interaction with port authorities and port services (pilots, towage providers, etc.) (Van Hooydonk, 2020, p. 92).

2.2 *Port State*

Under international law, ships do not enjoy a general right to access foreign ports. The port State instead has the authority to impose conditions for the entry of foreign ships into its ports, as reflected in UNCLOS Articles 25(2), 211(3), and 255. Port waters constitute internal waters and as such form part of the sovereignty of the state (Art. 2) signifying that the jurisdiction over foreign ships in this area is absolute, subject to international commitments that the port State might have undertaken. In this sense, a port State is entitled to refuse access to unmanned ships to its ports, provided that its right is exercised in accordance with the general international law principles of good faith, non-discrimination, and proportionality (the measure proportional to the objective) and definitely in a manner which would not constitute an abuse of right (UNCLOS, 1982, Article 300). If a port State determines that a foreign ship is unseaworthy and threatens marine environmental damage, it may prevent the ship from sailing until the deficiencies are corrected (UNCLOS, 1982, Articles 218 and 219). The port States, operating under administrative agreements such as the Paris Memorandum of Understanding on Port State Control—(Paris MoU)—have the authority to inspect those ships which they have grounds to believe not to be in compliance with SOLAS and if necessary, detain them (Paris MoU, s.3).

Port States play a pivotal role in the achievement of maritime safety and environmental protection, including pollution prevention. The role and responsibilities of the port State with respect to maritime safety and environmental protection are derived from a combination of international conventions and national laws as well as from bilateral and multilateral agreements (IMO Instruments Implementation Code (III Code, Resolution A.1070(28), at 53). If Port Officers have 'clear grounds' for believing that the ship does not comply with SOLAS, 1974 (SOLAS, 1974, Chapter 1, Regulation 19) or the ISPS Code, they must notify the ship and the flag State (ISPS Code, Part A, s 9.8.1.) and might require the ship to undergo further inspection or they may even deny entry into port.

The port State, exercising its rights as a Coastal State, may adopt laws and regulations relating to 'innocent passage'—the latter defined as 'not prejudicial to the peace, good order or security of the coastal state' (UNCLOS, 1982, Articles 19(1); 19(2) sets out a list of activities that shall be considered to be prejudicial)—*inter alia* in respect of the safety of navigation, the regulation of maritime traffic, the protection of navigational aids and facilities and other facilities or installations, the protection of cables and pipelines (UNCLOS, 1982 Article 21 (1)). Nevertheless, the port State, exercising its rights as a Coastal State, may not adopt laws and regulations relating to innocent passage that apply to the design, construction, manning, or equipment of foreign ships, signifying that it cannot prevent the innocent passage of a foreign unmanned ship through its territorial sea by laws and regulations that apply to the design, construction, manning or equipment, unless its laws are giving effect to generally accepted international rules or standards (UNCLOS, 1982, Article 21(2); Veal et al., 2019, p. 11).

3 COLREGs—Prevention of Collisions

The International Regulations for Preventing Collisions at Sea, 1972 (COLREGs, 1972) apply to all seagoing 'vessels' that are used or capable of being used as a means of transportation on water (COLREGs, 1972, Rules 1(a), 3(a)). Apparently, the COLREGs, 1972 are applicable to MASS as well. The latter is essential since manned and unmanned ships are sharing the same waterways.

The COLREGs, having as their primary aim the prevention of collisions at sea, provide for objective guidance Rules on vessel conduct in the context of safe navigation. In the context of Rule 18 which establishes a hierarchy of responsibility between vessels, it has been proposed to define the autonomous ship as 'not under command' (Rule 3 (f)) granting to her 'a navigable priority right of way' and thereby requiring that all other vessels keep out of her way (Gogarty & Hagger, 2008). This proposition contradicts the relevant case law though, which concedes that a ship is 'not under command' when she has, exceptionally, lost her ability to be controlled through some failure of equipment or damage rather than the absence of a crew as a normal or routine feature of the ship itself per Viscount Finlay in *Mendip Range v Radcliffe* [1921] 1 AC 556, at 571.

As long as the autonomous ship is operative and has the ability to navigate, whether autonomously or not monitored by the remote control of a shore-based operator, she will be deemed to be under command for the purposes of the COLREGs, 1972 (Carey, 2017, p. 14).

Despite the objective approach of the Rules addressing the ship, COLREGs, 1972 allows (subjective) deviations from the Rules, in accordance with the 'ordinary practice of seamen', if the special circumstances of the case so require, thusly confirming the primacy of good seamanship over strict compliance with the letter of the Rules (Ringbom, 2019, p. 15; Veal et al., 2019, p. 16) that relies as such on the presumption that a human is in the decision-making loop as in Rule 2 (Responsibility). In terms of the 'seamanship standard' which addresses the subjective cognitive, empirical, attributes innate to the humankind, and in particular, of a skillful, thoughtful and experienced mariner who is able to appraise, foresee and prevent disaster there has been significant debate among scholars as to whether unmanned and fully AI-enabled vessels can strictly comply with the COLREGs, 1972, in particular Rule 2 (Responsibility) and Rule 8 (action to avoid-collision). The main concern in the context of navigation is the automation of functions, that is, the replacement of key bridge functions by IT operational tasks, situational awareness, and decision-making. Decision-making with the use of AI represents autonomy in a strict sense, while other functions in the context of situational awareness such as hearing or seeing are better described as automation. The subjective attribute in the Rules reveals the inherent challenge in automating deviations from a set of rules, absent a human element. On the other hand, it is expected that since human error accounts for about 80–85% of all maritime accidents (Baker & McCafferty, 2016; Hasanspahic et al., 2021) reducing the involvement or even replacing the human element by automated procedures will prove beneficial in terms of avoidance of conventional, navigational accidents.

In the context of 'proper look-out' Rule 5 states that 'every vessel shall at all times maintain a proper look-out by sight and hearing as well as by all available means appropriate in the prevailing circumstances and conditions so as to make a full appraisal of the situation and of the risk of collision'. By analogy, the wording of SOLAS, 1974, Regulation V/19 (2.1.8) explicitly accepts the prospect that human functions may be replaced by technology in a totally enclosed ship's bridge, at least as far as situational awareness is concerned. In this regard, COLREGs Rule 5 may be interpreted accordingly (Ringbom, 2019, p. 13) The case law has similarly interpreted the wording 'available means appropriate in the prevailing circumstances and conditions' to include radar, which is specifically mentioned in the Rules (Rule 7], VHF radio, AIS, etc. As observed in *The Homer* [1973] 1 Lloyd's Rep 501 (CA), '... a proper look-out involves not only a visual look-out and not only the use of ears but it also involves the intelligent interpretation of the data received by way of various scientific instruments', whereas 'the possession of the radar equipment brings with it a concurrent duty to see that intelligent and reasonable use is made of the equipment provided' per Wilmer J in *The Nora* [1956] 1 Lloyd's Rep. 617. Furthermore, 'adequate training and experience in the use of the equipment' are required per Deputy Judge Brice QC in *The Contship Success* [1998] 2 Lloyd's Rep. 488. The courts have repeatedly emphasized the necessity of the radar's assistance for a proper lookout Maritime Harmony [1982] 2 Lloyd's Rep 400, maintaining poor radar lookout; *The Nordic Ferry* [1991] 2 Lloyd's Rep 591, master failing to keep a proper watch of radar; in *The Tenes* [1989] 2 Lloyd's Rep367 per Sheen J'..it is of course well known that with the assistance of an efficient radar lookout ships will continue to proceed at full speed in dense fog'; in *The Contship Success* [2000] 1 Lloyd's Rep 627 (CA) per Clarke LJ, '...the circumstances in which a vessel will not be found at fault for failing to use operational radar are likely to be exceptional'.

As far as automating situational awareness (replacing the human function of observation in the process of lookout) is concerned, from a technological point of view, it is probably feasible to create algorithms that comply with the Rules of the COLREGs, even considering unpredictable movements of other ships through an IT-driven collision avoidance system using enhanced AIS, GPS and radar in combination with sensors and cameras, in particular infra-red cameras (Wróbel et al., 2017, p. 161). By contrast, the reference in Rules 2 and 8, to 'the ordinary practice of seamen' and 'good seamanship' introduces the subjective element, the justification of which will eventually prevail in retrospect through a factual assessment of the ship's conduct based on all relevant prevailing circumstances, signifies that its incorporation into an automated navigation program constitutes a huge challenge and the result is questionable. Even if the autonomous ship is navigating without human control, it is anticipated that there might be in an emergency case human intervention by an operator from a shore-based remote-control center or pilot or even by Port Authority Officers.

Accordingly, navigation monitored by an operator at a shore-based remote-control center will have to contemplate automated solutions in advance at least to foreseeable risks, such as loss of or delay in communication, thusly safeguarding redundancy in order to identify in real time collision risks (Rule 7) for purposes of preventing a significant hindering impact on timely collision avoidance action on the part of the ship under Rule 8(a).

A critical issue that must be regulated as a matter of high priority, is the participation of the MASS and its interaction with the VTS in the port area, ensuring both the safety of navigation and exchange of communication and information. This is significant in terms of both preventing the risk of collision with other vessels and exposure to high risk of cyber-attacks.

IMO Resolution A.857 (20) on Guidelines for Vessel Traffic Services stipulates that VTS operations do not encroach upon the master's responsibility for safe navigation, or disturb the traditional relationship between master and pilot; when the VTS is authorized to issue instructions to vessels, these instructions should be result oriented only, leaving the details of execution, such as course to be steered or engine maneuvers to be executed, to the master or pilot on board the vessel. In the case of unmanned ships, this action would presumably be addressed to and executed by the operator at the shore-based control center. Furthermore, most ports have compulsory pilotage areas, whereas each state and port has enacted its pilotage laws and regulations. By virtue of the advent of unmanned MASS the relationship between the pilot, the VTS, and the operator at the shore-based control center must be defined anew (Carey, 2017; Van Hooydonk, 2020) and possibly uniformly regulated at the international level. In addition, under Article 22 of UNCLOS, the port State, exercising its rights as a coastal state, having regard to the safety of navigation, may designate sea lanes and traffic separation schemes for the regulation of the passage of ships. The latter will be indicated on charts to which due publicity shall be given. In this regard, unmanned MASS might be required to confine their passage to such sea lanes.

4 Seaworthiness Challenges in Respect of MASS in Litigation

Seaworthiness in contracts of carriage under a Bill of Lading according to Hague-Visby Rules (International Convention for the Unification of

Certain Rules of Law Relating to Bills of Lading 1924 as amended by 1968 Protocol), Article 3 (1), encompasses three aspects of seaworthiness requiring from the carrier, before and at the beginning of the voyage, to exercise due diligence to: (a) Make the ship seaworthy; (b) Properly man, equip, and supply the ship; (c) Make the holds, refrigerating and cool chambers, and all other parts of the ship in which goods are carried, fit and safe for their reception, carriage, and preservation. The 'prudent owner test' on unseaworthiness as set out *McFadden v Blue Star Line* [1905] 1 KB 697, at 706, is 'whether a prudent owner would have required the relevant defect, had he known of it, to be made good before sending his ship to sea'. The absolute duty to provide a seaworthy ship at common law 'that the ship should really be fit not merely that they should do their best to make the ship fit', per Lord Blackburn in Steel v State Line (1877) 3 App Cas 72 at p 86, is displaced by the 'due diligence duty' in Article 3 (1) of the Hague-Visby Rules. Accordingly, in marine insurance law, seaworthiness is defined in Section 39 (4) of the Marine Insurance Act 1906 which stipulates that 'a ship is deemed to be seaworthy when she is reasonably fit in all respects to encounter the ordinary perils of the seas of the adventure insured' whereby reference should be made to *The Miss Jay Jay* [1985] 1 Lloyd's Rep 264 at p. 271 for the assessment of perils as 'ordinary'. Although the 'seaworthiness' definition in marine insurance law and the contract of carriage of goods by sea is different, the meaning of seaworthiness is the same (Soyer, 2006, p. 50).

The 'due diligence' duty on the part of the carrier to make the ship seaworthy is an overriding obligation. 'If it is not fulfilled and the non-fulfilment causes the damage, the immunities of article IV cannot be relied on' *Maxine Footwear Co Ltd v Canadian Government Merchant Marine Ltd* [1959] AC 589, at 602–603. Hence, the carrier will not be able to benefit from the exclusion provisions from liability for negligence in the navigation or management of the ship, the so-called 'nautical fault' exception under Hague–Visby Rules Art IV r 2(a) or the other exceptions contained in Article IV rule 2, if the damage to or loss of the cargo is attributed to the unseaworthiness of the vessel. The 'due diligence duty to make the ship seaworthy' is a non-delegable, personal duty of the carrier at 862 per Lord Radcliffe in *The Muncaster Castle* [1961] 1 Lloyd's Rep 57 at 82; [1961] A.C. 807.

The components of the due diligence duty of the carrier to make the ship seaworthy, as illustrated by case law, are as follows: (1) The vessel must be in a suitable condition and suitably manned and equipped to meet the ordinary perils likely to be encountered while performing the services required of it. This aspect of the duty relates to the following matters: (a) The physical condition of the vessel and its equipment; (b) The competence/ efficiency of the master and crew (c) The adequacy of stores and documentation and (2) The vessel must be cargo worthy in the sense that it is in a fit state to receive the specified cargo. Also failing to comply with the ISM Code or to provide a proper ship safety management system will render the ship unseaworthy, per Creswell, J. at 128 in the 'Eurasian Dream' (*Papera Traders Co Ltd v Hyundai Merchant Co Ltd*) [2002] 1 Lloyd's Rep 719.

A ship may be rendered unseaworthy by the incompetency/inefficiency of the master or the crew, even despite being holders of certificates of competence due to lack of ability, knowledge, or training (*The Starsea* [1995] 1 Lloyd's Rep 651; Soyer, 2006, 66). The relevant test as to whether the incompetence or inefficiency of the master and crew has rendered the vessel unseaworthy is as follows: 'would a reasonably prudent owner, knowing the relevant facts, have allowed this vessel to put to sea with this master and crew, with their state of knowledge, training and instruction?' per Mr Justice Salmon in *Hong Kong Fir Shipping Co. Ltd v. Kawasaki Kisen Kaisha Ltd* [1961] 1 Lloyd's Rep 159 at 168; [1962] Q.B. 26 at 34. As to the competence or efficiency of the master and crew 'Incompetence or inefficiency may consist of a disabling want of skill or a disabling want of knowledge' per Creswell, J. at 129 in *The Eurasian Dream* [2002] 1 Lloyd's Rep 719. This principle applies where the master's inefficiency consists, whatever his general efficiency may be, in his ignorance as to how his ship may, owing to the peculiarities of her structure behave in circumstances likely to be met with on an ordinary ocean voyage. It is for the carrier to show that the latter has exercised proper care in relation to the appointment of 'a generally competent master and crew', *The Makedonia* [1962] 1 Lloyd's Rep 316 (at 337–338 per Mr. Justice Hewson), by inspection of the seaman's documents, interviews, or inquiries that he is reasonably fit to occupy the post to which he is appointed and the specific competence of the master in relation to the vessel and voyage in question (per Creswell, J. at 132 in *The Eurasian Dream* [2002] 1 Lloyd's Rep. 719).

Hence, it is argued that the unmanned MASS will be regarded as seaworthy according to the above-mentioned case law despite the absence of the human element on board, provided that it will operate efficiently and safely while being remotely monitored by an efficient, qualified and trained operator, or in the case of a fully autonomous ship, the latter's safe and efficient operation will have been programmed in advance by an efficient, qualified and trained IT programmer. The competence and the efficiency of the crew rather than the number of crew determine if a ship is seaworthy (*Hong Kong Fir Shipping Co v Kawasaki Kisen Kaisah* [1962] 2 WLR 474, at 481). Moreover, Seaworthiness is not an absolute concept, 'it is relative to the nature of the ship to the particular voyage and even to the particular stage of the voyage on which the ship is engaged', per Mr. Justice Moore-Bick in *The Fjord Wind* [1999] 1 Lloyd's Rep. 307 at 315 (approved by Lord Justice Clarke at [2000] 2 Lloyd's Rep. 191 at 197).

In addition, the seaworthiness of a ship must be judged by the standards and practices of the industry at the relevant time, at least so long as those standards and practices are reasonable' per Creswell, J. at 127 in '*The Eurasian Dream*'. Accordingly, the seaworthiness of unmanned MASS will be judged as to its compliance with the respective IMO instruments (that will apply to MASS) and the generally accepted standards and practices of the industry at the relevant time. Another aspect of seaworthiness, the documentation on board with regard to the ship's certificates, in compliance with the respective safety rules of IMO instruments, domestic laws, and regulation of the flag State, is expected to be replaced by fully digitized e-certificates which can be shared with the authorities concerned in the context of Port State Control.

Lastly, a defective passage plan may render a ship unseaworthy as established in *The CMA CGM Libra* (*Alize 1954 v. Allianz Elementar Versicherungs AG*) [2021] UKSC 51. Navigational decisions taken by the crew and defective passage planning prior to the commencement of a voyage do not fall within the 'nautical fault' exception in Art IV r2(a)) of Hague–Visby Rules and may render a ship unseaworthy. The provision of necessary equipment and competent crew alone does not suffice for the purposes of discharging the due diligence duty on the part of the carrier; the latter must also ensure that a proper passage planning is in place. In this regard, the passage planning of the unmanned MASS, whether automated or not, prior to the commencement of her voyage constitutes an element of her seaworthiness, therefore it should be given careful consideration. However, a real challenging issue that needs to be anticipated and addressed is the update of the unmanned MASS' navigational route after her sailing, in respect of the subsequent navigational constraints due to a change in political and environmental risks (Tsimplis, 2021a, 2021b, p. 300).

5 Conclusion

Seaworthiness is not an absolute concept; it evolves, following the advancements in technology, as reflected in the IMO Regulations and the generally accepted industry standards and practice. The advent of unmanned MASS has created safety concerns and seaworthiness challenges in the shipping and port sector and therefore calls for the design of a novel, comprehensive safety regulatory framework and safety management system relying on a holistic and risk-based approach that incorporates all the inter-operational and inter-relational aspects, the raising issues, the allocation of risks and the concerns of the stakeholders involved in the maritime sector. The concept of seaworthiness must be revisited as it has evolved through the introduction of automation and digitalization. To this effect, enhanced involvement and cooperation between all relevant stakeholders, from shipping, ports, and logistics, is essential in the digitalization process of shipping, thereby enhancing the latter's efficiency and sustainability as well as the resilience of the global supply chain.

References

Baker, C., & McCafferty, D. (2016). Accident Database Review of Human Element Concerns: What Do the Results Mean for Classification? Proceedings of the International Conference Human Factors in Ship Design and Operation. *Journal of Innovation in Digital Ecosystems*, *3*, 22–29. Available at: https://www.researchgate.net/publication/303320052_Cooperation_between_Intelligent_Autonomous_Vehicles_to_enhance_container_terminal_operations. Accessed 20 January 2022.

Carey, L. (2017). *All Hands Off Deck? The Legal Barriers to Autonomous Ships*. NUS Centre for Maritime Law (Working Paper 17/06). *JIML*, 23, 202–219, 3. Available at: https://law.nus.edu.sg/cml/wp-content/uploads/sites/8/2020/04/011_2017_Luci-Carey.pdf. Accessed 12 March 2022.

Chircop, A. (2019). Competencies of the International Seabed Authority and International Maritime Organization in the Context of Activities in the Area.

Commissioned Report to the ISA and IMO. Available at: https://www.academia.edu/es/44567757/Competencies_of_the_International_Seabed_Authority_and_International_Maritime_Organization_in_the_Context_of_Activities_in_the_Area_Commissioned_report_to_the_ISA_and_IMO_2019. Accessed 17 May 2022.

COLREGs. (1972). Convention on International Regulations for Preventing Collisions at Sea, Oct. 20, 1972, 28 U.S.T. 3459, T.I.A.S. 8587.

Gogarty, B., & Hagger, M. (2008). The Laws of Man over Vehicles Unmanned: The Legal Response to Robotic Revolution on Sea, Land and Air. *Journal of Law, Information and Science*, *19*, 73. Available at: https://ssrn.com/abstract=1796486. Accessed 23 March 2022.

Hasanspahić, N., Vujičić, S., Frančić, V., & Čampara, L. (2021). The Role of the Human Factor in Marine Accidents. *Journal of Marine Science and Engineering*, *9*(3), 261.

Hogg, T., & Ghosh, S. (2016). Autonomous merchant vessels: Examination of factors that impact the effective implementation of unmanned ships. *Australian Journal of Maritime & Ocean Affairs*, *8*, 206–222. https://doi.org/10.1080/18366503.2016.1229244.

Hong Kong Fir Shipping Co. Ltd v. Kawasaki Kisen Kaisha Ltd. [1961]. 1 Lloyd's Rep. 159.

International Ship and Port Facility Security Code. (2004). *Entered into Force under SOLAS chapter XI-2*, on 1 July 2004. Available at: https://www.imo.org/en/OurWork/Security/Pages/SOLAS-XI-2%20ISPS%20Code.aspx. Accessed 29 July 2022

JJ Lloyd Instruments Ltd v Northern Star Insurance Co Ltd (The Miss Jay Jay). [1985]. 1 Lloyd's Rep. 264.

Komianos, A. (2018). The Autonomous Shipping Era: Operational, Regulatory, Quality Challenges. *International Journal on Marine Navigation and Safety of Sea Transportation*, *12*(2), 335–348.

Lorenzon, F. (2016). Chapter 9, Safety and Compliance. In A. Attard, et al., (Ed.), *The IMLI Manual on International Maritime Law Volume II: Shipping Law* (pp. 343–344). Oxford University Press.

Lorenzon, F. (2020). Safety and Compliance. Y. Baatz, (Ed.), *Maritime Law* (5th ed.). Informa Law from Routledge.

Maxine Footwear Co Ltd v Canadian Government Merchant Marine Ltd. [1959]. AC 589.

McFadden v Blue Star Line. [1905]. 1 KB 697.

Mendip Range v Radcliffe. [1921]. 1 AC 556.

Porathe, T., Hoem, Å., Rødseth, Ø., Fjørtoft, K., & Johnsen, S. O. (2018). At Least as Safe as Manned Shipping? Autonomous Shipping, Safety and "Human Error". *Safety and Reliability—Safe Societies in a Changing World* (pp. 417–425). CRC Press.

Ringbom, H. (2019). Regulating Autonomous Ships—Concepts, Challenges and Precedents. *Ocean Development & International Law*.

Ringbom, H., & Veal, R. (2017). Unmanned Ships and the International Regulatory Framework. *Journal of International Maritime Law, 23*(2), 100–118.

Rødseth, Ø. J., & Burmeister, H. C. (2015). Risk Assessment for an Unmanned Merchant Ship. *International Journal on Marine Navigation and Safety of Sea Transportation, 9*(3), 357–364.

SOLAS. (1974). *International Convention for the Safety of Life at Sea*, Nov. 1, 1974, 32 U.S.T. 47, T.I.A.S. 9700.

Soyer, B. (2006). *Warranties in Marine Insurance* (2nd ed.). Cavendish Publishing Limited.

STCW. (1978). *International Convention on Standards of Training, Certification, and Watchkeeping for Seafarers, 1978*. With Resolutions Adopted by the International Conference on Training and Certification of Seafarers, 1978. London: International Maritime Organization, 1993.

Steel v State Line. (1877). 3 App Cas 72.

The 'Eurasian Dream' (*Papera Traders Co Ltd v Hyundai Merchant Co Ltd*). [2002]. 1 Lloyd's Rep. 719.

The CMA CGM Libra. [2021]. UKSC 51.

The Contship Success. [1998]. 2 Lloyd's Rep 488.

The Contship Success. [2000] 1 Lloyd's Rep 627.

The Fjord Wind. [1999]. 1 Lloyd's Rep 307.

The Homer. [1973]. 1 Lloyd's Rep. 501.

The Makedonia [1962] 1 Lloyd's Rep 316

The Muncaster Castle. [1961]. 1 Lloyd's Rep. 57

The Nora. [1956]. 1 Lloyd's Rep. 617.

The Starsea. [1995]. 1 Lloyd's Rep 651.

The Tenes. [1989]. 2 Lloyd's Rep. 367.

Tsimplis, M. (2021a). On the Carriage of Goods on Autonomous, Remotely Controlled, Crewed and Uncrewed Ships. *Maritime Organisation, Management and Liability: A Legal Analysis of New Challenges in the Maritime Industry*.

Tsimplis, M. (2021b). On the Carriage of Goods on Autonomous, Remotely Controlled, Crewed and Uncrewed Ships. In S. Girvin & V. Ulfbeck, (Eds.), *Maritime Organisation, Management and Liability: A Legal Analysis of New Challenges in the Maritime Industry* (pp. 283–306). Hart Publishing.

UNCLOS. (1982). United Nations Convention on the Law of the Sea, Dec. 10, 1982, 1833 U.N.T.S. 397.

Valdez Banda, O. A., Kujala, P., Goerlandt, F., Bergström, M., Ahola, M., van Gelder, P. H. A. J. M., & Sonninen, S. (2018) . *The need for systematic and systemic safety management for autonomous vessels in Marine Design*

XIII, Volume 2, 1st Edition, CRC Press. https://doi.org/10.1201/9780429440519

Van Hooydonk, E. (2014). The Law of Unmanned Merchant Shipping—An Exploration. *Journal of International Maritime Law, 20*(6), 403–423.

Van Hooydonk, E. (2020). Botport Law—The Regulatory Agenda for the Transition to Smart Ports. In B. Soyer & A. Tettenborn (Eds.), *New Technologies, Artificial Intelligence and Shipping in the 21st Century* (pp. 90–104). Informa from Routledge.

Veal, R., Tsimplis, M., & Serdy, A. (2019). The Legal Status and Operation of Unmanned Maritime Vehicles. *Ocean Development & International Law, 50*(1), 23–48.

Wróbel, K., Montewka, J., & Kujala, P. (2017). Towards the Assessment of Potential Impact of Unmanned Vessels on Maritime Transportation Safety. *Reliability Engineering and System Safety, 165*, 155–169.

CHAPTER 8

How to Ensure Safe Navigation: Navigation Safety Regulation in MASS

Mika Viljanen

1 Introduction

Maritime Autonomous Surface Ships (MASS) may soon navigate the seas. If and when this happens, navigation, a previously human-dominated activity, will be performed on a MASS by an ANS.

ANS are complex technological entities that consist of sensors, computing and connectivity equipment, software, and actuators. As ANS begin to replace a ship's master and crew, they become the primary determinants of navigational safety. Navigation is intensely regulated in manned ships. Chapter VIII of the Convention on Standards of Training, Certification and Watchkeeping, 1978 (STCW, 1978), for example, regulates watchkeeping and navigational decision-making in detail, while The International Convention for the Safety of Life at Sea (SOLAS,

M. Viljanen (✉)
Director of the Doctoral Program in
Law, Faculty of Law, University of Turku, Turku, Finland
e-mail: mivevi@utu.fi

© The Author(s), under exclusive license to Springer Nature Switzerland AG 2023

T. M. Johansson et al. (eds.), *Autonomous Vessels in Maritime Affairs*, Studies in National Governance and Emerging Technologies,
https://doi.org/10.1007/978-3-031-24740-8_8

1974) Chapter V contains numerous rules on technical navigational aids. As navigation transfers to a technological subsystem, the existing rules will become at least partly obsolete. The SOLAS (1974, Chapter V), for example, contains no rules on most autonomous navigation equipment. The STCW (1978) and Convention on the International Regulations for Preventing Collisions at Sea, 1972 (COLREGs, 1972) rules on watchkeeping and navigational decision-making are designed for manned bridges and will likely have little traction on Autonomous navigation subsytems (ANS). Consequently, navigational regulation must be translated to, and retrofitted for, ANS.

Work on MASS regulation has commenced within the International Maritime Organization (IMO). The Maritime Safety Committee (MSC) published a document setting out the conditions for MASS trials in 2019 (IMO, 2019). The same year, the Committee embarked on a Regulatory Scoping Exercise (RSE) to chart what amendments or new instruments would be needed to facilitate MASS commercial deployments. The final report was published in 2021 (IMO, 2021). Based on the RSE work, MSC agreed on a road map document in April 2022. The road map envisages a two-phase process with a goal-based non-mandatory Code to be adopted in the second half of 2024. The non-mandatory code will be followed by a full-blown mandatory goal-based MASS Code with a planned entry into force on 1 January 2028 (The Working Group on Maritime Autonomous Surface Ships, 2022).

Despite its crucial role in facilitating MASS deployments, the IMO RSE and the 2022 Road Map document contain few concrete hints on the future outlook of navigational safety regulation for Level 4 fully automated MASSs. RSE identifies SOLAS (1974, Chapter V) as a target for regulatory action suggesting that "additional performance standards for some navigational equipment of autonomously operated MASS will also need to be developed" (IMO, 2021, 33), but surprisingly, judges STCW (1978, Chapter VIII) irrelevant as "no trained and qualified seafarers serve on board" Level 4 MASS (IMO, 2021, p. 83). Other possible regulators fare no better. While some governments have published studies and road maps on MASS regulation, navigation has received relatively little attention (Ringbom et al., 2020 is, however, an exception). The theme has also been largely neglected in the burgeoning literature on MASS regulation (Ringbom et al., 2021; Soyer & Tettenborn, 2019).

This paper attempts to address the gap in our understanding of the future MASS navigational safety regulation by, first, outlining the regulatory setting for MASS's ANS. The section provides a high-level description of MASS as technological artefacts and lays out the option available to regulators for governing technological artefact safety. Secondly, the paper discusses the utility of rules-based safety regulation in an ANS context before moving to, thirdly, sketch out how ANS navigational safety could be regulated using performance-based instruments. The section on performance-based safety regulation remains the core of this chapter. The chapter argues that MASS safety regulation will likely converge around simulation-based black box testing, buttressed by real-world tests and a limited number of secondary design specification rules.

The paper has important limitations. First, the paper addresses Level 4, fully automated MASS only. In these ships, humans play no immediate role in navigating the ship, either as an onboard or a shore-based resource. Navigation is an entirely technology-reliant process. The paper will not delve into problems that may arise in manned or periodically manned MASS (for a treatment, see Ringbom et al., 2020). Secondly, the paper pays little attention to the disjointed nature of marine regulation and regulatory actors. Currently, the maritime safety regulator landscape is fragmented with regulatory actions taking place at multiple levels and in multiple modalities. The high-level SOLAS (1974), STCW (1978), and COLREGs (1972) rules emanate from the IMO. The rules are transposed into binding domestic rules by the flag states. The IMO Committees and other international organizations such as the International Hydrographic Organization, however, also issue a bevy of guidelines, recommendations, and interpretation documents. These documents are typically not legally binding but religiously followed by flag state administrations and classification societies that, in turn, are the ultimate rule-makers in shipping. The future MASS regulations will likely have to navigate an equally fragmented domain. The IMO MSC has signaled that its ultimate deliverable, the MASS code, will be goals-based (The Working Group on Maritime Autonomous Surface Ships, 2022). As a goals-based instrument, the Code will likely put in place high-abstraction rules that will be buttressed by countless lower level documents emanating either from the MSC, other regulatory organizations, or the classification societies. As a conceptual paper attempting to outline the most important focal points and design constraints of future MASS navigational safety regulation, the analysis in this paper will move on the level of the detailed implementing rules but will pay little attention to who will promulgate the rules and what their legal status will be.

2 The Regulatory Setting

2.1 *MASS as Technological Artefacts*

In contrast to the socio-technical manned ship, navigational systems dominated by humans, Level 4 autonomous ships rely entirely on technologies for navigation. These ships are complex technological cyber-physical subsystems that ANS operate during voyages.

MASS ANS typically contain three functionally separate but tightly integrated, sequentially ordered subsystems. A *situational awareness (SA) subsystem* is the first upstream component. The SA subsystem acquires and reconciles numerous data feeds and generates a digital map of the vessel's environment and its internal state. A *navigational planning and decision-making (NPDM) subsystem*, second, uses the SA subsystem outputs to generate navigational plans and make decisions that *actuators*, as the third subsystem, transform into physical movements (Ringbom et al., Chapter 1).

The SA and NPDM subsystems, essentially, constitute a technological navigational cognition. The subsystems replace the distributed socio-technical navigational cognitions (on distributed cognition theory and ships, in particular, see Hutchins, 1995) that ran manned ships as the entities capable of sensing and analyzing its environment, making decisions that, then, are actuated into the real world.

The SA subsystem consists of sensors, computing infrastructure, and software. A typical sensor setup consists of five blocks. *Fixed visual light and thermal cameras* and *robot pan-tilt -zoom cameras*, first, produce data used to primarily extract semantic information about the vessel's external environment. The sensors then allow the cognition to give semantic labels to the objects around the ship, but also contribute to the ship's spatial awareness. *Lidars, radars, and sonars* produce data that is used to map the vessel's external environmental spatially, fixing distances, movement vectors, and sizes to objects of various kinds. *Inertial navigation systems, Global navigation satellite systems* and *local position reference sensors* provide data on the vessel's location. *Automatic identification system transceivers, VHF radios* and *sound sensors* provide further data on the location of other vessels. *Machinery sensors, environmental sensors,* and *computing hardware sensors* produce data on the vessel internal state and its external environment with remote sensing providing additional data when connectivity conditions allow. In addition to the sensors, the SA subsystem has a significant computing infrastructure with tailored processors designed to match specific processing needs rising out of the sensor data feeds. Object detection, object recognition, and sensor fusion algorithms are the most important of the SA software. SA software varies greatly in its nature. Some software components, such as most spatial analysis software, are relatively simple algorithms. Semantic analysis algorithms, however, often contain complex proprietary machine learning algorithms (Ringbom et al., 2020, Chapter 1).

The NPDM subsystem weaves together a computing infrastructure and a variety of software components. The computers are likely standard off-the-shelf equipment. Most software components, instead, will likely be proprietary. Some of the algorithms are likely machine-learning based, but the brunt of navigational planning will likely be implemented by various path search and trajectory optimization algorithms (Ringbom et al., 2020, Chapter 1). Although sophisticated, these algorithms have a provenance in traditional mathematical and programming techniques (Campbell et al., 2012; Li et al., 2019; Polvara et al., 2018). The search algorithms will likely contain traffic rule translations that determine which objects in the ego ship's environment the ship should yield to or avert (in automotive contexts, see Pan et al., 2016). The NPDM subsystem also includes an ego ship model and trajectory models for target vessels and possibly algorithms that handle specific traffic situations. These models may have machine learning origins. Finally, actuators transform the electronic navigation plans into real-world action.

2.2 How to Regulate MASSs Technological Artefacts?

As ANS are technological artefacts and in Level 4 MASSs directly determine ship navigational capabilities, regulatory actions (should) center around affecting the artefacts' technological composition. To be successful, the regulatory interventions must fit the characteristics of the artefacts they seek to govern. Consequently, the characteristics of the ANS and their components determine what regulatory options are available.

Here, three important axes for regulatory intervention design appear. On the one hand, the regulatory objectives differ in terms of different types of equipment. For the SA subsystem and its sensors, the primary regulatory goal will likely be to ensure that the MASS always has sufficient situational awareness. To have sufficient situational awareness, the SA subsystem, in turn, needs to produce enough good enough data and process the data appropriately. The NPDM subsystem, in turn, has to be able to produce safe navigational plans, which the actuators, then, must be able to turn into efficient real-world movement.

On the other hand, the various equipment types share two primary regulatory surfaces on which interventions can find their effects. ANS performance and the MASS's navigational capabilities depend, firstly, on the mechanical and electrical performance of its ANS equipment and, secondly, on how its software and algorithms function. Importantly, the two regulatory surfaces differ from each other in crucial ways as engineering objects as software engineering and validation methods share little with mechanical and electrical engineering methods. As technological artefact regulation is mediated by engineering practices, the differences in available engineering methodologies play a crucial role in framing the universe of possible regulatory interventions.

The eponymous MASS autonomy adds a third dimension to regulatory design challenges. While most ANS software components are traditional programming products, ANS also contain machine learning algorithms, adding unique engineering challenges to the mix. Machine learning code is often intractable and evades formal validation methods. Even after comprehensive interpretation efforts, pockets of unpredictability will remain (Lipton, 2018). If the MASS contain software that implements *lifelong machine learning* approaches as, for example, Porathe (2019) has suggested, validation and verification troubles compound. Instead of validating an existing software object, however intractable, engineers would have to devise methodologies for validating either the learning methodology or the constantly changing software objects on demand (Chen & Chen, 2017).

In summary, when designing ANS regulation, the regulators must navigate a complex and layered technological landscape. ANS have at least three distinct technological components that each have a unique set of regulatory goals. Regulators must make sure that SA subsystems produce adequate situational awareness, NPDM subsystems generate safe navigational plans, and actuators actuate the plans reliably. The systems have mechanical, electrical, and software components. For each component type, engineering and, consequently, regulatory challenges and solutions differ. With machine learning code tossed into the mix with its unique verification and validation problems, the regulatory designs will likely be complex and layered.

2.3 The Regulatory Options

The technological regulatory focus pushes regulators towards two primary alternatives primary. The regulators may, first, attempt to force MASS manufacturers to choose particular technological ANS solutions (*rule-based technical regulation*). Second, regulators may establish performance-based regulatory requirements for ANS (*performance-based regulation*). In this section, the chapter will briefly try to map the strengths and weakness and future trajectories of both alternatives in the MASS space.

Potentially, regulators could also use transparency-based (e.g., Chesterman, 2021, Chapter 6), management-based (e.g., Coglianese, 2010), and liability-mediated regulatory instruments (e.g., Beckers, 2021; Chesterman, 2021, Chapter 4) to affect ANS design. While central to many scholarly treatments of robot regulation, these instruments will not be discussed. However, it is the view of the author that their utility in ANS regulation will be highly limited. In particular, liability-mediated regulation may lose much of its relevance as we transition to robot actors. *Ex post* liability-mediated regulatory processes typically move at a glacial speed that is unfit to govern fast-evolving technological fields, produce a small number of ad hoc decisions that are often contradictory, and are extremely resource-intensive.

3 Rules-Based Approaches to ANS Safety

3.1 Rules-Based Technical Regulation

Rules-based technical regulation comprises the traditional old-school core of safety regulation (e.g., Decker, 2018). In the above approach, regulators adopt a command-and-control attitude and set out detailed design standards for installations and products, imposing minimum requirements for product and installation configurations, materials, and design.

Ships are currently subject to intensive rules-based technology regulation. SOLAS (1974), for example, articulates at times detailed guidelines, for example, for ship construction, structure, stability, and machinery. The guidelines are further fleshed out in classification society rules. As IMO work on MASS rules is only starting, MASS ANS equipment, unsurprisingly, largely lack technical design standards. However, SOLAS (1974) contains a wide range of carriage requirements for existing navigational systems and equipment, some of which will remain in MASS. IMO has also issued high-level general requirements for electronic navigation aids and numerous performance standards for various navigational aids such as radars (IMO, 1981, 1991). These rules are buttressed by the equally numerous International Association of Classification Societies (IASC) standards. Nevertheless, important SA and NPDM subsystem components such as lidars, cameras, and path planning software lack dedicated standards.

3.2 Challenges and Pitfalls

Rules-based regulatory initiatives will likely face challenges and run into pitfalls. The idiosyncrasies and pitfalls flow from the cyber-physical nature of ANS. First, ANS perform extremely complex, interdependent, and cascading data collection and processing tasks. To do that, the system integrates hardware and software components into a single functional entity. How that entity performs, depends not only on its individual components but also on their interaction. ANS are, thus, frail systems where a failure in a seemingly insignificant component may lead to system failure. In addition, design constraints may be relatively relaxed in cyber-physical systems as different systems may drastically deliver similar performance. These equipment dynamics will likely decrease the utility of rules-based technical regulation in ANS contexts. Multiple alternative sensor configurations may be able to generate data feeds to provide adequate situational awareness. Thus, rigid rules on, for example, what sensors ships must carry, may be counterproductive.

Second, ANS software constitutes a major roadblock to rules-based technical regulation. The traditional safety engineering playbook is based on physical safety engineering practices. Physical system engineers leverage dependable knowledge from physics and materials sciences together with previous engineering artefacts to build designs. The designs are, then, subjected to tests and trials to gauge their performance in relevant operational domains with tests typically producing results that can be interpolated to neighboring world states. (Riehle, 2008). Redundancy, safety and design margins, and derating approaches all increase physical system reliability (Clarke & Hollister, 2010; Eckert & Isaksson, 2017; Huang, 2014). For software artefacts, these tricks are largely useless. While predictability-enhancing techniques exist—safety, robustness and resilience remain acute concerns. This entails that ANS cyber layers are more fragile engineering objects than their physical companions. In addition, the universe of possible designs is less constrained than for physical components. Again, technical regulation is bound to lose utility.

The regulatory environment is complicated by the machine learning components embedded in ANS. These components further destabilize rules-based regulatory approaches by introducing intractable black boxes into the system (Törngren & Grogan, 2018). Most machine learning code is unsimulatable: the code cannot be translated into discrete if, then structures that the engineers could analytically simulate to determine how the code transforms its inputs into outputs (Lipton, 2018). This unsimulatability entails that formal performance verification is typically impossible. Instead, the engineers are forced to use post hoc interpretability tools to inspect the code. The post hoc interpretability tools work on two levels. On the training data level, the tools allow the engineers to identify which training data set features drive outputs, analyze their relative significance, and feature interactions, and build visualizations. Similarly, the tools facilitate scoring what significance input data features have on individual predictions (Murdoch et al., 2019). The tools are important in enabling the engineers to understand the logic underlying the machine learning algorithms, ensure that the algorithms grasp important features in training data and inputs, and debug processes leading to outlier outputs (Nandi & Pal, 2022). However, uncertainty over system performance will remain with edge-case testing, thus, providing little solace. Research in the field also moves extremely fast, which will likely further diminish the utility of current rigid rulesets.

These equipment and software-related dynamics entail that drawing up detailed, rule-based technical guidelines for entire ANS configurations and their software components makes little sense. At best, regulators can articulate high-level design goals as the EU Commission attempted to do in the EU AI Act proposal (European Commission, 2021) Article 16.

3.3 *Pockets for Rules-Based Regulation Will Remain*

While rule-based regulation will likely face headwinds, pockets, where rules-based technical regulation remains relevant, will nevertheless persist. Sensor array composition and sensor and computing infrastructure mechanical and electrical designs will constitute a sensible regulatory target. In addition, SA equipment redundancy requirements should be set.

However, regulating sensor array composition surfaces as an important regulatory design concern. SA subsystem detection and labeling capabilities determine what actions MASS can take. If a MASS does not detect an object, the object does not exist under its purview. If a MASS detects an object but mislabels it, the ship will not take appropriate action. Sensor array capabilities constitute, thus, a crucial regulatory target. It is also worth noting that specifying which objects MASS should be capable of detecting and labeling in the operational design domain (an ODD ontology) is one of the prime ethical decision-making in MASS regulatory design processes (Ringbom et al., 2020). Consequently, regulators could implement a top-down reverse-engineering approach to designing sensor array capability rules. Instead of relying on a bottom-up approach, technology-driven process where existing sensor offerings determine what the arrays should contain, regulators should, first, describe the desired ODD ontologies together with detection distances. The sensor array standards should be configured to ensure that adequate detection and labeling capabilities will emerge. However, the heterogeneity of sensor array configurations will likely make rules-based regulation inefficient and accentuate the need for appropriate performance standards.

4 Regulating ANS Performance

4.1 *Performance-Based Regulation*

This chapter has thus far argued that rules-based technical regulation will likely have limited utility in MASS contexts. If rules-based design standards fail, performance-based standards offer a natural alternative.

The transition from rules-based design standards towards performance-based approaches is, in general, a relatively recent regulatory innovation with regulators, IMO included, increasingly deploying flexible regulatory approaches since the 1970s. The strategies are typically understood as reactions to increasing environmental and technological complexity that has made detailed rules-based regimes counterproductive (Coglianese & Mendelson, 2010; Decker, 2018; May, 2003). The proponents have, for example, argued that regulators, first, may lack the expertise to choose the best designs and end up imposing inefficient solutions, and the rigid design rulesets may, secondly, lock-in suboptimal designs, lead to "localized" regulatory capture, and stifle innovation. Focusing on "performance" instead of "design", then, would let the regulator, as domain experts choose which designs to adopt (Spinardi, 2019). This, the proponents argue, facilitates both efficiency and innovation as firms may either opt for the most cost-effective existing technologies or develop new ones (Coglianese et al., 2003). Critics, on the other hand, have argued that the strategies often constitute extensions of a neoliberal deregulatory agenda that has seen regulators bow to commercial interests and abdicate their regulatory responsibilities. The developments have, at times, also led to catastrophes, regulatory capture, and incumbency benefits (Brannigan & Smidts, 1999; Gunningham, 2010).

A performance-oriented goal-based MASS Code would not be a novelty in the IMO safety regulation mix. The IMO has used this approach on multiple occasions. For example, the Polar Code (1994) is perhaps the best IMO example of goal-based regulation. The Code builds on a three-fold regulatory structure. The safety-oriented provisions of the Code identify ten focal areas for regulatory interventions and establish a high-level goal for each area. Machinery installations, for example, must be "capable of delivering the required functionality necessary for the safe operation of ships" (Part I-A 6.1). The high-level goal is, then, buttressed by a more detailed set of "functional requirements" that identify, for example, the specific challenges such as "ice accretion and/or snow accumulation; ice ingestion from seawater; freezing and increased viscosity of liquids; seawater intake temperature; and snow ingestion" ships face in Polar waters (Part I-A 6.2.1.1). Detailed "regulations", finally, address the challenges and set out selected design parameters by, for example, providing that "seawater supplies for machinery systems shall be designed to prevent ingestion of ice" (Part I-A 6.3.1.2).

Goal-based and other performance-oriented regulatory approaches, however, come in many flavors. The IMO *goal-based approach* puts an emphasis on high-level qualitative goals. The performance standards are relatively vague semantic reference points. *Outcome-based regulation*, instead, conjures up an association with binary performance targets. *Performance-based regulation*, in turn, seems to accentuate measurable performance, often established through quantitative statistical benchmarks (Decker, 2018, pp. 14–15).

In the following section, the chapter will argue that a complex, layered, heavily statistical performance-focused regulatory approach will likely emerge for MASSs owing to the technological characteristics of autonomous navigation systems.

4.2 Designing Performance-Based ANS Standards

The ultimate objective of ANS regulation is to ensure that MASS can safely reach their destinations without causing damage to third-party interests during the voyage. The objective translates easily into a Polar Code generic high-level goal: MASS' ANS should be capable of navigating the ship safely under all foreseeable conditions and in all foreseeable traffic scenarios.

While the high-level goal may be relatively easy to formulate, the devil is in the details. First, regulators should specify the desired safety level. Secondly, a verification methodology should be developed to ascertain that the ships, in fact, attain the safety level. The problems are intertwined. The safety framing (Lundgren, 2021) must be commensurate with the methodologies used to ascertain safety. The interplay of safety framing and ascertainment methodologies will likely direct regulators to lengthy detours where different enactments of safety are fitted with various conceivable material assemblages that can produce information on ANS performance.

To illustrate how this process may play out, imagine that regulators coalesce on a "human crew equivalent" safety standard and allow commercial MASS deployments if manufacturers demonstrate that the ships are as safe as human-operated ships. In designing the detailed safety standard, the first question to be answered is a human one: how safe are ships navigated by human crews?

Regulators have two primary options for framing what safety should ideally embody. The first option disassembles safety into its "component" drivers. In this option, safe navigation arises as a function of the specific capabilities in both MASSs and manned ships. Regulators could, for example, require that the MASS can generate a situational awareness that is equivalent to the situational awareness competent MSS crews on average are able to maintain with equivalent path planning and collision avoidance capabilities. Safety certification would, then, be an exercise in which supervisors examine whether the required capabilities exist or not.

The other option is to treat both the MASS and manned ships as navigational black boxes. The black box approach would entail that the regulators would refrain from trying to disentangle what technical solutions or discrete capabilities ensure safe navigation. Rather the regulators would focus on navigational performance as the unit of analysis requiring, for example, that manufacturers demonstrate that their MASS is sufficiently safe. Such an approach could, for example, build on statistical analyses of how MSS would perform in various environmental conditions and traffic scenarios, and impose the measures as benchmarks for MASS.

Here, two regulatory design constraints seem to emerge. On the one hand, the software characteristics of both SA and NPDM subsystems will likely entrench the statistical orientation. First, formal verification of ANS performance will likely be impossible as the systems will likely contain intractable machine learning algorithms, at least with the current state-of-the-art methodologies. As a result, considerable uncertainty over performance will linger without testing-based validation. Secondly, limited scenario testing is unlikely to provide assurance of reliable functioning. While most testing in physical system engineering gauges system performance in edge-cases and interpolates the results to more benign conditions, machine learning code performance is typically non-linear and edge-cases hard to define in advance. Consequently, traditional edge-case focused testing strategies may have limited purchases.

On the other hand, even if regulators were able to articulate sensible bottom-up standards for ANS components, the cascading nature of ANS functions may render modular approaches infeasible as a stand-alone regulatory solution. ANS performance is dependent on the flawless functioning of each individual system component. Performing an upstream process such as SA generation flawlessly but failing at a later stage when navigational decisions are made will result in an undesired navigational outcome. Similarly, running a downstream process with bad inputs will also result in failure, consequently, while a modular regulatory approach targeting individual processes may be useful in improving safety, ensuring safe navigational outcomes will likely require a black box approach to sit on top of modular standards.

The outlines of a performance-based regulatory strategy emerge out of the aforementioned constraints. Regulators will likely impose detailed performance requirements for selected ANS components. Sensors, for example, will likely attract standards that resemble the current radar performance standards. Another primary set of performance standards gauging ship-level navigational performance will likely be layered upon the component standards. These standards will be statistics-oriented. The MASS ANS will be subjected to a wide range of environmental conditions and traffic scenarios, its performance monitored, and requirements for acceptable performance set in a statistical frame.

4.3 Designing the Testing Regime

Designing and building a testing regime capable of ensuring that ANS work as intended and attain an acceptable level of safety will not be a trivial exercise. To understand the scope of the challenge, consider the findings of the 2016 RAND Corporation study on how autonomous ground vehicle safety could be secured. The authors calculated that to demonstrate at a 95 percent confidence level that an autonomous car was safer than a human-driven car would entail a gargantuan testing effort. The car would have to be driven billions of miles to amass enough data, and, even with a hundred-car fleet in constant operation, the tests would take approximately 500 years (Kalra & Paddock, 2016, p. 10).

If the RAND calculations land anywhere near the right ballpark, the study lays bare two circumstances. First, relying on real-world testing alone will most certainly be insufficient. Real-world tests either in dedicated testing areas or even during operational use will simply take too long to be practicable. While real-world tests will be essential parts of the testing regime, the brunt of the validation efforts must, second, take place in virtual testing environments.

The UNECE ITC World Forum for Harmonization of Vehicle Regulations reached this conclusion as it outlined its future assessment framework for automated vehicles in June 2021. The framework comprises five pillars. The Forum envisions that automated vehicles will undergo "simulation/virtual testing", track testing, real-world tests, and audits before acceptance and will be subject to an in-service monitoring and reporting regime while in use. To facilitate testing, a scenario catalogue must be built. The catalogue will contain a large number of representative traffic scenarios in which the vehicle must be able to survive. The Forum further envisages that virtual testing will constitute the backbone of future regulatory framework and "an indispensable tool to verify the capability of the automated system to deal with a wide variety of possible traffic scenarios" (World Forum for Harmonization of Vehicle Regulations, 2021, p. 9). Virtual tests, the Forum holds, can provide qualitative and statistical confidence in the safety of the full system and its components, contribute directly to statistical confidence in the safety of the full system and discover challenging scenarios to test in the real world. Other testing modalities will supplement the virtual tests in a layered design.

There is no reason to think that the basic concept for validation testing would be any different in MASS than in automated vehicles. The brunt of testing will take place in simulation environments, with test areas and real-world online tests providing supplementary confidence to the risk assessments.

Some differences in emphasis may, however, emerge due to technical and environmental discrepancies of autonomous ships and vehicles. SA subsystem performance is one such area. SA subsystem capabilities may play a more central role in ANS performance determinants than in autonomous vehicles. While marine operational design domains are less congested and change slower than road ODDs, ships face significant maneuverability constraints. A ship must be able to plan its movement several minutes into the future and, consequently, be capable of detecting and identifying other traffic miles away. This will increase the importance of validating SA performance, but, simultaneously, validating the long-range detection capabilities necessary for safe MASS operations may be more difficult than ensuring adequate automotive SA capabilities. The problem is pressing in nature as simulation-based sensor testing remains technically challenging.

4.4 *Parameters for Simulation Environments*

Above, this chapter has argued that simulation testing will be the primary means for ensuring adequate ANS performance. To facilitate tests, simulation environments will have to be built. Designing and building the environments will, however, require significant expertise and investments and raise numerous important questions with regulatory implications.

Firstly, to gain statistically significant insights into ANS performance, the ANS need to undergo testing in a significant number of traffic and environmental scenarios of likely and unlikely circumstances to also explore the challenging edge cases which push MASS ANS to their limits. Developing the scenarios requires a considerable amount of localized data on both conceivable weather and traffic conditions. In addition, the designers must have an in-depth understanding of ANS's technological makeup to recognize what conditions will be demanded for MASS' ANS. Secondly, building the equipment and world models that make up the simulation environment will take considerable technical and domain expertise (Minami et al., 2021). In particular, sensor modeling for synthetic scenario generation will likely force considerable investments in technology as publicly available information suggests that standard modeling tools do not yet exist, even for autonomous vehicles (Chen & Liu, 2018; Cragun, 2022).

As testing environments will effectively determine how safe MASS will be, regulators have an inherent acute interest in controlling them. Consequently, the environments will likely morph into primary regulatory targets. This entails that future regulatory instruments should contain rules on simulation environment design setting out scenario type and scenario coverage requirements. The IMO MASS Code is unlikely to contain detailed rules on simulation environment design parameters. The regulatory gap will have to be filled by someone. Multiple alternative futures are conceivable, each with its own strengths and weaknesses. A large flag state with an interest in either promoting its shipbuilding or ship operating industry could emerge as a first mover and articulate its own set of standards for the simulation environments. Classification societies are also possible detail-level regulators.

Importantly, simulation environment design also blends into safety-level specifications. The number and type of scenarios MASS should be exposed to are directly dependent upon the safety confidence regulators choose to pursue. To develop high confidence in MASS capabilities requires that both normal and edge navigation cases are explored thoroughly. This probably requires hundreds of thousands of simulation runs and scenarios and is an issue that should be settled by legally binding rules. Here, one should note how the available validation technologies push the framing of regulatory objectives. If and when ANS performance can only be gauged by subjecting the systems to huge batteries of simulation tests, the regulatory objectives must be morphed into the language of tests. In practice, the weight of the testing arrangements will push the regulators to articulate safety requirements as statistical measures indicating test success or failure rates. A safety articulation might, under these circumstances, call for the ship to survive all scenarios without incidents or only fail a certain fraction of a scenario set.

In addition to design parameter determination, also building and running the environments is a safety critical process. Classification societies appear natural operator candidates alongside the ANS manufacturers. Both have their respective strengths and weaknesses as validators. On the one hand, manufacturers will likely have access to ready-made testing platforms as Testing is an integral part of all development processes. Further, the manufacturers' testing facilities would likely be built to fit the equipment configurations they plan to run, decreasing the need for customization work. Classification societies, in turn, would likely have no access to a ready-made environment but would have to develop the simulation capabilities solely for regulatory validation purposes. Similarly, the classification societies would likely have to work with several equipment configurations from multiple manufacturers. On the other hand, manufacturers will have a strong vested interest in demonstrating that their ANS are safe. The incentive misalignment might lead to suboptimal and "gentle" testing. Whether classification society testing will ameliorate the issue is unclear. Similar, although attenuated perverse incentives might also appear if tests are conducted by classification societies as testing will likely be a business for them. To make matters worse, the ANS manufacturers and shipowners will likely pay for certifications.

The landscape remains fragmented. MASS ANS regulation will likely center around simulation testing. Who regulates the testing and incurs the investment costs necessary for building testing environments are crucial but open questions with no simple answers.

5 Conclusion

This chapter focused on a largely neglected but likely important aspect of future MASS regulatory frameworks: navigational safety regulation. As MASS accident dynamics will likely be largely dominated by the technological composition of its autonomous navigation systems, the systems are prime regulatory targets. However, ANS regulation will likely be fraught with difficulties. ANS are complex technological artefacts that contain both hardware sensors and computing equipment and numerous software components of which some are machine learning algorithms. The technological nature of ANS will cause uncertainty over their performance to remain, complicating regulators' work as their traditional technology regulation playbook will likely lose much of its traction.

The chapter reviews the strengths and weaknesses of two primary safety regulation paradigms, rules-based technical and performance-based regulation, in MASS contexts. Based on the review, it has been argued that rules-based technical regulation will likely struggle to govern MASS ANS safety. While some pockets of rules-based regulation will likely remain, software component presence and the cascading nature of ANS data processing entails that technical regulation targeting ANS equipment will likely fail at securing overall performance. The variability in feasible ANS configurations further decreases the utility of rules-based standards. This entails that the future of MASS safety regulation will likely center around performance based-regulation and simulation-based testing in particular. ANS technological complexity and machine learning software components will likely entail that only comprehensive simulation-based testing allows regulators to explore navigational edge cases in sufficient detail to ensure safe operation. However, the simulation-based tests will be buttressed by real-world testing both in trial areas and in real traffic. Crucial questions over required safety levels, testing environment parameter specification, and operating responsibilities remain open. Further research and regulatory drafting work should concentrate on these areas.

References

Beckers, A. (2021). *Three Liability Regimes for Artificial Intelligence: Algorithmic Actants, Hybrids, Crowds*. Hart.

Brannigan, V., & Smidts, C. (1999). Performance Based Fire Safety Regulation Under Intentional Uncertainty. *Fire and Materials, 23*(6), 341–347. https://doi.org/10.1002/(SICI)1099-1018(199911/12)23:6<341::AID-FAM709>3.0.CO;2-1 (Accessed 12 June 2022).

Campbell, S., Naeem, W., & Irwin, G.W. (2012). A Review on Improving the Autonomy of Unmanned Surface Vehicles Through Intelligent Collision Avoidance Manoeuvres. *Annual Reviews in Control, 36*(2), 267–283. https://doi.org/10.1016/j.arcontrol.2012.09.008 (Accessed 12 June 2022).

Chen, J.-X., & Chen, J. (2017). Supply Chain Carbon Footprinting and Responsibility Allocation Under Emission Regulations. *Journal of Environmental Management, 188* (March), 255–67. https://doi.org/10.1016/j.jenvman.2016.12.006 (Accessed 12 June 2022).

Chen, Z., & Liu, B. (2018). Lifelong Machine Learning, Second Edition. *Synthesis Lectures on Artificial Intelligence and Machine Learning, 12*(3), 1–207. https://doi.org/10.2200/S00832ED1V01Y201802AIM037 (Accessed 12 June 2022).

Chesterman, S. (2021). *We, the Robots? Regulating Artificial Intelligence and the Limits of the Law*. 1st ed. Cambridge University Press. https://doi.org/10.1017/9781009047081 (Accessed 12 June 2022).

Clarke, D. M., & Hollister, I. (2010). Introduction to Redundancy. *Safety and Reliability, 30*(4), 4–15. https://doi.org/10.1080/09617353.2010.11690919

Coglianese, C. (2010). Management-Based Regulation: Implications for Public Policy. Paris. OECD. https://doi.org/10.1787/9789264082939-10-en (Accessed 12 June 2022).

Coglianese, C., & Mendelson, E. (2010). Meta-Regulation and Self-Regulation. In R. Baldwin, M. Cave, and M. Lodge (Eds.), *The Oxford Handbook of Regulation* (pp. 145–168). Oxford University Press. https://doi.org/10.1093/oxfordhb/9780199560219.003.0008 (Accessed 12 June 2022).

Coglianese, C., Nash, J., & Olmstead, T. (2003). Performance-Based Regulation: Prospects and Limitations in Health, Safety and Environmental Protection. *SSRN Electronic Journal*. https://doi.org/10.2139/ssrn.392400 (Accessed 12 June 2022).

COLREGs. (1972). Convention on International Regulations for Preventing Collisions at Sea, Oct. 20, 1972, 28 U.S.T. 3459, T.I.A.S. 8587. Available at: https://www.samgongustofa.is/media/log-og-reglur/COLREG-Consolidated-2018.pdf (Accessed 12 June 2022).

Cragun, M. (2022). DRIVE Sim Novel AI Tools Advance AV Deployment. NVIDIA Blog. Available at: https://blogs.nvidia.com/blog/2022/03/23/drive-sim-omniverse-neural-ai-digital-twin/ (Accessed 12 June 2022).

Decker, C. (2018). Goals-Based and Rules-Based Approaches to Regulation. *BEIS Research Paper No*. 8. Department for Business, Energy, and Industrial Strategy.

Eckert, C., & Isaksson, O. (2017). Safety Margins and Design Margins: A Differentiation Between Interconnected Concepts. Procedia CIRP (Complex Systems Engineering and Development Proceedings). *The 27th CIRP Design Conference*, 60 (January), 267–72. https://doi.org/10.1016/j.procir.2017.03.140 (Accessed 12 June 2022).

European Commission. (2021). Proposal for a Regulation of the European Parliament and of the Council Laying Down Harmonised Rules on Artificial Intelligence (Artificial Intelligence Act) COM(2021) 206 Final. Available at: https://eur-lex.europa.eu/legal-content/EN/TXT/?uri=CELEX%3A52021PC0206 (Accessed 12 June 2022).

Gunningham, N. (2010). Enforcement and Compliance Strategies. In *The Oxford Handbook of Regulation*. In R. Baldwin, M. Cave, and M. Lodge (Eds.), Oxford University Press (pp. 119–145). https://doi.org/10.1093/oxfordhb/9780199560219.003.0007 (Accessed 12 June 2022).

Huang, Z. (2014). De-Rating Design and Analysis for Safety and Reliability. *2014 Reliability and Maintainability Symposium*, 1–7. https://doi.org/10.1109/RAMS.2014.6798442 (Accessed 12 June 2022).
Hutchins, E. (1995). *Cognition in the Wild*. The MIT press.
IMO. (1981). Performance Standards for Radar Equipment (MSC.64(67)), as Amended.
IMO. (1991). Recommendations on General Requirements for Shipborne Radio Equipment Forming Part of the Global Maritime Distress and Safety System (GMDSS) and for Electronic Navigational Aids. Resolution A.694(17). Available at: http://www.imo.org/en/KnowledgeCentre/IndexofIMOResolutions/Assembly/Documents/A.694(17).pdf (Accessed 12 June 2022).
IMO. (2019). Interim Guidelines For Mass Trials. MSC.1-Circ.1604. https://wwwcdn.imo.org/localresources/en/MediaCentre/HotTopics/Documents/MSC.1-Circ.1604%20-%20Interim%20Guidelines%20For%20Mass%20Trials%20(Secretariat).pdf (Accessed 12 June 2022).
IMO. (2021). Outcome Of The Regulatory Scoping Exercise For The Use Of Maritime Autonomous Surface Ships. https://wwwcdn.imo.org/localresources/en/MediaCentre/PressBriefings/Documents/MSC.1-Circ.1638%20-%20Outcome%20Of%20The%20Regulatory%20Scoping%20ExerciseFor%20The%20Use%20Of%20Maritime%20Autonomous%20Surface%20Ships...%20(Secretariat).pdf (Accessed 12 June 2022).
Kalra, N., & Paddock, S. M. (2016). Driving to Safety: How Many Miles of Driving Would It Take to Demonstrate Autonomous Vehicle Reliability? RR-1478-RC. *Research Reports*. RAND Corporation.
Li, J., Wang, H., Zhao, W., & Xue, Y. (2019). Ship's Trajectory Planning Based on Improved Multiobjective Algorithm for Collision Avoidance. *Journal of Advanced Transportation*. Hindawi. e4068783. https://doi.org/10.1155/2019/4068783 (Accessed 12 June 2022).
Lipton, Z. C. (2018). The Mythos of Model Interpretability: In Machine Learning, the Concept of Interpretability Is Both Important and Slippery. *Queue, 16*(3), 31–57. https://doi.org/10.1145/3236386.3241340 (Accessed 12 June 2022).
Lundgren, B. (2021). Safety Requirements Vs. Crashing Ethically: What Matters Most for Policies on Autonomous Vehicles. *AI & Society, 36*(2), 405–415. https://doi.org/10.1007/s00146-020-00964-6
May, P. J. (2003). Performance-Based Regulation and Regulatory Regimes: The Saga of Leaky Buildings. *Law & Policy, 25*(4), 381–401. https://doi.org/10.1111/j.0265-8240.2003.00155.x (Accessed 12 June 2022).
Minami, M., Kokubun, K., Kobayashi, M., Hikida, K., Yoshimura, K., Sato, K., Saito, E., & Sawada, R. (2021). Development of Comprehensive Simulation System for Autonomous Ships. *Class NK Technical Journal* 4(II), 25–33.

Available at: https://www.classnk.or.jp/hp/pdf/research/rd/2021/04_e03.pdf (Accessed 12 June 2022).

Murdoch, W. J., Singh, C., Kumbier, K., Abbasi-Asl, R., & Yu, B. (2019). Interpretable Machine Learning: Definitions, Methods, and Applications. *Proceedings of the National Academy of Sciences, 116*(44), 22071–22080. https://doi.org/10.1073/pnas.1900654116 (Accessed 12 June 2022).

Nandi, A., & Pal, A. K. (2022). *Interpreting Machine Learning Models: Learn Model Interpretability and Explainability Methods*. Apress. https://doi.org/10.1007/978-1-4842-7802-4 (Accessed 12 June 2022).

Pan, S., Thornton, S. M., & Gerdes, J. C. (2016). Prescriptive and Proscriptive Moral Regulation for Autonomous Vehicles in Approach and Avoidance. In *2016 IEEE International Symposium on Ethics in Engineering, Science and Technology (ETHICS)* (pp. 1–6). https://doi.org/10.1109/ETHICS.2016.7560049

Polar Code. (1994). International Code for Ships Operating in Polar Waters (Polar Code) IMO Doc. MSC.385(94). Available at: https://www.icetra.is/media/english/POLAR-CODE-TEXT-AS-ADOPTED.pdf (Accessed 12 June 2022).

Polvara, R., Sharma, S., Wan, J., Manning, A., & Sutton, R. (2018). Obstacle Avoidance Approaches for Autonomous Navigation of Unmanned Surface Vehicles. *Journal of Navigation, 71*(1), 241–56. https://doi.org/10.1017/S0373463317000753 (Accessed 12 June 2022).

Porathe, T. (2019). Maritime Autonomous Surface Ships (MASS) and the COLREGS: Do We Need Quantified Rules Or Is 'the Ordinary Practice of Seamen' Specific Enough? *TransNav, International Journal on Marine Navigation and Safety of Sea Transportation, 13*(3). Faculty of Navigation, Gdynia Maritime University, Poland, 511–517. https://doi.org/10.12716/1001.13.03.04 (Accessed 12 June 2022).

Riehle, R. D. (2008). An Engineering Context for Software Engineering. Monterey, California. Naval Postgraduate School. Available at: https://calhoun.nps.edu/handle/10945/10379 (Accessed 12 June 2022).

Ringbom, H., Viljanen, M., Poikonen, M., & Ilvessalo, S (2020). *Charting Regulatory Frameworks for Maritime Autonomous Surface Ship Testing, Pilots, and Commercial Deployments*. Publications of the Finnish Ministry of Transport and Communications. Available at: https://julkaisut.valtioneuvosto.fi/handle/10024/162560 (Accessed 12 June 2022).

Ringbom, H., Røsæg, E., & Trond, S. (2021). Autonomous Ships and the Law. *IMLI Studies in International Maritime Law*. Abingdon, Oxon. Routledge. Available at: https://search.ebscohost.com/login.aspx?direct=true&db=nlebk&AN=2574023&site=ehost-live (Accessed 12 June 2022).

SOLAS. (1974). International Convention for the Safety of Life at Sea, Nov. 1, 1974, 32 U.S.T. 47, T.I.A.S. 9700, as amended.

Soyer, B., & Tettenborn, A. (Eds.) (2019). *New Technologies, Artificial Intelligence and Shipping Law in the 21st Century*. Informa Law from Routledge. https://doi.org/10.4324/9780429029172 (Accessed 12 June 2022).

Spinardi, G. (2019). Performance-Based Design, Expertise Asymmetry, and Professionalism: Fire Safety Regulation in the Neoliberal Era. *Regulation & Governance, 13*(4), 520–539. https://doi.org/10.1111/rego.12251 (Accessed 12 June 2022).

STCW. (1978). International Convention on Standards of Training, Certification and Watchkeeping, 1361 UNTS 2 as amended in 1995 and 2010 (Manila Amendments). 1361 UNTS 190.

The Working Group on Maritime Autonomous Surface Ships. (2022). Development of a Goal-Based Instrument for Maritime Autonomous Surface Ships (MASS). Report of the Working Group. MSC 105/WP.8.

Törngren, M., & Grogan, P. T. (2018). How to Deal with the Complexity of Future Cyber-Physical Systems? *Designs*, 2(4). Multidisciplinary Digital Publishing Institute, 40. https://doi.org/10.3390/designs2040040

World Forum for Harmonization of Vehicle Regulations. (2021). New Assessment/Test Method for Automated Driving (NATM) – Master Document. Available at: https://unece.org/sites/default/files/2021-04/ECE-TRANS-WP29-2021-61e.pdf (Accessed 12 June 2022).

PART IV

Global Environmental Change

CHAPTER 9

Autonomous Vessels in the Era of Global Environmental Change

Sean Pribyl

1 Introduction

The nexus between autonomy and sustainability efforts in the maritime industry remains in development but it is generally accepted that the marine industry will see more technological development in the next ten years than the last 100 years. Emerging legal frameworks and decarbonization goals are resulting in increased focus on managing the environmental impact of vessel operations through technological innovation. A key factor in shipping is the performance of a vessel during transits to which an owner or charterer is bound under terms of a charter party and which obligates the vessel to maintain certain speed to arrive at its destination at an agreed upon time. When vessels do not maximize efficiency, they can waste fuel and omit more emissions. Autonomy can assist in this regard as augmented technology can assist with voyage planning

S. Pribyl (✉)
Holland & Knight LLP, Washington, DC, USA
e-mail: sean.pribyl@hklaw.com

© The Author(s), under exclusive license to Springer Nature Switzerland AG 2023

T. M. Johansson et al. (eds.), *Autonomous Vessels in Maritime Affairs*, Studies in National Governance and Emerging Technologies,
https://doi.org/10.1007/978-3-031-24740-8_9

and onboard course corrections and can improve efficiency in dull, dirty, and dangerous operations such as surveys and oil spill response, among other operations.

In particular, the US maritime sector is facing ever-growing challenges with stricter environmental emission regulations, unprecedented supply chain disruptions, navigational safety concerns with congested waterways, incidents caused by human error, increasing security risks with cyber security, and crew challenges caused by the COVID-19 pandemic. The emergence of the so-called "Blue Economy" and innovative smart ship and port technologies, digital data exchanges, and advanced automated processes aboard vessels are indicative of a technological revolution in the maritime sector as these smart technologies may improve operational efficiency, resiliency, and safety with more sustainable solutions (NOAA, 2021a). Moreover, the implementation of smart technologies could bolster the US position as a global leader in innovation and maintain a competitive edge over competitor nations. US goals toward decarbonization of shipping and new environmental regulation are demanding innovative solutions to increase efficiencies in vessel and oceanographic data optimization, improved risk management, and environmental performance. However, questions abound as how to maintain safety in the absence of clear standards or applicable domestic and international regulations which calls for consideration of a risk-based approach to manage the risk. Moreover, the reliance on digitalization, integration, and automation leads increasingly to marine cyber security risk management concerns which are being addressed by the International Maritime Organization (IMO) and by the US Coast Guard (USCG) to ensure the security of operations with data protection and reliable and safe marine operations (Wärtsilä Voyage, 2021).

2 The Role of Digitalization and Advanced Automation in shipping—A Framework for Sustainable Operations

The perceived benefits of smart autonomy are well-known, as is the understanding that technology is being developed and deployed at a faster pace than the regulatory development and consensus on uniform standards. Over the past few years, industry conversations on digitalization and maritime autonomy have struggled to adequately describe their application in a uniform manner, an important consideration as markets look to build to scale. Shipboard autonomy exists on a spectrum with varying degrees of automation ranging from fully crewed vessels with augmented decision-making support to fully uncrewed vessels. Generally, innovative technological applications aboard vessels must take into account the unique role that autonomous ships may play in decarbonization efforts while assessing their use against the looming technological and regulatory challenges that remain unresolved and which may vary depending on vessel type and size as well as a respective vessel's location of operations, for example, in internal waters or on the high seas. The use cases are emerging with a new trend that focuses on sustainable operations that preserve the environment, though an overview of these applications is warranted.

The use of innovative digitalization to support so-called smart autonomy is touted as a means to improve cost efficiency, enhance vessel safety, and relevant here, improve environmental performance through advanced robotics, data collection, and analytic processing with the assistance of artificial intelligence (AI), machine learning, or cloud computing supported by the Internet of Things. Through integration in the vessel's operations, AI could assist with providing risk data in useful formats through automated exchange of communication on situational awareness, navigation matters, and cargo delivery timing. Such digital technologies aboard vessels are evolving to either augment or replace the human in the loop of vessel operations, and can re-assign tasking from the human to the machine with the use of advanced sensors and cameras for "sight and hearing" with increased electronic navigation solutions that improve prediction and reliability by utilizing increasing levels of AI systems to recognize hazardous situations through these sensor inputs. This in turn can augment crew performance and lessen the demands on vessel workloads during continuous at-sea operations. For example, this could lead to a so-called "uncrewed bridge" on long sea transits with minimal traffic or course corrections needed. This could support efficiency and resiliency and mitigate risk in cases historically attributed to human error, such as those involving fatigue, which in turn could reduce manpower and operational costs.

For purposes of environmental compliance, smart autonomy can purportedly support decarbonization goals by utilizing smart autonomy to optimize ship routing and fuel consumption and thus reduce environmental impacts, such as pollution and air emissions. This can ostensibly be seen during long open ocean transits, short sea shipping or constrained waterways with congested traffic, and even during docking and undocking. Smart autonomy could aid the mariner with augmented situational awareness and decision-making which could increase safety and mission effectiveness, thereby potentially reducing marine casualties like groundings, collisions, or allisions, all of which pose a heightened risk to environmental damage. Regardless, the industry cannot sit idly by and still meet emerging environmental regulations and goals which now dominate commercial decisions and remain at the forefront of initiatives put forth by government bodies, issues discussed next.

3 International Regulatory Framework

Put simply, global trade relies on the shipping industry. However, if the maritime industry was a country, it reportedly would be the sixth largest greenhouse gas (GHG) polluter. Internationally, there are around 90,000 merchant ships in a wide variety of services with diverse operational parameters, routing requirements, and unique commercial risks (Reid, 2022). Maritime shipping accounts for approximately 80 percent of international goods transportation by volume (Gray et al., 2021). The IMO considers decarbonization of shipping to be a monumentally transformative and complex regulatory challenge impacting the full spectrum of the supply chain to include charterers, shipowners, banks, investors, and consumers. Stakeholders are realizing that they will be required to demonstrate environmental regulatory compliance with reliable and credible data (Palmejar & Chubb, 2021). This is where smart autonomy may evolve.

As with other segments of the transportation sector, shipping is considered a major contributor of GHG emissions. The IMO estimates that the international shipping sector is the source of 2.8% of annual global emissions (IMO, 2020). Left unchecked, the IMO suggests that GHG emissions from shipping may grow by 50–250% by 2050 due in large part to anticipated growth in international maritime trade (IMO, 2015).

In response, in 2018 the IMO developed a strategy to combat climate change by addressing GHG emissions from international shipping and developed aggressive targets for the shipping industry when it agreed on GHG targets to align with the 2015 Paris Agreement to limit global warming to 1.2–2 degrees increase (IMO, 2020). More specifically, the IMO developed an Initial IMO Strategy to assess the reduction of GHG emissions from ships followed by four IMO greenhouse gas studies (IMO, 2020). The IMO Initial Strategy strives to phase out GHG emissions from international shipping as soon as possible before the end of the century, and includes ambitious goals to reduce the carbon dioxide (CO2) emissions per transport work (carbon intensity) by at least 40% by 2030 and total annual GHG emissions by at least 50% by 2050 compared to 2008 levels—a clearly daunting task (IMO, 2018). In the US, GHG emissions from the transportation sector have been considered the largest contributor of US greenhouse gas emissions, with 2% of total transportation emissions, including CO2, sulfur oxide (SOx), nitrogen oxide (NOx), and methane, attributed to various ships and boats depending on propulsion type, operational parameters, and efficiency (EPA, 2021a). Indeed, the US has also made net-zero GHG emissions (by no later than 2050) from the international shipping sector a national priority and offers incentives to help industry meet these goals (US State Department, 2022).

4 Work of the IMO on Reducing GHG Emissions in Shipping

In response to the IMO's GHG initiatives, the maritime industry is taking steps to mitigate environmental impact, including through the use of advanced autonomy and data analytics which could help meet collateral GHG reduction goals. Understanding the role smart autonomy can play in decarbonization requires an overview of the primary means by which the IMO administers global and regional regulatory guidelines to combat shipping emissions, which is through the International Convention for the Prevention of Pollution from Ships 73/78 (MARPOL). Inter alia, MARPOL sets the standards for global compliance for prevention of air pollution from ships under MARPOL Annex VI (EPA, 2021b).

In June 2021, the IMO's Marine Environment Protection Committee (MEPC) adopted new amendments to MARPOL Annex VI to reduce emissions as part of the IMO's near-term ambitions toward the 2050 carbon emissions reduction plan (Kongsberg, 2022). These changes will implement significant new technical rules called the Energy Efficiency Existing Ship Index (EEXI) and Carbon Intensity Indicator (CII). The EEXI is a technical measure setting new minimum requirements for the energy efficiency of existing ships (Barreiro et al., 2022). The EEXI is evaluated based on the vessels' design parameters such as equipment and technical data and is applicable to certain vessels falling under MARPOL Annex VI (ibid.). The CII is measured in grams of CO2 emitted by passenger or cargo carrying capacity and nautical mile and incentivizes industry through an annual indicator of the ship's transport efficiency rated from A (best) to E (worst) (DNV, 2022). Vessels will have to demonstrate improvements in their operational carbon intensity beginning in 2023 through 2030 with the regulations due to come into force on January 1, 2023 and the first ratings issued in 2024. Shipowners therefore have an incentive to urgently take implementing actions for EEXI compliance and to best position themselves for favorable CII ratings, in particular as one-third of the world fleet is predicted to potentially fall short of CII ratings (Blenkey, 2021).

The Ship Energy Efficiency Management Plan (SEEMP) also provides shipping companies with a method to manage ship and fleet efficiency performance over time using the Energy Efficiency Operational Indicator (EEOI) as a monitoring tool (Tran, 2017). The SEEMP includes guidance on best practices and emerging options for fuel efficient ship operations, and the EEOI allows operators to measure the fuel efficiency of a ship and variations while in operation, which in turn could drive decisions on better-quality voyage planning and innovative considerations (IMO, 2022). Indeed, the intent of the SEEMP, at least in part, is to urge the ship owner and operator at each stage of the plan to consider new technologies and practices when seeking to optimize the performance of a ship.

The above referenced environmental considerations are meant to show the gaps in compliance that smart autonomy and AI may fill to best position shipowners to support human operations by gathering data that can be converted into usable data from which shipowners can understand and improve operational efficiency. Such steps could potentially increase commercial and market position in the most optimal manner. Indeed, regulatory decarbonization measures will likely become more rigorous over time, and non-compliance could result in enforcement measures such as fines and related interruption of a vessel's operations, which in turn could lead to increased costs and disputes. Thus, shipowners seeking the highest environmental ratings (e.g., CII) may seek to install innovative technologies and novel systems on their vessels that assist in monitoring GHG emissions and augment net-zero emission solutions.

5 US Contributions Related to GHG

As previously discussed, the US government believes that GHG emissions from the shipping sector are significant and projected to increase by up to 50% from 2018 levels, a trajectory incompatible with the goals of the Paris Agreement (US State Department, 2022). Such international efforts were underpinned at the United Nations Climate Change Conference in Glasgow in November 2021 where 22 signatory countries to the Clydebank Declaration (including the US) pledged to support the establishment of so-called "green shipping corridors" (ibid.). The US is taking a multi-agency approach to maritime decarbonization in a concerted attempt to move away from a "business-as-usual" attitude through guidance, initiatives, and innovative solutions. Such efforts are receiving support from the USCG and US Maritime Administration (MARAD), and notably also from non-traditional maritime agencies such as the US Department of Energy (DOE) (Hume & Ramsey, 2022). The US Department of the Navy has also promulgated Climate Action 2030 to reduce its GHG emissions and support the US' commitment to net-zero emissions by 2050 (Department of the Navy, 2022).

Indeed, the US government is spurring investment in efforts needed to meet aspirational commitments, including research, development, demonstration, and deployment on a larger industry scale in tandem with enabling policies that incentivize the advent of innovate technologies at the earliest opportunity (US State Department, 2022). Such efforts will bring to bear international collaboration on technologies to serve as part of the solution to achieving net-zero emissions from maritime transportation over the coming years and decades, including smart autonomy, port technologies, novel vessels, and other supply chain stakeholders driven by data to demonstrate improvement over time (ibid.).

In fact, emissions data is a powerful tool in curbing emissions to fight climate change and achieve net-zero emission operations (SailPlan, 2022). For example, stakeholders could use lifecycle emissions assessment tools and analyses that incorporate accepted methodologies to implement a plan that includes energy efficiency and optimization technologies that lead to reduced overall energy consumption and reduce GHG emissions for ocean-going vessels, support vessels, and commercial harbor craft (US State Department, 2022).

6 The Role of Smart Autonomy to Support Decarbonization

Autonomy is sometimes referred to as a journey and technologies are being developed for which the industry still cannot predict their ultimate purpose and value. Whether or not smart autonomy will reach a critical mass and permeate the entire marine sector is unclear, though what is clear is that various vessels in different classes are already implementing smart autonomy for divergent purposes. Some vessels may become fully autonomous and uncrewed, though the industry continues to look in the near term for opportunities to implement advanced automation in a set of solutions that involve augmented navigation, high-tech sensors, sonar and lidar, weather predicting analytics, and improved connectivity to encourage faster data analytic processing. The goal with maritime autonomy is less about the idea of autonomous ships and is now shifting more toward approaches assessing how to automate the operations of a ship to achieve optimal operational efficiency with the latest and most advanced technology. This shift is, at least in part, being driven by decarbonization efforts in the marine sector, and smart autonomy is being hailed as a means to that end.

More specifically, the ambitious GHG reduction goals of the IMO and the US require a pathway by which the marine industry can not only utilize a variety of emerging alternative fuels to complement current fossil fuels, but equally will enlist technologically innovative solutions to assist the mariner in developing more efficient operations, turning the data collected into decipherable formats on which regulatory reporting and critical decision-making can be based. This need for technological solutions is spurring shipowners to implement solutions to improve the energy efficiency and sustainability of their fleet through urgent and viable means, a process all the more complicated by the dearth of a clear regulatory framework for novel technologies such as autonomous functions. Advanced smart autonomy in the shipping sector thus could offer valuable contributions to decarbonization efforts in the shipping sector and this includes perceived benefits of improved environmental safety and GHG reductions (Kongsberg/Massterly, 2021).

Several factors are spurring increased desire for technology that can assist in this regard. Shipowners, operators, charterers, and managers use CII to meet decarbonization targets and implement sustainability shipping measures. Banks and investors are also implementing regulatory requirements and standards as financial institutions seek to align ship finance portfolios with responsible environmental impacts and incentivize decarbonization efforts (Poseidon Principles, 2022). Port States and Flag States will seek to implement audits and inspections to ensure compliance with GHG standards. Customers are also demanding more GHG reporting from shippers and logistics providers to verify sustainable shipping measures.

At the forefront of ensuring compliance with environmental regulations and GHG reduction targets is the need for new data sources to better predict operational risk. The regulatory landscape is shifting, and smart autonomy and AI could offer meaningful information for vessel-specific scenarios that assist with the management of a voyage, including through better monitoring and adjusting for fuel oil consumption, improved route optimization and weather predictions, greater clarity on the status of hull and propeller fouling, and other predictive maintenance and diagnostics, all of which are intended to enhance operational decision-making.

To this end, proponents of AI and smart autonomy suggest that such technology is vital to future vessel operations since the way a vessel is operated can dramatically impact its fuel consumption and its resulting GHG emissions, by some estimates as much as 5–10% decrease in fuel savings annually (Wärtsilä, 2021). However, only with appropriate measuring, monitoring, and reporting of GHG emissions from ships can stakeholders understand a vessels' environmental impacts and performance. The need to modernize vessel operations to meet data driven regulatory requirements is nearly a foregone conclusion, and the role of smart autonomy is touted as offering, inter alia, improved safety, flexible and cost-effective design options for new-build or retrofit vessels, and CO2 reducing capabilities when paired with hybrid or low fuel consumption modeling.

In many cases, such technologies would be used to augment the human interactions taking place onboard the vessel. More specifically, commercial operators are looking at smart autonomy as a means by which they can increase productivity and reduce operational risk and costs under current goal-based regulatory compliance measures (ABS, 2022). This could be viewed in the context of the onboard mariner if routine tasks in low-risk areas of the navigational watch are removed or redirected to allow for the human mariner to direct greater attention to operational needs. Such support could be developed through increased reliance on various sensors installed on the ship and the use of algorithms and other AI systems to analyze the large amount of information from the ship in real time and instantaneously make decisions that best ensure performance and safe navigation (Smith, 2022). If managed properly and in keeping with regulatory requirements (or lawful interpretations of same), such re-tasking could conceivably offer more rest to the mariner and reprieve from fatigue, a common contributor to human error in decision-making (Rothblum et al., 2002).

The collateral benefits of smart autonomy to the mariner could, at least ostensibly, reduce marine insurance claims related to human error, although more analytical data and peer review analysis is needed on this point. For example, a maritime casualty or incident, such as a grounding or collision, can result in serious impacts on the environment, and in some cases, these incidents are attributed to human error and loss of situational awareness (ibid.). Through the use of advanced autonomy technologies, a vessel operator can receive additional assistance in constantly monitoring a vessel's operational parameters, such as its position compared to hazards and surrounding traffic and maintain a safe distance from other vessels and avoid navigational risks which in turn leads to prevention of accidents and the environmental consequences that could follow. Such enhanced awareness through smart autonomy could be in the form of geofencing-type applications to comply with areas with environmental discharge and emission restrictions, or other protected areas such as marine sanctuaries.

To many in the marine industry, data is considered the "new gold", although in many cases collecting the data is not the problem, rather it is how to distill the data into practical formats on which decisions can be made in real-time and over the course of a voyage. Smart autonomy could provide better and more accurate data to enable superior decision-making by onboard mariners and shoreside personnel. To this end, a threshold consideration to enable decision-making is that a vessel's daily emissions must be accurately measured. Most current emissions measures, such as the IMO's CII indices (IMO, 2022), fail to account for other dynamic factors, such as weather, vessel routing, and navigational interactions. Some operational parameters are not easily measured, like hull fouling. Thus, in order to benefit from the evolving net-zero emissions market, such considerations require continual data collection, resources, and time. Over time, stakeholders can then leverage new expertise along with actionable options and information.

Another potential benefit of autonomous or automated navigation exists in the form of increased voyage efficiency which could lead to more sustainable shipping operations and support decarbonization efforts, for example, by saving fuel and reducing emissions both at sea and in port. More specifically, emerging technology could potentially improve productivity and fuel efficiency through continuous voyage data monitoring that in turn directs the vessel to take slight actions to respond to more trivial changes as opposed to human corrections to larger changes that could involve more significant actions. Over the course of a voyage, such AI-assisted navigation and operations could lead to reduced emissions. Indeed, advocates of smart autonomy suggest that operational solutions involving advanced autonomy to optimize speed routing and speed could lead to a 10 percent savings (or more) on longer voyages (Wärtsilä Voyage, 2021). Digital optimization that utilizes connectivity with port congestion data could conceivably improve vessel arrival times by making incremental schedule adjustments to limit vessel queuing outside ports, and thus reduce port air emissions. Besides the voyage itself, some suggest that smart autonomy optimization during docking times could reduce fuel consumption by 2–3 percent per minute (ibid.).

Another entry point for discussions on smart autonomy may be seen at the design and shipbuilding stages of a vessel. The lifespan of a vessel is generally considered to be 30 years and thus forethought must be given to environmental compliance through the integration of emerging technologies to meet current and ever-changing regulatory requirements. However, as vessels age, retrofitting may become a less economically attractive option for shipowners looking to utilize state-of-the-art technologies. Even so, the means by which the shipping sector could reduce emissions are several, and could include more efficient ships, the utilization of alternative propulsion and low-sulphur fuels (e.g., LNG, biofuel, methanol, hydrogen), and operational improvements. However, given the wide variety of vessel types and operational profiles, there is no "one-size-fits-all" solution that can be applied across the entire shipping industry. Examples of these efforts are developing in the US on several fronts, discussed next.

7 US Autonomy Vessel State-Of-Play

The US is a maritime nation with 95,471 miles of shoreline (NOAA Ocean Facts, 2021b). The US maritime industry is a combination of the

US merchant marine, shipbuilding and repair facilities, port systems, and supporting industries that involves waterborne transportation through its port system (Buzby, 2019). Approximately 41,000 vessels serve the domestic maritime market (ibid.) The maritime sector also plays a critical role in research and development to facilitate environmental compliance and enhance sustainability (ibid.). As a maritime nation with extensive marine activities, the US serves as a prime example of where innovate technological solutions should develop.

Smart autonomy is gradually permeating various aspects of the US maritime sector, including long-range surface and subsurface survey vehicles, smart harbor tugs, commercial outer space support vessels, cargo vessel docking assistance, and government and defense vessels. The US is also a leader in the technological development of AI for data analytics from the private sector as well as within academia. The advent of smart autonomy in the US has generally evolved along the same historical lines as other technological advancements and national priorities in the US transportation sectors wherein the lion's share of US efforts and investment first occur in the defense sector with the commercial and private market relying on private investment at a much more measured pace. Such defense-focused priorities include federal investment of close to half a billion US dollars in maritime autonomy, which in turn has created a market of short-term lucrative defense contract opportunities. With a guarded approach to open collaboration in the US, early movers in the market are treading cautiously with a philosophy on implementing advanced degrees of autonomy on vessels though no one wants to be "the first one through the wall". Indeed, many companies seem inclined to take a wait-and-see approach as they monitor early movers. Regardless, the US market (and more notably the US defense sector) is offering beneficial use-case precedent in answering oft-debated questions as to whether so-called autonomous vessels can, in fact, comply with domestic and international laws, regulations, and conventions.

One of the prevailing examples of the use of smart autonomy in the US sector is that of the use of uncrewed survey vehicles to provide ocean data, maritime security, and ocean mapping. In the government sector, this is being led by investment into uncrewed surface vehicles (USVs) by the National Oceanic and Atmospheric Administration (NOAA) in conformity with their Uncrewed Systems Strategic Plan 2021–2025 (NOAA, 2021c) and Artificial Intelligence Strategic Plan 2021–2025 (NOAA, 2021d). NOAA is leveraging the private sector in their autonomy efforts and partnered with California-based provider Saildrone to collect meteorological and environmental data above and below the sea surface.

Besides NOAA, in March 2021 the US Navy and Marine Corps released their Unmanned Campaign Plan which includes the Department of the Navy's strategy for incorporating unmanned systems into future surface and subsurface assets, including Medium and Large Unmanned Surface Vessels (Navy, 2021). The US Navy's Surface Development Squadron One has also created a new division for its unmanned-vessel operations with the Unmanned Surface Vessel Division 1 (USVDIV One) which will oversee the squadron's two unmanned vessels, the Sea Hawk and Sea Hunter (Decker, 2022). USVDIV One will also include two commercial crew boats, the Nomad and Ranger which were modified and developed by the Pentagon's Strategic Capabilities Office under the Ghost Fleet Overlord program (Decker, 2022). The US Navy has also established Task Force 59 Bahrain, a first of its kind task force intended to rapidly integrate unmanned systems and AI with maritime operations.

US government sector efforts in autonomy use cases must also be underscored in terms of the precedent they are potentially setting for compliance with various vessel requirements under international maritime law, in particular the International Regulations for Preventing Collisions at Sea, 1972 (COLREGs, 1972) and the United Nations Convention on the Law of the Sea, 1982, which should lead to increased implementation of advanced autonomy in the commercial sector (Swain, 2018). Indeed, the US position is that unmanned systems (e.g., warships) can be compliant with the COLREGs even when autonomous or remotely navigated (Commander's Handbook, 2022). For example, as part of the Ghost Fleet Overlord Surface program, US Navy vessels have transited from the US Gulf Coast to the West Coast via the Panama Canal with command and control conducted from a shoreside remote operations center and in which case the vessel reportedly operated under 98 percent of the voyage in an autonomous mode. Those transits followed earlier high seas voyages of an Overlord vessel from California to Hawaii. Similar precedent could be developing through NOAA's partnership with a Saildrone USV involving over 200,000 nautical miles of missions (Meinig et al., 2019).

The USCG is also exploring opportunities for use of uncrewed systems and has conducted tests to evaluate the performance and potential applications of unmanned surface vehicles and vessels, though it has not reached the scale of the Navy or NOAA. Even so, the US Congress has directed the USCG to develop a detailed strategy to implement unmanned systems across their mission areas, based in large part on recommendations from a 2020 National Academies of Sciences consensus study report (National Academies, 2020). Beyond its limited test cases, the USCG has been active as a regulator and in February 2022 promulgated guidelines for human-supervised testing of remote controlled and autonomous systems on vessels, which builds on the USCG's continued support to the IMO's work on Maritime Autonomous Surface Ships (MASS) (USCG, 2022).

US use cases extend beyond government applications as the commercial sector continues to explore options for smart autonomy. Boston-based Sea Machines Robotics (SMR) autonomous technology involves comprehensive integration with a vessel, particularly with the propulsion system. This integration allows the autonomy system to collect and process data concerning critical aspects of the vessel's operation, including prime mover speed(s), vessel speed, sea conditions, and the resulting vessel motions. The system can then optimize for efficiency by constantly adjusting operational parameters like throttle and heading, all while dynamically avoiding collisions based on data from onboard sensors. This voyage optimization using autonomous control, combined with tools like advanced weather routing, can increase the safety of vessel operations while reducing fuel consumption and GHG emissions.

The US government has also cooperated with the private sector on environmentally related tests in scenarios involving hazardous material spills, which can occur anywhere and cause serious environmental damage to inland waterways, coastal waters, and offshore. In 2019, SMR was awarded a cooperative agreement under MARAD's maritime environmental and technical assistance program to demonstrate their remote and autonomous control system aboard a Kvichak MARCO Boom skimmer with the intended benefit of improving safety, efficiency, and productivity, which resulted in a representative use case for illustrating the value of autonomy on vessels.

US-based SailPlan has been developing an intelligent maritime navigation platform for scalable autonomy while offering technology to support ESG goals and carbon reduction through vessel-specific true emissions monitoring, AI-assisted emissions optimization, and simplified emissions reporting. According to Jacob Ruytenbeek, CEO and Founder of SailPlan: "Deploying SailPlan's technology enables the maritime industry to understand their emissions accurately and in real-time with one-click software. The current status quo for maritime emissions reporting is via calculations—SailPlan's technology allows the maritime industry to go straight to measurement, omitting both the bias that comes with estimation and the need for manual calculations" (SailPlan, 2022; see Fig. 1). As the maritime industry grapples with becoming net-zero, SailPlan's technology may offer a part of the solution. In addition to acquiring a comprehensive view of emissions, SailPlan's technology enables users to understand how to optimize and reduce their emissions, which also generates fuel savings.

US-based Ocean Power Technologies (OPT), the manufacturer of autonomous power generating wave buoys and unmanned surface vehicles, develops carbon free and low-carbon emitting autonomous systems. These systems enable persistent monitoring offshore across the world's oceans and in landlocked bodies of water while removing the requirement to put humans on the water (see Fig. 2). These technologies

Fig. 1 Sailplan technology installed on vessel (*Source* SailPlan [2022])

enable greater efficiencies and provide persistent monitoring/inspections all the while using renewable energy. This technology is instrumental in maturing and supporting essential markets like the defense and security, hydrographic, and energy markets, and helping to prevent illegal unreported and regulated (IUU) fishing. California's Marine Advanced Robotics, an OPT company, has been developing autonomous surface vehicles (ASVs) called Wave-Adaptive Modular Vessel (WAM-V) that can operate autonomously or by remote control (see Fig. 3).

Another novel use case in the US has emerged in the convergence of outer space operations and autonomous vessels related to both national security and commercial missions. Specifically, SpaceX has been operating "autonomous drone ships" to support launch and reentry operations as the drone ships are towed to international waters and then operated in an uncrewed autonomy mode that reduces risk to the environment and the public. While other commercial cases exist, a full survey of all US autonomy efforts is beyond the scope of this chapter, though these emerging and novel use cases are noteworthy as the marine sector

Fig. 2 Ocean Power Technologies PowerBuoy operating in the North Sea generating power from the waves (*Source* Ocean Power Technologies)

Fig. 3 Ocean Power Technologies WAM-V OPT unmanned surface vehicle performing a hydrographic survey and inspection of a port (*Source* Ocean Power Technologies)

looks for means by which to incorporate technology and data into more sustainable operations.

8 Conclusions: Tying the Threads Toward a Future with Smart Autonomy

The nexus between autonomy and sustainability remains in development but it is becoming clearer as it remains likely that the marine industry will see more technological development in the next ten years than the last 100 years. As technology rapidly develops, the potential to support sustainable operations is yet to be fully realized, though shipowners are already exploring opportunities for incorporating digitalization and data monitoring as a means to assist with meeting decarbonization goals. Implementation of advanced degrees of autonomy in survey operations and other commercial operations is also reducing carbon footprints while relieving mariners of tasks that could lead to undue fatigue, and in turn, accidents caused by human error. Sustainable operations are requiring innovative solutions and as autonomy use cases continue to develop further implementation can be explored.

Indeed, smart autonomy may develop as a piece of the decarbonization puzzle, but it is likely not a panacea. One of the key challenges to implementing smart autonomy on either new-build or retrofit vessels will be those related to design and technical considerations due to the lack of an international consensus on standards. Even under domestic technical design frameworks in the US, approvals are still being achieved through ad hoc processes with the USCG, and generally require the commercial entity to present the USCG with a comprehensive risk model framework to achieve a "design basis" approval. This will be the norm for the foreseeable future as the US industry awaits the development of domestic and international regulatory frameworks in which design and operation of autonomous vessels under varying degrees of automation and control can be safely managed in existing traffic schemes to conform to navigational rules and regulations. Absent more comprehensive regulations, the industry is left to operate under existing legal frameworks which presuppose a human onboard a vessel. This begs the question of whether current regulations are sufficient to permit innovation and commercial growth in the US maritime sector, and whether new or modified laws are required to address varying degrees of automation and control, including decision-making without humans aboard, augmented intelligence, or remote operation directed from a remote location.

In the US, the progress being made by the US government will continue to offer useful precedent on which commercial cases can develop. Even so, the technology used in advance autonomy will continue to resonate with commercial operators seeking to develop more sustainable operations that can rely on machine and AI data collection and processing to guide decision-making and reporting. Much will depend on the extent to which current regulations will support or inhibit innovation, though the US market indicates that both the government and commercial are vying for the technology that will assist in reaching more efficient operations.

References

American Bureau of Shipping (ABS). (2022). Whitepaper. Autonomous Vessels, 4–8. Available at: https://absinfo.eagle.org/acton/media/16130/autonomous-vessels. Accessed 3 May 2022.

Barreiro, J., Zaragoza, S., & Diaz-Casas, V. (2022). Review of Ship Energy Efficiency. *Ocean Engineering, 257*, 111594.

Blenkey, N. (2021). Over One-Third of World Fleet Could Fall Short on CII ratings. Marine Log. Available at: www.marinelog.com/legal-safety/environment/over-one-third-of-world-fleet-could-fall-short-on-imo-cii-ratings/. Accessed 7 May 2022.

Buzby, M. (2019). US Maritime and Shipbuilding Industries: Strategies to Improve Regulation, Economic Opportunities and Competitiveness. U.S. Department of Transportation. Available at: https://www.transportation.gov/testimony/us-maritime-and-shipbuilding-industries-strategies-improve-regulation-economic. Accessed 6 May 2022.

COLREGs. (1972). Convention on International Regulations for Preventing Collisions at Sea, Oct. 20, 1972, 28 U.S.T. 3459, T.I.A.S. 8587.

Decker, A. (2022). Overlord Program Officially Transferred to Navy. Inside Defense. Available at: https://insidedefense.com/insider/overlord-program-officially-transferred-navy. Accessed 3 June 2022.

Department of the Navy. (2021). Unmanned Campaign Framework. Available at: https://www.navy.mil/Portals/1/Strategic/20210315%20Unmanned%20Campaign_Final_LowRes.pdf?ver=LtCZ-BPlWki6vCBTdgtDMA%3D%3D. Accessed 15 May 2022.

Department of the Navy. (2022). Climate Action 2030. Available at: https://media.defense.gov/2022/May/24/2003004208/-1/-1/0/220524-N-NO191-0001.JPG. Accessed 6 May 2022.

DNV. (2022). CII – Carbon Intensity Indicator Frequently Asked Questions (FAQs). Available at: www.dnv.com/maritime/insights/topics/CII-carbon-intensity-indicator/answers-to-frequent-questions.html. Accessed 13 June 2022.

EPA. (2021a). Fast Facts: U.S. Transportation Sector Greenhouse Gas Emissions 1990–2019. EPA-420-F-21-076. Available at: www.epa.gov/greenvehicles/fast-facts-transportation-greenhouse-gas-emissions. Accessed 12 May 2022.

EPA. (2021b). MARPOL Annex VI and the Act to Prevent Pollution From Ships (APPS). Available at: https://www.epa.gov/enforcement/marpol-annex-vi-and-act-prevent-pollution-ships-apps. Accessed 12 May 2022.

Gray, N., McDonagh, S., O'Shea, R., Smyth, B., & Murphy, J. D. (2021). Decarbonising Ships, Planes and Trucks: An Analysis of Suitable Low-Carbon Fuels for the Maritime, Aviation and Haulage Sectors. *Advances in Applied Energy, 1*, 100008.

Hume, D., & Ramsey, T. (2022). Annual Report: An Overview of Ocean Energy Activities in 2021 (United States). Ocean Energy Systems, 198–205.

IMO. (2015). Third Greenhouse Gas Study 2014. Available at: https://greenvoyage2050.imo.org/wp-content/uploads/2021/01/third-imo-ghg-study-2014-executive-summary-and-final-report.pdf. Accessed 8 May 2022.

IMO. (2018). Initial IMO Strategy on Reduction of GHG Emissions from Ships. *Resolution MEPC, 304*(72).

IMO. (2020). Fourth Greenhouse Gas Study 2020. Available at: www.cdn.imo.org/localresources/en/OurWork/Environment/Documents/Fourth%20IMO%20GHG%20Study%202020%20-%20Full%20report%20and%20annexes.pdf. Accessed 12 May 2022.

IMO. (2022). Energy Efficiency Measures. Available at: https://www.imo.org/en/OurWork/Environment/Pages/Technical-and-Operational-Measures.aspx. Accessed 13 May 2022.

Kongsberg. (2022). EEXI Compliance Through Power Limitation Solutions. Available at: www.kongsberg.com/maritime/campaign/eexi_cii/. Accessed 11 May 2022.

Kongsberg/Massterly. (2021). One Sea: Autonomous Shipping Has Clear Environmental Benefits. The Maritime Executive. Available at: https://maritime-executive.com/editorials/one-sea-autonomous-shipping-has-clear-environmental-benefits#:~:text=%E2%80%9CThis%20saves%20fuel%20and%20reduces,a%2030%20percent%20decrease%20in. Accessed 19 May 2022.

Meinig, C., Burger, E. F., Cohen, N., Cokelet, E. D., Cronin, M. F., Cross, J. N., & Zhang, C. (2019). Public–Private Partnerships to Advance Regional Ocean-Observing Capabilities: A Saildrone and NOAA-PMEL Case Study and Future Considerations to Expand to Global Scale Observing. *Frontiers in Marine Science, 6*, 448.

National Academies of Sciences, Engineering, and Medicine. (2020). *Leveraging Unmanned Systems for Coast Guard Missions*. The National Academies Press.

NOAA (National Oceanographic and Atmospheric Administration). (2021a). Blue Economy Strategic Plan for 2021–2025. NOAA Blue Economy Pillars: Marine Transportation, Seafood Production, Ocean Exploration, Coastal Resilience, Tourism & Recreation.

NOAA. (2021b). Ocean Facts. How long is the U.S. shoreline? Available at: https://oceanservice.noaa.gov/facts/shorelength.html. Accessed 2 June 2022.

NOAA. (2021c). Uncrewed Systems Strategic Plan 2021b–2025. Maximizing Value for Science-based Mission Support. Available at: https://sciencecouncil.noaa.gov/Portals/0/NOAA%20Uncrewed%20Systems%20Strategic%20Plan%201.19.2021b.pdf?ver=2021b-01-22-134232-833. Accessed 9 June 2022.

NOAA. (2021d). Artificial Intelligence Strategic Plan 2021c–2025. Analytics for Next-Generation Earth Science. Available at: https://sciencecouncil.noaa.gov/Portals/0/Artificial%20Intelligence%20Strategic%20Plan_Final%20Signed.pdf?ver=2021c-01-19-114254-380. Accessed 10 June 2022.

Palmejar, E., & Chubb, N. (2021). *The Learning Curve: The State of Artificial Intelligence in Maritime*. Thetius.

Poseidon Principles. (2022). Available at: https://poseidonprinciples.org/. Accessed 4 May 2022.

Reid, B. (2022). Arriving at Decarbonization Generating Methanol-to-Hydrogen on Vessel, On Demand. *Sea Technology, 63*(3), 22–25.

Rothblum, A. M., Wheal, D., Withington, S., Shappell, S. A., Wiegmann, D. A., Boehm, W., & Chaderjian, M. (2002). 2nd International Workshop on Human Factors in Offshore Operations (HFW2002), Human Factors in Incident Investigation and Analysis. *Coast Guard Research and Development Center Groton Ct, 11*, 32–34.

SailPlan. (2022). Sailplan Whitepaper. The Benefits of Tracking Emissions in Real-Time. Available at: https://www.sailplan.com/whitepaper. Accessed 16 May 2022.

Smith, A. (2022). Autonomous Perception Technologies Continuing Advancement Creates Competitive Advantage. *Sea Technology, 63*(3), 15–19, 16. Available at: https://lsc-pagepro.mydigitalpublication.com/publication/?i=741069. Accessed 29 May 2022.

Swain, C. C. (2018). Towards Greater Certainty for Unmanned Navigation, a Recommended United States Military Perspective on Application of the" Rules of the Road" to Unmanned Maritime Systems. *Geo. L. Tech. Rev., 3*, 119, 120–123. Available at: https://georgetownlawtechreview.org/wp-content/uploads/2019/01/3.1-Swain-pp-119-61.pdf. Accessed 27 May 2022.

The Commander's Handbook on the Law of Naval Operations. (2022). U.S. Navy NWP 1-14M/U.S. Marine Corps MCTP 11-10B / U.S. Coast Guard COMDTPUB P5800.7A.

Tran, T. A. (2017). A Research on the Energy Efficiency Operational Indicator EEOI Calculation Tool on M/V NSU JUSTICE of VINIC Transportation Company, Vietnam. *Journal of Ocean Engineering and Science, 2*(1), 55–60.

US Department of State. (2022). Green Shipping Corridors Framework Fact Sheet. Available at: www.state.gov/green-shipping-corridors-framework/. Accessed 1 June 2022.

USCG (US Coast Guard). (2022). CG-CVC Policy Letter 22–01. Guidelines of Human-Supervised Testing of Remote Controlled and Autonomous Systems on Vessels.

Wärtsilä Voyage. (2021). E-report. The future of Smart Autonomy is here. Available at: https://www.wartsila.com/docs/default-source/whitepapers/smart_autonomy_e-report_2021-final.pdf?sfvrsn=31024843_3. Accessed 7 June 2022.

PART V

Autonomous Passenger Transportation

CHAPTER 10

Autonomous Urban Passenger Ferries—A New Mobility Mode in Need of Appropriate Regulation

Øyvind Smogeli

1 Introduction

Around the globe, urban areas are growing. It is projected that 70% of the world's population will live in cities by 2050, an increase of 58% from today's 4.3 billion people to 6.8 billion (The World Bank, 2020). Humans tend to flock to the waterfront, and today 90% of urban areas are coastal (UN habitat, 2022). We also see a global trend where cities

This work has been supported by the industry collaboration project ZAWAS, financed by Innovation Norway, and the research project TRUSST, supported by the Research Council of Norway through grant 313,921. The author would like to extend his gratitude towards industry and research partners, as well as to the reviewer, that have all provided valuable input and guidance to this chapter.

Ø. Smogeli (✉)
Zeabuz AS, Trondheim, Norway
e-mail: oyvind.smogeli@zeabuz.com

© The Author(s), under exclusive license to Springer Nature Switzerland AG 2023

T. M. Johansson et al. (eds.), *Autonomous Vessels in Maritime Affairs*, Studies in National Governance and Emerging Technologies,
https://doi.org/10.1007/978-3-031-24740-8_10

increasingly convert old industrial areas by the waterfront to attractive residential and commercial areas. A consequence of this development is that the current city transport infrastructure is about to reach its breaking point: there is simply not enough capacity on the roads to meet the growing demand for personal mobility and transport logistics. This challenge is further increased by the introduction of zero-emission zones and public demand for more sustainable transport solutions, a much-needed development given that cities already account for more than 70% of global CO2 emissions (UN Environment Programme, 2022).

Today, our urban waterways are often perceived as blockers of transportation flow, crossed by bridges and tunnels that become bottlenecks for road-based mobility. However, there is a great and unrealized potential in these waterways as part of the solution for sustainable, livable cities. This trend shift can be seen, e.g., in the European Green Deal from 2019, which calls for a substantial part of the 75% of inland freight carried today by road to shift onto rail and inland waterways (European Commission, 2019). A recent report from the European Commission (EC) and the Central Commission for the Navigation of the Rhine (CCNR) identifies urban waterborne transport as a major market opportunity (European Commission, 2022).

While electrification is essential to achieve a future-proof environmental footprint, there is also a need to re-think how these transport solutions are designed and operated. An increasing number of initiatives and references point to varying levels of autonomy and small purpose-built vessels as the key to achieve desired system qualities such as high availability, redundancy, flexibility, and cost efficiency, see, e.g., Reddy et al. (2019) and Čorić and Nikšić (2022). The European Parliament report "Towards future-proof inland waterway transport in Europe" stresses the importance of autonomy for increased use of inland waterways (European Parliament, 2021).

Looking at these needs, trends, and initiatives, it appears inevitable that we will see the emergence of a new mobility segment based on electric, autonomous urban ferries. The market pull for sustainable urban mobility solutions is present, while the enabling technology is maturing rapidly.

Centre for Autonomous Marine Operations and Systems (AMOS), Dept. of Marine Technology, Norwegian University of Science and Technology, Trondheim, Norway

The missing piece in order to mature and scale this new segment is the availability of fit-for-purpose regulation.

Introduction of autonomy for urban mobility is a many-faceted topic, and not all are addressed here. Some important aspects not further discussed in this chapter are improvements in communication and navigation infrastructure needed to provide the necessary aids to navigation (AtoN) also for higher levels of automation, and the complex interactions between different transport modes needed to realize the full benefits of autonomous operation.

2 Urban, Autonomous Waterborne Mobility—An Emerging Segment

Over the past few years, an increasing number of commercial and research initiatives have explored and helped mature both concepts and technologies for the emerging urban waterborne mobility segment. It is beyond the scope of this chapter to provide a complete overview of these initiatives; for a comprehensive list of references see, e.g., Čorić and Nikšić (2022), Cheemakurthy et al. (2017), and Tarkowski and Puzdrakiewicz (2021). An additional source is the overview published by the CCNR Secretariat listing relevant national and international projects including the assessment of their specific level of automation (CCNR, 2022).

The key commonality of these initiatives is that they all attempt to provide novel mobility solutions by deploying vessels with varying degrees of automation on urban waterways. Cheemakurthy et al. (2017) proposed classifying the navigation routes of urban environments into three basic types (a)–(c), see also Čorić and Nikšić (2022).

a. Routes of type (a) are also called linear ferry systems, and refer to typical "water bus" routes where the vessel navigates along an urban waterway with several stops along the way.
b. Routes of type (b) refer to "shortcuts" across an urban waterway, typically with two or three stops with the main purpose of moving passengers efficiently across a water barrier. Travel times are typically short, departure frequencies high, and passenger comfort is not a main focus.

c. Routes of type (c) refer to longer routes that typically connect urban areas with the wider urban and suburban areas. Due to the longer travel time, the frequency of ship departures on these lines is lower, vessel speed is higher, and passenger comfort is increasingly important.

Based on research that was conducted in 23 cities with established waterborne mobility systems, type (a) routes accounted for 37%, type (b) routes 43%, and type (c) routes 20%. While the (a)–(c) categorization is useful to roughly distinguish between these three main types of service, there will be large differences between individual services within each category, and also services that do not fit directly in one category. To support the introduction of autonomy it is, therefore, necessary to establish a more comprehensive taxonomy to describe a given service including both characteristics of the operational design domain (ODD), the vessel operation, and availability of sound minimum risk conditions (MRCs). For details on the MRC concept see, e.g., Det Norske Veritas (DNV) (2021a). The main goal of this service taxonomy is to describe the key properties of a range of operations as they pertain to risk subject to varying levels of autonomy and manning. The taxonomy will be useful when discussing Levels of Automation in Sect. 4, and support argumentation towards the need for a differentiated regulatory approach.

A proposed set of parameters for the service taxonomy and their range can be found in Table 1. This parameter set is likely to be expanded and changed as new knowledge and new use cases emerge.

It is beyond the scope and space of this chapter to analyze a range of different services in terms of the above taxonomy or perform associated generic risk assessments. Rather, the author believes that is pertinent to analyze a particular service and determine its hazards and risk levels on a case-by-case basis. As experience grows, it will hopefully be possible to mature a more rigid framework with a clear set of regulations that makes the establishment of a new service both efficient and predictable.

Looking for example at route type (a) defined above, the size and capacity of the vessel could vary greatly depending on the service, as could parameters such as route complexity, traffic complexity, weather exposure as well as most of the others. As a consequence, the suitable Level of Autonomy, availability of remote support, and needed safety manning will vary greatly between different service concepts.

Table 1 Taxonomy of parameters to describe a specific urban mobility service

Parameter	*Explanation*	*Range indication*
Route type	a—linear ferry systems; b—shortcuts; c—longer routes; custom	a, b, c, custom description
Payload	Payload carried by the vessel; may also be a combination	Passengers, cargo, parcels, materials, waste, ...
PAX	Number of passengers. Strongly influenced by current regulations that set thresholds to requirements based on this parameter	None (cargo etc.), <5 pax, <12 pax, <35 pax, larger
Vessel size	Determined by vessel length as primary parameter. Strongly influenced by current regulations	<5 m, <15 m—depending on local regulations
Route duration	How long is the journey?	<3 min, <10 min, longer
Vessel speed	Regular operational speed	<5 knots, <10 knots, faster
Distance to closest quay	What is the maximum distance to quay in case of an emergency?	<100 m, <500 m, longer
Traffic complexity	Influenced by type of vessels, density of traffic, speed, etc	Low to High
Damage potential	The damage potential in case of an accident	Low to High, divided in terms of life, material, and the environment
Weather exposure	How much influence does the weather have on the operational risk?	Shielded to Exposed
Environment sensitivity	How vulnerable is the operating environment to the operation?	None, vulnerable sea floor, etc
Availability of emergency support	Operator provided or existing services, e.g., from local fire departments or port authorities	<2 min, <5 min, longer
MRCs	Availability of suitable MRCs to mitigate operational risk	Stay in position (on DP), return to dock, drop emergency anchor, drift freely, ...

(continued)

Table 1 (continued)

Parameter	*Explanation*	*Range indication*
Level of knowledge uncertainty	Key influencing factor on the risk assessment pertaining to potential consequences, operational complexity, or abilities of the system	Low to High

Source Author

3 Relevant Areas of Regulation/Governance

European nations are subject to various rules, laws, and regulations depending on the respective membership(s) and affiliation(s) of each particular state. The regulation of maritime or waterborne crafts and activities can come from several sources, including international agreements, EU-wide law, national legislation, and even local regulations. Examples of regulatory agencies at the international level include United Nations Economic Commission for Europe (UNECE), and the International Maritime Organization (IMO). At the regional level, governance in the European Union include the European Committee for Drawing up Standards in the Field of Inland Navigation (CESNI) promulgated by both the European Council and the Parliament of the European Union. At a local level relevant governing bodies include national maritime and coastal authorities. Also, other organizations play key roles in governance of maritime autonomy, including classification societies, and member organizations such as the International Association of Marine Aids to Navigation and Lighthouse Authorities (IALA), and the Central Commission for the Navigation of the Rhine (CCNR). It is worth noting that, in areas where national and international traffic is sailing in the same area, national laws must be compatible with international regulations to maintain safety.

In December 2020, the European Commission enacted the *Sustainable and Smart Mobility Strategy* that calls for the European transport system to develop mobility sources that are sustainable, smart (i.e., digitalized), and resilient. As a part of the effort, the European Parliament (2021) recently issued its "Report Towards Future-proof Inland Waterway Transport in Europe", which calls on member states and cities to develop waterborne public transport as part of their urban mobility planning, including digital mobility platform services. However, a review of European laws and regulations reveals that a void exists when it comes to passenger ferries, in general, and autonomous passenger ferries in particular.

As seen in earlier chapters there have been significant efforts to develop a regulatory framework on maritime autonomy over the past years. However, most of the work, such as the IMO regulatory scoping exercise (IMO, 2021) and classification guidelines (Bureau Veritas, 2017; DNV, 2021a), have had their focus fixated on the traditional shipping segments. For example, the Bureau Veritas Guidelines apply to larger ships, typically 500 gross tonnage (GT) or more and not below 20 meters (m). While many of the discussions and perspectives in the above references provide important insights, they are only partly relevant to the emerging segment discussed in this chapter. For urban passenger ferries, it is the national regulations that are of importance. These ferries could be subject to regulations that cover both inland waterways and seagoing vessels, of course depending on the classification of the waterway and national requirements. In Norway, for example, all passenger ferries are regulated by the Norwegian Maritime Authorities (NMA). In 2020 the NMA published a guideline which outlines the process required to obtain permission to operate an autonomous vessel (NMA, 2020a). This includes a gap analysis, definition of a Concept of Operations (CONOPS) and supporting procedures, hazard identification, risk assessment, and third-party verification. For areas where exceptions from current regulations are needed, the NMA requires that equivalent safety can be proven through the process defined in MSC.1/Circ.1445 (IMO, 2013). However, noting the emergence of entirely new segments as discussed in this chapter, the "equivalence principle" may be challenging to apply since: (1) there is no historic benchmark; and (2) parts of existing regulations may be entirely unfit for this new segment. It remains to be seen how many gaps towards existing legislation that will be identified for the first autonomous urban passenger ferries, and what will be deemed appropriate measures to prove equivalent safety.

In the European Union, the CCNR is in the process of developing a framework for the authorization of pilot projects which require temporary derogations from CCNR regulations (CCNR, 2021). In order to face the specific challenges posed by automated navigation, the CCNR has revived its Small Navigation Committee, originally established to tackle and coordinate innovative and cross-sectoral developments in Rhine navigation.

Another pertinent legislative document enacted by UNECE is the European Code for Inland Waterways (CEVNI). The 6th Edition was issued in December 2021 (CEVNI, 2021); however, this does not address highly automated or autonomous vessels—as with current IMO regulations the wording clearly assumes that all vessels will be manned.

4 Levels of Automation and Vessel Functions

When discussing various types of autonomous and unmanned operation, the so-called level of automation (LoA) is a key concept. The original LoA taxonomy was published as "The 10 Levels of Automation" by Sheridan and Verplanck (1978). Later various similar taxonomies have been published for different purposes. In recent years a number of LoA taxonomies aimed at specific autonomous operation have also been published. It should be noted that some references use the terms "Level of Autonomy", "Degree of Autonomy", or "Degree of Automation" instead of "Level of Automation", however the intention remains, to a great extent, the same. In the automotive industry, the standard taxonomy is published by the Society of Automotive Engineers (SAE, 2021), defining 5 levels of autonomous driving. Here, the key concept is a division of tasks and authorities between a human operator and the machine. Other taxonomies, like the one published by the National Research Council (2005) to support naval operations, also include various levels of remote operation as a second dimension. In a maritime context, and especially in the context of passenger transport, there are really three dimensions to account for in the LoA:

1. The level of autonomous operation;
2. The level of remote control capability; and
3. The level of (and capability/role of) onboard manning.

To further complicate this picture, a maritime operation may be divided into a subset of functions that all can have different levels of automation along these three dimensions. A typical functional division is proposed in Sect. 2.6 of DNV (2021a). This Guideline further categorizes the functions into two main groups, Navigational functions and Engineering functions, and argues that we should discern between the

LoA for these. For passenger ferries, we need to add a functional category for Passenger handling and safety. Finally, we argue that there needs to be a separate category for Supervisory control functions, which is typically where the strategic operational choices are made. An overview of these four functional groups and a generic, non-exhaustive list of example functions within the groups is shown in Fig. 1. Such a functional overview must necessarily be adapted to a particular vessel and operation. In Sect. 6 we will propose functional groups for our case study of urban shortcuts.

Finally, in many maritime operations, the level of automation along these dimensions and functions could vary throughout different phases of the journey. Correspondingly, the distribution of tasks and responsibilities between different agents that are active in the operation (humans and machines) could vary based on the prevailing phase and associated risk picture.

There have been numerous attempts at defining taxonomies for maritime autonomy. Some of the more prominent ones from recent years are the preliminary taxonomy defined in the IMO regulatory scoping exercise (IMO, 2021) that attempts to blend all three dimensions into four distinct levels, the 5-level taxonomy defined by NMA (2020a), the two-dimensional setup defined by EMSA (2020) dividing between level of autonomous operation and level of qualified operators onboard, and the taxonomy defined by Bureau Veritas (2017) focusing only on the level of autonomy, but more clearly distinguishing between actions and authority. There is also ongoing work on an ISO standard. For

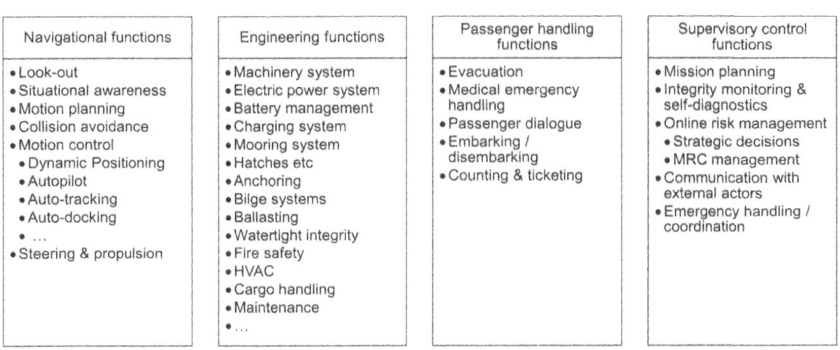

Fig. 1 Generic functional groups for autonomous vessel operation (*Source* Author)

inland waterways, the CCNR has adopted the first international LoA definitions for inland navigation (CCNR, 2021). The CCNR levels of automation go from "0"—no automation, to "5"—full automation, and is apparently much inspired by the taxonomy published by SAE (2021). The CCNR taxonomy also distinguishes clearly between who is in command (authority), who is monitoring and responding to the operational environment (action), and who is responsible for fallback of dynamic navigation tasks.

For the case of urban passenger ferries, which is a rather new segment with its own special characteristics and needs—we argue that none of the taxonomies proposed thus far have the sufficient nuances needed in order to accelerate development towards higher levels of automation. There are several reasons for this:

1. They will be operating close to shore at all times;
2. Velocities and damage potential will mostly be low;
3. Emergency response will usually be close by;
4. Some of them will be very small and carry few passengers;
5. Traffic complexity will often be limited (but may also be high);
6. Many of them will operate in mobility networks with a number of vessels in a small area; and
7. New and innovative approaches to monitoring, control, and operation are available.

In Sect. 6 we will suggest a suitable taxonomy for our case study of urban shortcut ferries.

5 Trustworthiness and Assurance

To successfully deploy urban passenger ferries as a new mobility mode it is paramount to prove its trustworthiness towards an extensive set of stakeholders: passengers, the general public, marine traffic, regulators, insurance companies, municipalities, and transport system operators and owners.

It is essential to take an interdisciplinary approach to building trust. This is clearly stated in a recent report from the European Parliament Think Tank (Schroten et al., 2020) which confirms the need for addressing not only the technical, but also the social, ethical, environmental, and regulatory aspects of smart mobility. The TRUSST research project (DNV, 2021b), therefore, innovates digital assurance concepts that integrate methods, tools, simulation-based testing, use of digital twins, full-scale testing, citizen engagement methodologies, and environmental impact assessment. The main deliverable from the project is a new framework for assurance of complex, digital assets that we are adopting in our development.

The new assurance framework is built on an iterative and goal-based assurance process. This process for assuring digital assets is split into two distinct stages. The first stage focuses on establishing an in-depth profile of the digital asset, its use, and all the relevant actors involved, while the second stage focuses on substantiating claims by building and assessing knowledge in an assurance case. Key features of the assurance framework are deemed as being: iterative, modular, and continuous. Iterative, since it is building trust over repeated cycles throughout the asset lifecycle. Modular, since it breaks the complex asset into smaller fragments or components, and then assures those and their inter-connections. And finally Continuous, since it builds and maintains assurance as assets are developed, deployed, and modified.

It is not sufficient to prove that the system is safe from a technical point of view; the perceived safety—which is what builds the societal trust—is just as important and might be just as hard to achieve. A mobility system design process should, therefore, focus on managing the delicate balance of technical safety, perceived safety, and system performance, see Fig. 2.

A central method of our trust-building process is the creation of an assurance case (see Fig. 3). This is a structured set of claims with associated evidence backing up those claims. A well-designed assurance case can be modular and dynamic, capture requirements from all kinds of stakeholders, and be used for continuous assurance through a system's lifecycle. It can incorporate both technical and non-technical claims and basically any kind of evidence, and it is flexible to adapt to new or changed requirements. A key feature of an assurance case is to trace every assurance activity back to its claims. This helps to ensure that assurance efforts are focused, transparent, replicable, and reusable.

The traceability of the reasoning and evidence used to substantiate claims also allows us to update the assurance case in light of potential changes to the mobility system, its use, and context. A modular assurance

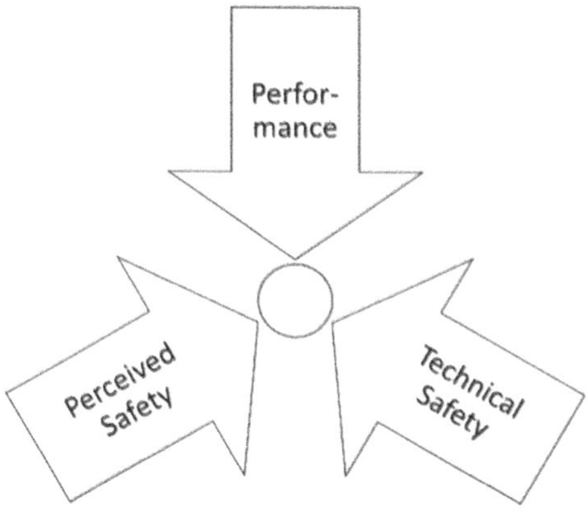

Fig. 2 A balanced approach to mobility system design (*Source* Author)

case also allows re-use of previous analyses for new system deployments, where only the changes between cases need to be addressed.

By addressing the needs of all stakeholders in one common assurance case, individual subsets of claims can be extracted and presented to any particular stakeholder in a consistent and uniform way. This enables consistency and transparency, which is inherently trust-building.

A special type of assurance case is a so-called safety case, which only focuses on the safety aspects of the asset subject to assurance. We increasingly see the adoption of these safety cases in the automotive industry, including the release of ANSI/UL 4600 Standard for Safety for the Evaluation of Autonomous Products (ANSI/UL 4600, 2022).

An essential part of an assurance case is to perform a thorough hazard identification and risk assessment. This pertains both to new risks that emerge, primarily due to autonomous operation and reduced manning, and to traditional maritime risks that are still applicable in an urban waterway setting. Risk assessment of autonomous vehicles in general and autonomous marine vessels in particular is an extensive subject which is beyond this chapter to address. That being said, it is important to realize that traditional methods for hazard identification often will fall short due to their reliance on past experience, as well as failing to address the new systemic risks arising from the interaction of the autonomy, humans, and the operating environment.

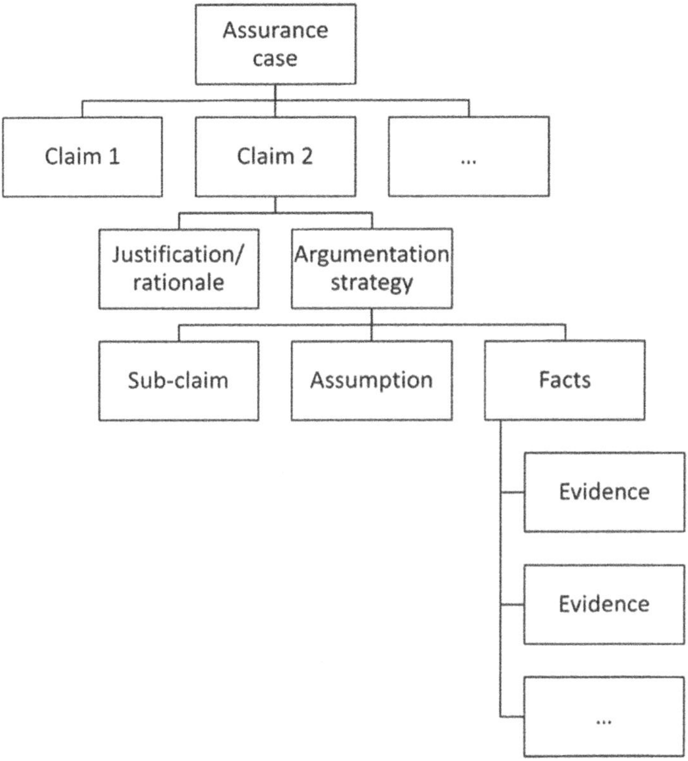

Fig. 3 Structure of an Assurance Case, adopted from IEEE/ISO/IEC 15,026-1 (2019) (*Source* Author)

6 Case Study: Urban Shortcuts with Small, Electric Passenger Ferries

To illustrate the challenges appearing in the intersection of current regulations and business needs we will, as an example, discuss a simple urban shortcut service in more detail. This new segment emerges as a response to the societal needs introduced as background in Sect. 1, with denser cities requiring new, sustainable transport infrastructure. We believe that small, electric, autonomous passenger ferries in network operation will be a key part of this solution, providing cities and citizens with a democratic, compelling and efficient mobility solution, available around the clock and easily adaptable to changing societal needs. Autonomous, crewless operation will be key to make this segment financially scalable and provide ubiquitous availability. Referring to the service taxonomy defined in Table 1, this new segment is described in Table 2.

In its simplest form, the urban shortcut closely resembles the operation of a traditional small cable ferry. The major difference is that the autonomous ferry follows a "virtual cable" instead of a physical one, and in doing so remains untethered towards land. The operation as it pertains to passenger safety and navigation, however, remains largely the same. However, the analogy with existing cable ferry operation is only partly

Table 2 Description of an urban shortcut based on the proposed service taxonomy in Table 1

Parameter	*Urban shortcut*
Route type	b—shortcut
Payload	Passengers, cargo bikes
PAX	Up to 12 (based on current EU legislation)
Vessel size	Less than 15 meters
Route duration	Less than 10 minutes
Vessel speed	Up to 7 knots
Distance to closest quay	Less than 500 meters
Traffic complexity	Sparse traffic, mainly leisure boats, kayaks etc
Damage potential	Low. A potential impact between the ferry and other objects will likely not result in major loss potential. Low speed and electric propulsion ensure limited material and environmental loss potential. Similarly, impact with a small object such as a kayak will likely worst-case result in the kayak capsizing
Weather exposure	Calm waters, limited wind exposure, small environmental loads
Environment sensitivity	Site specific
Availability of emergency support	Onshore safety operator present at quay-side with the ferry within visual contact range and with a motorboat readily available for assistance if needed
MRCs	Primary MRC: Stay on DP; secondary MRC: Anchor drop
Level of knowledge uncertainty	Medium. The service is new with very limited experience per se, but it can be analyzed in in terms of knowledge inferred from other operations

Source Author

helpful to the discussion in this section, since a review of European legislation for cable ferries turned out to be surprisingly difficult—the author did not come across available regulation or standards to aid their safe building and operation, let alone clearly established definitions.

The apparent lack of appropriate regulation does not only pertain to the operational mode, but also to the vessel size and carrying capacity. For example, various regulatory definitions of "passenger vessel" explicitly note that it is a "vessel" equipped or constructed with the purpose of carrying more than 12 passengers, see, e.g., CCNR (2016), CESNI (2021), European Parliament (2016). The length of the craft itself is not taken into consideration in this definition, only its carrying capacity for would-be passengers.

The most recent edition of the European Code for Inland Waterways (CEVNI, 2021) seems to be cognizant of this gap in regulations by revising the definition of "vessel" by including "small craft" and "ferry-boats". A "ferry-boat" is loosely defined as any vessel providing a transport service across a waterway that is classed as a ferry-boat by the competent authorities, and includes vessels that do not move independently. This latter definition, hence, also includes cable ferries. A "small craft" is defined as a vessel with a hull of less than 20 meters in length, except craft authorized to carry more than 12 passengers and ferry-boats. Hence, both of these categories may apply to different urban shortcut use cases, depending on the route type and carrying capacity. It is important to note no technical requirements for vessels in the categories "ferry-boat" and "small craft" have been provided.

In Norway this regulatory gap has been addressed by passing legislation that specifically addresses requirements for vessels that aim to carry 12 passengers or less (NMA, 2020b). However, this regulation only applies to manned vessels. Hence, the question on how to regulate a small, autonomous, "virtual cable ferry" remains largely unanswered, and will need to be addressed through the guidance on autonomous and remote operation discussed in Sect. 3.

As discussed in Sect. 4, having a suitable definition of the applicable LoA and vessel functions to which they pertain is a key starting point for establishing fit-for-purpose regulation. It was also argued that none of the established LoA taxonomies are fit-for-purpose in relation to urban passenger ferries. In the following, we will suggest such a taxonomy and functional breakdown for this segment, to serve as a starting point for future regulatory development.

Figure 4 shows an overview of functional groups for the case study, based on the generic overview in Fig. 1. The functional groups have been further sub-divided into eight groups with descriptive names for convenience in the further analysis. It should be noted that the presented sub-division is merely a simplification, and would need to be re-assessed considering a real case.

For the urban shortcut case, we have identified a possible taxonomy consisting of five distinct LoA:

0—Manual operation This is the baseline with all operational functions handled by the onboard crew. There could be one or several operators handling the ferry and passengers manually—no autonomy or remote control involved.

1—Automatic operation A safety operator manually controls the ferry velocity along a predefined path, which includes the departure, transit, and docking sequences. This could also be viewed as a combined "auto-track" and "auto-dock" function. Movement along the track and the maneuvering sequences are handled by the motion control system, while situational awareness and decisions are made by the safety operator. The safety operator is responsible for all operations, including passenger service and safety.

2—Onboard supervised autonomy The autonomy system manages navigation of the vessel and gives input to motion control, meaning

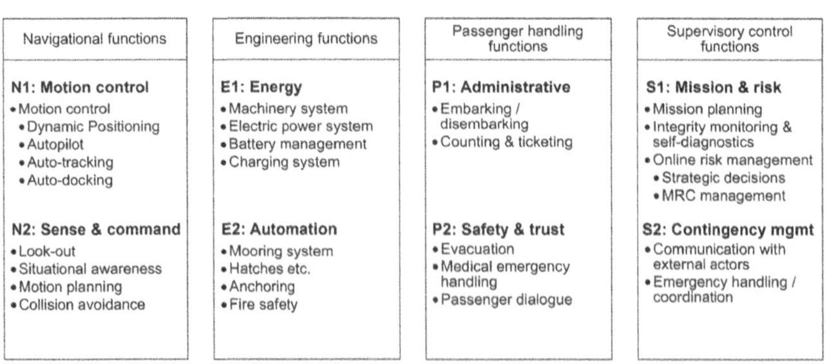

Fig. 4 Functional groups for an urban shortcut passenger ferry, further divided into eight subgroups (*Source* Author)

that the full quay-to-quay operation is performed autonomously. The operation and vessel are continuously monitored by an onboard safety operator, who can take manual control at any time. The safety operator is responsible for all operations, including passenger service and safety. As long as the operator has the necessary certifications, there should normally be no regulatory difference from level 1.

3—Onshore supervised autonomy In this mode of operation, the safety supervisor is moved onshore, but in immediate vicinity of the operation with visual overview and with a boat nearby for on-demand assistance to the ferries. The vessel will monitor itself and the passengers, and ask for assistance when needed. The safety operator will have capabilities for remote monitoring and control, two-way communication with passengers, and contact with additional local emergency response. One operator may be responsible for a network of ferries operating in the same area.

4—Full autonomy with remote support The highest LoA is full autonomy, where the vessels are self-sufficient for all regular operations. The vessel will monitor itself and the passengers, and ask for assistance when needed. The operators are located at a remote support center where they monitor a fleet of mobility systems similar to an air traffic control center. They can interact with and control the vessel on-demand and communicate with passengers. An emergency will be handled by local emergency response.

For LoA 2 and 3 we foresee the need for a remote support center, providing technical and operational assistance to the onboard or onshore supervisor. Note that we deliberately use the term "Remote Support" and not "Remote Control" as is in commonly parlance, since the primary role of the remote support center staff will be monitoring, diagnostics, and coordination. The operational concepts for LoA 2, 3, and 4 are illustrated in Fig. 5.

Having defined a set of suitable LoA for the urban shortcut segment and identified the applicable functional groups in Fig. 4, it remains to show how the responsibility for each functional group is distributed between the relevant agents:

1. The autonomy system;
2. The onboard supervisor;

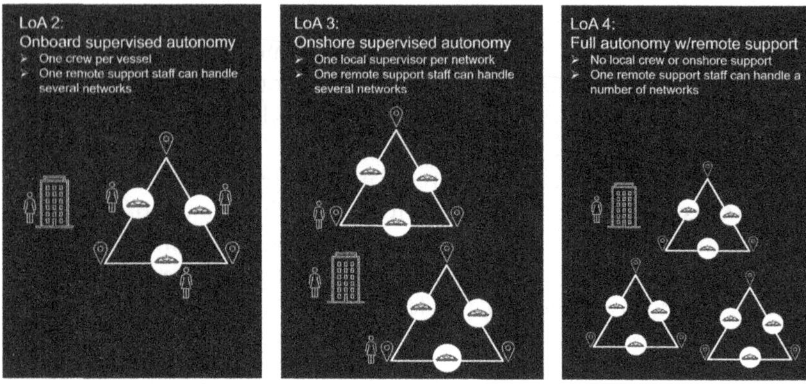

Fig. 5 Operational concepts for the urban shortcut at LoA 2, 3, and 4 (*Source* Author)

3. The onshore supervisor; and
4. The remote support center.

Notably, higher LoA functions will increasingly be handled by the autonomy system, with the human operators increasingly distanced from the operational decisions and actions. For each LoA, the operational functions are distributed with respect to:

- Action: Who initiates and performs the operational function?
- Authority: Who is responsible for the function?

Note that both action and authority may be shared between several agents. For example, a local safety supervisor and a remote support center could both have the ability and authority to initiate the transition to an MRC. In case both the autonomy system and a human have authority with respect to a given function, the human decision would normally prevail. Furthermore, it is essential that an agent with a given authority also has the necessary capabilities to fulfill its role. In general, this balance between authority and capability is a prerequisite for any well-working agent in an autonomous system. The LoA proposal for the urban shortcut segment is shown in Table 3.

Table 3 Division of action and authority between agents for different Levels of Autonomy. For Levels 2 and 3, the remote support center role is optional and depends on the capabilities and capacity of the local supervisors

Level of Automation (LoA)	*Functional group*	*Autonomy system*	*Onboard safety supervisor*	*Onshore safety supervisor*	*Remote support centre(on-demand)*
Level 0: Manual operation	All		Action Authority		
Level 1:	Navigation 1:	Action	Action Authority		
Automatic	Motion control	Action	Action Authority		
operation	Navigation 2:	Action	Action Authority		
	Sense and	Action	Action Authority		
	command		Authority		
	Engineering 1:		Authority		
	Energy		Authority		
	Engineering 2:		Authority		
	Automation				
	Passengers 1:				
	Administrative				
	Passengers 2:				
	Safety and trust				
	Supervisory 1:				
	Mission and risk				
	Supervisory 2:				
	Contingency				
	mgmt				

(continued)

Table 3 (continued)

Level of Automation (LoA)	*Functional group*	*Autonomy system*	*Onboard safety supervisor*		*Onshore safety supervisor*	*Remote support centre(on-demand)*	
Level 2: Onboard Supervised Autonomy	Navigation 1: Motion control	Action	Action	Authority		(Action)	(Authority)
	Navigation 2: Sense and command	Action	Action	Authority		(Action)	(Authority)
	Engineering 1: Energy	Action	Action	Authority		(Action)	(Authority)
	Engineering 2: Automation	Action		Authority			
	Passengers 1: Administrative	Action		Authority			
	Passengers 2: Safety and trust	Action		Authority			
	Supervisory 1: Mission and risk			Authority			
	Supervisory 2: Contingency mgmt			Authority			

Level of Automation (LoA)	*Functional group*	*Autonomy system*		*Onboard safety supervisor*		*Onshore safety supervisor*		*Remote support centre(on-demand)*	
Level 3: Onshore Supervised Autonomy	Navigation 1: Motion control Navigation 2: Sense and command Engineering 1: Energy Engineering 2: Automation Passengers 1: Administrative Passengers 2: Safety and trust Supervisory 1: Mission and risk Supervisory 2: Contingency mgmt	Action Action Action Action Action Action Action	Authority Authority Authority Authority Authority Authority			Action Action Action	Authority Authority Authority	(Action) (Action) (Action)	(Authority) (Authority) (Authority)

(continued)

Table 3 (continued)

Level of Automation (LoA)	*Functional group*	*Autonomy system*		*Onboard safety supervisor*	*Onshore safety supervisor*	*Remote support centre(on-demand)*	
Level 4: Full Autonomy with remote support	Navigation 1: Motion control Navigation 2: Sense and command Engineering 1: Energy Engineering 2: Automation Passengers 1: Administrative Passengers 2: Safety and trust Supervisory 1: Mission and risk Supervisory 2: Contingency mgmt	Action Action Action Action Action Action Action	Authority Authority Authority Authority Authority Authority			Action Action Action	Authority Authority Authority

Source Author

There are many possible nuances between these LoAs coupled with a more fine-grained distribution of operational functions. Especially between LoAs 2 and 3: there will probably be a gradual transition where authority for some time is shared among the autonomy system, the onboard safety supervisor, and the onshore safety supervisor. It should also be noted that the remote support center has an on-demand role, with actions and authorities that duplicate those of other agents for all LoAs except level 4.

7 Conclusions

Both European and international private and governmental entities have identified the need to transition to cleaner, smarter, and eventually unmanned forms of transportation on inland waterways. However, despite recent regulatory developments both on the international, regional, and national level, there is still no readily available governance for autonomous and unmanned operation. Projects with this ambition will, therefore, need to carve out the necessary measures to close any gaps through equivalent safety principles in close cooperation with regulators.

Looking at the case study for urban shortcuts as discussed in Sect. 6, we believe this new segment can provide a compelling starting point for autonomous, unmanned passenger transport through the concept of onshore supervised autonomy. These ferries will typically be small and could fit within the current regulatory void for vessels carrying 12 passengers or less. They will be operating close to the shore at all times, with emergency response remaining in close proximity. The availability of a safety supervisor on shore with a readily available boat for intervention will solve many of the communication and cognitive challenges associated with a fully remote support center, and will serve as a stepping stone towards the latter.

Finally, it should be emphasized that for autonomous urban passenger ferries to be deployed successfully into society and fit seamlessly into people's everyday lives, there is a strong need for proving their trustworthiness. This will require a fit-for-purpose assurance process focusing on the needs of an extended set of stakeholders and the construction of a systematic assurance case, providing evidence both for technical safety, perceived safety, societal trustworthiness, and sustainability.

References

ANSI/UL 4600. (2022). Evaluation of Autonomous Products, 2nd edition.

Bureau Veritas. (2017). Guidelines for Autonomous Shipping. Guidance Note NI 641 DT R00 E.

CCNR. (2016). Regulations for Rhine Navigation Personnel (RPN), Art. 1.01 (2) "passenger vessel". Available at: www.ccr-zkr.org/files/documents/reglementSTF/stfl_072016_en.pdf. Accessed 4 April 2022.

CCNR. (2021). Press Release, Strasbourg. Available at https://www.ccrzkr.org/files/documents/cpresse/cp20211117en.pdf. Accessed 3 March 2022.

CCNR. (2022). Listing of Pilot and Research Projects in the Field of Automation in Inland Navigation. Available at: https://automation.ccr-zkr.org/. Accessed 18 May 2022.

CESNI. (2021). European Standard laying down Technical Requirements for Inland Navigation vessels (ES-TRIN), Edition 2021/1, Art. 1.01 (6). Available at: https://www.cesni.eu/wp-content/uploads/2020/10/ES_TRIN_2021_en.pdf. Accessed 16 April 2022.

CEVNI. (2021). European Code for Inland Waterways 6th Ed., Art. 1.01 I(4). Report ECE/TRANS/SC.3/115/Rev.6. Available at: https://unece.org/sites/default/files/2021-12/2109540_E_pdf_web%2BCorr1.pdf. Accessed 20 May 2022.

Cheemakurthy, H., Tanko, M., & Garme, K. (2017). Urban Waterborne Public Transport Systems: An Overview of Existing Operations in World Cities. Report TRITA-AVE 2017:92. Royal Institute of Technology, Stockholm Sweden.

Čorić, M., & Nikšić, M. (2022). Possibilities of Using Autonomous Green Vessels for Passenger Transport in Urban Environments. In M. Petrović, L. Novačko, D. Božić, T. Rožić (Eds.), *The Science and Development of Transport—ZIRP 2021*. Springer, Cham. https://doi.org/10.1007/978-3-030-97528-9_7

DNV. (2021a). Autonomous and Remotely Operated Ships. Class Guideline DNV-CG-0264.

DNV. (2021b). Autonomous Urban Mobility: Taking Digital Assurance to the Next Level. Available at: https://www.dnv.com/feature/autonomous-urban-mobility.html. Accessed 6 April 2022.

EMSA. (2020). Study of the Risks and Regulatory Issues of Specific Cases of MASS (SAFEMASS)—Part 2. Available at: http://www.emsa.europa.eu/mass/. Accessed 7 May 2022.

European Commission. (2019). The European Green Deal. Communication. Document 52019DC0640. Available at: https://eur-lex.europa.eu/legal-content/EN/TXT/?uri=COM:2019:640:FIN. Accessed 12 May 2022.

European Commission. (2022). Thematic report: An assessment of new market opportunities for inland waterway transport. Available at: https://inland-navigation-market.org/wp-content/uploads/2022/03/Thematic-report_20212022_EN_BD.pdf. Accessed 6 May 2022.

European Parliament. (2016). Directive (EU) 2016/1629 of the European Parliament and of the Council of 14 September 2016 Laying Down Technical Requirements for inland waterway vessels, Art. 3 (f). Available at: https://eur-lex.europa.eu/legal-content/EN/TXT/?uri=CELEX%3A32016L1629. Accessed 19 March 2022.

European Parliament. (2021). Towards Future-proof Inland Waterway Transport in Europe. Report. A9–231/2021. Available at: https://www.europarl.europa.eu/doceo/document/A-9-2021-0231_EN.pdf. Accessed 19 May 2022.

IEEE/ISO/IEC 15026–1. (2019). Systems and Software Engineering—Systems and Software Assurance—Part 2: Assurance Case.

IMO. (2013). Guidelines for the Approval of Alternatives and Equivalents as Provided for in Various IMO Instruments. MSC.1/Circ.1455.

IMO. (2021). Outcome of the Regulatory Scoping Exercise for the use of Maritime Autonomous Surface Ships (MASS). MSC.1/Circ.1638.

National Research Council. (2005). *Autonomous Vehicles in Support of Naval Operations*. The National Academies Press.

NMA. (2020a). Guidelines for the construction or installation of automated functionality, with the intention of being able to perform unmanned or partially unmanned operation. Circular letter RSV 12-2020a.

NMA. (2020b). New Regulations on vessels of less than 24 metres carrying 12 passengers or less. Circular letter RSR 01-2020b.

Reddy, N. P., et al. (2019). Zero-Emission Autonomous Ferries for Urban Water Transport: Cheaper, Cleaner Alternative to Bridges and Manned Vessels. *IEEE Electrification Magazine, 7*(4), 32–45.

SAE. (2021). Taxonomy and Definitions for Terms Related to Driving Automation Systems for On-Road Motor Vehicles. Society of Automotive Engineers. J3016_202104.

Schroten, A. et al. (2020). Research for TRAN Committee – The Impact of Emerging Technologies on the Transport System. European Parliament, Policy Department for Structural and Cohesion Policies, Brussels. Available at https://bit.ly/32hJzpH. Accessed 20 June 2022.

Sheridan, T. B., & Verplanck, W. L. (1978). Human and Computer Control of Undersea Teleoperators. Technical Report. Man–Machine Systems Lab, Dept. of Mechanical Engineering, MIT. Cambridge, MA.

Tarkowski, M., & Puzdrakiewicz, K. (2021). Connectivity Benefits of Small Zero-Emission Autonomous Ferries in Urban Mobility—Case of the Coastal City of Gdańsk (Poland). *Sustainability, 13*(23), 13183.

The World Bank. (2020). Urban Development Website, Last Updated Apr 20, 2020. https://www.worldbank.org/en/topic/urbandevelopment/overview#1. Accessed 26 May 2022.

UN Environment Programme. (2022). Cities and Climate Change. Available at: https://www.unep.org/explore-topics/resource-efficiency/what-we-do/cities/cities-and-climate-change. Accessed 7 June 2022.

UN Habitat. (2022). Climate Change. Available at: https://unhabitat.org/topic/climate-change. Accessed 7 June 2022.

CHAPTER 11

New Design Solutions and Procedures for Ensuring Meaningful Human Control and Interaction with Autonomy: Automated Ferries in Profile

Christoph A. Thieme, Marilia A. Ramos, Even A. Holte, Stig O. Johnsen, Thor Myklebust, and Øyvind Smogeli

1 Introduction

For the operation of ships with a certain degree of autonomy, the International Maritime Organization (IMO, 2013) and state authorities, such as the Norwegian Maritime Authority (NMA), require a gap analysis to

C. A. Thieme (✉)
SINTEF Digital, Software Engineering, Safety and Security, Trondheim, Norway
e-mail: Christoph.thieme@sintef.no

M. A. Ramos
The B. John Garrick Institute for the Risk Sciences, University of California, Los Angeles (UCLA), Los Angeles, CA, USA
e-mail: marilia.ramos@ucla.edu

© The Author(s) 2023

T. M. Johansson et al. (eds.), *Autonomous Vessels in Maritime Affairs*, Studies in National Governance and Emerging Technologies,
https://doi.org/10.1007/978-3-031-24740-8_11

identify disparities between the proposed design solution and the applicable regulations (IMO, 2013; NMA, 2020). Gap analysis is used to describe how the design and operational solution address particular regulatory requirements. For automated passenger ferries, two key aspects need to be addressed: (1) the distribution of tasks between the automated functions and the operators, and (2) the safe execution of tasks through meaningful information exchange and clear procedures. Since automated passenger ferries are a recent phenomenon, there is little guidance for efficient completion of these processes.

The classification society Det Norske Veritas (DNV) (2021) provides a framework for implementing novel technologies to achieve automated, autonomous, or remotely controlled ships. The framework is risk-based and aim to assist users to get approval for new design concepts. For this purpose, the document describes functional and technical guidance where possible (Holte et al., 2021) analyzed the safety requirements for automated passenger vessels by evaluating the current legislation. Based on their evaluation, they assign functions either to automated control systems, on board operators, or human remote supervision located in a remote supervision center (RSC). This is described for several scenarios, such as evacuation, collision, stranding, water ingress, fire on board, and man overboard. The term Remote Control Center is often used in the context of autonomous ships (IMO, 2021), since the ferry concept is normally supervised RSC was deliberately chosen to differentiate from a remotely controlled ferry.

E. A. Holte
SINTEF Ocean, Energy and Transport, Trondheim, Norway
e-mail: even.holte@sintef.no

S. O. Johnsen · T. Myklebust
SINTEF Digital, Software Engineering, Safety and Security, Trondheim, Norway
e-mail: Stig.O.Johnsen@sintef.no

T. Myklebust
e-mail: Thor.Myklebust@sintef.no

Ø. Smogeli (✉)
Zeabuz AS, Trondheim, Norway
e-mail: oyvind.smogeli@zeabuz.com

The human element is an important aspect of an automated passenger ferry concept, both onboard the ferry and in the RSC. The operators need to have sufficient situational awareness, however technical failures or sabotage may lead to loss of situational awareness and thus increase the risk related to operating the ferry (Thieme et al., 2019). To achieve a high level of situational awareness, information needs to be tailored to the users' needs, avoiding unnecessary or distracting information (Endsley et al., 2021).

This chapter describes the process of gap analysis of automated passenger ferries and their closure through new operational procedures and meaningful information exchange between remote operators, passengers, and the automated functions. For this purpose, a task analysis is conducted using concurrent task analysis (CoTA), building on the principles of safety critical task analysis (SCTA). Finally, the chapter points out shortcomings in the existing regulations regarding the operation of automated passenger ferries and their land-based infrastructure. The use-case is taken from the AutoSafe project, where the main objective is to develop safety solutions for automated and autonomous passenger ferries. The work presented focuses on the operational phase and emergency procedures relating to accidental events of an autonomous ferry. Events related to terror, sabotage, and vandalism are not explicitly covered. The details of the use-case are given in the respective section later in this chapter.

2 Relevant Rules and Regulations

For ships and ferries operating in domestic waters mainly national rules apply. These cover design, construction, equipment, and operational arrangements. Two particular regulations are frequently referred to and relevant for navigation, International Regulations for Preventing Collisions at Sea, 1972 (COLREGs, 1972) and the International Convention for the Safety of Life at Sea, 1974 (SOLAS, 1974). Especially, SOLAS is often referred to regarding safety equipment and demonstration of safety compliance.

FSA-Formal Safety Assessment (IMO, 2018)) is the safety assessment process to be used for decision-making regarding maritime regulations. The FSA emphasizes using risk assessment as a tool to determine the benefit of measures to improve passenger safety. Ship operators can also use the process to demonstrate the safety of their implemented safety system in case this is required. MSC.1/Circ.1455. (IMO, 2013) provides guidance on demonstrating equivalent safety of a proposed solution that deviates from the prescribed safety measures of novel concepts.

The NMA, in its circular letter RSV 12-2020, picks up on IMO's MSC.1/Circ.1455 and adopts it for the requirements and guidance for the building or installation of automated functionalities on ships to achieve partly or fully uncrewed ship operation. One of several requirements stated in the circular RSV 12-2020, is a gap analysis of the proposed ship system concerning the rules, identifying where the design deviates from these rules (Norwegian Maritime Authority, 2020). For each deviation and novel solution introduced in the ship system, a risk assessment is necessary to demonstrate equivalent safety. Following IMO's requirements, the relevant authorities need to be involved from the early system design phase. Relevant documents need to be presented, such as the concept of operations (CONOPS), safety concept, hazard assessment of the ship system, and risk analysis. For areas that deviate from the current rules, e.g., procedures and technical solutions, a third-party verification is required. The documentation of deviations is similar to the requirements outlined in the IMO rules, MSC.1/Circ.1455 (IMO, 2013).

In an analysis of regulations applicable to autonomous passenger ferry operations in Norway, five were found to be particularly relevant (Holte et al., 2021). They are used as basis for the gap analysis presented herein. These regulations relate to the involvement of human operators for safe operation of passenger ships, and ultimately which tasks that need to be overtaken by automated functionalities. The considered regulations for this chapter are:

1. Safety in passenger spaces (Reg. 2021-12-17-3666);
2. Manning of Norwegian ships (Reg. 2009-06-18-666);
3. Watchkeeping on passenger ships and cargo ships (Reg. 1999-04-27-537);
4. Concerning operating arrangements on Norwegian ships (Reg. 1992-09-15-704); and
5. Life-saving appliances on ships (Reg. 2014-07-01-1019).

The regulation on *Safety in Passenger spaces* (Norwegian Maritime Authority, 2021) sets requirements to design-related safety measures on passenger vessels. For ships under the length of 15 m, simplified rules apply regarding equipment and ship design. With respect to operation, §14 and §15 are highly relevant for the automated passenger ferries since they pertain to steering position in passenger spaces (e.g., uninterrupted lookout) and the non-obstructive stowage of passengers' luggage, respectively. Additional requirements are made for the operation and maintenance of the passenger vessel.

The regulations on the *Manning of Norwegian ships* (Norwegian Maritime Authority, 2009) apply to all ships transporting passengers. It summarizes requirements to on board crew and minimum level of safety crew. The minimum crew level is determined based on safety assessment, risk analysis, and an evacuation analysis, among others. The regulation is highly relevant for the current chapter since some functions and roles are transferred to automated systems (or supported by automation).

The regulation on *Watchkeeping on passenger ships and cargo ships* (Norwegian Maritime Authority, 1999) prescribes arrangements and principles for watchkeeping for passenger vessels over 50 tons or operating in areas defined as Great coasting or larger. In addition, requirements are provided for certification of crew, voyage planning, watchkeeping and engineering watchkeeping. These tasks will be carried out by the automated ferry and to a lesser degree by human crew.

The regulations *Concerning operating arrangements on Norwegian ships* (Norwegian Maritime Authority, 1992) applies to all Norwegian passenger ships, and provides requirements for operational aids and watch arrangements in the engine room. Functional tests are required for automated functions and systems. If an engine room is (periodically) uncrewed, this needs to be approved by the NMA.

The regulations on *Life-saving appliances on ships* (Norwegian Maritime Authority, 2014) is based on the SOLAS requirements, whereas reduced requirements apply to ships solely used in national operation (SOLAS, 1974). Among others, the regulation specifies requirements for number of life-vests, marine evacuation equipment, alarm systems, and other appliances on board based on passenger capacity.

3 Method

A four-step process is applied to identify operational procedures and requirements to information:

1. Gap analysis—Identification of gaps that need procedures for human–operator interaction;
2. Development of the relevant scenario;
3. Concurrent Task Analysis focusing on safety critical tasks;
4. Development of operational procedures with decision criteria and information needs.

3.1 Gap Analysis

The gap analysis identifies the areas where the planned solution deviates from the applicable international and domestic rules laid. The relevant rules need to be mapped out beforehand. The identification of applicable rules depends highly on different parameters, such as the ship's length, the number of passengers, trade area the ship will operate in, length of journey, cruising speed, and tonnage (Holte et al., 2021). For the gap analysis the existing information on the ferry and its planned operation is reviewed, i.e., CONOPS, safety concept, design drawings, etc. For each applicable regulation (i.e., the five key regulations identified), each paragraph is assessed for its relevance (some may not apply due to design or other factors mentioned previously). If a paragraph applies, the CONOPS and design documentation are used to evaluate if the requirements in the paragraph are implemented or not. If not, it is noted how this requirement will be addressed: (a) through modifying design and operation to implement it, (b) through an alternative design/operation, (c) through compensating measures, i.e., increasing robustness, (d) through applying for dispensation of the requirement. Additionally, the relevant person/party is noted for both the design phase and the operation phase where necessary. To support such an analysis, a spreadsheet-based tool is being developed by the AutoSafe project for autonomous ships planning to operate in Norway.

3.2 Development of Scenarios

In this step, the relevant scenarios for which procedures are needed have to be described. This process is supported by available documentation, such as hazard analysis, CONOPS, safety concept, etc. The resulting scenarios should be documented in an event sequence diagram or operational flowchart.

3.3 Concurrent Task Analysis

The required procedures and tasks are developed with the Concurrent Task Analysis (CoTA) framework (Ramos et al., 2020a, 2020b), addressing safety critical tasks (Smith & Roels, 2020). The CoTA builds on task analysis (TA) theory (Shepherd, 2001) and introduces new elements: specific stop rules, parallel tasks, interface tasks, and trigger tasks. The system is analyzed as a whole and concurrently, for all agents, and stop rules to provide guidance when decomposing smaller tasks into sub-tasks, so-called redescription.

TA is "the collective noun used in the field of ergonomics, which includes human computer interaction, for all the methods of collecting, classifying, and interpreting data on the performance of systems that include at least one person as a system component" (Annett & Stanton, 2000). The tasks must be carried out in a certain order to achieve the higher-level goals, described by plans. In many complex systems, some tasks should be performed constantly, while others are carried out only on demand. This includes, for example, but is not limited to, information collection (by a system), transferring data between different agents, or monitoring systems while executing other tasks. In CoTA, these are represented by parallel tasks.

In addition to parallel tasks, the CoTA introduces interface tasks to account for interactions between the different agents of a system. Interface tasks either depend on input from another agent's task or give output to another system agent's task.

The redescription of tasks into sub-tasks could technically go on infinitely. For obtaining comparable and reproducible results, the CoTA uses clear stop rules for the redescription. These stop rules are based on the Information, Decision, Action (IDA) model, originally developed for modeling Nuclear Power Plants operators (Smidts, Shen, & Mosleh, 1997). The CoTA extends IDA to modeling the technical aspects of the autonomous system as, similarly to humans, they collect and pre-process information (I-Phase), make decisions and assess a situation (D-Phase) and take necessary actions (A-Phase).

The guidelines for developing the CoTA from an operational flow chart can be summarized as follows:

- Definition of agents to be analyzed;

- Definition of Task 0: the main task to be accomplished by the system's agents. This may be to recover successfully from a disturbing initiating event or to perform normal operation;
- Definition of high-level tasks;
- Identification of parallel tasks;
- Re-description of tasks until stop rules are satisfied:
  - The sub-tasks are associated with only one of the IDA phases;
  - The interface tasks are explicitly identified: if the accomplishment of the task is dependent on another agent, or if the output of the task is an information or command to be sent to another agent, the task is re-described until this interaction can be clearly characterized;
  - The trigger tasks are explicitly identified: if the performance of a task is dependent on the outcome of a previous task, i.e., if the task should be performed only if an earlier task "triggers" it, the task is re-described until this interaction can be clearly characterized.

The CoTA can be visualized through graphical symbols These symbols are explained in Fig. 1. In addition, the plans for the CoTA are described in Fig. 2:

3.4 Developing Operational Procedures

Having analyzed the tasks in the operation, the procedures can be developed based on the necessary steps identified in the CoTA. A tabular form is suggested that records the steps in a parallel order for the agents. Additionally, through the CoTA exchanged information can be identified and should be recorded. This information has the purpose of developing decision criteria and build the foundation for identifying information requirement, such as necessary HMI.

4 Use-Case—Highly Automated Local Passenger Ferry

To demonstrate and exemplify the gap analysis process and procedure development, a use-case from the AutoSafe project is analyzed. The use-case ferry is planned to transport up to 25 passengers in the Norwegian city of Florø between the city center and an offshore supply base, which

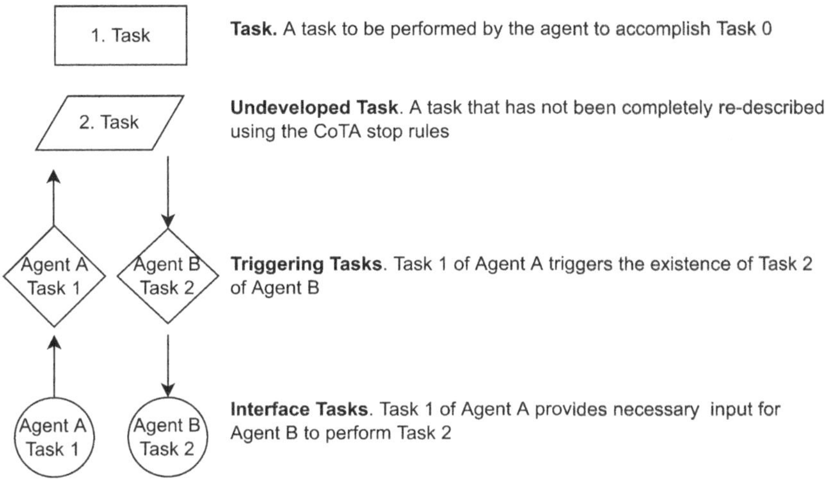

Fig. 1 Symbols used in the CoTA with explanation (*Source* Authors)

is a few kilometers outside the city center. Sailing distance and time is 2.6 km and 15–20 minutes when cruising at 5–6 knots. The battery powered ferry has a planned length of 11 m and width of 4.5 m and charging points located at both quays.

The ferry is designed based on a "safety by design" philosophy. Through hull compartmentation and strategic use of floatation foam in the hull, the ferry will only have a small angle of inclination in conditions where ship stability is compromised. Other important safety design choices are redundant physically separated power and propulsion systems, and an emergency anchor drop.

The ferry is uncrewed during normal operation and supported by two people located on land. One safety supervisor and one permanent crew, both located in the RSC. An emergency button is available for passengers to call for assistance from the people in the RSC. The crew in the RSC will be able to communicate with the passengers. Additionally, both the safety supervisor and the permanent crew in the RSC can communicate with local emergency services if necessary. The permanent crew in the RSC has a better possibility to communicate and coordinate necessary efforts, but also share needed information in a timely manner compared to the safety supervisor assisting the passengers on the ferry.

Type	Notation	Definition
Sequential tasks	1 -> 2	*Perform task 1 then 2*
Non-Sequential tasks	1.2 and 1.3	*Perform task 1.2 and 1.3 at any order*
Exclusive tasks	1.2 or 1.3	*Perform task 1.2 or 1.3*
Parallel tasks	[1 -> 2] // 3	*Perform task 1, then 2. Perform 3 at all times*
Triggered tasks	[1 -> 2 --- 3]	*Perform task 1, then 2. Perform 3 only if triggered by 2*
Example tasks 1	1 -> 2 -> [(2) --- 3 or (2) --- 4]	*Perform task 1, then 2. Perform 3 only if triggered by 2, or 4 only if triggered by 2*
Example tasks 2	1 -> 2 -> [(OA 2) --- 3]	*Perform task 1, then 2. Perform 3 only if triggered by Other Agent task 2*

Fig. 2 Explanation of the plan notation used in the CoTA (*Source* Authors)

In case of an emergency, the safety supervisor can reach the ferry with a dedicated boat within minutes. In previous work on the ferry concept, fire, water ingress due to a collision or grounding, evacuation, and passenger medical emergencies were deemed as the main hazards (Johnsen et al., n.d.). When on board the ferry, the safety supervisor has available a simple user interface with basic functions to control the ferry, whereas the main task will be to take care of passengers and their needs. Upon arrival, the safety supervisor can thus assess the situation of the ferry visually, interact with external parties, maneuver the ferry, or tow it to the shore. While the RSC permanent crew has a full overview over the ferry state and can give additional information and assistance to the safety supervisor. The autonomous system, safety supervisor, and RSC are carrying out the tasks as summarized in Table 1.

The ferry will only be operated in weather conditions and sea states that are compatible with its design and the capabilities of the safety supervisor's boat. Four minimum risk conditions (MRC) are identified, ensuring passenger safety in case of an accident However, there may be conditions where none of the described MRC's can be attained, and these issues are treated later in this section (e.g., in case of a fire onboard or if the ferry is sinking):

1. Stay at quay—the ferry remains at the current quay, i.e., in adverse weather conditions, problems with the ferry control system, low battery level, etc.;
2. Head to closest quay—the ferry is returning/continuing to the closest quay. This will be the primary choice for the safety supervisor in case of a safety critical situation, such as failure on the propulsion system, a medical emergency, partial loss of power, etc.;
3. Stop and stay in position—using its dynamic positioning system, the ferry remains at the current position by station keeping. This may be necessary, for example, if the ferry leaves its designated operational

Table 1 Functions and tasks to be carried out by the autonomous system, safety supervisor, and RSC (*Source* Authors).

Autonomous system	*Safety supervisor*	*Remote Supervision Center crew*
Transit and docking	Monitor system and respond to calls or alarms	On-demand passenger and safety supervisor support
Lookout and navigation	Assess and confirm ferry state visually in emergency situations, request emergency support	Call and coordinate supporting emergency assistance, if necessary
Safe dis-/embarkment, passenger counting, and passenger monitoring and counting	Manual control and operational decision making, in required situations	Fleet management
	Passenger handling in emergency situations	Condition monitoring and maintenance

area or a malfunction in the autonomous navigation system, etc. The ferry is then maneuvered or towed to a nearby quay for passengers to safely disembark. An evacuation of the ferry through a Marine Evacuation System (MES) is not included in the design; and
4. Drop of the emergency anchoring system—a physical anchor is released, preventing the ferry from drifting. The anchor is released automatically if the ferry loses power or if the safety supervisor deems it necessary. The ferry can be towed to the closest shore, where the passengers can leave the ferry.

When viewed in isolation, this use-case with basically two crew needed to support one ferry operation is not highly attractive from a commercial point of view. However, the solution with a safety supervisor and a permanent RSC crew enables the future support of several ferries. The RSC is designed to support a series of ferry networks at different locations. However, the role of an RSC or Emergency Response Center must be defined with agreed response times.

5 Results

5.1 Gap Analysis

Table 2 summarizes the findings of the gap analysis. Regulation (3) on Watchkeeping on passenger ships and cargo ships was assessed not to apply and hence not covered by the analysis. For regulation (1) on Safety in passenger spaces, most of the requirements are met through ship design measures. However, the paragraph on steering position in the passenger area is quite relevant for the procedures. As stated, the safety supervisor will have a portable joystick control interface available when on board, enabling freedom to choose the most beneficial steering position with good visibility. Facilitated by an appropriate HMI-solution, the safety supervisor is provided with critical and correct information of the technical status of the ferry and its position.

Regarding (2), the regulations on Manning of Norwegian ships, all functions will be carried out through either the autonomous ferry system (watchkeeping, navigation, counting of passengers), the safety supervisor (emergency handling, emergency exercises, watchkeeping, medical help to passengers), or the RSC crew (supporting the safety supervisor). Even though the safety supervisor is located on land, the functions of timely

Table 2 Regulation addressed and assessed for the case study (*Source* Authors)

#	*Regulation*	*Applicable*	*Identified Gaps*
1	Safety in passenger spaces (Reg. 2021-12-17-3666)	Yes—§3–§13 do not apply	All requirements can be met. One particular points should be paid attention to: • §14 Steering position in passenger spaces—the operator is required to have a good view from the dedicated steering position. In this case, the local safety supervisor will have the possibility to control the ferry through a remote-control joystick. This will enable a good view from the ferry and the boat the safety supervisor will arrive with, due to the flexible position possibilities

(continued)

Table 2 (continued)

#	*Regulation*	*Applicable*	*Identified Gaps*
2	Manning of Norwegian ships (Reg. 2009-06-18-666)	Yes	All required functions are covered by the safety supervisor, the autonomous system, and the RSC. Particular attention needs to be paid though to the procedures for fulfilling the requirements: • Watchkeeping during voyage and while at the quay, including rescue and emergency preparedness exercises • Emergency situations that may arise, such as, fire, collision, man over bord, or evacuation • First aid, injury treatment and medical assistance Through the proximity of the safety supervisor these functions can be executed in an adequate time frame if required. The boat of the safety supervisor needs to be chosen, such that it can fulfill the required tasks, such as towing

#	*Regulation*	*Applicable*	*Identified Gaps*
3	Watchkeeping on passenger ships and cargo ships (Reg. 1999-04-27-537)	No—tonnage below requirement and not operating in small coastal trade area	Not relevant
4	Concerning operating arrangements on Norwegian ships (Reg. 1992-09-15-704)	Yes	§7 Normally the engine-room shall be continuously manned. The ferry concept does not have an engine room, only a compartment for the batteries. These are directly connected to the thruster units. Even if two thrusters fail the ferry will be able to maintain position and propulsion power, due to the redundant arrangement. The condition of batteries and thrusters is remotely monitored through the autonomous sensors and the RSC. The regulation is assuming a fossil fuel-based machinery system, which is more maintenance intensive than electrically driven propulsion systems. Thus, it is argued that the thrusters ("engines") do not need to be accessed during normal operation §11 Automatic pilot systems sets out requirements for the control of the vessel using an automated system using the ship's steering gear. The requirements set out are highly relevant for the design of the autonomous system and should be considered. Regarding the safe operation the requirements for alarm and warning signals are implemented such that the safety supervisor will be notified of a failure and the ferry goes to MRC 2, MRC 3, or MRC 4, depending on the failure §12 Internal communications only applies in point (2) e), that all communication systems should be connected to an emergency power supply source

(continued)

Table 2 (continued)

#	*Regulation*	*Applicable*	*Identified Gaps*
5	Life-saving appliances on ships (Reg. 2014-07-01-1019)	Yes	§3 General emergency alarm system will be integrated with the public address system §7 Life-saving appliances for ships on domestic voyages are only partly fulfilled and are planned to be addressed through the safety supervisor and the RSC: • A marine Evacuation System (MES) will not be installed and will be handled by the safety supervisor • SOS flares—are available to the safety operator but not deemed necessary, since the ferry will be operated close to share. and being equipped with several tracking technologies • VHF- radio communication will be available for the safety supervisor. Additionally, the RSC will handle VHF communication with other ships nearby and maintain direct communication channels with the ferry §8 A survival craft will not be installed nor an alternative, see also the comment on MES in §7 §9 A rescue boat will not be on board the ferry; the safety supervisor will be responsible for these tasks. A risk assessment is required to demonstrate an acceptable safety level §10 Evacuation Systems (MES) will not be installed, see comments on §7, §8, and §9

assistance can be ensured through the proximity of the ferry operation to shore and the use of a sufficiently powerful boat that can intervene or assist rapidly. However, further analysis and documentation is needed to validate that this operational profile is indeed as safe as a conventional crewing scheme.

Concerning the regulation (4) on Operating arrangements on Norwegian Ships, two main gaps are identified. Firstly, the electrical propulsion system will not require an engine room in the traditional sense, meaning that the rules regarding the crewing of the engine room cannot apply. Secondly, the ferry control system can be considered as automated system using the ship's steering gear. Therefore, the control system needs to be able to switch over to manual control within the allowable limits, under any conditions. Systems need to be in place ensuring remote control is possible from the RSC under foreseeable conditions, and that the ferry control system has an equivalent safety level as conventional systems.

The most significant gaps regarding existing rules were identified for regulation (5) on Life-saving appliances on ships. The ferry concept will deviate from the regulations regarding §8, §9, §10, and partly §7. These are all concerned with rescue boats, rafts, or MES. Due to the safety by design approach ensuring stability and flotation in damaged conditions, the ferry is not planned to have any of these on board. The safety supervisor will be taken over by the safety supervisor who will either control or tow the ferry to shore. Since this is the most critical gap, this chapter will further assess the procedure of reacting to a critical situation, before deciding on and implementing the best emergency procedure. Additional gaps in §7 concern SOS flares and VHF radio, as these will be with the safety supervisor and hence not on board the ferry.

Two gaps are related to the rigidity of the regulations. Firstly, the regulations require that an engine room must be crewed with the possibility of exception. In the described ferry concept, the propulsion unit is located in the actual thruster unit, making the engine room obsolete. Moreover, modern electrically driven propulsion systems do not fit in the current regulations and exemptions from the rules must be applied for.

Secondly, the operational environment and concept of the ferry do not fit well with existing rules on life-saving appliances. For small passenger ferries, as in this case, the required life-saving appliances will lead to an unnecessary complex design solution, which could be solved differently given the operational environment (sheltered water, close to shore). As such, regulations should be amended to also apply to these types of cases, without impacting passenger safety.

5.2 Developing Operational Procedure

The remainder of this chapter describes the development of the operational procedure for handling emergency situations where the ferry has entered MRC 3 or MRC 4. These situations generally occur if a failure in the autonomy system occurs, rendering further autonomous operation unsafe, if a fire is detected on board, or if there is water ingress due to, e.g., a grounding or collision. In these scenarios, the ferry must alarm the personnel at the RSC and go to either MRC 3 or MRC 4. The safety supervisor, supported by the RSC, will then promptly navigate to the ferry, estimate the damage, and take action accordingly. The scenario is summarized in Fig. 3, as a flowchart of actions. Evacuation by means of life rafts or similar was deemed one of the major hazards, and thus the emergency procedure and ship design should ensure that passengers always have the possibility to safely evacuate to land.

The CoTAs for the autonomous ferry, the safety supervisor, and the RSC are shown in Figs. 4, 5, and 6, respectively. The tasks identified in Fig. 3 are presented in more detail, highlighting triggers and interactions. These dependencies and triggers are the points where the agents interact. The task redescription in the CoTA focuses on the safety critical tasks, meaning those related to assessing the condition of passengers, technical status of the ferry, and the immediate help of these. Please note that due to the space limitations, not all tasks are further detailed.

Table 3 shows the proposed procedure, with decision criteria and information requirements for the autonomous ferry and the RSC, including the safety supervisor. The decision criteria and required information were identified from the CoTA through the involvement of partners in the AutoSafe project. The information requirements need to be addressed in the ferry design, through the inclusion of necessary sensors, human–machine interfaces with the right information and algorithms that can infer the technical status of the ferry. Examples are a fire detection system that can determine the location and severity accurately, and sensor that can detect the position of damages to the hull and level of water ingress.

The ferry's role in the covered scenario is mainly to provide information and follow the commands of the safety supervisor. The safety supervisor's tasks are the physically most demanding: going to and entering the

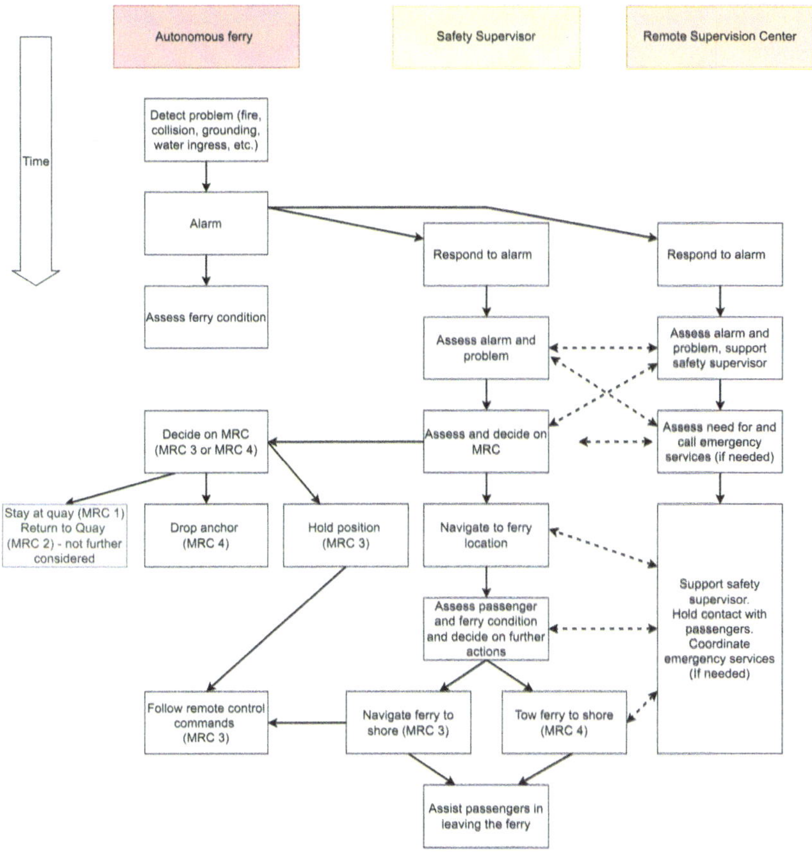

Fig. 3 Summary of the scenario being considered for developing operational procedures. Arrows represent flow of events, and Arrows with broken lines represent bi-directional information exchange. Abbreviations: MRC—Minimum Risk Condition (*Source* Authors)

ferry, assisting passengers, and navigating the ferry safely to shore. The safety supervisor is supported by the RSC through exchanging important information. In addition, the RSC communicates with the passengers, while the safety supervisor is busy, and coordinating emergency services, such as police, ambulances, or firefighters, if needed.

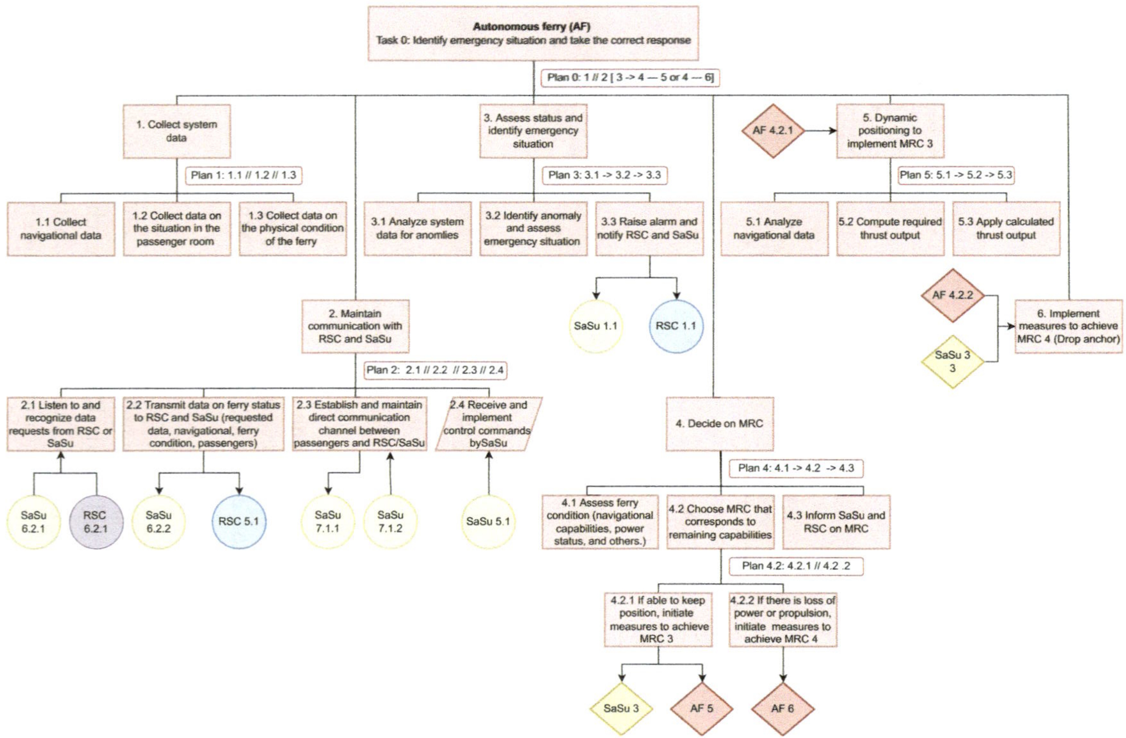

Fig. 4 Concurrent Task Analysis for the autonomous ferry, regarding an emergency on board the ferry. Abbreviations: AF—Autonomous ferry, SaSu—Safety supervisor, RSC—Remote Supervision Center (*Source* Authors)

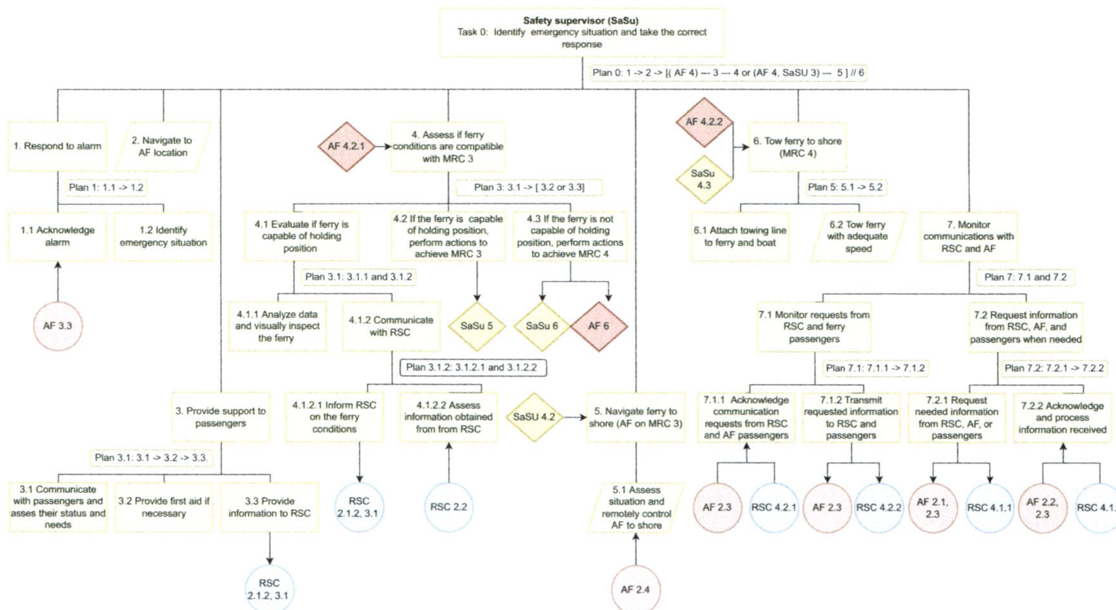

Fig. 5 Concurrent Task Analysis for the safety supervisor, regarding an emergency on board the ferry (*Source* Authors)

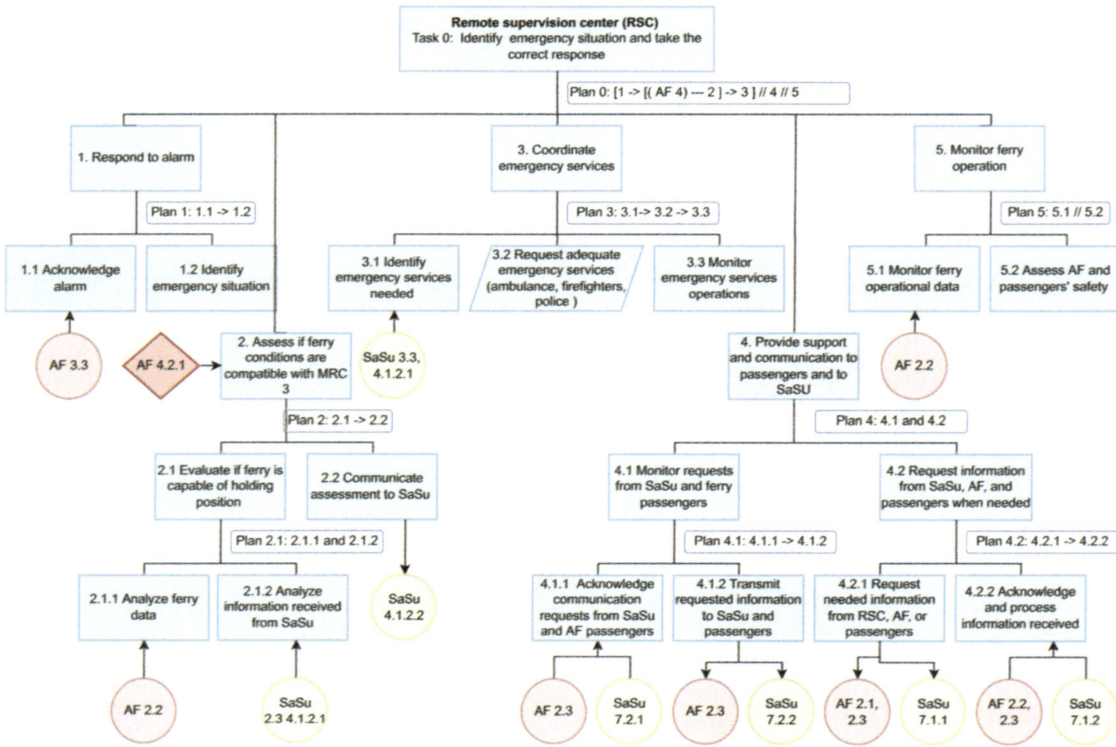

Fig. 6 Concurrent Task Analysis for the RSC, regarding an emergency on board the ferry (*Source* Authors)

Table 3 Developed operational procedure for the autonomous ferry, the safety supervisor, and the remote supervision center, including decision criteria and information needs

Step	*Autonomous ferry (AF)*	*Safety supervisor (SaSu)*	*Remote supervision Center (RSC)*	*Decision criteria Decision-maker indicated in brackets*	*Information needs Recipients indicated in brackets*
1	Detect problem				Navigational status and current capabilities (AF) Sensor information on collision, grounding, water ingress or fire Sensor information from the passenger room
2	Send Alarm Go to applicable MRC Start firefighting (if applicable)	Respond to alarm Assess ferry condition	Respond to alarm Assess ferry condition	Status of power supply and propulsion power (AF) Navigational and position holding capabilities (AF) Status of water ingress, damage, and fire (AF)	Damage type, severity, and location (all) Sensor information on collision, grounding, water ingress or fire (all) Sensor and camera information from the passenger room (all)

(continued)

Table 3 (continued)

Step	*Autonomous ferry (AF)*	*Safety supervisor (SaSu)*	*Remote supervision Center (RSC)*	*Decision criteria Decision-maker indicated in brackets*	*Information needs Recipients indicated in brackets*
3	Implement MRC Provide requested data	Navigate to AF location	Assess ferry condition and MRC applicability Communicate relevant information to SaSu Communicate with passengers Assess need for assistance from emergency services Call and coordinate emergency services if needed (ambulance, firefighters, and/or police)	Status of power supply and propulsion power (RSC) Navigational and position holding capabilities (RSC) Status of water ingress, damage, and fire (RSC)	Position of AF (SaSu, RSC) Damage type, severity, and location (all) Sensor information on water ingress or fire (all) Video and voice communication with passengers (RSC) Passenger injury status (RSC, SaSu)

Step	*Autonomous ferry (AF)*	*Safety supervisor (SaSu)*	*Remote supervision Center (RSC)*	*Decision criteria Decision-maker indicated in brackets*	*Information needs Recipients indicated in brackets*
4	Provide requested data	Assess AF condition and MRC applicability Communicate directly with passengers and provide help Assess need for help from emergency services and communicate need to RSC Communicate and coordinate with RSC	Monitor ferry status Communicate relevant information to SaSu Communicate with passengers Coordinate emergency services if needed	Extent of damage on AF through visual assessment (SaSu) Navigational and position holding capabilities (SaSu) Status of water ingress, damage, and fire (SaSu)	Damage type, severity, and position (all) Sensor information on water ingress or fire (all) Passenger injury status (RSC, SaSu) 2-way video and voice communication with passengers (RSC) Status of SaSu operation (RSC) Status of emergency services (RSC)
5	Provide requested data Follow SaSu control commands	Attach towing equipment to AF (only if AF in MRC 4) Navigate to shore with AF (remote control of AF or towing) Communicate and coordinate with RSC	Monitor ferry status Communicate with passengers Communicate relevant information to SaSu Coordinate emergency services if needed		Damage type, severity, and location (all) Sensor information on water ingress or fire (all) Passenger injury status (RSC, SaSu) 2-way video and voice communication with passengers (RSC) Status of SaSu operation (RSC) Status of emergency services (RSC)

(continued)

Table 3 (continued)

Step	*Autonomous ferry (AF)*	*Safety supervisor (SaSu)*	*Remote supervision Center (RSC)*	*Decision criteria Decision-maker indicated in brackets*	*Information needs Recipients indicated in brackets*
6		Assist passengers disembark AF Communicate and coordinate with RSC	Coordinate emergency services if needed Communicate relevant information to SaSu		

Source Authors

6 Discussions

Despite the Norwegian focus and domestic regulations in force, key elements of this chapter are assumed transferable to other countries. Firstly, the method is generic and risk-based, and can be applied to other operational environments and countries, with the corresponding relevant regulations. Additionally, the Norwegian regulations are based and founded on international regulations ratified by the IMO, such as, SOLAS (1974), COLREGs (1972), and principles of safe manning (IMO, 2011).

Since more than ten different regulations could apply to the case study, the analyzed regulations do not cover all aspects of design and ship operation. However, due to the focus of this chapter on the safety supervisor and crew in the RSC, the early maturity stage of the case study and the limitation of available space these regulations are not further discussed here. Most of the regulations not covered in this chapter refer to the design and design elements of the ferry, i.e., how certain facilities should be designed, which materials should be used, etc. Regarding regulation (3) on Watchkeeping on passenger ships and cargo ships (Norwegian Maritime Authority, 1999), which is not applicable to the case study, appendix 1 of the said regulation may give guidance for the implementation of automated functions (navigational and watchkeeping).

The CoTA does not cover all identified tasks, but only those deemed most important with respect to risk. A full analysis may reveal further information needs and associated requirements. It is necessary to address the identified information needs through design of the ferry, human–machine interfaces, and the RSC, which may require additional analysis.

7 Conclusions

This chapter presents an approach to develop procedures for autonomous systems with remote human supervision. The process is applied to the case of an uncrewed automated passenger ferry with shore-based safety supervisors and remote supervision centers. The approach is based on a gap analysis of the solution regarding regulatory requirements and a Concurrent Task Analysis of the tasks to be executed by the different agents. The operational procedure for an emergency that requires the safety supervisor to board the ferry are developed from the Concurrent Task Analysis. The approach highlights decision criteria and information needed for the different agents. The application to the use-case revealed several gaps that need to be addressed through design solutions and demonstrated to be closed by verification and validation of the concept. These gaps relate to the navigational tasks, passenger handling in emergencies, and life-saving appliances on board the ferry.

The work described in this chapter is the basis for further analysis concerning design requirements and risk. One approach that will be further investigated is the exploration of the Crisis and Intervention Operability (CRIOP) method for selected critical scenarios, which has been applied successfully to control rooms of autonomous maritime surface ships and in other industries.

Acknowledgements The input and feedback from the AutoSafe partners are highly appreciated. The work presented in this chapter was supported by the Norwegian Research Council through the projects Automated safety solutions for passenger ferries (Project No. 320798) and MAS—Meaningful Human Control in autonomy/digitalization of safety critical systems (Project No. 326676).

References

Annett, J., & Stanton, N. A. (2000). Research and Developments in Task Analysis. In Annett, J., & Stanton, N. A. (Eds.), *Task Analysis*. Taylor & Francis

DNV. (2021). Autonomous and Remotely Operated Ships (DNVGL-CG-0264).

Endsley, M. R., Barrett, S., Caldwell, E. K., Chiou, N. J., Cooke, M. L., Gonzalez Cummings, C., Lee, J. D., Nathan, McNeese, J., Miller, C., Roth, E., & Rouse, W. B. (2021). *Human-AI Teaming*. National Academies Press.

Holte, E. A., Wennersberg, L. A. L., & Pobitzer, A. (2021). *Smartere Transport Møre Og Romsdal—L4.3 Sikkerhetskrav Til et Autonomt*. Sjøverts Persontransportsystem.

COLREGs. (1972). Convention on International Regulations for Preventing Collisions at Sea, Oct. 20, 1972, 28 U.S.T. 3459, T.I.A.S. 8587.

SOLAS. (1974). International Convention for the Safety of Life at Sea, Nov. 1, 1974, 32 U.S.T. 47, T.I.A.S. 9700.

IMO. (2011). Resolution A.1047(27) Principles of Safe Manning, 1047(27), 14.

IMO. (2013). MSC.1/Circ.1455: Guidelines for the Approval of Alternatives and Equivalents as Provided for in Various Imo Instruments. MSC.1/Circ.1455 44(0).

IMO. (2018). MSC-MEPC.2/Circ.12/Rev.2. Revised Guidelines for FSA for Use in the IMO Rule-Making Process, 44(2).

IMO. (2021). MSC.1/Circ.1638 *Outcome of the Regulatory Scoping Exercise for the Use of Maritime Autonomous Surface Ships* (Mass), 44.

Johnsen, S. O., Thieme, C., Myklebust, T., Holte, E., Fjørtoft, K., & Rødseth, Ø. J. (2022). Hazards and Risks of Automated Passenger Ferry Operations in Norway. International Conference on Applied Human Factors and Ergonomics 2022.

Norwegian Maritime Authority. (1992). Regulation of 15 September 1992 No. 704 Concerning Operating Arrangements on Norwegian Ships.

Norwegian Maritime Authority. (1999). Watchkeeping on Passenger Ships and Cargo Ships. Vols. 1999–04–27. Haugesund, Norway.

Norwegian Maritime Authority. (2009). Manning of Norwegian Ships. Vols. 2009-06-18. Haugesund, Norway.

Norwegian Maritime Authority. (2014). Life-Saving Appliances on Ships. 2014-07-01.

Norwegian Maritime Authority. (2020). Rundskri V 12-2020. Føringer i Forbindelse Med Bygging Eller Installering Av Automatisert Funksjonalitet, Med Hensikt å Kunne Utføre Ubemannet Eller Delvis Ubemannet Drift.

Norwegian Maritime Authority. (2021). Regulations on Safety in Passenger Spaces.

Ramos, M. A., Thieme, C. A., Utne, I. B., & Mosleh, A. (2020a). Human-System Concurrent Task Analysis for Maritime Autonomous Surface Ship Operation Safety. *Reliability Engineering and System Safety, 195*. https://doi.org/10.1016/j.ress.2019.106697

Ramos, M. A., Thieme, C. A., & Yang, X. (2020b). Human-System Concurrent Task Analysis: An Application to Autonomous Remotely Operated Vehicle Operations, 978–981.

Shepherd, A. (2001). Diaper, D., & Stanton, N. A. (Eds.), *Hierarchical Task Analysis*. Taylor & Francis.

Smidts, C., Shen, S. H., and Mosleh, A. (1997). The IDA Cognitive Model for the Analysis of Nuclear Power Plant Operator Response under Accident Conditions. Part I: Problem Solving and Decision Making Model. *Reliability Engineering and System Safety*, *55*(1), 51–71. https://doi.org/10.1016/S0951-8320(96)00104-4

Smith, E., & Roles, R. (2020). *Guidance on Human Factors Safety Critical Task Analysis*.

Thieme, C. A., Guo, C., Utne, I. B., & Haugen, S. (2019). Preliminary Hazard Analysis of a Small Harbor Passenger Ferry-Results, Challenges and Further Work. *Journal of Physics: Conference Series, 1357*, 1.

Open Access This chapter is licensed under the terms of the Creative Commons Attribution 4.0 International License (http://creativecommons.org/licenses/by/4.0/), which permits use, sharing, adaptation, distribution and reproduction in any medium or format, as long as you give appropriate credit to the original author(s) and the source, provide a link to the Creative Commons license and indicate if changes were made.

The images or other third party material in this chapter are included in the chapter's Creative Commons license, unless indicated otherwise in a credit line to the material. If material is not included in the chapter's Creative Commons license and your intended use is not permitted by statutory regulation or exceeds the permitted use, you will need to obtain permission directly from the copyright holder.

PART VI

Liability & Insurance

CHAPTER 12

Autonomy, Autonomous Shipping and Coastal Authorities' Concerns

Matti Eronen

1 Introduction

Maritime transport is a part of the national logistics system, which is an integral part of society at large. Full automatization in one transport mode affects other transport modes. Development of the transport system, in turn, is an improvement that will have societal implications. Harbors are hubs for all transport modes and serve as meeting places for fairways, railroads and roads. Development of any one of these will influence the others. Enhanced digitalization is particularly focused on ports and their access routes. Realizing the full benefits of automatization would require digitalized unity of all transport modes.

Patently, "transport" is a cornerstone of European integration and is vital for fulfilling the free movement of individuals, services and goods. The main purpose of the European Union (EU) transport policy is to

M. Eronen (✉)
Finnish Transport Infrastructure Agency, Helsinki, Finland
e-mail: matti.eronen@ftia.fi

© The Author(s), under exclusive license to Springer Nature Switzerland AG 2023

T. M. Johansson et al. (eds.), *Autonomous Vessels in Maritime Affairs*, Studies in National Governance and Emerging Technologies, https://doi.org/10.1007/978-3-031-24740-8_12

keep the European economy running. This is reflected when observing how developing a modern infrastructure network makes transport fluid as well as making traveling faster and safer. A concrete example is the development of the European maritime single window (EMSW), which takes into account the needs of marine transport by combining and harmonizing the exchange of information and acting as a platform for value-added services. The European Commission has launched a legislative proposition for the regulation of artificial intelligence (AI) (KOM [2018] 206 final). It aims to make the EU an environment that is amenable to the development and application of internet of things (IOT) that will boost investment, make companies more competitive and improve the function of the internal market.

It is the duty of coastal States to safeguard and ensure the safety of navigation around the coastline in respective jurisdictions. When ships are sailing in challenging shallow waters and where traffic is heavy in merchant fairways, the traffic control and safeguarding systems have an important role in preventing collisions and environmental disasters. The primary task is to conduct the traffic in a navigationally and environmentally safe and efficient way (Bievre, 1985). This requires sufficient traffic control and safeguarding systems. In practice, this means proper vessel traffic services (VTS), effective pilotage systems and modern aids to navigation (AtoN); and how the above complement the ships' seaworthiness requirements (Abdulla, 2011). The more "roles and responsibilities" of coastal States are becoming crucial due to digitalization and increasing automated shipping—the more important these safeguards become. This will inevitably change the liability regime in cases of accidents and loss or damage at sea.

The sailing of remotely controlled and completely autonomous vessels in coastal waters imposes new requirements on the coastal States. Successful monitoring and assistance of the merchant fairways is based on proper situational awareness. Digitalization, and especially autonomous shipping, introduces new challenges for coastal States. This primarily corresponds to communication and accessibility between ships and authorities. Digitalization and new digital services are changing the business models, services and transportation chains. From the administration's viewpoint, there is a need to identify and anticipate the potential impacts and changes in logistics chains and the development needs and opportunities of these transport systems. As it is, intelligence-based traffic control is an evolving area. This is natural because the more automatic and remote-controlled the traffic is, the more important and significant the role of control systems are. However, the larger the digitalized system is, the more sensitive and vulnerable it is. This is related to the misuse of digital networks. A major new challenge is cybersecurity, which aims to ensure the reliability of the transport environment whereby enhancing cybersecurity is essential.

Increasing automation and the declining human factor pose a number of challenges for coastal States as the services provided to maritime transport in the coastal waters are affected. The development of information and communication technology has increasingly brought real-time connections to the outside world and various electronic information services supporting navigation to ships. In principle, the information provided to the ship is intended to support and help the navigator make the right decisions. As false or conflicting information has the potential to cause confusion or even distract and mislead the decision-maker, the accuracy and timeliness of information have become increasingly relevant.

2 Safety of Merchant Fairways

The task of "fairway maintenance" is to ensure that the maritime safety devices operate in accordance with the regulations and instructions and, subsequently, correspond to the information presented in the nautical chart data. It requires management of maritime warnings, baseline design data and management of disturbance data such as safety equipment failures, water traffic signal failures, site-related failures and water traffic disturbances. The above contribute to what is known as "safe navigation". Such systems are AtoN, VTS and pilotage services.

Especially intelligence-based traffic control is an evolving area because of the increased role of automatization. It is crucial to define the content of AtoN in the assessment of coastal States' liabilities. This is due to the fact that the "liability" clause in many international conventions exonerates the owners from liability when the main reason for a maritime casualty is a failure in the maintenance of navigational aids (e.g., Nairobi Convention Art 10).

It is important to re-emphasize on the importance of coastal States' roles and responsibilities in the context of digitalization and increased automated shipping. It is the administration's task to provide safe and functional infrastructure for traffic as well as ensure safe traffic routes and their maintenance. The administration's liability for accidents and damage at sea is to be reconsidered in the new situation arising from autonomous shipping. In the new situation, the concept of AtoN comes under review. This will inevitably lead to a re-examination of the concept of "maintenance of the fairways". However, due to the principles of good governance, there seems to be barriers to algorithmic-based decision-making in public administration (Suksi, 2018). The authorities must take into account the legal implications if there is a shipping accident caused by their traffic control systems (Hughes, 2009).

The navigational fairways and their safety are less regulated than ships' operational legal matters. Mostly, they are regulated by national legislation as the coastal areas are subject to a country's exclusive sovereignty. However, because of the nature of the international maritime business where ships sail into unknown waters, there has been a need to harmonize the rules concerning coastal fairways. This is the reason behind the adoption of Maritime Organization (IMO) legislation, International Convention for the Safety of Life at Sea 1974 (SOLAS) Chapter V Rule 12 and 13 (SOLAS, 1974). However, as the mandate of the International Maritime Organization (IMO) is to regulate ships, these questions have been left to coastal States themselves. In their own waters, they arrange such aids to navigation as the volume of traffic justifies and the degree of risk requires. However, during this arrangement, the states are bound to follow international recommendations and guidelines, such as SOLAS V:12 and 13. As these matters are left to be governed by national legislation, the role of International Organization for marine aids to navigation (IALA) is intrinsically important in harmonizing the navigational aid mechanisms such as AtoN and VTS.

Coastal States also have a similar role concerning VTS in SOLAS V:12. They develop the systems according to the guidelines developed by the IMO. This refers to IMO Resolution A.857 (20), "Guidelines on vessel traffic services".

The IALA has defined AtoN as a "device or system external to vessels that is designed and operated to enhance the safe and efficient navigation of vessels and/or vessel traffic". It has included VTS in AtoN in its "Navguide" (IALA Navguide, 2018). However, this, to date, remains unclear. The United Nations Convention on the Law of the Sea 1982 (UNCLOS) seems to refer to physical installations rather than a system referred to in AtoN in article 21: "[i]n respect of ... the protection of navigational aids and facilities ... or other facilities or installations", etc. SOLAS has separate regulations for VTS and AtoN (12 and 13) (UNCLOS, 1982). Additionally, in several national legislation, these are regulated separately. In the case of *MT José Marti*'s grounding, the Swedish Supreme Court communicated that the pilotage was not considered a part of AtoN (*M/T José Marti*'s case, 1987). There seems to be no case in law as to whether VTS would be included in the concept of AtoN.

Failure in AtoN has the same kind of consequences for liability on environmental damage as VTS. Alteration of VTS's role leads to a re-evaluation of its legal basis. Traditionally, it has been a general informative and assisting system for all ships sailing in fairways. However, the deeper the liaison between ship and authority, the closer the situation where the control system as VTS performs services for an individual; case-in-point: assisting a particular ship and its master in navigational decision-making processes. This has a remarkable impact on coastal States' traditional liability regimes. In several international conventions, it has been ruled that the ship is responsible for the damage caused by those that perform services for the ship. This is interpreted such that liability pre-supposes that the work is connected with the ship in question and its operations. As long as the assistance is generally maritime administrative in nature, it is not included as a part of the owner's responsibility (Wetterstein, 2004a). This means that in the case of vessel traffic service operator (VTSO) actually performing a service to a ship in its navigational decision-making process, the ship owners would carry liability pertaining to VTS's action. In such a situation, the liability would be transferred from the coastal State to the ship owner, and it also would have a consequence of VTS being subject to a limitation of liability.

This may also have a significant impact on liability arising from environmental damage. Coastal States would be held responsible for the oil pollution in the case of VTS contributing to the risk of pollution by an individual ship. Liability for compensation of environmental damage may have relevance in this case. Of interest in this respect is the *Commune de Mesquer* solution following the wreck of the oil tanker *MT Erika*. In the Criminal Court of First Instance following the accident, the Criminal Court's provision on liability and channeling in the Convention applied only to persons that work for the ship and participate directly in the ship's maritime activities (Jacobsson, 2014). The classification society was held liable for the oil spill disaster because it had a direct connection to the ship's condition (Wetterstein, 2004b). Based on the resolution, liability is incurred by those that contribute to an increased risk of pollution by failing to meet their obligations. This may have a great impact on coastal States as the cooperation between VTS and ship is expanding extensively with VTS likely to render increasing assistance to an individual vessel.

3 Situational Awareness is of Cardinal Importance

The primary objective of traffic control is to conduct the traffic through merchant fairways in a navigationally and environmentally safe and efficient way (Bievre, 1985). In order to perform this task, the controlling system must be aware of the movements of the vessels in real time. This is termed as situational awareness, which means always having good knowledge of the ship's surrounding environment. Shipside, situational awareness is a significant part of good seamanship.

The vessel tracking system is a collection of equipment that enable the tracking, identification and monitoring of a ship's position and any other detailed information in maneuvering and stabilizing the ship's route and course. VTS is based on vessel tracking, which is dependent on sensors such as automatic identification system (AIS). Radars are located around the coast and cover all merchant fairways. The system is similar to all transport modes, such as air and road traffic centers.

Ships communicate with VTS and other ships via very high frequency (VHF) radio or satellite-based communication systems. The AIS delivers on-time information about the ship, its position and its destination, which has not only made it possible to follow a ship but has also made situational awareness possible and significant. VTS uses all available information, such as various authorities' radar images and ships' AIS information to form the graphical situational picture and to present real-time navigational circumstances in merchant fairways in order to strengthen situational awareness.

However, the sensor network works both ways during the communication process between the ship and VTS. It is used to control vessel traffic by providing various services such as information services, traffic management services and navigational assistance services. It also provides information about other vessels in the VTS area as well as weather, ice conditions, water level, operation of pilots and icebreakers, condition and availability of fairways and safety equipment, possible hazards to the vessel and other factors affecting the safe operation of vessels.

The more "activity" and "control" exists human control, the more "autonomous" the "system" (Aawa White Paper, 2018). This concerns the control of ships navigating the merchant fairways, but it also sets requirements for the coastal States' controlling and safeguarding systems. VTS needs to be aware of ships' movements and plans for the purposes of situational awareness. This has introduced new technical challenges, as described in the following section.

4 Technical Challenges

The idea of automatization, as such, is considered to have started around the year 1720 when James Hargreaves invented the "Spinning Jenny" in the United Kingdom of Great Britain and Northern Ireland (UK). Since then, automatization has evolved but liability issues have remained more or less unaltered. The electrification of maritime transport, i.e., digitalization and IT, is seen as the next major technological leap.

Digitalization has been said to have a revolutionary impact on people's lives with IOT serving as a new element (Pöysti, 2018). Algorithmic transparency requires that different parties can trust the systems and make decisions that affect their safety and security (Viljanen, 2018). This is particularly important in the interaction between man and machine when dealing with AI. IT systems and data transmission technologies are evolving at an unexpected pace. While this creates new business opportunities for energy technology and service companies, it simultaneously exerts pressure on the practices and forms of action of major maritime players and parties. Ports' operation has also been affected by electrification, changing the port infrastructure and connecting them as integral parts of smart grids.

A major new challenge introduced by digitalization is the vulnerability and misuse of digital networks. Cybersecurity aims to ensure the reliability of both transport environment and marine environment.

Maritime transport is part of a nationwide transport system that is shaped by the needs of users, *inter alia*. Therefore, it is safe to assert that the development of the transport system means societal development. The biggest change in the transport system is related to intelligent transport, for which electrification creates good conditions. Intelligence-based traffic control in particular is an evolving area. It requires a new category of cooperation between public authorities and companies (Tapaninen, 2018). Digitalization and electronic data transmission will play an increasingly important role in future logistics solutions. Administrations play an important role in supporting the development and operating conditions of maritime actors, i.e., the maritime cluster. In traffic digitalization, information is utilized to control traffic. The use of information and communication technologies improves the flow and security of traffic. Transport telematics means targeting information where it is deemed required.

The development of remotely operated and autonomous vessels also means the development of communication between ships and services at shore. Remote piloting and VTS are expected to converge as functions (to some extent). In this case, the significant content of the navigation service is changing and its interface to pilotage is becoming obscure. For some time now, the arrival and departure notifications of vessel traffic have been communicated electronically to the vessel traffic notification system.

As long as the human element exists, certain areas will require concentration, such as communication protocol, shared situational awareness and standardized data sharing. International maritime standards are being changed to meet the new challenges posed by automation. The IMO has put the development of international standards for digitalization and unmanned ships on its agenda. As a first step, the organization has launched a study into how current maritime legislation is able to respond to the use of unmanned and fully autonomous vessels in merchant shipping. Following this background study, the actual legislative development projects will begin.

In cooperation with the IMO and IALA, a special electronic tool called e-Navigation is being developed to support the bridgework of ships. It refers to a harmonized system for the exchange and management of maritime information, which transmits all information relevant to the movement and control of a ship in digital form from ship to ship and between the ship and the land organization. This is expected to have an impact not only on the prevention of accidents at sea but also on future automated ship movement solutions.

The European Parliament has invested interest in AI, and to that end, published a response in 2018, which dealt specifically with liability issues. This examines the different forms of liability and the primacy of national liability law. It highlights the importance of the EU Product Liability Directive and sets out topics for further research, including the development of AI and IOT and their importance in terms of liability issues.

In this respect, the Commission has identified insurance as a possible solution. It suggested that consideration should be given to whether it would be necessary to impose an insurance obligation on autonomous systems. In this way, victims would receive compensation regardless of the debtor's ability to pay. Insurers would also have sufficient expertise and resources to pursue potential recourse actions against manufacturers of autonomous products. Similar views have also been expressed in scientific discussions, but it is clear that this does not solve the issue of liability itself.

The development of information and communication technology has brought increased real-time connections to the outside world, and various electronic navigation support services to ships. In principle, the information provided to the ship is intended to support and help the navigator to make the right decisions. However, as is observed in general, too much information, misunderstood information or conflicting information from different sources can cause confusion or even distract and mislead the decision-maker. The ship's bridge may also face serious challenges related to the general flood of information. The IMO has made efforts to tackle this problem by harmonizing the use of electronic navigation information by launching the so-called e-Navigation project. This project has been a success and the standardization of systems has increased maritime safety. Many of the items that need development are directly related to a ship's bridge equipment and information presentation. The list of matters requiring international standardization also includes the actual electronic information services provided to ships. In this context, standardization means agreeing on harmonized data content, data models and data transmission technologies for services. The standardized electronic services in the e-Navigation implementation plan prepared by the IMO are grouped into information service packages called Maritime Service Portfolios. It is the duty of the coastal State to monitor and participate in the development of international e-Navigation. This is vital in order to effectively offer standardized information services for vessels.

The harmonization of information services will ensure that ships throughout the world and at all stages of their voyage have access to the best possible navigational information in a harmonized, unambiguous and user-friendly format. The project has especially highlighted the importance of information accuracy. Relevant areas for development are electronic information services for ships, weather services and nautical chart services.

It is the duty of a coastal State to ensure that its traffic control system is capable of safeguarding the navigation in the merchant fairways. This requires capability and preparation on the part of administrations to interact with the traffic and to respond to traffic situations in coastal waters. This has a direct connection to liability, more specifically, system liability.

5 Coastal State's Legislative Challenges

As digitalization increases and ships shift toward autonomy-mode of operation, national laws and regulations must keep pace with changes. They must be able to react to the development of digital infrastructure. It is up to the administrations to go through and prepare their legislative systems so that there are no regulatory barriers that would hinder merchant ships arriving through fairways. Bottlenecks in this would have a negative effect on international trade and the smooth movement of goods.

Automation itself does not have a big impact on the basic causality-based liability regime. The customary rules of indemnity concern the automotive systems that assist humans in controlling and steering the ships. As long as the traffic is not fully automatic and ships are still under control, the normal rules of liability seem to apply when an accident occurs (van Hooydonk, 2015). The more significant the autonomy, the more important is the question on the level of human presence (Ringbom, 2019).

However, the usage of automatization on remote-controlled ships, and especially fully autonomous ships, will certainly alter the traditional liability regime in some respects (CMI, 2018). This is with regard to human machine interface (HMI). The human element comes into question when an individual person has caused damage by his/her action or negligence by failing to act to prevent the accident. In the context of this chapter, this means that a marine accident would be caused by the action or negligence of a VTSO or pilot or by a wrongful act in the maintenance of AtoN. The level of autonomy here is significant whereby the main question is the level of human attention. As noted earlier: the more the activity and control is out of human hands, the more the system itself is autonomous. As far as safety is concerned, this has been demonstrated as a positive factor as it diminishes the probability of accidents.

The IMO is scrutinizing international conventions and is preparing the necessary alterations to these in order to enable the movement toward increased automation, and even fully autonomous shipping. The latter refers to ships without seafarers on board. Coastal States experts are participating in this work in order to address important issues, and also to remain cognizant of technical solutions. Authorities of flag state control (FSC) and port state control (PSC) inspections need all possible information to carry out their tasks. All technical details and alterations to international regulations are central to their work.

When evaluating legislative sovereignty, the decisive factor is the geographical area in which ships sail. This can be broken down into coastal waters, territorial waters, exclusive economic zone and international waters. Coastal States have the sovereign right to impose regulations on the passage of ships in cases where their passage is directed to a port or to areas within the so-called baseline. This applies to the traditional manned, as well as unmanned vessel. In territorial waters, i.e., state waters outside the baseline, control is observed as being more limited.

Regarding coastal States' legislative jurisdiction, UNCLOS Article 21(2) stipulates that a state may not impose its national requirements on the construction, design, equipment or manning of foreign ships in its territorial sea, unless those requirements give effect to "generally accepted international rules and standards". This requirement sets the obligation for coastal States to participate in the development of up-to-date international maritime legislation.

Changes in international legislation may widen the liability regime. This may be a consequence faced by a State because of a wrongful act or negligence when carrying out its responsibilities. The International Law Commission (ILC) has considered the principles of international law concerning State responsibility and liability. Its working group produced draft articles in 2001 (ILC, 2001a) which include general principles concerning damages a state may cause to another state. However, it has left open the question of dispute settlement and proposed that it could be dealt with in a different international arrangement under a separate legal basis. Hence, these rules are on the level of draft. As this question of settlement is still open, this topic is dealt mostly via the traditional system. There is an internationally wrongful act when an action or omission constitutes a breach of an international obligation of the State (ILC, 2001b). Such a wrongful act may consist of one or more actions or omissions, or a combination of both. Whether there has been an internationally wrongful act depends firstly, on the requirements of the obligation which is said to have been breached and secondly, on the framework conditions for such an act (ILC, 2001a). The conduct in question must be attributable to the State under international law and constitute a breach of an international legal obligation. Negligence in implementing an international convention may go against the tenets of Vienna Convention and lead to liability (van Hooydonk, 2010). Coastal States are bound to justify their decision-making through the rules of general international law that is enforced at the national level (van Hooydonk, 2010). It is a state's duty to arrange the administrative system so that it fulfills the tasks at hand (Mac William—Cooke). This applies to the internal organization of the Authority and to the handling of matters that fall within its competence (Kulla, 2015).

6 Traditional Indemnity Regime is Challenged

As a coastal entrance, fairways pose challenges to navigation since traffic is heavy and ships are sailing in shallow waters. Traffic control carried out by coastal authorities has been important in preventing collisions and environmental disasters. They have been very successful in preventing marine accidents with early contact and alerting. Maritime transport is part of the national logistics system and an integral part of the society as a whole. The development of transport system means improving society, which can clearly be seen with harbors being hubs for all transport modes. The nexus cannot be clearer.

The movement of remotely controlled and completely autonomous vessels in coastal waters imposes new requirements for the authorities. These mainly relate to communication and accessibility between ships and the authorities per se. Digitalization and new digital services are changing business models, services and transportation chains.

As noted earlier, VTS, AtoN and pilotage play key roles in ensuring the safety of the marine environment and maritime transport as they complement ships' seaworthiness requirement (Abdulla, 2011). The new modes of cooperation, the land-based and remote-controlled pilotage as well as plans to merge VTS and pilotage are starting to take place, and calls for the establishment of a seamless cooperation between authorities and the industry concerned.

It has been proposed that new kinds of command centers would be built, including VTS as an integral part of the ship's navigation control mechanism (Aawa project). This is yet to be materialized. Extensive work lies ahead. Also stressed earlier: the deeper the liaison between ship and authority is, the more the control system as VTS is considered to perform what is known as a "service" for an individual ship. The same is not considered in the case of physical navigation aids as they are placed on the fairways and serve all ships sailing there. It can be argued that VTS would no longer be a general informative system for all ships sailing in the fairways but would instead be assisting a particular ship and its master in navigational decision-making processes.

This may also have a significant impact on the liability for environmental damage. On the basis of the *Commune de Mesquer*'s decision following the oil disaster of *MT Erika*, those who have contributed to the risk of pollution would be liable. The Finnish Supreme Court (KKO, 2011, p. 62) has come to a generic conclusion: the party that had the ability to control the environmental risk was found responsible. The same principle has been observed in the case law of the Court of Justice of the European Union (EUTI), even if the pollutant is not subject to physical control. Both the producer and the holder of the waste/pollution were held liable, as there was a causal link between their obligations and actions and the cause of the damage (Van de Walle Case, 2004). It is worth considering whether a failure in the VTS, FSC or PSC would have such an impact that it would lead to liability for environmental damage as noted above.

7 System Operability and Administrative Burden

A states' liability may come into question when the state has not been able to arrange its administration in accordance with national legislation to be adequately built to answer the challenges presented to it (Hakalehto-Wainio, 2008). According to UNCLOS Article 235(2) and the general principles regarding the liability of States for internationally wrongful acts, the Administrations are responsible for fulfilling their international requirements. States have the responsibility of implementing the international norms so that the legal implications are similar (Wetterstein, 2004a). The Vienna Convention posits that States bear the responsibility to implement international conventions and treaties as soon as they come into force. A treaty shall be interpreted in good faith in accordance with the ordinary meaning to be given to the terms of the treaty in their context and in the light of its aims and objectives.

The authorities must take into account the legal implications that may arise if there is a shipping accident emanating from problems associated with vessel control. Coastal States have responsibility for the safety of navigation around the coastline of their jurisdiction. This means that they have to arrange sufficient traffic control at fairways. In addition, it means that the fairways must be safe to navigate and properly marked. In practice, this means proper VTS and AtoN. In cases such as the *MT Exxon Valdez* grounding or *MV Karen Danielsen* colliding with the Big Belt Bridge in Denmark, the investigation reports have included observations about VTS's role. A significant lack of due diligence in traffic control and safeguarding systems was observed.

In the Finnish High Court case, the court investigated the role of pilot organization in accidents. The main point of investigation was whether the system itself was robust enough to have prevented the accident. The court found that the system was in order, but the main issue was "system-liability". In the Swedish *Tsesis*-case (1983), the Administration was held liable for failure in nautical charts, as there was a subtle nexus between the failure and the state officers' awareness. Again, in the Swedish *M/T José Marti*-case (1987), the court found that pilotage is not part of AtoN. It is worth mentioning that this decision was made in the 1980s and therefore, the outcome may differ in the international regulatory systems found today. IALA includes VTS and pilotage to AtoN in its recommendations. This could lead to a situation where these would be included in the strict liability of fairway maintenance.

According to SOLAS Chapter V: 12, the coastal States should arrange VTS when the volume of traffic or the degree of risk justifies such services. VTS is a marine traffic monitoring system established by authorities to keep track of vessel movements and provide navigational safety in a limited geographical area. When building such a system, the States shall follow the guidelines developed by IMO. Such rules are set in the IMO Regulation A.857 (20) and IALA recommendations and guidelines. This means that the VTS authority should retain sufficient staff that are appropriately qualified, suitably trained and capable of performing the tasks required taking into account the type and level of services to be provided.

Resolution A.857 (20) is under alteration in the IMO. In its new form, the liability of service providers and administration is more clearly stated. This means that in cases of expanding digitalization and automatization, the duty rests with the coastal States' administration be able to provide service to individual ships sailing their merchant fairways.

8 Conclusions

A cascade of innovation leading to automatization and the decline in the human factor has markedly set challenges for traditional legal thinking. As the role of human actors is diminishing, the traditional principles concerning "human based causality" are unable to shed light on liability issues. In other words, the existing laws do not seem to be sufficient to lead to the right answers on questions of liability regarding autonomous operations.

Liability questions regarding autonomous shipping have been studied at length. The normal rules of liability still apply as long as the ship can be controlled and where an error has taken place. Those responsible for a specific activity are still liable for any damage emanating from that activity. However, increased automation and autonomous shipping have brought new challenges to coastal States' authorities when tracking and controlling the traffic on merchant shipping fairways. The central question has been whether the traditional indemnity regime provides sufficient solutions to concerned administrations.

In this continuum, cooperation between ships and coastal States may change the traditional liability regime. In some cases, administrative activities are considered as providing services to individual ships in their navigational decision-making processes. This would transfer the primary liability from the State to the ship. This would also have an impact on environmental liability. The liability may apply to persons whose work revolves around the ship or participates through the execution of direct tasks in relation to the ship's maritime activities.

The coastal States' authorities must be up to date and are obliged to participate in all changes to international maritime legislation. Particularly intelligence-based traffic control requires a new kind of cooperation between authorities and the shipping industry.

The effects of increased digitalization and autonomous shipping for coastal States should be taken into consideration. International regulations, conventions and agreements need to be studied and legislative action must be taken in order to avoid unintended consequences. The liability clauses in international conventions should be adapted to respond to the new situation.

References

Aawa White Paper. (2018). *Remote and Autonomous Ships—The next step.*
Abdulla, A. M. (2011). *Regulating Vessel Traffic Services (VTS) to Mitigate Maritime Accidents at Port Approaches*. World Maritime University.
Alfons Lütticke v Commission. [1971]. ECR 325.
Bievre, A. (1985). *Vessel Traffic Services and The Law*. Final Report.
CMI. (2018). International Working Group Position Paper on Unmanned Ships and the International Regulatory Framework.
European Commission. (2018). Artificial Intelligence for Europe. COM 2018 237 final.
Hakalehto-Wainio, S. (2008). Valta ja vahinko, Julkisen vallan käyttäjän vahingonkorvausvastuu vahingonkorvauslaissa. Talentum.
Hughes, H. (2009). When Is a VTS Not a VTS? *Journal of Navigation, 62*(3), 439–442.
IALA Navguide. (2018). Available at: https://www.iala-aism.org/product-category/publications/manuals/. Accessed 4 May 2022.
International Law Commission. (2001a). Yearbook.
International Law Commission. (2001b). Report A/56/10.
Jacobsson, M. (2014). The French Court of Cassation and the Erika Case; Some Issues Relating to Civil Liability. *International Maritime Law, 20*(1), 18–29.
KKO (Finnish Supreme Court). (2011). Case 2011:62.
KOM. (2018). 206 final. Based on White Paper on IOT.
Kulla, H. (2015). *Hallintomenettelyn perusteet*. Talentum.
M/T José Marti case. (1987). ND (*Nordisk Domssamling*), 64.
Pöysti, T. (2018). Kohti digitaalisen ajan hallinto-oikeutta. *Lakimies, 7*, 868–903.
Ringbom, H. (2019). Regulating Autonomous Ships—Concepts, Challenges and Precedents. *Ocean Development & International Law, 50*(2–3), 141–169.
SOLAS. (1974). International Convention for the Safety of Life at Sea, Nov. 1, 1974, 32 U.S.T. 47, T.I.A.S. 9700.
Suksi, M. (2018). Förvaltningsbeslut genom automatiserat beslutsfattande–statsförfattnings-ochförvaltningsrättsliga frågor i en digitaliserad myndighetsmiljö, *JFT, 5*, 329–337.
Tapaninen, U. (2018). *Logistiikka ja liikennejärjestelmät*. Gaudeamus/Otatieto.
Tsesis case. (1983). NJA, 3.
UNCLOS. (1982). United Nations Convention on the Law of the Sea, Dec. 10, 1982, 1833 U.N.T.S. 397.
van De Walle case. (2004). *Criminal Proceedings v. Paul Van De Walle, Daniel Laurent, Thierry Mersch, and Texaco Belgium SA* (Case C-1/03), ECR I-07613.
van Hooydonk, E. (2010). *Places of Refuge*. International Law and The CMI Draft Convention. *Lloyd's List*.

van Hooydonk, E. (2015). The Law of Unmanned Merchant Shipping—An Exploration. *The Journal of International Maritime Law, 20*, 403–423.

Viljanen, M. (2018). Robotteja vakuuttamassa: autonimiset alukset esimerkkinä. *Lakimies*, 7–8, 954–974.

Wetterstein, P. (2004a). *Redarens miljöskadeansvar*, Åbo Akademis Förlag.

Wetterstein, P. (2004b). Miljöskadeansvaret till sjöss efter Erika-och Prestigeolyckorna. *JFT*, 5.

CHAPTER 13

Remote Control and Remote Risk of Liability?—Vicarious Liability for Remotely Controlled Vessels in Scandinavian and English Law

Vibe Ulfbeck and Aslı Arda

1 Introduction

Tesla patent 'Method of and Apparatus for Controlling Mechanism of Moving Vessels or Vehicles' which was granted in 1898 covers 'any type of vessel or vehicle which is capable of being propelled and directed, such as a boat, a balloon or a carriage' (Tesla, 1898). The initial demonstration of the first ever wireless remotely controlled device was performed in a pool

V. Ulfbeck (✉) · A. Arda
Faculty of Law, Centre for Private Governance (CEPRI), University of Copenhagen, Copenhagen, Denmark
e-mail: vibe.ulfbeck@jur.ku.dk

A. Arda
e-mail: asli.arda@jur.ku.dk

© The Author(s), under exclusive license to Springer Nature Switzerland AG 2023

T. M. Johansson et al. (eds.), *Autonomous Vessels in Maritime Affairs*, Studies in National Governance and Emerging Technologies,
https://doi.org/10.1007/978-3-031-24740-8_13

of water by Nikola Tesla before the public in the same year at Madison Square Garden, New York City. Some 120 years later, the concept of unmanned ships is now again a trending topic.

Remotely controlled and autonomous vessels are now being tested (IALA Report, 2022). It is projected that they will operate in a hybrid way including remote control and autonomy for a considerable amount of time depending on the purpose and type of the vessel (Jokioinen et al., 2016). The roles of the Remote Control Centers (RCCs) and shore-based controllers (SBCs) are expected to continue to be essential ones as the vessels will lack full automation for quite some time, and therefore involvement and, indeed, intervention from these in the case of emergencies must be expected (Bugra, 2019). This raises the question of who can be held liable in case something goes wrong. For example, if a ship that is remotely controlled collides with another ship due to errors committed by the SBC, who should then be held liable? The shipowner or the SBC, or both?

In many legal systems, the legal status of the SBC will have an impact on the appertaining liability that may arise as a result of the operation of the remotely controlled vessel. However, it is still unclear how the organizational structure will be established. The essential question is: will the SBC be an employee of the shipowner or simply work as an independent contractor? Following from the above, in this article, English law and Scandinavian law will be examined to ascertain to what extent it would be possible to hold the shipowner liable for the acts of SBC if a third party suffers a loss due to SBC errors.

2 The SBC as an Employee

'An employee is one who is paid a wage or salary to work under some, if only slight, control of his employer in his employer's business' (*E v English Province of Our Lady Charity*). Historically, the concept of employment has been distinguished from other type of relationships, such as the one between the independent contractor and the engager/principal by means of ascertaining the extent to which the engager/principal has a right to direct the worker both regarding what to do and how to do it (*Market Investigations Ltd v Minister of Social Security*). The control test, which evaluates 'the level of retained power of the engager over controlling the work to be done' (*Sadler v Henlock*) has traditionally been accepted as the test to be applied (*Performing Right Society Ltd v Mitchell and*

Booker Ltd) to ascertain whether the relationship of employment exists (Gray, 2018). Some provided methods of assessment are, indeed, quite antiquated as they tend to oversimplify the criteria of assessing whether the relationship of employment is established in a way corresponding to the realities of the modern professional life. This comes more into focus where some tasks require a special skill, expertise, and professionalism, which may not possibly be 'controlled' in the straightforward sense by the engager or employer simply because they may not be expected to have such a specific skill (Carrigan, 2016). It is noted in *Morren v Swinton and Pendlebury Borough Council* that it would not be possible for an employer to tell an employee how to do their job concerning the employment of a professional or someone with specific skills.

The legal position of the SBC of an unmanned ship will likely constitute a similar situation. For clarity, now we turn to the assessment of the potential liability of the owner of an unmanned ship where the SBC undertakes tasks as an employee in the conventional sense.

In English law, the doctrine of vicarious liability imposes liability on the employers for the wrongdoings of their employees and it constitutes a part of the English tort law. Markedly, it has its roots in the early common law (Todd, 2020). Vicarious liability, constituting an extension of strict liability, would be attached to the employer even if they have not committed an error and the culpable conduct may not be personally traced back to them. Under English law, employers are vicariously liable for the negligence of their employees exhibited during the course of their employment (*Joel v Morison*). Consequently, the owner as an employer may be vicariously liable for damages that occurred as a result of the negligent operation of the unmanned ship by the controllers and programmers, who are employed by the employer, i.e., the shipowner. Demonstrating that the owner exercised prudence in the process of employment of the SBC would not remove the vicarious liability of the owner of the unmanned ship.

Scandinavian law, similar to English law, recognizes vicarious liability where the defendant is not personally at fault but responsible for the negligence of others (Falkanger et al., 2017). The employer's liability for the acts of employees is the classic example of vicarious liability in Scandinavian law. Notably, it also applies to maritime law (Falkanger et al., 2017).

The liability of the shipowner arises where the damage is caused by the negligence of an employee. The relevant liability ensues even if it is not possible to identify the particular employee that has been negligent (Falkanger et al., 2017). It should be noted that Scandinavian law puts forth some criteria in a fashion similar to English law with a view to making it fair, just, and reasonable to impose vicarious liability. The error that may potentially impose vicarious liability should have been committed both within the scope of the employment during the time of the employment and in connection with the duties of the employee (Falkanger et al., 2017).

As described above, both under Scandinavian law and English law, the shipowner will be liable for the negligent acts of the SBC if the SBC is an employee. This raises the question as to what can be considered a negligent act of an SBC. Since the SBC will take over the role played by both the master of the ship and seafarers on board the ship, the issue of negligence has a direct correlation with the concept of 'good seamanship'. Questions remain as to what it entails in the unmanned shipping context.

The concept of 'good seamanship' may be subject to a twofold evaluation: firstly, it has something to do with the appropriate knowledge, and secondly, it indicates a certain type of behavior (Stevens, 2021). Concerning the former aspect of this evaluation, the SBC would be expected to have appropriate technical and nautical knowledge (Stevens, 2021). The concept of 'technical' knowledge must necessarily include knowledge of how to operate the IT system through which the vessel is now controlled. This adds a new layer of qualifications to what has previously been required from seafarers and consequently also transforms the test of negligence. A lack of technological skills may indicate negligence (and perhaps unseaworthiness) and this may trigger the liability of the shipowner. Concerning the latter aspect of the relevant evaluation—'good seamanship' would also indicate a certain type of behavior that may be categorized as 'bad', if the situation is handled poorly, and 'good' if it is handled correctly (Stevens, 2021). This twofold evaluation would, indeed, potentially lead to different results depending on the factual circumstances. Notwithstanding, and generally speaking, it would be possible to argue that the seamanship was overall a good one in situations where the above two boxes can be ticked. This would mean that no vicarious liability would arise for the shipowner. On the contrary, the insufficient technical or nautical knowledge of the SBC or their inadequate conduct to avoid the unwanted outcome (or both) may be regarded to exhibit 'bad seamanship' and could accordingly, lead to the liability of the shipowner.

3 The SBC as an Independent Contractor

As mentioned, the concept of vicarious liability, historically, relies on a distinction between workers that are employees and workers who are independent contractors (Gray, 2018). Whereas an employee is guaranteed payment for work, 'the independent contractor works in and for his own business at his risk of profit or loss' (*E v English Province of Our Lady of Charity*). Currently, it seems a likely scenario that at least to some extent that maritime management companies will take over the management of unmanned ships. In fact, the first standard contract for outsourcing the task of remote control is yet to be introduced to the market (Arda, 2021). Ship management companies usually operate as independent contractors. This raises the question of to what extent the shipowner is liable for the acts of an independent contractor.

Under English law, the owner of the unmanned ship is not liable to compensate for damage that is caused by fault or negligence of an independent contractor during the course of the service provided. The fundamental issue to be ascertained, to put the legal relationship into its correct place, is to identify the elements in a contract that are creating an 'employer-employee relationship' and some other elements that prompt the emergence of an 'engager/principal-independent contractor relationship' (Todd, 2020). English law provides a substantial test examining 'whether the person who has engaged himself to perform services is performing them as a person in business on his own account?' (*Market Investigations Ltd v Minister of Social Security*). If the answer to this question is 'yes' then this would mean that the contractual relationship constitutes a form of 'service providing' relationship whereby the provider is an independent contractor, and the contract is a 'contract for services'. On the other hand, if the answer is 'no' then the contract would be a 'contract of service' where the person concerned is an employee (Todd, 2020). Common law, in a way traceable back to 1840 (*Quarman v Burnett*), essentially distinguishes employees and independent contractors and it adopts the general rule that employers would not be held liable for independent contractors.

It should be noted that the general rule of 'non-establishment of the vicarious liability of the engager/principal for the independent contractor', in English law, as in many other legal systems, is subject to some exceptions (Galand–Carval, 2003). The main exceptions are the 'non-delegable duties', 'retention of control', and 'the peculiar risks'

(Ulfbeck & Ehlers, 2019). Briefly explained: where the duty is a non-delegable one, or where the engager/principal retains the right to control over the work done by the independent contractor, or where the work is inherently dangerous, then the vicarious liability of the engager/principal will be triggered. In other words, even if the work is done by an independent contractor where the work in question falls under one of the above categories—the engager/principal will not be able to avoid liability. With regard to the operation of unmanned ships, it should be ascertained whether the tasks of the SBC fall under the scope of any of the mentioned categories. Such categorization would only be possible subsequent to the clarification of the tasks and responsibilities of the SBC and the examination of whether these would fall into the scope of one of the defined categories of exceptions.

At this juncture, a few deductions may be made. Non-delegable works are crucial that due to the weight they bear they simply cannot be delegated to other entities (Henderson, 1979; Morgan, 2015). The owner's task of making the vessel seaworthy can be characterized as non-delegable. Owners may not contract out of it or in any way be relieved from their responsibilities with regards to ensuring seaworthiness through delegation (Alize, 1954 *& Anor v Allianz Elementar Versicherungs AG & Ors*). Normally, the task of carrying out remote control must be categorized as a delegable duty as the task is 'navigational' in character. However, if the delegation of remote control is conducted in a way making such a delegation resulting in impairment of ship's seaworthiness (for instance, because of delegation to be made to an unqualified SBC) then the shipowner would not be able to escape liability. As described by Lord Blackburn in *Hughes v Percival*: 'if such a duty was cast upon the defendant, he could not get rid of responsibility by delegating the performance of it to a third person. He was at liberty to employ such a third person to fulfil the duty which the law cast on himself ... but the defendant still remained subject to that duty, and liable for the consequence if it was not fulfilled'.

The retention of control, on the other hand, would indeed depend on the dynamics and the framework of the established contractual relationship between the engager/principal and the independent contractor. Where the former retains the control over the work to be done significantly, then the former may possibly be vicariously liable for the latter (Douglas, 2010). Although, the assessment of this would be subject to the objectively assessed level of such control depending on the facts of each case.

Concerning the last category, it is a general rule in many legal systems that the delegation of inherently dangerous work to an independent contractor would not waive the liability of the original engager/principal for such a work (Ulfbeck & Ehlers, 2019). This is also a general rule of English law. In *Bower v Peate* the court found that an employer that hires someone to perform work '[f]rom which in the natural course of things, injurious consequences ... must be expected to arise...is bound to see to the doing of that which is necessary to prevent the mischief, and cannot relieve himself of his responsibility by employing someone else'.

Although, the task of carrying out the remote control of a ship may not be categorized as an inherently dangerous task that creates peculiar risks, it would indeed be technically possible for the remote control of the ship to become dangerous because of the way in which the navigation or control was carried out. However, such a possibility would not render tasks of remote control 'inherently' dangerous.

Noting the deductions made above, it would be rare for an engager/principal to be vicariously liable for an independent contractor under English law. Accordingly, in the context of unmanned shipping, where the SBC happens to be an independent contractor it would be very unlikely for the owner of the remote-controlled ship to be liable for the independent SBC under this particular legal system. However, the implementation of unmanned vessels, as all substantial market developments do, will blur some lines regarding the roles undertaken in this particular industry. Not being specific to the shipping market, there is observed difficulty in distinguishing the independent contractors from employees in many markets due to many tasks and works being outsourced.

From the perspective of English law, it should be noted that in *The Catholic Child Welfare Society*, the well-established definition of the 'employee and employer relationship' was interpreted in a more sophisticated way so that the emerging liability would include 'those whose relationship was akin to that between an employer and an employee' (Bell, 2013). However, in *Cox v Ministry of Justice* it was emphasized that a relationship that is akin to employment would only apply to individuals and not to legal entities, which are constituting independent businesses (*Cox v. Ministry of Justice*, para 29). This indicates that in English law, the concept of a relationship 'akin to that between employer and employee' cannot be used for establishing the vicarious liability of the owner of an unmanned ship for the damage caused as a result of the negligence of the management company, which is an independent business.

Furthermore, Paula Giliker uses the terms 'non-independent' independent contractor or the 'dependent contractor' to define independent contractors that undertake work which was formerly assumed by employees in the conventional sense (Giliker, 2010). These 'not-that-independent contractors' are difficult to distinguish from the employees and, also, in terms of the tasks they so undertake, they mostly, and of course, fairly, deserve to be subject to generic employment protection. It is at present difficult to conclude whether the position of the SBC will constitute one of the 'not-that-independent contractors'.

In Scandinavian law, it is also the clear starting point that there is no vicarious liability for independent contractors (von Eyben & Isager, 2019). However, in the maritime sector, a special rule has been developed. In Scandinavian shipping law, it is a basic principle that vicarious liability of the shipowner arises for the personnel that are performing work in relation to the service of the vessel (Solvang, 2021). In Danish law, the principle is stated in the Maritime Code § 151 reading: 'The Shipowner (reder) shall be liable to compensate the damage caused in the service by the fault or negligence of the master, crew, pilot, tug or others performing work in the service of the ship'. Identical rules are found in the other Scandinavian legal systems. In other words, contrary to English law, the shipowner under Scandinavian law may also be potentially liable for the independent contractors that are not the employees of the shipowner. The shipowner would be liable for those that are performing pilotage, towing and loading under a contract as these jobs would be considered as falling into the scope of the liability regime adopted in Scandinavia. However, also negligent acts of 'others' performing work in the service of the ship could potentially trigger vicarious liability. This raises the question of whether the owner would also be liable for the negligent acts of an independent contractor—for instance, a ship management company—to whom the remote control of the ship has been outsourced through contract. When determining for which independent contracting actors the shipowner is vicariously liable, the decisive criterion is whether the independent contractor is exercising an activity that is a 'typical shipowner activity' (Falkanger et al., 2017).

Relevantly, the navigation of the ship is indeed a typical shipowner activity. This speaks in favor of assuming that remote control of a ship will also be regarded as a 'typical shipowner activity', even if remote control will largely require technological skills rather than traditional seamanship skills. In addition, it is a requirement under § 151 of the Danish

Maritime Code that the 'work in question must be connected to a particular ship and be carried out in service of that ship' (Falkanger et al., 2017). If the SBC operates just one vessel, this requirement will evidently be fulfilled. However, if the SBC operates several ships belonging to different shipowners, the matter inevitably becomes more questionable. As a parallel, it is generally assumed that there is no vicarious liability for lighthouse services and public charting since these services are provided as services for all ships and not in the service of a particular ship (Falkanger et al., 2017). Against this background and depending on the way in which remote control will be organized more generally, it could be argued that there may be situations in which the shipowner cannot be held vicariously liable for the negligent acts of an SBC under Scandinavian law.

In determining whether the acts of SBS are to be categorized as negligent, the same criteria as described above with regard to the SBC as an employee will be relevant. However, in the event where the SBC acts as an independent contractor, there is a duty to ensure that the IT system used for the remote control is functioning adequately and appropriately, and does not suffer from any defects (Arda, 2021).

4 Recourse Actions

As explained above, under both English (for instance, through the exceptions to the general rule of 'non-establishment of the vicarious liability of the engager/principal for the independent contractor') and Scandinavian laws, the shipowner may be held vicariously liable for the negligent acts of the SBC as an independent contractor. If both the owner of the vessel and the management company carrying out the remote-control function can be held liable to a third party, then the question is how can liability be evenly distributed between the two.

The first standard contract that governs the outsourcing of the task of remote control in shipping, AUTOSHIPMAN, is expected to be introduced to the market by Baltic International Maritime Council (BIMCO) in 2023 (BIMCO, Upcoming contracts and Clauses). This raises the question of whether AUTOSHIPMAN will create a basis for recourse actions between the shipowner and the management company. For instance, in a situation where the shipowner is held vicariously liable towards a third party, could the shipowner file a recourse action against the management company?

Clause 17 (b)(i) of the AUTOSHIPMAN, similar to the relevant section of BIMCO SHIPMAN 2009 from which it is derived, states in the 'Responsibilities' section that '…the Managers shall be under no liability whatsoever to the Owners for any loss, damage, delay or expense of whatsoever nature, whether direct or indirect … UNLESS same is proved to have resulted solely from the negligence, gross negligence or willful default of the Managers or their employees or agents, or sub-contractors employed by them in connection with the Vessel, in which case … the Managers' liability for each incident or series of incidents giving rise to a claim or claims shall never exceed a total of ten (10) times the annual management fee payable hereunder'.

In the context of remote control of ships, this means that—as a starting point—the owner will be able to pass on the loss to the management company on the basis of its negligent acts. As explained above, it is not (yet) entirely certain what will in fact constitute 'negligence', 'gross negligence', and 'willful default' in the context of remote-control shipping due to the contemporary nature of the remote operation. Although inherently, the tasks are undertaken by the SBCs and therefore, the ones that would potentially be committed in 'negligence, gross negligence or by willful default' in the context of ship management would essentially be relevant to navigation, control, and duty of care.

However, what is certain is that, the ship being remotely controlled or not, the ship management companies enjoy wide protection against liability. Similar to SHIPMAN 2009, also AUTOSHIPMAN creates a basis for actions between the shipowner and the management company and limits the liability of the ship manager. In compliance with the well-settled limitation formula in the ship management industry, also in the remote-control context the liability of the managers will be capped at ten times the annual management fee, even if it is established that they have acted recklessly or intentionally (Hunter, 2021).

Moreover, the cap has a broad coverage range in the sense that it applies even if the blameworthy act gives rise to a whole series of incidents and more than one claim. Presumably, the formulation seeks to avoid the difficulties in distinguishing between what is 'one incident' and 'more incidents' under the global limitation rules (Falkanger et al., 2017).

5 Conclusions

The role of the SBC is a new one. The assessment of the legal status of the SBC will clearly bear importance in the context of liability issues. The way in which the organizational structure of the operation of the unmanned ship will be established still remains unclear. Consequently, it is unknown for the time being whether the SBCs will be employees of the shipowners or will work as independent contractors. This categorization is significant. Looking into English law and Scandinavian law, this research concludes that where the SBC is an employee, the owner of the unmanned ship will be vicariously liable under both legal systems; where the SBC is an independent contractor, the liability of the owner of the ship would normally not arise under English law. However, under the special maritime law principle on vicarious liability in Scandinavian law, the owner may be vicariously liable for the actions of an SBC in respective legal systems.

References

Alize 1954 & Anor v Allianz Elementar Versicherungs AG & Ors. (2021). UKSC 51.

Arda, A. (2021). Testing the Water: Applying BIMCO AUTOSHIPMAN to Remotely Controlled Ships, Cyber Incidents and Events of Force Majeure. *Journal of International Maritime Law, 27*, 399–413.

Bell, J. (2013). The Basis of Vicarious Liability. *The Cambridge Law Journal, 72*(1), 17–20.

BIMCO. (2022). *Upcoming Contracts and Clauses*https://www.bimco.org/contracts-and-clauses/upcoming-contracts-and-clauses.

Bower v Peate. . (1896). 1 QBD, 326.

Bugra, A. (2019). *Insuring Remotely Operated Vessels: Tempestuous Waters for Hull Insurers. CML Working Paper Series*, 19/08.

Carrigan, F. (2016). Class Analysis and the Contract of Employment. *Canterbury Law Review, 22*, 207–234.

Core Advodkatfirma and Cefor Report. (2018). Maritime Autonomous Surface Ships: Zooming in on Civil Liability and Insurance. https://static.mycoracle.com/igpi_website/media/article_attachments/maritime_autonomous_ships_report_dec_18_6URrRcy.pdf

Cox v Ministry of Justice. (2016). UKSC 10.

Douglas, B. (2010). *Enterprise Liability and the Common Law*. Cambridge University Press.

E v English Province of Our Lady of Charity. . (2013). QB 722.

Falkanger, T., et al. (2017). *Scandinavian Maritime Law—The Norwegian Perspective* (4th ed.). Universitetsforlaget.

Galand-Carval, S. (2003). Comparative Report on Liability for Damages Caused by Others. In Spier, J. (Ed). *Unification of Tort Law: Liability for Damage Caused by Others* (pp. 289–308). Kluwer Law International.

Giliker, P. (2010). *Vicarious Liability in Tort*. Cambridge University Press.

Gray, A. (2018). *Vicarious Liability: Critique and Reform*. Hart Publishing.

Henderson, E. J. (1979). Liability to Employees of Independent Contractors Engaged in Inherently Dangerous Work: A Workable Workers' Compensation Proposal. *Fordham L. Rev., 48*, 1165.

Hughes v Percival. (1882–83). LR 8 App Cas 443.

Hunter, G. (2021). Standard Contract for the MASS(es)—Charter Parties and Other Agreements for Autonomous Ships. Soyer, B., and Tettenborn, A. (Eds.). *Ship Operations: New Risks, Liabilities and Technologies in the Maritime Sector*. Informa Law, 207–220.

IALA Report. (2022). The International Association of Marine Aids to Navigation and Lighthouse Authorities (IALA) on the 'Developments with Autonomous Ships, Possible Case Studies from a VTS Perspective. https://www.iala-aism.org/content/uploads/2022/02/Possible-case-studies-Operations-and-Trials-of-Autonomous-Ships-24-Jan-22.pdf

Joel v Morison.. (1834) 172 ER 1338.

Jokioinen, E., et al. (2016). Advanced Autonomous Waterborne Applications (AAWA) Position Paper, Remote and Autonomous Ships: The Next Steps. Rolls Royce. https://www.rolls-royce.com/~/media/Files/R/Rolls-Royce/documents/customers/marine/ship-intel/aawa-whitepaper-210616.pdf

Market Investigations Ltd v Minister of Social Security. (1969) 2 QB 173.

Morgan, J. (2015). Liability for Independent Contractors in Contract and Tort: Duties to Ensure that Care is Taken. *The Cambridge Law Journal, 74*(1), 109–139.

Morren v Swinton and Pendlebury Borough Council. (1965). 1 WLR 576.

Performing Right Society Ltd v Mitchell and Booker Ltd (1924). 1 KB 762.

Quarman v Burnett. (1840). 6 M & W 499, 151 ER 509.

Sadler v Henlock. (1855). 4 E & B 570; 119 ER 209.

Solvang, T. (2021). Shipowners' Vicarious Liability Under English and Norwegian Law. With an Eye to Technical Failure of Autonomous Ships. *Marius, 541*, 5–129.

Stevens, F. (2021). Seaworthiness and Good Seamanship in the Age of Autonomous Vessels. In Ringbom, H., Røsæg, E., & Solvang, T. (Eds). *Autonomous Ships and the Law* (pp. 243–260, 252). Routledge.

Soyer, B., Tettenborn, A., & Leloudas, G. (2022). *Remote Controlled and Autonomous Shipping: UK Based Case Study. Assuring Autonomy International Programme* (pp. 1–47). Institute of International Shipping and Trade Law,Swansea University.

Tesla, N. (1898). *Method of and Apparatus for Controlling Mechanism of Moving Vessels or Vehicles*. U.S. Patent No. 613,809-A. Grant 1898/11/08. Washington, DC. U.S. Patent and Trademark Office.

Todd, S. (2020). Various Liability on the Move-But Where Should It Stop? *Journal of International and Comparative Law, 7*(1), 1–40.

Ulfbeck, V., & Ehlers, A. (2019). Direct and Vicarious Liability in Supply Chains. In Ulfbeck, V., Andhov, A., & Mitkidis, D. (Eds.), *Law and Responsible Supply Chain Management. Contract and Tort Interplay and Overlap*. Routledge.

von Eyben, B., & Isager, H. (2019). *Lærebog i erstatningsret*, 10th edn. Djøf Forlag.

CHAPTER 14

Maritime Autonomous Surface Ships (MASS): Precarious Legal Position of the Shore-Based Remote Controller

Proshanto Kumar Mukherjee

1 Introduction

1.1 The Title

Let me first say a few words about the title. I was assigned to write on a topic bearing the draft title "Operating Remotely Controlled Ships: An Analysis of the Legal Position of the Shore-Based Controller from English Perspectives" under the thematic strand "autonomy from an English perspective". I take that to mean "English law perspectives" in both instances but I have chosen to deal with the topic in more general terms, not necessarily confined to English law as such. The expression "Maritime Autonomous Surface Ships" or "MASS" in short, I believe, was

P. K. Mukherjee (✉)
Dalian Maritime University, Dalian, China
e-mail: Proshanto.Mukherjee@hotmail.com; proshanto.mukherjee@yahoo.com

© The Author(s), under exclusive license to Springer Nature Switzerland AG 2023

T. M. Johansson et al. (eds.), *Autonomous Vessels in Maritime Affairs*, Studies in National Governance and Emerging Technologies,
https://doi.org/10.1007/978-3-031-24740-8_14

coined by the IMO. "MASS" is defined as a ship that, to a varying degree, can operate independent of human interaction (LEG 108/WP.1/Rev.1, 2021, Annex 2, p. 3, para. 3.4).

In light of the above definition, the term "autonomous" is synonymous with "unmanned". Why "ship" and not "vessel" which has a wider connotation, was chosen, is unclear. The term "surface" alludes to "not being underwater"; in other words, the appellation does not cover submarine craft. Again, it is not clear why that is so given that there are submersibles operating in tourism, for example, in some Caribbean resorts. But MASS is now accepted jargon which is why it features in the title. The IMO has created this phraseology (IMO Doc (2021a), IMO Doc (2021b)). Finally, what if any, legal implications might there be for "inhuman" interaction (no pun intended) with regard to MASS? Is there a human–inhuman dichotomy in the offing? Doubtless, there is a serious concern among many over the plight of the world's seafaring community which today hails predominantly from the so-called global south. The technologically advanced sector of the human race seems to be less concerned with that aspect of international shipping. In my humble opinion, depriving a certain community of humans of the right to make a living from seafaring is inhuman. One delegation to the IMO Legal Committee drew the Committee's attention to the "serious effects the introduction of MASS may have on seafarers' careers and lives", and referred to how it might "negatively influence young men and women to pursue a career at sea" (LEG 108/WP.1/Rev.1, 2021, p. 26). A view that seems to be floating around in some quarters is that seafarers will become "techies". In my own view, the proposition is unrealistic at best and manifestly absurd at worst, at least for the near future and in respect of the present generation of active seafarers from the developing and less developed countries. It is notable that vessel autonomy has thus far been articulated as Degrees one, two, three and four (MSC.1/Circ.1638, 2021, pp. 3–4, para. 3.4).

Where there is a shore-based remote controller with the hi-tech equivalent of a joystick at his/her disposal, the situation falls primarily under the second and third degrees. Under these categories, there is the concept of the Remote-Control Station or Center which is basically a facility providing regular shore to ship connection through communication satellites (MSC.1/Circ.1638, 2021, Annex, p. 8, para. 5.6).

Finally, the legal position of the remote controller is described in the title as "precarious". The term alludes to the uncertainty surrounding the potential liability of that person. The matter is presently under consideration by the Legal Committee of the IMO (LEG 108/WP.1/Rev.1, 2021, Annex 2, p. 7, para. 5.4). Until its deliberations are completed, any such person in a MASS operation is at serious risk of being held liable under the extant maritime legal regimes for any casualty attributable to faulty navigation (LEG 108/WP.1/Rev.1, 2021, Annex 2, p. 7, para. 5.5). The "precarious legal position of the shore-based remote controller" addressed in this chapter mainly concerns the two categories of MASS mentioned above, namely, Degrees two and three.

1.2 Purpose

The principal purpose of this chapter is to focus on the liability of the shore-based remote controller in relation to collisions at sea and in "all waters connected therewith" as stated in the International Regulations for Preventing Collisions at Sea, 1972 (COLREGs 1972). It necessarily involves the regulatory law manifested through the COLREGs 1972 as well as the so-called Collision Liability convention (1910). The COLREGs 1972 commonly referred to as "the rules of the road" evolved from the international custom of seamen and can be traced back to a number of rules established in 1840 by the Trinity House pilots associated with pilotage for the port of London (Cockroft & Lameijer, 2011, p. xi). In the context of COLREGs 1972 a fundamental observation is the concept and usage of the term "good seamanship" and the expression "ordinary practice of seamen" on which I have elaborated further in this chapter. It is of trivial interest in this regard that the word "seaman" is of ancient vintage, and although for the sake of gender neutrality which is absolutely essential, the term used today is "seafarer" exemplified in the International Convention on Standards of Training, Certification and Watchkeeping for Seafarers, 1978 (STCW Convention, 1978) and other legal instruments, there is no such word as "seafarership", although it is quite feasible to substitute "seamen" with "seafarers" in the phrase "ordinary practice of seamen" in the COLREGs 1972.

2 MASS in Motion

2.1 Evolution of MASS

It has been said that shipping is a relative newcomer in the autonomous technology arena in the transportation field and that airplanes fly mostly in autopilot mode except while landing or taking off (Munim & Haralambides, 2022, p. 181). Actually, the use of autopilot in maritime navigation has been around at least since the early 1920s. The m.t. J.A. Moffett owned by the Standard Oil Company of New Jersey was the first ship to use an autopilot (Marineinsight, 2022). In my personal experience, it was common practice to put a ship on autopilot as soon as it departed pilotage waters and proceeded toward what was then the high seas, namely, beyond 3 nautical miles from the territorial sea baselines. The development of autonomous ships dates back to the advent of the project named maritime unmanned navigation through intelligence in networks (MUNIN) which was launched in 2012 by the Faculty of Technology, Natural and Maritime Sciences, University of South-Eastern Norway. It was ostensibly the precursor of today's MASS. There were eight project partners from five European countries operating collaboratively. The principal object of investigation was to conduct a feasibility test through a case study involving a dry bulk carrier (Munim & Haralambides, 2022, p. 181).

The genesis of autonomy in maritime navigation was the creation of a guidance and control system in combination with a dynamic unmanned vessel algorithm. The guidance system provides for navigation as well as obstacle detection and avoidance (ODA) (Chinmayi et al., 2018). There are also integrated systems comprising varieties of radar applications, light detection and range (LIDAR), thermal ranging and high-definition cameras (GISGeography, 2021). Algorithms have been developed incorporating various rules contained in IMO conventions. All these can be employed as backup devices when connectivity from land is needed to intervene with the shipboard operation to ensure navigational safety and environmental protection. In addition to these, technologies like artificial intelligence and robotics have become essential parameters of autonomous shipping.

Given the overwhelming dominance of seaborne international trade, the demand for autonomous cargo vessels is bound to increase rapidly. Ships must prove to be reliable and the technology must be sustainable in order to support the enhancement of the global economic order. Needless to say, maritime safety and marine environmental protection remain matters of core concern in shipping. Meeting them poses a formidable challenge, and in some quarters which includes my own personal estimation, there is creeping doubt that in the realm of MASS, it will be fully possible.

2.2 The Master and the Controller

Whether in MASS, the shore-based remote controller is the master of the vessel in question is a thought-provoking issue. As a former seafarer, I am quite familiar with the age-old adage "master under God" which has conceptually all but disappeared over time. In pilotage, for example, one of the earliest instances of diminution of the master's authority, even though the master remains in command, the pilot has the conduct of navigation. In numerous instances of vessel traffic management systems (VTMS) such as in the Eastern Canada Vessel Traffic Services Zone Regulations (ECAREG) operating in the Atlantic coast of Canada including the Gulf of St. Lawrence and the approaches to the St. Lawrence River, ships are subject to shore-based navigational control (Canadian Coast Guard, 2022). The potential disempowerment of the master has also been exemplified in the European Union project "Motorways and Electronic Navigation by Intelligence at Sea" known by its acronym MONALISA, which is somewhat of a progenitor of MASS. The central core of the MONALISA project is "Dynamic and Proactive Route Planning" (DPR) in which is embedded the concept of sea traffic management (STM) akin to Air Traffic Management in aviation. In a Report written by me for the Swedish Maritime Administration in 2013 on the MONALISA project, I stated that shipboard control of navigation and shoreside control through electronic communication between shore and ship is dichotomous. I also pointed out that—

Whether it is navigation conducted by the ship's navigators or by pilots in pilotage waters, those who belong to the conservative cadre of navigation professionals are die-hard supporters of shipboard control of navigation and are opposed to any attempt by shore-based personnel (desktop navigators) to control shipboard navigation (Mukherjee, 2013).

Admittedly, changes in popular perceptions within the shipping community are inevitable and concomitant with technological advancements. As may be expected, the diminution of the master's authority is happening rapidly. Much worse than being stripped of empowerment, in terms of the growing ill-fate of masters, in several relatively recent instances of oil spills, they have been criminalized and held in prison or police lock-ups without trial for extended periods. Striking examples are the infamous episodes of the Erika, Prestige, Tasman Spirit and Hebei Spirit incidents, to name a few (Mukherjee, 2016). Whether a shore-based controller of a second- or third-degree MASS should suffer the same personal perilous consequences in similar situations is a concern no doubt. Some may cynically and unabashedly say—why not? It is a verity that neither woman/man nor machine is infallible. This has been proven time and again in cases of driverless automobiles (Clifford Law Offices, 2022). While the machine element is prima facie unpunishable, should the human element go scot-free if the action or inaction of the individual is found to be the proximate cause of the accident?

On the question of whether the shore-based remote controller is the equivalent of the master, it is postulated that in a conventional ship, the master with the crew as servants of the shipowner or operator must uphold the law of the flag state and invoke flag state jurisdiction as and when required. Correspondingly, with respect to an autonomous vessel, these matters should squarely be attributed to the shipowner and the shore-based remote controller who is its servant (LEG 108/WP.1/Rev.1, Annex 2, p. 6, para. 5.3).

3 Collision Liability in the Realm of MASS

3.1 Introductory Remarks

That human society whether at sea, on land or in the air, or even in space, revolves around the law in some shape or form, is a verity that is not always appreciated by those in the know on the technology side of things. That is no less true than in the context of MASS, a phenomenon which spreads across the spectrum of international, regulatory and private law in the maritime field. Almost all maritime law today is contained in international conventions of sorts adopted under the auspices of the United Nations, the IMO or the International Labor Organization (ILO). MASS involves virtually all extant maritime conventions, The vast majority of them will need to be reviewed and probably revised in light of this unprecedented phenomenon. Indeed, even new conventions may be needed to address the new technologies, which could be through the adoption of a MASS Code (LEG 108/WP.1/Rev.1, Annex 2, p. 9, para. 5.12) although in some instances, market practice relating to MASS operations formalized through standard form contracts may well be adequate. Aside from all the maritime regulatory conventions of IMO and ILO, the Legal Committee of IMO has identified 19 private law conventions associated with MASS (LEG 108/WP.1/Rev.1, Annex 2, pp. 5–6, para. 4.4). In the present discourse, we are concerned only with the law of collisions which contains in almost equal proportion, regulatory and private law elements. The former regulates navigational conduct in respect of which, violations of rules designed to prevent collisions are subjected to penal sanctions. The latter essentially deals with civil liability and associated remedies in light of collision at sea being a maritime tort.

3.2 COLREGS, 1972 and MASS

It was apparently concluded, in the 2012 MUNIN study referred to earlier, that autonomous navigation is feasible because there is virtually no concentrated density of traffic in the high seas, which can be dealt with by utilizing advanced collision avoidance algorithms (Munim & Haralambides, 2022, p. 181). As conceded by the authors of the cited work, this is not the case in approaches to ports and harbors or in coastal waters. The study involved the introduction of a control system centered on the COLREGs 1972. Several of the rules in the COLREGs 1972 are predicated on traffic density and the application of good seamanship and the concept of "ordinary practice of seamen" mentioned earlier (COLREGs, 1972, Rules 2a and 8a). In every action taken to avoid collision, good seamanship must be observed. In the realm of autonomous vessels, there is ample cause for careful caution, concern and consideration in this regard (UK P&I Club, 2019, pp. 3–4). A pertinent question is whether a shore-based remote controller can exercise good seamanship or conduct him/herself according to the ordinary practice of seamen given that he/she is not a seafarer and is not operating at sea.

Another development that took place in 2016, namely, the Advanced Autonomous Waterborne Applications (AAWA) was spear-headed by Rolls-Royce (2016). The participants in that project came up with integrated electronic systems aimed at navigational safety and collision avoidance (DNV, n.d.). Given that the focus in the present discussion is on MASS of the Degrees 2 and 3 varieties, where the vessel is remotely controlled from the Remote-Control Center or Station, the operator or controller must have full and uninterrupted access to the shipboard sensors and communication systems.

With regard to safety of navigation, COLREGs 1972 is indubitably of utmost importance. Rules for the prevention and avoidance of collisions at sea became an absolute necessity for international shipping when it underwent the transitions from sail to steam propulsion and from wooden to steel hulls. Gone were the days of the proverbial "wooden ships and iron men". It became evident, however, that the rapid acceleration of technology required further expansion of the collision avoidance rules as the consequences of collisions at sea became increasingly more serious. As maritime technology continues to advance in leaps and bounds, the law must keep pace. This is no less true with respect to MASS (Liu, 2022). The COLREGs 1972 must be revisited on several fronts, and in this context, it must be stressed that whereas the COLREGs, 1972 primarily fall in the category of regulatory law, all such law is penal in scope. In other words, a COLREGs 1972 violation may be characterized as an offence, and its seriousness will define the severity of the sanction that the law will impose. In the N.F. Tiger case, for example, which involved a violation of Rule 10 dealing with the requirement for ships to traverse on the designated lane in a traffic separation scheme, the court's finding was that there was an absence of men's rea on the part of the master (Lloyd's Rep. 564, 1982). Thus, the violation did not amount to a criminal offence.

An important noteworthy point about the COLREGs 1972 is the use of the term "vessel". The broad definition of "vessel" which is "every description of water craft used or capable of being used as a means of navigation" would ostensibly cover MASS as presently conceived (Komianos, 2018, p. 341). The term "water craft" in the definition can include just about anything that floats, including a raft, or arguably a ski jet. It is therefore somewhat surprising why the word "ship" which is a relatively narrow concept by comparison, features in the expanded depiction of MASS.

There are some COLREGs 1972 rules that feature in almost all collision cases. These are the lookout rule (Rule 5) and safe speed rule (Rule 6). Both these rules can be adequately dealt with by the shore-based remote controller. Notably, "lookout" by definition includes visual or by sight as well as radar lookout, and also lookout by hearing or sound. The actual words in the rule are "all available means appropriate in the prevailing circumstances". One commentator has opined in this context that there is a presumption that when technical aids to keeping a lookout such as radar are exhausted, the human senses must be resorted to, which will inevitably require a judgment call on the part of the on-board navigator (Komianos, 2018, p. 342). Good seamanship instincts will obviously feature in such a decision. In this regard, the shore-based remote controller in the MASS scenario can surely keep a radar lookout from the Remote-Control Station. At sea, a visual lookout or lookout by sight is not possible in poor visibility; only a radar lookout would be feasible. Lookout by remote control from a shore station would ostensibly be the same. Regarding Rule 6, it is notable that previous to the 1972 version of the COLREGs 1972 the term "moderate speed" was in use, the judicial definition of which was the speed at which a vessel can be stopped within half the visibility. That term has now been changed to "safe speed" with which the shore-based remote controller can comply in the same manner as an on-board navigator at sea.

There are three important rules relating to navigational maneuvers which warrant some attention, but first, it is necessary to understand the concept of risk of collision because the teleology of COLREGs 1972 is not just collision avoidance but also avoidance of risk of collision. This was held by the English Court of Appeal in The Nowy Sacz (Lloyd's Rep 91 (C.A.), 1977, p. 94 and p. 138; Tettenborn & Kimbell, 2021, para. 5-01). In the MASS context, ascertaining whether or not the risk of collision exists is not problematic as it is based on a simple geometric determination. According to Rule 7, the risk of collision is deemed to exist if the compass bearing of an approaching vessel does not *appreciably* (emphasis added) change; in other words, the relative bearing between two vessels approaching each other is more or less steady. The mathematical part is relatively easy to determine, but how a shore-based remote controller can conclude whether or not the bearing change is "appreciable" is, in my view, not simply a matter of geometry. It is to be determined by the objective standard of a professional navigator well-versed in seamanship. The three rules relating to maneuvers are the overtaking situation (Rule 13), the head-on situation (Rule 14) and the crossing vessels situation (Rule 15).

An overtaking vessel under Rule 13 is defined in mathematical terms, namely, that a vessel is considered to be overtaking when it is coming up with another vessel from a direction more than 22.5 degrees abaft the beam. Again, apart from what is meant by "coming up", which was discussed at length in the appeal decision of The Nowy Sacz, this can be determined by the remote controller by computer-based devices. The rule requires that the overtaking vessel must keep out of the way (emphasis added) of the overtaken vessel, and no subsequent change in the bearing between them will make the overtaking vessel a crossing vessel. To comply with the requirement to keep out of the way, a navigator at sea will have to make a judgment call based on good seamanship. Whether a shore-based remote controller can make a similar judgment is a question to be considered. In a practical situation, drawing on the application of the adage "ordinary practice of seamen", a navigator at sea can choose how best to keep out of the way but whether that state of mind can be replicated by a shore-based operator is a question mark. The same goes for Rule 15 which requires the burdened vessel to keep out of the way in a crossing situation. The circumstances will dictate the choice a navigator makes to comply with the Rule. In these two situations, probably a shore-based desktop navigator will resort to the deployment of an artificial intelligence (IT) device.

Rule 15 which deals with a head-on situation is manifestly different. If two vessels are proceeding on reciprocal or nearly reciprocal courses, both will have to alter course specifically to starboard so that they will pass "port-to-port"; however, when exactly that should be done will require a judgment call on the part of both vessels depending on the nature of the risk of collision. Presumably, advanced collision avoidance systems will be at the disposal of the shore-based remote controllers of both vessels. But what if only one is a MASS and the other, a manned vessel? In the words of one author—

> It will be virtually impossible for unmanned ships under the fourth degree referred to above to comply with, among others, the aforementioned rules requiring navigational judgments to be made to prevent collisions in specific situations. (Liu, 2022)

In my own view, that observation would apply no less to autonomous vessels falling under the second and third degrees as well.

In respect of navigational maneuvers, Rule 17 is another rule of great importance. It provides that if a burdened vessel fails to keep out of the way in good time and finds itself too close to the stand-on vessel, it must "take such action as will best aid to avoid collision". How a shore-based remote controller can comply with this rule in the case of a MASS, is another question mark. In such instances, communications must be reliable and safe, and the transfer of information from shore to ship must be swift and secure (Komianos, 2018, p. 342).

A positive aspect of MASS pertaining to the COLREGs 1972 is that voyage plans of vessels are easily accessible to shore-based remote stations through which the controller will become aware of its routing and other relevant information to guide the vessel remotely and control its movements so as to avoid any collision or grounding. However, the efficacy of the autonomous system will depend a lot on the traffic density which will invariably change, sometimes quite frequently.

3.3 Collision Liability and MASS

Liability can be penal or civil; in many cases, both. Penal liability is almost exclusively governed by the COLREGs 1972. Violations of the COLREGs 1972 inevitably result in penal sanctions of sorts, usually in the form of fines, but more seriously, punishment imposed on the master or navigator, which may result in suspension or withdrawal of certificates issued under the STCW Convention. If the collision happens when the vessel is under the conduct of a pilot, the pilot's license may be suspended or revoked. Violations of conventions like COLREGs 1972 must be transformed into offences under national law. If the offence is serious resulting in a catastrophe involving loss of life, for instance, the offence may be characterized as criminal as distinguished from regulatory, and the sanctions will obviously be considerably more severe. Whereas penal liability is imposed on the navigator or pilot as servant or agent of his/her principal, that is, the owner or operator, by contrast, civil liability which involves big money, is imposed on the principal.

Even though COLREGs 1972 is mainly concerned with potential penal liability because it is a regulatory instrument, civil liability features in a tangential way which is no less important.

Civil liability for collision damage, in most cases, is governed by the Collision Liability Convention of 1910. As mentioned earlier, in terms of private law, collision is a maritime tort. Among the salient features of the convention, perhaps the most striking one is that in a collision between two vessels, pursuant to Article 4 of the 1910 Convention, liability is apportioned between them according to the degree of fault of each; if the faults are equal, liability is apportioned equally. In this sense, apportionment of collision liability is akin to the notion of contributory negligence in English tort law (Parliament of the United Kingdom, 1945). Compared with ship-source pollution damage, which is another maritime tort governed by several conventions stipulating strict liability of the registered owner, collision liability is based on fault. Previously, fault was presumed if a rule under the COLREGs 1972 or similar regulatory rule under domestic law was violated. The presumption was expressly removed by Article 6 of the 1910 Convention.

Among other principal features of this convention, Article 2 provides that where the cause of the collision is accidental or is attributable to force majeure or the cause is left in doubt, the loss lies where it falls; regardless of whether the vessels are underway (COLREGs, 1972). Pursuant to Article 8, the master of each vessel in a collision situation has a duty to render assistance to the other vessel provided no danger is caused to his/her own vessel, the crew or passengers. This corresponds to Regulation 33 in Chapter 5 of the International Convention for the Safety of Life at Sea, 1974 (SOLAS, 1974). It is doubtful that this requirement in the Collision Liability Convention or in SOLAS, 1974 for that matter, can be fulfilled by a shore-based remote controller. Another provision is Article 13 of the Collision Liability Convention which makes the convention applicable even if no collision has occurred but one vessel causes damage to another by faulty maneuvering or non-observance of the COLREGs 1972. An example is the damage suffered by a relatively small vessel caused by the heavy backwash of a large vessel even if there has been no physical contact between the two.

One suggestion that I have seen made in respect of collision liability relating to MASS is to change it from fault-based to strict, which will pre-empt the need for claimants to discharge the burden of proof. I am not sure I am in full agreement with this proposition. Presumably, it will be the principal of the remote controller on whom the strict liability will be imposed. It may be the shipowner or some other entity in respect of whom, the controller is the servant in law. At any rate, there are other issues involved as pointed out below.

We are all aware that pollution liability under the conventions is strict; it works well simply because no contributory negligence is involved and liability is exclusively that of the registered shipowner once it is shown that the pollution in fact occurred and that it was ship-generated. In the case of collision liability, in the vast majority of cases, both vessels involved are at fault, albeit in the same or in different proportions. In that sense, it is a kind of strict liability except where there is a finding of 100% fault on the part of one vessel and the other is totally without fault, which is relatively rare. It may work, if both colliding vessels are MASS in which case, the court will simply have to deal with the issue of apportionment of fault assuming both vessels are at fault in the first place. However, it will be impossible to implement strict liability if there is a collision between a manned and an unmanned vessel. In this regard, I think that manned vessels at sea will remain in the majority well into the distant future, in which case there is little or no rationale for changing the status quo of fault-based liability with regard to them.

3.4 Correlation Between the Civil and Penal Liability Regimes

The civil liability regime governed by the 1910 Convention and the COLREGs 1972 are inextricably correlated in most instances. In practical terms, the two instruments are virtually inseparable. In collision, the civil liability arises by reason of commission of a maritime tort. The nature and extent of damage inflicted by one vessel on the other dictate the remedy that the court provides in respect of each vessel (Mukherjee, 2013).

Whereas COLREGs being a regulatory convention mainly concerns penal sanctions to be imposed in the event of a violation, there are tangential civil liability implications. For example, it is provided in Rule 2 of the COLREGs 1972 that no owner, master or member of the ship's crew is exonerated from "the consequences of any neglect to comply with the rules...". Arguably, therefore, aside from penal consequences, there may be pecuniary damages imposed on the owner, master or crew member in question; but the two latter entities may successfully plead that the owner as their principal, is vicariously responsible in terms of the civil liability. The same argument can be made in respect of the provision which states that none of them are exonerated from the consequences of any neglect to take precautions necessitated by the "ordinary practice of seamen". The consequences are potential liability in respect of the master or crew member, no doubt.

In relation to the legal position of the shore-based remote controller, a valid question regarding liability is whether good seamanship can be demonstrated through the use of computer software (UK P&I Club, 2019). To comply with the aforementioned Rule 2, control centers will need to employ personnel well-versed in seamanship to avoid potential liability. One commentator has pointed out that autonomous vessels in the fourth-degree category will have no qualified crew onboard and therefore, in practical terms, the requirement of "ordinary practice of seamen" will not be met (Komianos, 2018). The same situation will apply to vessels of the second and third degrees with which this discussion is concerned. Like numerous other rules and requirements, the question arises as to whether the relevant instruments must be amended. Another relevant observation is that Rule 2 permits a departure from the requirements if that is needed to avoid immediate danger which is another instance of a judgment call based on ordinary practice of seamen.

Negligence liability involves a standard of care that must be determined by the application of an objective test. As mentioned earlier in this chapter, COLREGs 1972 refer to "ordinary practice of seamen" and "good seamanship" which are objective standards albeit ones associated with a particular calling or vocation. Even though the presumption of fault by reason of a violation of the COLREGs 1972 has been effectively abolished by the 1910 Collision Liability Convention, non-compliance with COLREGs 1972 is nevertheless strongly indicative of fault or negligence in most cases. When COLREGs 1972 are inapplicable, good seamanship or ordinary practice of seamen dictates whether or not there has been negligence (The Heranger, 1939).

The dichotomy between what is a crossing and what is an overtaking situation is one that has baffled nautical and legal minds. The matter has not been definitively resolved in relation to real factual situations. Liability and its apportionment in private law terms rest on differences in individual circumstances. In my own view, the case law jurisprudence is somewhat obscure and convoluted. A case in point is The Dream Star, a decision of the Singapore High Court (2017). Two other cases from a few decades ago were The Nowy Sacz, already mentioned, and The Auriga (Lloyd's Rep.384, 1977) both decisions of the English courts. It is also notable in this context that the viewpoints of judges in this matter are distinctively different from those of professional mariners (Mukherjee, 1992).

The long and short in terms of MASS is that the above-mentioned situations, namely, vessels meeting head-on, and crossing and overtaking situations, all call for the application of good seamanship which translates into skill and proficiency acquired through rigorous training and years of first-hand experience at sea on different types of vessels. It is not something that a shore-based remote controller is likely to possess unless he/she is an experienced "real" master or mariner who has served at sea and is not just a desktop navigator. It cannot simply be learnt in theory. It is instructive to note the EU initiative suggesting that shore-based remote controllers dealing with MASS should have the know-how and qualifications possessed by shipboard personnel (European Commission, 2020). But perhaps that is a tall order. I am personally not aware of any individuals with the kind of dual expertise that is needed although such skill and proficiency will eventually come about in due course, no doubt. The question is—when?

It is said that technology moves at the speed of sound; by contrast, the law develops at a snail's pace. It is also said that in the maritime field, the law is reactive. A cynical view in this regard is that nothing changes or no new law is created until a major maritime catastrophe occurs. The sinking of the Titanic, the Torrey Canyon disaster, the Herald of Free Enterprise and the Achille Lauro incident are prime examples. At any rate, maritime safety remains at the core of concerns in the world shipping community. Even with phenomenal technological advancements in shipping, accidents continue to happen. The 2012 foundering of the Costa Concordia is a striking and exemplary case of over-reliance on technology. In consonance with others, I am of the firm view that regardless of the huge technological advancements, regulatory control of ships must never be compromised (Schröder-Hinrichs et al., 2012). Pioneers who are at the forefront of cutting-edge technology contend that MASS provides the answer to all shipping problems. But those of us who belong to the conservative cadre of mariners, are skeptical and less enthusiastic. Autonomous ships like all other vessels plying the waterways of the world must be regulated through international instruments to ensure that maritime safety is always maintained. The novel characteristics and peculiarities of MASS of all descriptions are reason enough for their proper and effective regulation through international maritime conventions (Kim et al., 2020, p. 19).

On the liability front, given that in the realm of autonomous ships, computers and other sophisticated hi-tech equipment will carry out the same tasks that trained and experienced humans are doing at present, an important matter in the context of collisions as a maritime tort, is the issue of negligence. That is the variety of fault that prevails in collision liability law. If the remote-control operator is incompetent or operates the computer or equipment in a negligent fashion which is the proximate cause of the collision, then negligence and the ensuing liability can be imputed to that individual. But if the computer or equipment malfunctions without any fault on the part of the operator, negligence cannot be imputed to the inanimate object, that is, the computer or hi-tech equipment. One must ponder over who in such a case should be held liable. A viable possibility is to pursue the seller and/or manufacturer of the equipment in question. That will inevitably lead to the arena of product liability.

4 Conclusion

This chapter is premised on my view and observation, that collision law is probably the most important element in terms of the potential liability of the shore-based remote-control operator involved in MASS operations. As elaborated in the text, collision liability is imposed on the owner or operator of the vessel in question, and more often than not, is based on violations of rules committed by the master or navigator of the vessel concerned. In the extant scenario of collision liability law, the master or navigator onboard is the servant or agent of the owner or operator and the latter is vicariously liable in law. In the MASS scenario, the shore-based remote controller corresponds to the onboard master or navigator. It is that person's actions or failure to act for which the owner or operator is liable; therefore, prima facie, there is no reason why the remote controller should not be held accountable one way or another.

Where it is a matter of application of penal law for a COLREGs 1972 violation, the remote controller should be held personally responsible. In terms of application of civil liability, needless to say, the owner or operator as principal, will be held liable for the fault of the remote controller. I have heard murmurs about holding the manufacturer of equipment in the MASS context liable under product liability law, but that, in my view, is a question of proximate cause as a parameter of liability in tort which is a function of the particular factual situation.

Apart from collision law, there are fundamental issues within the framework of public and private maritime law regarding such matters as what constitutes a ship and the roles and responsibilities of the master and navigator in the MASS context, including the tricky question of whether the shore-based remote controller fits those descriptions. Related to the liability of that person is the question of insurance which will have to be revisited in terms of the basic tenets of that regime. In the final analysis, the expertise of multifarious sorts will have to be perused including those of professional navigators, maritime lawyers and technologists in the fields of artificial intelligence, computers and associated disciplines.

In legal terms, to accommodate all the above-noted elements, probably a convention in the nature of a MASS Code will have to be introduced for international application. My concluding observation is that the liability regime in respect of MASS is as yet underdeveloped.

The roles and functions of the flag state, port state and coastal state will have to change in the face of MASS. It will involve substantial and significant changes to the extant legal regimes, including questions of jurisdiction and enforcement in the public law sphere and liability in private maritime law matters including the regime of marine insurance which is relevant to all aspects of private law. On the whole, MASS will only become a workable practical reality when all vessels become autonomous in some shape or form. That is unlikely to happen in the short term, especially with regard to ships owned or operated by entities in developing countries. Only time will tell what may transpire in the future.

References

Canadian Coast Guard. (2022). *Radio Aids to Marine Navigation 2022 Part 3—Vessel Traffic Services*. Available at: https://www.ccg-gcc.gc.ca/publications/mcts-sctm/ramn-arnm/part3-eng.html. Accessed 5 July 2022.

Chinmayi, R., Jayam Y. K., Tunuguntla, V., Dammuru J. V., Nadella, H., Dulla, S. S. K. A., Raja, L. S. K., & Nair, J. G. (2018). Obstacle Detection and Avoidance Robot. *2018 IEEE International Conference on Computational Intelligence and Computing Research (ICCIC)*.

Clifford Law Offices. (2022). The Dangers of Driverless Cars, *The National Law Review*, *XII*(170).

Cockroft, A. N., & Lameijer, J. N. F. (2011). *A Guide to the Collision Avoidance Rules* (7th ed.). Butterworth-Heinemann.

COLREGs. (1972). Convention on the International Regulations for Preventing Collisions at Sea 1050. *UNTS* 16, *UKTS* 77 (1977), 28 *UST* 3459 Cmnd. 6962.

DNV. (n.d.). *Autonomous and Remotely-Operated Ships* (webpage). Available at: https://www.dnv.com/maritime/autonomous-remotely-operated-ships/research-activities.html. Accessed 5 July 2022.

European Commission. (2020). EU Operational Guidelines for Operational Guidelines for Operational Guidelines for Safe, Secure and Sustainable Trials of Maritime Autonomous Surface Ships (MASS). Available at: https://transport.ec.europa.eu/news/european-commission-encourages-maritime-future-which-includes-autonomous-and-sustainable-ships-and-2020-11-30_en. Accessed 6 July 2022.

GIS Geography. (2021). *A Complete Guide to LiDAR: Light Detection and Ranging* (webpage). Available at: https://gisgeography.com/lidar-light-detection-and-ranging/. Accessed 2 July 2022.

IMO Doc. MSC.1/Circ.1638. (2021a). *Outcome of the Regulatory Scoping Exercise for the Use of Maritime Autonomous Surface Ships (MASS)* (June 3, 2021).

IMO Doc. LEG 108/WP.1 Rev.1 (2021b). *Draft Report of the Legal Committee on the Work of its 108 Session* (August 4, 2021).

International Convention for the Unification of Certain Rules of Law with Respect to Collision Between Vessels. (1910). [130] ATS 14.

Komianos, A. (2018). The Autonomous Shipping Era. Operational, Regulatory, and Quality Challenges. *International Journal on Marine Navigation and Safety of Sea Transportation, 13*(18) 335–348. https://doi.org/10.12716/1001.12.02.15

Liu, H (2022). Maritime and Aviation Law: A Relational Retrospect and Prospect on Unmanned Ships and Aircraft. In A. Basu Bal (Ed.), *Revisiting Trade, Transport, and Marine Law: Risk and Technology in Perspective, Liber Amicorum Lars-Goran Malmberg*, Brill.

Lloyd's Law Reports. (1977). Lloyd's Rep 91 (C.A.) The "Nowy Sacz" Available at: https://www.i-law.com/ilaw/doc/view.htm?id=147620

Lloyd's Law Reports. (1977). Lloyd's Rep 384. The "Auriga". Available at: https://www.i-law.com/ilaw/doc/view.htm?id=147580. Accessed 5 July 2022.

Lloyd's Law Reports. (1982). Lloyd's Rep. 564. Bradshaw (acting on behalf of the Secretary of State for Trade) v. Ewart-James (The "N.F. TIGER"). Available at: https://www.i-law.com/ilaw/doc/view.htm?id=148179. Accessed 4 July 2022.

Marineinsight. (2022). *10 Things to Consider While Using Auto-Pilot System on Ships* (webpage). Available at: https://www.marineinsight.com/marine-navigation/10-things-to-consider-while-using-auto-pilot-system-on-ships. Accessed 6 July 2022.

Mingyu Kim, K., Joung, T.-H., Jeong, B., & Park, H.-S. (2020). Autonomous Shipping and its Impact on Regulations, Technologies, and Industries. *Journal of International Maritime Safety, Environmental Affairs, and Shipping, 4*(2), 17–25. https://doi.org/10.1080/25725084.2020.1779427

Mukherjee, P. K. (1992). Overtaking or Crossing: Judicial Interpretation and the Mariner's Dilemma. *Journal of Maritime Law & Commerce, 23*(2), 247–262.

Mukherjee, P. K. (2013). *Impact of the MONALISA Project on the International Legal Framework for Navigation at Sea*. Report submitted to the Swedish Maritime Administration in April 2013.

Mukherjee, P. K. (2016). The Fundamental and Human Rights of Seafarers: Legal Issues in Perspective. *Human Rights Law Journal*, *1*(1), 56–75. National Law University Odisha.

Munim, Z. H., & Haralambides, H. (2022). Advances in Maritime Autonomous Surface Ships (MASS) in Merchant Shipping. *Maritime Economics & Logistics, 24*, 181–188.

Parliament of the United Kingdom. (1945). *Law Reform (Contributory Negligence) Act 1945, c. 28*. Available at: https://www.legislation.gov.uk/ukpga/Geo6/8-9/28/contents. Accessed 4 July 2022.

Rolls-Royce. (2016). *(AAWA) Project, Led By Rolls-Royce, Introduced the Project's First Commercial Ship Operators* (webpage). Available at: https://www.rolls-royce.com/media/press-releases/2016/pr-12-04-2016-aawa-project-introduces-projects-first-commercial-operators.aspx. Accessed 4 July 2022.

Schröder-Hinrichs, J.-U., Hollnagel, E., & Baldauf, M. (2012). From Titanic to Costa Concordia—A Century of Lessons Not Learned. *WMU Journal of Maritime Affairs, 11*, 151–167.

Singapore High Court. (2017). The "Dream Star". SGHC 220.

STCW. (1978). International Convention on Standards of Training, Certification and Watchkeeping, 1361 *UNTS* 2 as amended in 1995 and 2010 (Manila Amendments). 1361 *UNTS* 190.

Tettenborn, A., & Kimbell, J. (2021). *Marsden & Gault on Collisions at Sea* (15th ed., p. 2021). Sweet and Maxwell.

The Heranger. (1939). S.S. (Owners) v Diamond, S.S. (Owners) [1939] AC 94.

UK P&I Club. (2019). *Legal Briefing: Autonomous Shipping—Revolution by Evolution*. Available at: https://www.ukpandi.com/news-and-resources/briefings/2019/legal-briefing-autonomous-shipping-revolution-by-evolution/. Accessed 4 July 2022.

CHAPTER 15

Navigating the Turbulent Waters of Liability: Making the Case for the Application of Risk-Management-Based Liability Approach to Autonomous Vessels

Anil Ozturk

1 Introduction

In simple terms, Maritime Autonomous Surface Ships (hereinafter MASS) refer to vessels that can self-execute some or all of their operational processes on their own. The display of autonomy, i.e., the characteristic that differentiates MASS from the rest of the ships, lays a specific spectrum. Presently, there are MASS, specifically short-distance passenger ferries, that perform some of the operational tasks autonomously. Although the level of technological development allows the production of such ships, there are no commercial oceangoing MASS that are

A. Ozturk (✉)
School of Law and Criminology, Maynooth University, Co. Kildare, Ireland
e-mail: aniluozturk@gmail.com

© The Author(s), under exclusive license to Springer Nature Switzerland AG 2023

T. M. Johansson et al. (eds.), *Autonomous Vessels in Maritime Affairs*, Studies in National Governance and Emerging Technologies,
https://doi.org/10.1007/978-3-031-24740-8_15

capable of self-navigation. Still, as the combined initial and working costs of MASS become relatively inexpensive compared to the constantly increasing costs associated with running crewed vessels, facilitated by the constantly decreasing numbers of available seafarers worldwide, it is assessed that MASS will emerge and become widespread, perhaps sooner than anticipated. Nonetheless, just as the core domains of private law fail to recognise that some functional artefacts could make decisions and implement them without human intervention—the legal regime that governs the operations of ships is based on the presumption that ships are either operated by crews on board or somehow under human control. That being the case, determining how the legal regime should respond to the unwelcome outcomes of MASS' independent activities is critical for preserving the principles of legal security and certainty, two of the core principles of the rule of law.

2 Conceptual Framework

2.1 Characteristic of Autonomy

MASS are ships set apart from other ships in how they complete their tasks. Unlike conventional ships that are manually operated by crew members on board, MASS carry out at least some of their operations autonomously. The display of the characteristic of autonomy is not approached from a binary perspective. Instead, it is assessed that different MASS have various degrees of autonomy. That assessment is based on the definition provided by the International Maritime Organization (IMO) in its regulatory scoping exercise (as discussed in detail in Chapter 3 of this volume). In that exercise, the IMO specified four degrees of autonomy that MASS might display. Taking these specifications as the reference baseline, it can be argued that most MASS on the market merely have some of the processes automated, and on-board crew members otherwise operate them (corresponding to Degree 1 and Degree 2 of the IMO definition). Other types of MASS are teleoperated ships (corresponding to Degree 3) (IMO, 2018; MSC.1/Circ.1638, 2021). Though MASS may have some of their operational processes automatised, they still depend on human control to complete their tasks maintaining the degrees of autonomy. In other words, though MASS are not altogether new technological contraptions, most of those produced up until the present day do not display the characteristic of autonomy at levels that would pose challenges to the effectiveness of existing legal frameworks. Be that as it may, at the current level of technological development, it is also possible to build more autonomous MASS that can make and execute decisions regarding their navigation without any humans in the loop (corresponding to Degree 4). According to available statistical data, at least one thousand such MASS are already in use, though none of these genuinely independent MASS is deployed commercially (Dougherty, 2021).

Considering that the term 'ship' refers to the functional artefacts that are intended to be used in maritime transportation, we submit that MASS that display Degree 4 autonomy are robots. The categorisation of these self-navigating MASS as robots makes the solutions proposed for determining civil liability for robots relevant to the questions concerning legal responsibility for independent activities of the MASS.

The definition of autonomy as 'being able to operate freely from real-time human interaction' is not sufficiently specific since it also encompasses automatic devices that do not make their own decisions. For example, that definition applies to thermostats. Once the desired temperature is entered, thermostats bring the ambient temperature to the desired temperature without human interaction, but they are not considered autonomous. Therefore, instead of adopting that simplistic definition, the present study follows the trend in the literature and embraces the sense-think-act paradigm as the operational definition of the characteristic of autonomy. As suggested by the name, devices that can operate according to the sense-think-act paradigm have three sets of capabilities allowing them to carry out the processes of sensing, thinking, and acting (Siegel, 2003).

First, sensing capabilities refer to artefacts' ability to observe and perceive whatever might happen in their surroundings. These abilities require artefacts that have sensors instead of the sensory organs of living beings, so they can monitor the environment they operate in. Without sensing capabilities, functional artefacts cannot process or react to any stimuli, no matter how developed their evaluating abilities might be (Rubio et al., 2019). Then sensing capabilities are sine qua non for any artefact to display the autonomy characteristic.

Secondly, thinking capabilities refer to the competence of artefacts to subject the information gathered through sensors to analytical and evaluative algorithms, allowing them to plan the course of action they need to follow to achieve their specified tasks. In short, thinking capabilities are artefacts' problem-solving and decision-making skills (Krach et al., 2008). The complexity and sophistication of these capabilities determine the degree of artefacts' autonomy. If artefacts can incorporate outcomes of past experiences into decision-making processes and improve the accuracy, efficiency, and precision of the said processes, they can be considered as being more autonomous than the others.

Thirdly, acting capabilities refer to artefacts' ability to carry out courses of action planned through the 'thinking' capabilities. Through these capabilities, artefacts can affect the environments they operate in or be 'active'. Indeed, if artefacts cannot 'act', they would be little more than some advanced measuring instruments or computational devices.

Regardless of the degree of autonomy, the capabilities that facilitate that characteristic under no circumstances mean that robots' independent activities are driven by their own needs, desires, and goals. On the contrary, robots have no individual interests that drive their activities. Instead, their autonomous behaviours are driven by the individual interests of their owners, users, and manufacturers—the entity that determines and specifies tasks.

Consequently, it is established that robots—functional artefacts that have the capabilities that facilitate the characteristic of autonomy in levels allowing them to operate according to the sense-think-act paradigm, including independent MASS beyond Degree 4 according to the IMO definition of the MASS, can also be categorised as 'autonomous artificial agents'. Unlike other artefacts, robots can carry out courses of action that they plan through their decision-making processes. Only MASS that perform their core progress—navigating in oceans—according to the sense-think-act paradigm can be considered robots under the discussions speared through in the present chapter.

2.2 Concept of Effectiveness

The present chapter does not discuss the functionality of the balances between conflicting interests safeguarded by the existing legal mechanisms. Instead, it presumes that specific balances that each legal mechanism seeks to maintain between conflicting interests signify the unique purpose of that mechanism. To this end, this chapter supports the concept of 'effectiveness' that denotes the success of any given legal mechanism in achieving its unique purpose. Most legal mechanisms that address the questions of civil liability are devised to restore the balances between interests of equal members of society, disrupted by members' unlawful interferences on one another's personality, property, or other legally protected interests. To which degree these damages would be restored is determined by the relevant legal principles and applicable legal mechanisms. In that regard, most civil liability disputes could be addressed as conflicts between the defendant's interest in freedom of action and the plaintiff's interest in legal security.

The freedom of action, primarily when expressed as the freedom of enterprise, is one of the interests that propel the general progress in society. In most modern economic systems based on voluntary exchange, competition in the market is prompted by the legal protection extended to the interest in freedom of action. That competition, in turn, motivates the actors in the market to offer better products at lower prices, thereby boosting economic dynamism and scientific research and eventually maximising the general welfare. In conflicts of interest involving the interest in freedom of action, severely restricting that freedom in favour of the defendant's interest in legal security can result in economic stagnation that in turn slows the rate of scientific or technological progress (McMullen et al., 2008). Nonetheless, when unwelcome outcomes arise in everyday life—it almost always concerns one party's exercise of the freedom of action.

Legal security refers to the protection afforded by the law to the integrity of material and immaterial rights of society's members. According to social contract theorists, perhaps the most significant reason for human beings to live together in society is the assurance that another would arbitrarily violate no one's rights. Should such violations occur, they would be made good. In that regard, the interest in legal security protects the assurances of social life (Palombella, 2009).

When the plaintiff's interest in legal security conflicts with another's interest in freedom of action, if the balance foreseen by the law gives priority to the freedom of action over the interest in legal protection and therefore, does not sufficiently remedy the damages, the assurances underlying the maintenance of social life would inevitably weaken. Indeed, using the phraseology of Hobbes, the prominent social contract theorist, the lack of protection afforded to the interest in legal security would result in humankind's U-turn back to the state of nature, where life was 'nasty, brutish, and short' (Hobbes & Shapiro, 2010).

Which of the conflicting interests would be protected to what degree differs according to conditions and circumstances foreseen for each legal mechanism. For instance, contract law mechanisms, in general, give more weight to the plaintiff's interest in legal security since disputes in contract law often relate to legally enforceable promises—voluntary commitments that the parties make about their future courses of conduct. Contracts can be regarded as self-imposed constraints on the freedom of action. Then, it is rational for the law to try and uphold the reliance on the promise made and prioritise the interest in legal security. When it comes to disputes addressed by tort law mechanisms, however, conflicts between the injured party's interest in legal security and the injuring party's interest in freedom of action are more perceptible. Across national legal systems and even in the context of different torts within the same legal system, the weight given to these interests also differs. For instance, while the French Civil Code emphasises the good in legal security, the German Civil Code prioritises the interest in freedom of activity when putting forward the general rule for negligence-based tort liability. The legal mechanisms relevant to the questions of civil liability for MASS and their purposes are discussed in the following section.

In addition, per the core principles of the rule of law, any 'effective' legal mechanism must also be fair, just, and reasonable. If the party held liable was unaware of what conduct they should adopt or what actions they should refrain from to avoid liability—that party would not be allowed to regulate their behaviours. In such cases, even if the existing legal mechanisms maintain the balance between conflicting interests when applied to the disputes, their application will still violate the principle of legal certainty, one of the core principles of the rule of law. No legal mechanism that fails to conform to the principles of the rule of law can be regarded as effective.

3 Challenges: Current Legal Regime

3.1 Regulatory Framework

Thanks to their ability to operate autonomously, it is likely that some MASS can appear as initiators and parties to some interactions themselves. Much like the interactions that are initiated by and take place between human beings, it is inevitable that some of the independent activities of MASS are going to damage other entities' legally protected interests, and thereby bringing about disputes on civil liability.

The domain in which MASS operate—the maritime domain—does not always allow for fair winds and smooth sailing. On the contrary, the seas are full of perils, and when accidents occur at sea, they often also bring about many types of unwelcome outcomes, such as loss of life, personal injury, damages to other ships, harms to other property and harbour works, not to mention environmental damages. Because of the treacherous nature of the seas, the damages that may arise in the maritime domain are often more difficult for the concerned parties to foresee, circumvent, and eventually remedy. Nonetheless, a significant part of the global trade is still conducted through international maritime shipping, calling for the creation of some sort of international regulatory framework.

In the present day, one such framework is created, mostly by the IMO to provide for safe, secure, and efficient operations of ships (De Burgh, 2009). That regulatory framework does not often explicitly address questions that are civil liability in nature. Instead, it specifies ideal behaviours or standards of care to be followed by shipowners and crews during seafaring activities to prevent potential damages. If these standards of behaviours are not observed, it means that shipowners or crew members are not displaying the levels of care and attention expected of them, and as such, they can be held liable in the event of damages on the basis of their carelessness, or negligence (De Bruyne, 2019).

Though the regulatory framework sets out behavioural standards to be followed in seafaring activities, that framework and the behavioural standards contained therein are primarily developed before the emergence and commercial usage of the independent MASS. Consequently, in literature there exists debate as to whether MASS can be regarded as ships or vessels and fall under the scope of application of the regulatory framework. When the international statutory instruments that constitute the regulatory framework are examined, it is revealed that most of these instruments do not provide explicit definitions of ship and/or vessel, even when their scopes of application are defined. For example, most prominently, the United Nations Convention on the Law of the Sea, 1982 (UNCLOS) contains provisions that specify that the Convention applies to ships and vessels, but it does not provide the much-needed definitions. In the same manner, the International Regulations for Preventing Collisions at Sea, 1972 (COLREGs, 1972) specify that they apply to 'all vessels upon the high seas and in all waters connected therewith navigable by seagoing vessels', but do not define what is a seagoing vessel. In contrast, the

International Convention on Salvage, 1989 (Salvage Convention, 1989) that applies to 'vessels or any other property in danger', defines vessel as 'any ship or craft, or any structure capable of navigation', and property includes anything that is 'not permanently and intentionally attached to the shoreline'. So, while MASS can fall within the scope of application of Salvage Convention, 1989, the same cannot be said with the same certainty in relation to other statutory instruments.

On the presumption that MASS fall within the scope of international statutory instruments that set out the regulatory framework that is currently in force, applying most of their provisions to MASS' independent activities would not make much sense.

These statutory instruments are not intended to apply in cases where ships manage themselves, evidenced by references made to on-board crews. For example, one UNCLOS provision requires flag states 'to take such measures as are necessary to ensure safety at sea with regard to the manning of ships, labour conditions and the training of crews'. The same provision further stipulates that such measures must ensure that each ship is in the charge of a master and officers who possess appropriate 'qualifications'.

Considering that the provision makes explicit reference to 'manning of ships' refers to some crew operating the vessel, it is clear that its application would not make much sense in the context of self-navigating MASS. Similarly, and perhaps more explicitly, the International Convention for the Safety of Life at Sea, 1974 (SOLAS, 1974) requires that 'all ships shall be sufficiently and efficiently manned'. Rule 5 of COLREGs, 1972 requires every vessel at all times to 'maintain proper look-out by sight as well as by hearing as well as by all available means appropriate in the prevailing circumstance and conditions so as to make a full appraisal of the situation and of the risk of collision'.

These provisions, even though they were clearly intended to denote the presence of 'on-board' crews operating ships, can be interpreted to apply to the MASS that are up to level 3 of autonomy, including the MASS that are remotely controlled and therefore, under direct human control. For example, 'manning' of the ship, for the purposes of the COLREGs, 1972, can be construed to include the personnel that operate the vessel from another location, thereby expanding the scope of the notion of 'crew'. Equally, the obligation to continuously maintain a proper lookout, imposed by the COLREGs, 1972, Rule 5, could also be conducted by seafarers located elsewhere but still have real-time access to the data generated by the ship's cameras and sensors. Be that as it may, even then, the regulatory framework that is in force would not apply to or allow for fully independent ships with no human crew continuously controlling them. In closing, the regulatory framework would not work at all for independent MASS that operate without the constant control or supervision of some human being.

Then, if the independent MASS are considered to fall outside the scope of the regulatory framework that applies to the rest of the ships, as suggested by the analysis above, then, it is surmised that manufacturers, owners, and users of independent MASS are not provided with any clarity about what is expected from them. With no regulatory framework that addresses the independent MASS, there are no standards of care to guide the conduct of concerned parties over the MASS. Therefore, these parties do not have their duty of care defined sufficiently. Consequently, as these parties have no legal certainty as to what is expected of them, if any civil liability is imposed on them for damages arising from independent activities of MASS, that situation would run the risk of disrupting parties' interests not only in terms of freedom of action but also in relation to legal security. Under the rule of law, arbitrary imposition of any form of liability unjustified, and unjustified infringements of one's personal rights and assets, even by the State cannot be sanctioned. The present chapter, therefore, defends that the existing regulatory framework should be expanded to address the independent activities of MASS and elucidate the duties of their manufacturers, owners, and users.

3.2 Existing Legal Mechanisms

Most of the existing legal mechanisms that are intended to resolve civil liability disputes in maritime law are based on the same purposes that guide the distribution of liability in general private law. Relevantly, in both domains of private law—contract law and tort law—the general principle for restoring the balance between interests is the fault principle. The fault principle is assessed to reflect the influence of morality in the rebalancing of competing interests, in other words, which of the parties should ultimately bear the damages. To put it simply, existing legal mechanisms based on the fault principle provide that the protection of the damages should be borne by the party who is morally blameworthy for the occurrence of these damages, and the morally blameworthy party is the one that use their free will with fault to cause damages or inflict injuries on another party (Gray, 2021).

There are two types of faults: intent and negligence. When the fault is 'intent', the responsible party knowingly and willingly uses their free will to inflict injury, and when the fault is 'negligence', the party fails to use their free will to prevent injuries even though these outcomes were foreseeable and preventable.

More specifically, in maritime law, shipowners are often held liable for the damages caused during the operation of ships, so long as these damages do not relate to the breaches of contracts. The tortious liability of shipowners is based on the fault principle (though the fault that provides the primary basis of liability is that of the crew) rendering the shipowner's liability as one that takes the form of vicarious and secondary liability (Todd, 2020). Though the general rule for establishing liability is the fault principle, the systems already recognise that the fault principle may not consistently achieve the fair distribution of risks that arise in the ordinary course of everyday life in industrial society. Consequently, under some exceptional circumstances, the imposition of liability on the defendant is allowed regardless of their fault. When strict liability is applied, the criteria for moral justification for the assignment of liability—fault of the defendant—is not sought. Considering the fault principle provides the basis for the legitimacy of liability under normal circumstances, each form of strict liability, to be seen as legitimate, must be justified through some alternative principle. One of these alternative principles is the risk principle.

Accordingly, if one engages in potentially dangerous activities, they are expected to take all measures to prevent any damages from arising. If damages still occur despite measures undertaken, one is held responsible for damages regardless of whether they were at fault, since they were engaged in activities that they knew or should have known. The risk principle applies to the damages that are caused by ultra-hazardous activities, as well as the possession of dangerous animals, and environmental damages, as well as liability incurred from traffic accidents. Another alternative basis for the imposition of liability is the duty to control: when one employs another, the employer must also take necessary measures to prevent damages being caused by the behaviour of their employees in the course of their employment, if not, they can be held liable for damages since they avail from the benefits brought by their behaviour (Gray, 2021).

In the context of maritime law, the IMO framework provides strict liability for pollution damages. According to the International Convention on Civil Liability for Oil Pollution Damage, 1969 (CLC 69), vessels involved in pollution incidents are held both individually and jointly liable for the damages without any need to establish their fault. Similarly, the Athens Convention Relating the Carriage of Passengers and their Luggage at Sea (2002 Protocol) provides that strict liability could be applied in cases where maritime accidents result in loss of life or bodily injury of the passengers.

When it comes to damages caused by independent activities of MASS; there may be no crew on board, or no personnel off board that are obliged to exercise control over the ship. Some or all of the crew roles on traditional ships are performed by MASS themselves, depending on the degree of autonomy. However, the law does not recognise that any artefact can have 'free will' or agency and as such, no fault can be attributed to the MASS themselves. Consequently, it is uncertain how or whether the fault-based liability regime would work in relation to MASS in scenarios where the human element is absent. The characteristic that distinguishes MASS from other ships, i.e., autonomy, is the reason behind this uncertainty.

Self-navigating MASS, by definition, are able to decide which behaviours they are going to perform themselves. Even though the human element designs the vessel and determines the voyage destinations—they are controlled by their own operating systems without human involvement. The fact that these vessels are autonomous means that human beings are out-of-the-loop.

One could also ask the question whether the fault principle can be applied to impose liability on manufacturers of such vessels. The decision-making algorithms of these vessels are programmed, after all, by their manufacturers. That being said, autonomous vessels operate in uncontrolled environments, and even though the variety of actions that they can perform are limited by their operating systems, manufacturers cannot reasonably foresee the types of actions vessels might take in every possible circumstance. Decision-making algorithms or operating systems of these vessels determine which actions are going to be performed, and in which sequence those will be performed. There are potentially infinite number of action plans that could be adopted by these vessels, and it is simply not possible for manufacturers to foresee the consequences of all possible behaviours. Since the fault principle appears to be ineffective when it comes to liability for autonomous vessels, it must be assessed whether the legal mechanisms that espouse strict liability could be applied to damages caused by MASS.

Though the imposition of strict liability for the damages caused by MASS would provide for the recovery of damages, it would not necessarily strike the balance between competing interests of manufacturers, owners, users, and that of injured parties. Here, it must be noted that the purpose of the existing liability mechanism is not to award compensation to the damaged party in all cases, rather to provide for fair re-distribution of the damages. Then, to impose strict liability for the damages caused by MASS, there needs to be some reason apart from the non-existence of fault that justifies abandoning the fault principle. Indeed, for liability for damages caused by defective products, the reasons are the necessities of economic life, and for damages that are caused by ultra-hazardous activities or certain animals, the justification is the danger principle. The present chapter submits that none of these principles finds any practical application when it comes to MASS.

First of all, the utilisation of MASS does not increase the likelihood and gravity of potential damages. Autonomous vessels are said to observe and analyse changes in their surroundings without any interruptions and respond to risky situations much faster than the human element. Today, human error results in maritime incidents and maritime casualties. It is therefore expected that the introduction of fully autonomous ships will reduce the general level of risk for marine accidents. As such, the 'danger' principle cannot be used to legitimise strict liability for autonomous vessels' behaviours (de Vos et al., 2021).

The other prominent form of liability, i.e., strict product liability, is addressed in the European Union by the Product Liability Directive. Under the Directive, manufacturers are held strictly liable for the damages caused by their defective products. With the exception of the United States, most of the prominent legal systems have introduced product liability regimes similar to the regime produced by this Directive. The present chapter holds that the Directive may not quite apply to autonomous vessels. First of all, it is not clear that whether the definition of 'product', determined by the Directive, includes the autonomous vessel, or more specifically, the decision-making algorithms.

Indeed, there is some consensus in literature on that robots, including MASS, are not products for the purposes of the Directive since they are not static once put into circulation. This point of view is strengthened by the presence of the state-of-the-art defence provided in the Directive, absolving the manufacturer from any liability on the condition that they prove that the defects could not have been identified under the level of technological development and scientific knowledge at the time when the product was released. Moreover, it is also not entirely certain whether all the damages caused by decisions taken by autonomous vessels themselves can be seen to be caused by some 'defects'. The present chapter holds that so long as sensory errors or software bugs remain outside the liability scope, the damages cannot be linked to any 'defect' and therefore the product liability provisions cannot be applied.

4 Beyond the Challenges: Overcoming the Shortcomings of the Current Legal Regime

The current legal regime is presumed to be effective for answering the civil liability questions for damages caused by functional artefacts under the control of human beings. However, as the analysis of existing legal mechanisms and the regulatory framework that is currently in force establishes, that legal regime is ineffective and inadequate for determining liability for undesirable outcomes of independent activities of MASS. To be regarded as adequate, answers to question on civil liability for MASS must balance the interests of owners, users, and manufacturers of MASS injured parties in manners similar to those struck by existing legal mechanisms when applied to disputes that do not involve non-autonomous functional artefacts.

The existing legal mechanisms, when applied to disputes involving the independent activities of MASS, might still vindicate the interest of the injured party. In doing so, they run the risk of having manufacturers, owners, or users shoulder all the damages without allowing them to avail the protection they would have afforded if the ships were not autonomous. In other words, applying existing legal mechanisms to civil liability questions would likely result in the prioritisation of the interests of the injured party beyond what is intended by existing legal mechanisms.

In that regard, the present chapter holds that the questions of civil liability for MASS cannot be answered effectively by existing legal mechanisms, and therefore improvements to the current legal regime are critical. Since MASS belong to the group of functional artefacts that are identified as robots, it is assessed that proposals for determining civil liability for robots may be utilised to answer the liability question for MASS.

Perhaps the most innovative proposal is one that advocates granting legal personhood to robots. Accordingly, the conferral of legal personhood on robots means that these specific functional artefacts would be equipped with two legal capacities: the capacity to have rights and obligations and the capacity to perform legally meaningful actions. It is argued that granting robots personhood allows for the direct imposition of liability for the damages arising from robots' behaviours on robots without disrupting the balance of interests that the existing legal mechanisms were designed to maintain.

That said, robots—including MASS—regardless of what degree of autonomy they may display, do not have any desires, objectives, needs, purposes, and wants of their own. In fact, they perform each and every one of the independent activities to fulfil certain predetermined functions, specified by either the manufacturer, owner, or user. In other words, no robot or MASS can possess any individual interests to guide their external behaviours. If the concept of right is defined as 'legally protected individual interest', then in this case, there is nothing to extend legal protection to. As such, even if robots are granted legal personhood, their capacity to hold rights would only serve as some sort of straw-man to limit the potential liability of their owner.

Moreover, it should be reiterated that robots, including MASS, regardless of their capabilities, are ultimately 'artefacts'. They are objects that emerge following the exertion of engineering and programming skills on raw materials. Despite the growth of autonomy and the increasing variety of roles they can undertake, at the end of the day, they are still devices deployed by their manufacturer, owner, and user. Considering that, any or all of the above maintain their right to use, benefit, and dispose of the robot. In which case, it can be said that robots including MASS, for all intents and purposes, remain as a 'property'.

Falling short of full personhood, some proposals focus on the recognition of robots' capacity to act but refrain from giving them the capacity to have rights and obligations. According to these proposals, robots (including MASS) can be given some sort of semi-personhood. In the realm of semi-personhood, independent activities of robots will create legal consequences, but these consequences would be borne by whatever parties have the duty to control the artefacts. Proposals that advocate the introduction of semi-personhood vary in their content, especially to what degree the consequences of robots should bind the concerned parties (Chopra & White, 2011).

One proposal for semi-personhood is put forward by Pagallo that suggests that robots could be treated as 'the new agents in town' and admits that giving them the legal capacity to have rights and obligations is neither necessary nor practical. Instead, Pagallo suggests the revival of one of the defunct legal instruments from Roman law (Pagallo, 2013). Indeed, Roman Law recognised that there could be some agents whose behaviours were attached to legal consequences but could not possess neither rights nor obligations. Much like robots and MASS, these agents interacted with third parties and sometimes ran businesses on behalf of their principals. The law, in the interest of economic dynamism and legal security, introduced the legal instrument of 'peculium' that would allow for the fulfilment of obligations assumed by these agents. Principals designated some part of their patrimony as their agents' 'peculium', and though 'peculium' still remained as principals' property, legal consequences of agents' behaviours were borne on that part of the patrimony, limiting principals' liability to that extent. Pagallo argues that the challenge that faces 'the new agents in town' in the present find is not at all different from the situation of the above-mentioned non-person agents in Roman Law. Accordingly, it follows that the solution devised by Romans, with some modifications, could be applied to the question of liability for artificial autonomous agents. Pagallo calls this proposed revival of an ancient legal instrument as 'digital peculium' and suggests that this peculium can be jointly funded by the masters and manufacturers, or some other funds, such as compulsory insurance (Izumo, 2018).

The present chapter finds that proposal suitable for robots, but when it comes to MASS, its application may be problematic. First off, in specific circumstances, ships are already personified to some degree. For instance, when no fault that can be attributed to the shipowner or to the crew, the liability is imposed on the shipowner. Indeed, in most countries of the world, the State regulates ships as some sort of legal enterprise. This is in addition to a ship's status as 'property'. Since the current legal status of ships also includes lability provisions—the present study believes that the creation of an additional legal status to address liability questions has the potential to create confusion and inconsistency. Considering that one of the precepts of rule of law is legal security, knowing what rules apply in which cases, granting ships some sort of further legal status, even if it does not include recognition of the capacity to have rights and obligations, seems inconsistent with the rule of law, and may result in more problems than it solves.

Another alternative that answers the question of civil liability suggests a risk-based management approach. The proposal developed by Bertolini can be distinguished from the general rule in that it relaxes elements pertaining not only to the 'fault' side of things but also legal causation required for the establishment of liability. For the damages caused by robots, Bertolini agrees that none of the existing legal mechanisms is able to provide solutions that are both effective and fair. Bertolini argues that liability should be borne by the party that is placed best to '(i) identify a risk (ii) control and minimize it through its choices, and (iii) manage it'—ideally pooling and redistributing it among all other parties—eventually through insurance, and/or no-fault compensation funds. Even though Bertolini suggests that the liable party may change 'from one class of applications to another', it is evident that the party that is in the best position for risk management would be the manufacturer, since owners and users are not expected to be familiar with the inner workings of their devices (Bertolini, 2013).

Adoption of the risk-based liability management approach to answer the question of civil liability for MASS does not necessarily mean, however, that all responsibility for damages caused by independent activities of MASS would ultimately be borne by ship manufacturers. Under Bertolini's risk-based liability management approach, it is possible to construct the liability in a fashion as to be divided between ship manufacturers and owners/users of MASS, since they are, unlike the owners and users of ordinary robots, have some degree of expertise with regard to MASS. That being said, Bertolini's approach focuses on the compensation of the injured party as the sole criteria for efficacy of legal instruments (Bertolini & Episcopo, 2021).

The present chapter establishes that the above viewpoint cannot alone preserve the legal balance of interests as it potentially sacrifices both interests in the process of making damages good. To achieve the legal balance of interests, the author stresses that liability be only imposed when the autonomous vessel's decisions can be regarded as both the factual and legal causes of the damages arising.

References

Bertolini, A. (2013). Robots as Products: The Case for a Realistic Analysis of Robotic Applications and Liability Rules. *Law, Innovation and Technology, 5*(2), 214–247.

Bertolini, A., & Episcopo, F. (2021). The Expert Group's Report on Liability for Artificial Intelligence and Other Emerging Digital Technologies: A Critical Assessment. *European Journal of Risk Regulation, 12*(3), 644–659.

Chopra, S., & White, L. (2011). *A Legal Theory for Autonomous Artificial Agents*. University of Michigan Press. IMO Doc. MSC.1/Circ.1638 2021. Outcome of the Regulatory Scoping Exercise for the use of Maritime Autonomous Surface Ships (MASS).

De Bruyne, J. (2019). Tort Law and the Regulation of Classification Societies: Between Public and Private Roles in the Maritime Industry. *European Review of Private Law, 27*(2), 429–450.

De Burgh, W. (2009). *The Elements of Maritime International Law*. BiblioLife.

de Vos, J., Hekkenberg, R., & Valdez Banda, O. (2021). The Impact of Autonomous Ships on Safety at Sea—A Statistical Analysis. *Reliability Engineering and System Safety*, 210, 107558.

Dougherty, J. (2021). *Autonomous Vessels Are Becoming a Commercial Reality*. The Maritime Executive. Available at: https://www.maritime-executive.com/editorials/autonomous-vessels-are-becoming-a-commercial-reality. Accessed 20 May 2022.

Gray, A. (2021). *The Evolution from Strict Liability to Fault in the Law of Torts*. Hart.

Hobbes, T., & Shapiro, I. (2010). *Leviathan or The Matter*. Yale University Press.

IMO Doc. MSC.1/Circ.1638. (2021). Outcome of the Regulatory Scoping Exercise for the Use of Maritime Autonomous Surface Ships (MASS).

International Convention for the Safety of Life at Sea (SOLAS), Nov. 1, 1974, 32 U.S.T. 47, T.I.A.S. 9700.

International Convention on Salvage (Salvage Convention), Adopted in London, 28/04/1989, entry into force on 14 July 1996, UNTS 1953.

International Maritime Organization. (2018). *IMO Takes First Steps to Address Autonomous Ships*. Available at: https://www.imo.org/en/MediaCentre/PressBriefings/Pages/08-MSC-99-MASS-scoping.aspx. Accessed 20 May 2022.

International Regulations for Preventing Collisions at Sea (COLREGs), Oct. 20, 1972, 28 U.S.T. 3459, T.I.A.S. 8587.

Izumo, T. (2018). Digital Specific Property of Robots. *Delphi—Interdisciplinary Review of Emerging Technologies, 1*(1), 14–19.

Krach, S., Hegel, F., Wrede, B., Sagerer, G., Binkofski, F., & Kircher, T. (2008). Can Machines Think? Interaction and Perspective Taking with Robots Investigated via fMRI. *PLoS ONE, 3*(7), e2597.

McMullen, J., Bagby, D., & Palich, L. (2008). Economic Freedom and the Motivation to Engage in Entrepreneurial Action. *Entrepreneurship Theory and Practice, 32*(5), 875–895.

Pagallo, U. (2013). *The Laws of Robots*. Springer.

Palombella, G. (2009). The Rule of Law Beyond the State: Failures, Promises, and Theory. *International Journal of Constitutional Law, 7*(3), 442–467.

Rubio, F., Valero, F., & Llopis-Albert, C. (2019). A Review of Mobile Robots: Concepts, Methods, Theoretical Framework, and Applications. *International Journal of Advanced Robotic Systems, 16*(2).

Siegel, M. (2003). *The Sense-Think-Act Paradigm Revisited*. 1st International Workshop on Robotic Sensing. ROSE' 03.

Todd, P. (2020). *Advanced Introduction to Maritime Law*. Edward Elgar.

CHAPTER 16

Insurance of Marine Autonomous Surface Ships: Risk Allocation, Seaworthiness and Technological Challenges from an Underwriter's Perspective

Manuel Varela Chouciño, Jonatan Echebarria Fernández, and Johanna Hjalmarsson

1 Introduction

Marine insurance contracts are instruments where an insurer undertakes to indemnify the assured, in a manner and to the extent agreed, against marine losses, that is to say the losses incident to a marine adventure (Marine Insurance Act 1906). This definition has represented the cornerstone of the global marine insurance sector for centuries but is now under scrutiny with the rapid emergence of Maritime Autonomous Surface Ships (MASS) and the implications that these new marine vehicles bring.

M. Varela Chouciño (✉)
Shipping & Transport, Business Management Department, MAPFRE Insurance, Madrid, Spain

© The Author(s), under exclusive license to Springer Nature Switzerland AG 2023

T. M. Johansson et al. (eds.), *Autonomous Vessels in Maritime Affairs*, Studies in National Governance and Emerging Technologies,
https://doi.org/10.1007/978-3-031-24740-8_16

The notion of the insurance contract as a contract of indemnity is a general principle which is internationally accepted whether the policy is construed under Common Law or Continental Law and requires an actual or future insurable interest for a valid insurance contract. There will be no indemnity under a marine insurance contract if an insurable interest cannot be identified under the policy, or if no loss or liability is suffered in connection to that interest. This principle avoids financial speculation and wagering under marine insurance contracts. It is preliminary to other conditions for recovery that the assured must suffer an identifiable loss caused by an insured peril (*Leyland Shipping v. Norwich Union Fire Insurance Society* [1918] AC 350) or proximately caused by an insured peril in connection to a non-excluded situation (*JJ Lloyd Instruments Ltd v. Northern Star Insurance Co Ltd., The Miss Jay Jay* [1987] 1 Lloyd's Rep 32) according to the terms and conditions of the policy.

The emergence of MASS has obliged the industry to review its traditional approach to marine insurance contracts as it provides a new generation of vessels, which potentially exposes insurance contracts to a new set of proximate causes not yet identified. As a consequence, can we maintain the traditional understanding of concepts like seaworthiness, safety on board or the duty of fair presentation in the formation of the contract? Are MASS more likely to produce claims under insurance policies than are traditionally manned vessels? Can the standard terms adequately respond to the new risks associated with MASS?

This chapter addresses these questions to achieve a better understanding of the challenges that the marine insurance industry will face in relation to MASS. The following sections identify concepts crucial to every insurance policy, such as the fair presentation of the risk and the nature of the concept of seaworthiness, which may be affected by the technical developments that MASS have introduced. Additionally, the

J. Echebarria Fernández
The City Law School, City, University of London, London, UK
e-mail: jonatan.echebarria-fernandez@city.ac.uk

J. Hjalmarsson
Institute of Maritime Law, Southampton Law School, University of Southampton, Southampton, UK
e-mail: jhj@soton.ac.uk

most relevant types of marine insurance terms and contracts will be analysed to assess to what extent there is effective insurance protection with respect to risks strictly connected to MASS.

2 The Nature of MASS Risks as a Question of Marine Insurance

The evolution of operational technology of MASS raises the issue of whether the insurability of MASS should be a question of marine insurance or general insurance. The sophistication of the navigational technology of MASS may attract the contract to some sector of insurance other than marine insurance, e.g. specific property insurance, cyber property insurance; or it may even qualify as a sub-category under engineering insurance. However, there appears to be a consensus among the most relevant authorities in the maritime industry, e.g. Maritime Safety Committee (MSC) of the International Maritime Organization (IMO), *Comité Maritime International* (CMI), International Union of Marine Insurers (IUMI) or the International Association of Classification Societies (IACS), that the challenges to which MASS have given rise ought to be studied from a transport perspective, and particularly from a maritime and shipping approach.

In 2017, IMO initiated a scoping exercise, to which key players and stakeholders in the shipping industry contributed. The exercise considered revision of a substantial number of IMO treaties and international instruments: International Convention for the Safety of Life at Sea, 1974 (SOLAS, 1974), International Regulations for Preventing Collisions at Sea, 1972 (COLREGs, 1972), International Convention on Maritime Search and Rescue, 1979 (SAR, 1979), etc., to assess how MASS could be regulated (Veal, 2017).

The outcome of the regulatory scoping exercise for the use of MASS of the MSC, as approved by the Committee, was published in June 2021 (IMO, 2021). This document identified as high priority issues a list of themes which were defined as common potential gaps, which may thematically shape the course of how MASS operations should be addressed (Veal, 2021). These gaps and themes are the meaning of master, crew or responsible person; and their role depending on the degree of autonomy of the ship; the definition of remote-control station/centre and operational technology; and the qualifications, responsibilities and the roles of a remote operator.

From an insurance perspective, it seems that the evolution of MASS will affect concepts of manning, watchkeeping, seaworthiness and the position of classification societies established in marine insurance practice. Some of these concepts inscribe themselves into the context of the formation of marine insurance contracts. Analysis from a marine insurance perspective may reveal an impact of these changes on the concepts of the fair presentation of the risk and particularly, the concept of seaworthiness. In any case, MASS must be considered in the context of maritime law (Veal and Tsimplis, 2017), and consequently MASS insurability may be analysed within the context of marine insurance.

2.1 The Duty of Fair Presentation in Relation to MASS Underwriting and Cyber Risk Management

A contract of marine insurance governed by English law is said by Section 17 of the Marine Insurance Act 1906 to be a contract based upon the utmost good faith. To effect a contract of insurance, the proposer (insured) must make to the underwriter a fair presentation of the risk, i.e. the assured must disclose "every material circumstance which the insured knows or ought to know", or failing that, make "disclosure which gives the insurer sufficient information to put a prudent insurer on notice that it needs to make further enquiries for the purpose of revealing those material circumstances" (UK Insurance Act 2015). The presentation of the risk must be clear and accessible; representations as to fact must be substantially correct and representations as to belief must be provided in good faith (UK Insurance Act 2015). In the absence of enquiry, the proposer is not required to disclose circumstances that diminish the risk, that the insurer knows or ought to know, circumstances that the underwriter is presumed to know or circumstances as to which the underwriter waives information (UK Insurance Act 2015). But what are the particular circumstances introduced by MASS vehicles which must be disclosed to a marine underwriter?

Specific disclosure of material information will vary between the different types of marine insurance policies, but a marine underwriter aiming to assess a MASS risk will necessarily need to obtain information related to the degree of automation of the vessel, mainly in relation to the applicable operational technology (OT). OT can be defined as the integration of hardware and software with network connectivity to control industrial processes and particularly the operation and control of a vessel (BIMCO, 2016).

The distinction between information technology (IT) systems and OT systems is important. IT systems are founded on the use of data as information. OT systems are focused on the use of data to control or monitor physical processes (IMO, 2017a). Considering this, the protection of information and data exchange within these systems becomes crucial and introduces a new concern: might the physical safety of the marine adventure be affected by a lack of cyber protection in the systems remotely operating the vessel? Although computer-based systems in relevant parts of vessels (IMO, 2021) have provided undeniable gains in the shipping industry, they also present new risks such as cyber threats coming from malicious or negligent actions. Effective cyber risk management needs to be considered as a countermeasure in relation to cyber vulnerabilities in MASS operation. These cyber vulnerabilities may have implications on the security, integrity and availability of information and, due to the interconnection of systems it can produce implications on safety, particularly where critical control systems (e.g. bridge navigation or main propulsion systems) are compromised. Consequently, a causal link can be established between cyber security and the safe operation of MASS using fully or partially autonomous and connected systems. As Meixian Song has argued (Song, 2020), cyber risks or vulnerabilities may become entangled with traditional risks and losses in marine navigation.

This is why cyber risk management becomes crucial to MASS. Cyber risk management means the process of identifying, analysing, assessing and communicating a cyber-related risk and accepting, avoiding, transferring or mitigating it to an acceptable level, considering the costs and benefits of actions taken by stakeholders (IMO, 2021). As of 1 January 2021, all vessels must comply with IMO Resolution MSC.428(98) (2017b). This resolution provides a regulatory framework aiming to safeguard shipping from current and emerging cyber threats and vulnerabilities and includes functional elements that support effective cyber risk management.

The potential level of damage that cyber risks can produce to the vessel itself, but also to the environment, crew on board and the reputation of the company, identify such risks as requiring the involvement of senior managers of the company (BIMCO, 2016) to avoid computer-based exposures. If owners have not acted diligently in the protection of their vessels in relation to cyber risks, the basic level of diligence required for a prudent shipowner or manager will not be satisfied and insurance cover may not be granted in some situations.

But what should a marine underwriter consider while assessing the cyber risks in relation to a vessel? The Guidelines on cyber marine risks management (IMO, 2017a) provide a model of the elements which should be complied with to procure an effective cyber risk management of the company.

Hence a prudent marine underwriter, according to the IMO Guidelines (IMO, 2017a, 5) should evaluate if the shipowner at a minimum complies with the five measures identified by the IMO:

1. *"Identify":* Define personnel roles and responsibilities for cyber risk management and identify the systems, assets, data and capabilities that, when disrupted, pose risks to ship operations.
2. *"Protect":* Implement risk control processes and measures, and contingency planning to protect against a cyber event and ensure continuity of shipping operations.
3. *"Detect":* Develop and implement activities necessary to detect a cyber event in a timely manner.
4. *Respond":* Develop and implement activities and plans to provide resilience and to restore systems necessary for shipping operations or services impaired due to a cyber event.
5. *"Recover":* Identify measures to back up and restore cyber systems necessary for shipping operations impacted by a cyber event.

The effectiveness of cyber risk management will need continuous updates and cyber protection will have to be considered by shipping companies' loss prevention departments. Cyber risk management must be considered by marine underwriters as material information in relation to MASS. Depending on the degree of automation, cyber security measures will specifically impact on the MASS' safety. To comply with the duty of fair presentation of the risk, the shipowner will have to disclose the cyber risk management programme in place for MASS, to obtain an effective marine insurance policy.

2.2 Contract Terms in the Marine Insurance Contract: The Paramount Concept of Seaworthiness

We may now consider that the issues introduced by MASS in insurance practice are brand new, but underwriting practice was also updated when vessels began to incorporate steam engines in the merchant navy, or to be propelled by new sources of power. Insurance cover is not generally immediately updated to respond to technological progress, but underwriters have a wide range of contractual tools at their disposal to construct insurance policies.

One such tool which merits reflection is the promissory warranty. A promissory warranty is a condition on which the contract is founded (*Bean v Stupart* (1778). 1 Dougl 11, 14). When a promissory warranty is identified in the contract as such a term, the compliance with that warranty is a condition precedent to the attachment of the risk (*Thomson v Weems* (1884) 9 App Cas 671), and underwriters may not be found liable to honour a claim if that warranty is not strictly complied with (*De Hahn v Hartley* (1786) 1 T.R. 343). Until the Insurance Act 2015, the law provided that if an assured fails to comply with a promissory warranty, the insurer is automatically discharged from liability under the policy (*Bank of Nova Scotia v Hellenic War Risk Association Ltd (Bermuda), The Good Luck* [1991] 3 All ER 1). This is now ameliorated by Sects. 10 and 11 of the Insurance Act 2015. These provisions in turn are subject to contracting out, which is frequently done in the marine insurance market segment. Warranties can be expressly defined in the policy, but certain warranties are implied in the marine insurance policy by statutory implication. Under Section 39 of the Marine Insurance Act (MIA) in respect of voyage policies, the seaworthiness of the vessel is an implied warranty in a voyage policy. In a time policy, the seaworthiness requirement is implied by s39(5). In addition, there is a vast number of relevant authorities identifying seaworthiness as a condition precedent to the policy.

Section 39(4) MIA establishes the standard test to determine when a ship can be considered seaworthy, namely *when she is reasonably fit in all aspects to encounter the ordinary perils of the seas of the adventure insured* (*Papera Traders Co Ltd. v Hyundai Merchant Marine Co Ltd, The Eurasian Dream* [2002] 1 Lloyd's Rep 719). The burden of proving unseaworthiness rests on the underwriters (*Pickup v Thames and Mersey Marine Insurance Co, Ltd* [1878] 3 QBD 594; *Ajum Goolam Hossen & Co v Union Marine Insurance Co* [1901] AC 362).

Nevertheless, MASS have introduced a degree of automation that has made necessary an update of fundamental concepts of shipping which have been established for centuries. Even implied warranties like seaworthiness require evaluation to determine if the traditional tests are still applicable to MASS. The competence of the crew and *good seamanship* has for centuries been considered a crucial factor to determine if a vessel is in a seaworthy condition (*Manifest Shipping Co Ltd v Uni-Polaris Insurance Co Ltd (The Star Sea)* [2001] 1 Lloyd's Rep. 389). The level of importance of this concept is such that it can also be confirmed that a vessel is unseaworthy if, for example, the Master cannot deliver their functions due to physical disability, illness or in some other circumstances, such as an addiction.

But the competence of the crew is not the sole aspect which determines the seaworthy—or otherwise—condition of a vessel. The number of crewmembers is also paramount to confirm seaworthiness (*Forshaw v Chabert* (1821) 3 Brod Bing 158). The reduction of crewmembers due to the automatization of process on board is strictly connected to the developments that MASS have introduced. The crew on board must be sufficient in number to ensure that the marine adventure can be effected in a safe manner, but also having enough substitutes on board to secure a safe journey is a consideration in respect of seaworthiness (*Clifford v Hunter* (1827) Moo & M 103).

MASS are technologically able to navigate (depending on the degree of autonomy) with fewer crew on board than a traditional vessel (The Nippon Foundation, 2022). The goal of every marine adventure is to reach its destination in a safe manner and the human element plays a key role in this respect. The compatibility between "technologies, environments, and organisations" with an "optimal human performance" (Rothblum et al., 2002) is a source of friction that may lead to accidents at sea (Christodoulou and Echebarria Fernández, 2021).

As pointed out by Christodoulou and Echebarria Fernández (2021), and according to the IMO's Sub-Committee on Flag State Implementation, the human element is the cause of about 80% of groundings and collisions (Listewnik and Wiewóra, 2007; Mindykowski, 2017). Ship design will still play a key role since "hardware, software, and the physical environment associated with the system" (Riahi et al, 2012) when liaising with offshore personnel and MASS operations, especially at port. However, it is expected that casualties will be reduced since crew fatigue and other factors in MASS will decrease, but dangers still lurk in respect of other ships and marine infrastructures.

If developments in OT support a reduction of crew members on board MASS, the traditional standards to determine that a vessel is seaworthy in respect of the number of crew on board may be affected. As a consequence, an underwriter willing to provide insurance cover to a MASS will have to take into consideration the material circumstances of that specific MASS, i.e. level of autonomy; OT technology on board and specific-risk management. When the risk assessment is complete, the underwriter can incorporate contractual provisions in the policy to determine specific safety measures that must be complied with. The Minimum Safe Manning Certificate can provide a reference for the underwriter in respect of the minimum crew on board to ensure the safety of navigation. In addition, any prudent underwriter may rely on specific contractual terms e.g. conditions precedent or exclusions expressly incorporated in the policy to mitigate the exposure of the insurer if a substantial reduction of crewmembers affects the MASS.

How insurance markets deal with the evolution of the concept of seaworthiness for MASS is uncertain. It can be suggested that if the operational technology in MASS is sufficient to produce the same result as a traditional manned vessel, the implied warranty of seaworthiness for MASS in respect of the number of crew on board may require an update. However, the contractual remedies which can be incorporated in the policy rest on the underwriters' choice to preserve their position.

3 Is Traditional Marine Insurance Cover Sufficient to Address MASS Risks?

Most marine insurers incorporate one of a number of internationally accepted sets of standard clauses. Whether we refer to Hull & Machinery (H&M) insurance (through its various forms of Time (LMA—Institute Time Clauses—Hulls, 1983a), Voyage (LMA—Institute Voyage Clauses—Hulls, 1983b), Fishing (LMA—Institute Fishing Vessels Clauses, 1987), etc.), cargo insurance i.e. Institute Cargo Clauses (A), Institute Cargo Clauses (B), Institute Cargo Clauses (C) (Lloyd's Market Association, 2009a, 2009b, 2009c) or shipbuilding risks under Institute Builders Clauses, the use of such standard terms is accepted by international markets LMA, 1988.

The aforementioned clauses have been designed, in some cases, several decades ago and are periodically updated. But can these standard terms provide insurance cover to MASS risks or is it necessary to update their content? The correct approach seems to be the analysis of each type of insurance contract to determine if the standard terms are appropriate to provide insurance cover to MASS.

3.1 Analysis of Marine Shipbuilding Insurance Cover in Relation to MASS

Shipbuilding is the process of construction and sea trials of the vessel which leads to its delivery to the shipowner. Even though construction techniques for MASS are not different from a traditional vessel, the most important innovations from a shipbuilding perspective affect the sea trial techniques. The European Maritime Safety Agency has published a guide to help EU member states to address MASS sea trials (European Union, 2020), however, each flag state has the power to establish its own requirements to guarantee the safe performance of sea trials for vessels under construction.

In respect of the insurance cover available for shipbuilding, most shipbuilding contracts are insured internationally under standard terms. The most relevant standard clauses are the Institute Builders Risks Cl. 351 and the shipbuilding cover provided by the Nordic Marine Insurance Plan of 2013 which is generally used in Scandinavian markets (LMA, 1988, CEFOR, 2013). Shipbuilding insurance cover grants protection on an *all risks basis*, i.e. the insurance policy covers all risk of loss or damage to the subject matter insured, caused and discovered during the period including the cost of repairing, replacing and renewing any defective part [...] according to Section 5.1 of the Institute Builders Risk Cl 351.

MASS can be considered vessels with special features which can be graded (Veal, 2017) in relation to their autonomous responses or operational technology on board, but they share structural, stability and hydrodynamic principles with traditional vessels. Therefore, apart from spearhead technology applicable to the operational control, construction techniques are similar in MASS and in traditional vessels.

Although risks related to the construction remain unaltered in terms of the assessment of shipbuilding risks, sea trials for MASS (which are also covered under clause 9.1 of the Institute Builders Risk Cl 351) require a different risk evaluation than a traditional sea trial. The evaluation of risks has to be focused on the relevant operational systems and the countermeasures provided to develop a safe sea trial, speed, propulsion system, position lighting, onboard sensors, software to prevent collisions, object recognition through its radar systems and object recognition systems, among others. An additional premium may be required if a wider range of navigation is required than the 250 nautical miles granted by clause 9.1 of the Institute Builders Risk Cl 351, or if the underwriter considers that the level of exposure under the applicable insurance clause is more likely to produce a claim under the insurance policy. Therefore, sea trials must be considered from an underwriter's perspective as a material element in the analysis of the risks involved in MASS construction.

But what is the material information that a prudent underwriter should evaluate in assessing MASS sea trials? Depending on the degree of autonomy of the vessel, sea trials should be performed in a designated test area/ship safety zone suitable for effective tests of MASS systems and sub-systems in a safe, secure and environmentally friendly manner (European Union, 2020). The evaluation of sea trial areas should analyse the maritime traffic density of the trial zone, which is a crucial factor to prevent alterations in the navigation area. Designated test zones for MASS will have to be coordinated with flag state authorities and the shipyard. In order to determine an optimal area for sea trials, relevant factors may be the following: is the designated area open to or closed to maritime traffic? Is the area sufficiently connected to conduct safe tests? Is the area going to be identified with buoys and reported on radio systems as an area which is going to be closed to maritime navigation for MASS sea trials? A prudent underwriter will pose at least these questions but will also consider whether the Vessel Traffic Services (VTS), Search and Rescue teams, communications systems and navigational systems will take part in the safe control of the whole operation.

The use of Integrated Maritime Services satellite information and access to maritime, oceanographic, terrestrial data and Traffic Density Maps can be crucial to help flag states identify trial areas adequate for MASS. In addition, the use of automated behaviour monitoring (ABM) tools helps to develop sea trials with an adequate level of safety. ABM are used to provide position reports for the detection of and alerts on ship's behaviours to detect MASS movement patterns, encounters at sea, approaches to shore or deviation from the designated route, and they are an important asset to confirm a safe sea trial for a MASS.

A Ship Safety Zone will also have to be established to construct a "bubble" area around the MASS which may prevent other vessels nearby from getting closer to the vessel currently on trial tests. Flag states depending on the level of automation can determine the level of collision avoidance tests which should be performed, but it is recommended that trial awareness is raised to inform third parties of the navigational situation.

The manning during sea trials is also a crucial element. Whether the vessel is fully autonomous or not, MASS will have to be operated by qualified and sufficient personnel to guarantee the safe operation of the sea trials. If a failure of the operational systems occurs, appropriate strategies should be put in place to respond to emergencies and mitigate the effects of harmful consequences.

Would a specific exclusion designed for the construction of MASS be a valuable addition to the arsenal of available clauses? Institute Builders Risk Cl 351 provides insurance cover for *all risks* which are not expressly excluded. The main exclusions identified under the clause are those included in the earthquake and volcanic exclusion, collision liability, protection and indemnity liability, war exclusion, strike exclusion, malicious acts and nuclear exclusions. It should be noted that even though a literal interpretation of the malicious acts exclusion (Lloyd's Market Association, Malicious Acts Exclusion, 1982) may be interpreted to exclude malicious acts, the clause was developed to exclude damage proximately caused by a detonation of an explosive or by any weapon of war, not cyber damage.

Although the current wording of the Institute Builders Risk Cl 351 can provide insurance cover for cyber events because such perils are not expressly excluded, it is also accepted that most shipbuilding policies are subject to specific cyber exclusion clauses such as Cl. 370; Cl. 5402; or Cl. L5403 (Lloyd's Market Association, 2003a, 2003b, 2019a, 2019b, 2019c), which in the end, exclude insurance cover if some damage or liability arises from the use or operation of any computer-based systems.

We may conclude that an adequate risk evaluation can be made by a prudent underwriter on the basis of the standard terms currently available in the market and that insurance cover can adequately respond to the particular needs arising from the construction of MASS. However, sea trials are the most challenging part of the shipbuilding insurance policy for a MASS. Particular provisions and warranties should be established in the contract by a prudent underwriter.

3.2 *Hull & Machinery Insurance*

When testing of a MASS is completed and it is delivered to shipowners, H&M insurance contract should be effected. The applicable terms will mainly depend on where the contract is issued. The most relevant terms are those provided by the Joint Hull Committee of the Lloyd's Market Association or under the Nordic Marine Insurance Plan.

According to the international market, marine insurance cover is provided on a time or voyage basis under the Institute Hull Clauses. Depending on the type of insurance, different insurance clauses can be chosen to define the cover: Institute Time Clauses—Hulls, Institute Voyage Clauses—Hulls or even Institute Fishing Vessels Clauses. Even though the inception of the Institute Hull Clauses is dated in 1983, their wording has been revised at intervals, with the latest edition dating from 2003.

The scope of cover under an H&M insurance policy under these standard terms is different from that of Institute Builders Risk Cl 351, the latter providing insurance cover using an *all risks* approach. Time, Voyage or Fishing Vessels clauses provide insurance cover for a series of named perils which are indicated in clause 6 of the Institute Time Clauses—Hulls and Institute Fishing Vessels Clauses and clause 4 of the Institute Voyage Clauses—Hulls.

Insured perils may be grouped as follows:

1. Loss or damage caused by a marine peril, irrespective of that peril being caused by a lack of due diligence from the assured. These perils are: perils of the seas, rivers, lakes or other navigable waters, fire or explosion, violent theft by persons outside of the vessel, jettison, piracy, breakdown of or accident to nuclear installations or reactors (provided that specific nuclear exclusion (Lloyd's Market Association [2003a, 2003b]. Cl 370) is not expressly included in the contract, Lloyd's Market Association, 2003b, Cl 370), Contact with aircraft or similar objects falling therefrom, land conveyance, dock or harbour equipment or installation, earthquake, volcanic eruption or lightning.
2. Loss or damage caused by a peril insured against when that peril has not resulted from want of due diligence by the Assured, Owners or Managers. These perils are: accidents in loading discharging or shifting cargo or fuel, bursting of boilers breakage of shafts or any

latent defect in the machinery or hull, negligence of Master Officers Crew or Pilots, negligence of repairers or charterers provided such repairers or charterers are not an Assured under the policy, barratry of Master Officers or Crew and loss of or damage to the vessel caused by any governmental authority acting under the powers vested in it, to prevent or mitigate a pollution hazard or damage to the environment.

3. Three-quarters of collision liabilities against other vessels. The non-covered quarter can also be covered by hull underwriters subject to additional premium, however, it has been traditionally allocated under the P&I contract.

But could damage caused by a cyber-related risk or vulnerability result in a right to produce a claim under the H&M insurance? The terms above prevent the assured from making a claim to its underwriters, because cyber risks are not expressly covered under the International Hulls Clauses. In addition, hull underwriters count on express exclusion clauses which can be incorporated in the policy to exclude insurance cover if the damage is proximately caused by a peril insured against in connection to a cyber-related cause.

3.3 Cargo Insurance

The use of MASS in international transport raises the issue of whether there are any implications on the cargo cover currently available in the market. Under a cargo insurance policy, the underwriters will agree to indemnify the insured for loss or damage to the cargo proximately caused by a peril insured against. The cover is internationally provided on the terms of the three sets of clauses which were developed over the course of the twentieth century, with the current update introduced in 2009: Institute Cargo Clauses (A), Institute Cargo Clauses (B) and Institute Cargo Clauses (C). Institute Cargo Clauses (A) is the most common and provides the widest scope of cover because it is defined as *all risks* cover. ICC B and C are scarcely used, and they are usually applicable for low value cargo or when insurance in international transport is not required on ICC(A) terms.

All three sets of cargo clauses contain a general exclusion clause included in clause 4. The standard terms also include further relevant exclusion clauses, e.g. a war exclusion in clause 6, a strike exclusion in clause 7 and the unseaworthiness and unfitness clause in clause 5. In relation to MASS risks, the exclusion which can produce a severe impact is the unseaworthiness and unfitness clause. If the vessel or MASS is to be regarded as unseaworthy or unfit according to this exclusion, cargo cover can be excluded and no underwriter will be found liable under the insurance contract if privy to such unseaworthiness or unfitness. The incorporation in every cargo insurance of the Cyber Attack Exclusion Cl. 380 also prevents the assured from effecting any claim in connection to a cyber risk causing damage to the insured cargo.

Usually, a prudent underwriter will require relevant information about the vessel performing the carriage of high valuable cargo. Alternatively, the policy may to some extent determine certain specifications which have to be fulfilled by the carrier (Lloyd's Market Association, 2001) IMO number of the means of conveyance is required in order to make further inquiries in respect of its construction year, classification society or Protection & Indemnity (P&I) club. Thus, if the carriage of goods is effected by a vessel which does not comply with certain requirements e.g. Institute Classification Clause, *ibid.* under a cargo policy, insurance cover of a specific cargo can be waived by cargo underwriters.

It is assumed that cargo underwriters may have to consider cyber risks in relation to cargo insurance. The Joint Cargo Committee, following the PRA's requirement to identify, quantify and manage cyber risks established a working group to address the implications of cyber security in cargo policies (2019a, 2019b, 2019c). The result was the production of a new Cyber Coverage Clause JC2019-004 which was published on 18 July 2019 and is one of the first steps forward by the insurance market to recognize that cyber-related risks can be addressed by cargo underwriters. This clause includes a condition precedent to the contract: insurance coverage can be provided if an insured provides evidence that reasonable measures have been executed to ensure cyber risk recommendations at the inception of the insurance cover.

Although cargo insurance may seem to have a weak connection with MASS evolutions, insurance practice may impose relevant specifications on the side of the carrier which may have indirect influence in the level of premium or the insurance cover provided by the policy.

3.4 P&I Insurance Cover

Mutual protection granted by the P&I clubs provides insurance cover for liabilities which may arise in connection with the operation of a vessel. The rules of International Group P&I clubs do not generally exclude claims arising from cyber incidents, unless such incident is considered as an act of war or terrorism. But depending on specific drafting on the rules of each club, each member should analyse their exposure in consultation with the P&I club. If an incident is caused e.g. by a failure in the ship's navigation systems rooted in a criminal act or cyber incident, it may be argued that if any exclusion is not met, liabilities may be subject to usual P&I cover depending on the rules of each club.

The International Group of P&Is has established a working group to assess specific risks which are crucial to MASS. Undoubtedly MASS risks are strictly connected to cyber-related events. However, it is generally accepted that shipowners would have to evaluate cyber risks within their loss prevention departments. Usually, loss prevention departments of the shipowners work in connection with the loss prevention departments of their P&I to mitigate risks on board. Cyber risk will also have to be considered from a loss prevention perspective. Therefore, any P&I cover can be prejudiced by the failure to take reasonable steps to prevent foreseeable loss or liability, and as more and more potential cyber risks are being identified, P&I clubs will expect shipowners to develop their cyber risk management programme to avoid potential liabilities.

4 Conclusions

MASS represent an evolution from the traditional manned shipping practice. Relevant industry players (IMO, Baltic and International Maritime Council (BIMCO), CMI, IUMI and IACS, among others) and stakeholders have studied the main implications and challenges that are connected to MASS, and important updates and recommendations have been made.

Marine insurance is not an exception and it is necessary that the industry provides a flexible approach to insure MASS risks. The physical protection of the marine adventure which has been deeply studied for centuries has now evolved according to the technological developments in operational technology and autonomous navigation. The traditional tests to ascertain concepts such as seaworthiness, safety on board or the fair presentation of risks must be broadened. In addition, there is a new concept which has emerged in connection to MASS and that is *cyber risk management* which can be considered as a new feature, paramount to the marine insurance contract.

Marine underwriters are required to strengthen their practices to understand MASS material circumstances: the level of autonomy of the vessel, the degree of operating technology and safety measures to control the vessel and the cyber security management practices of the shipowners. However, even though insurance cover provided on an *all risk basis* can provide insurance cover to MASS, specific cyber exclusions are generally incorporated in marine insurance policies to prevent underwriters to insure cyber-related causes.

Even though it is more likely that the increase in automation will reduce the level of damages, losses and liabilities in MASS, loss prevention departments of shipowners will have to confirm that they have taken the necessary steps to comply with cyber security measures so insurance cover shall not be prejudiced by lack of exercise of due diligence.

From an underwriter's perspective, insurance terms currently available can provide an adequate scope of insurance cover for MASS risks. In addition, insurance practitioners must strengthen their knowledge of cyber risk management and the material circumstances related to MASS to develop a solid practice in relation to the new challenges ahead.

References

Ajum Goolam Hossen & Co v Union Marine Insurance Co (1901) AC 362.

Bank of Nova Scotia v Hellenic War Risk Association Ltd. (Bermuda) The Good Luck (1991) 3 All ER 1.

Bean v Stupart (1778) 1 Douglas 11, 14 per Lord Mansfield.

BIMCO (2016). The guidelines on cyber security onboard ships. V4. https://www.bimco.org/about-us-and-our-members/publications/the-guidelines-on-cyber-security-onboard-ships (Accessed 28 June 2022).

CEFOR (2013). Nordic Marine Insurance Plan of 2013. Edition 2019 revised. http://www.nordicplan.org/The-Plan/ (Accessed 28 June 2022).

Christodoulou, A., and Echebarria Fernández, J. (2021). Maritime Governance and International Maritime Organization Instruments Focused on Sustainability in the Light of United Nations' Sustainable Development Goals. In *Sustainability in the Maritime Domain* (pp. 415–461). Springer. https://www.springerprofessional.de/en/maritime-governance-and-internationalmaritime-organization-inst/19209912 (Accessed 21 June 2022).

Clifford v. Hunter (1827), Moo & M 103.

COLREGs (1972). International Maritime Organization (IMO). *Convention on the International Regulations for Preventing Collisions at Sea*. Oct. 20, 1972, 28 U.S.T. 3459, T.I.A.S. 8587. https://www.imo.org/en/About/Conventions/Pages/COLREG.aspx (Accessed 23 January 2022).

De Hahn v Hartley (1786) 1 T.R. 343.

European Union (2020). *EU Operational Guidelines for Trials of Maritime Autonomous Surface Ships (MASS)*. https://europeanshippers.eu/eu-guidelines-on-trials-of-marine-autonomous-surface-ships/ (Accessed 28 June 2022).

Forshaw v Chabert (1821) 3 Brod Bing 158.

IMO (2017a). Guidelines on Maritime Cyber Risk Management. MSC-FAL.1/CIRC.3/REV.1.

IMO (2017b). Maritime Cyber Risk Management in Safety Management Systems. MSC.428(98).

IMO (2021). Outcome of the Regulatory Scoping Exercise for the Use of Maritime Autonomous Surface Ships (MASS). MSC.1/Circ.1638.

Leyland Shipping v Norwich Union Fire Insurance Society (1918) AC 350.

Listewnik, J., and Wiewióra, A. (2007). Considerations on Limiting the Elements of Human Factor Influence on Breakdowns of Ship's Machinery Illustrated by Some Case Studies. *Problemy Eksploatacji*, 147–157.

Lloyd's Market Association (1982). CL266 Malicious Acts Exclusion.

Lloyd's Market Association (1983a). CL280 Institute Time Clauses-Hulls.

Lloyd's Market Association (1983b). CL285 Institute Voyage Clauses-Hulls.

Lloyd's Market Association (1987). CL346 Institute Fishing Vessel Clauses.

Lloyd's Market Association (1988). CL351 Builders Risks.

Lloyd's Market Association (2001). CL354 Institute Classification Clause.

Lloyd's Market Association (2003a). CL380 Institute Cyber Attack Exclusion Clause.

Lloyd's Market Association (2003b). CL370 Institute Radioactive Contamination, Chemical, Biological, Biochemical, and Electromagnetic Weapons Exclusion Clause.

Lloyd's Market Association (2009a). CL252 Cargo (A).

Lloyd's Market Association (2009b). CL253 Cargo (B).

Lloyd's Market Association (2009c). CL254 Cargo (C).

Lloyd's Market Association (2019a). CL5402—Marine Cyber Exclusion.

Lloyd's Market Association (2019b). CL5403—Marine Cyber Exclusion.

Lloyd's Market Association (2019c). Joint Cargo Committee. Cyber Coverage Clause. JC2019c-004.

Manifest Shipping Co Ltd v Uni-Polaris Insurance Co Ltd (The Star Sea) (2001) 1 Lloyd's Rep. 389.

Marine Insurance Act (1906). Section 1, https://www.legislation.gov.uk/ukpga/Edw7/6/41/contents (Accessed 2 February 2022).

Mindykowski, J. (2017). Towards Safety Improvement: Implementation and Assessment of New Standards of Competence for Electro-Technical Officers on Ships. *Maritime Policy & Management, 44*(3), 336–357.

Papera Traders Co. Ltd v Hyundai Merchant Marine Co. Ltd The Eurasian Dream (2002) 1 Lloyd's Rep. 719.

Pickup v Thames and Mersey Marine Insurance Co. Ltd (1878) 3 QBD 594.

Riahi, R., Bonsall, S., Jenkinson, I., and Wang, J. (2012). A seafarer's reliability assessment incorporating subjective judgements. *Proceedings of the Institution of Mechanical Engineers, Part M. Journal of Engineering for the Maritime Environment, 226*(4), 313–334.

Rothblum A. M., Wheal D., Withington, S., Shappell, S. A., Wiegmann, D. A., Boehm, W., and Chaderjian, M. (2002). Human Factors in Incident Investigation and Analysis. In Excerpts *from Proceedings of the 2nd International Workshop on Human Factors in Offshore Operations (HFW200)*, Houston, Texas. https://www.bsee.gov/sites/bsee.gov/files/tap-technical-assessment-program//401aa.pdf (Accessed 21 July 2022).

SAR (1979). IMO. International Convention on Maritime Search and Rescue, amended by IMO Resolution MSC. 70(69) (1998), 27 April 1979, 1403 UNTS. Available at: https://treaties.un.org/doc/publication/unts/volume%201405/volume-1405-i-23489-english.pdf (Accessed 28 June 2022).

SOLAS (1974). IMO. International Convention for the Safety of Life at Sea, Nov. 1, 1974, 32 U.S.T. 47, T.I.A.S. 9700. Available at: https://www.imo.org/en/About/Conventions/Pages/International-Convention-for-the-Safety-of-Life-at-Sea-(SOLAS),-1974.aspx (Accessed 28 June 2022).

Song, M. (2020). Moving forward by looking back: Insuring autonomous vessels under English hull and machinery cover and law. In Ringbom, H., Røsæg, E., and Solvang, T. (Eds.), *Autonomous ships and the law* (p. 229). Routledge. https://eprints.soton.ac.uk/cgi/eprintbypureuuid?uuid=96f91ab3-0adf-41bd-b138-aa5edc536a87 (Accessed 5 May 2022).

The Nippon Foundation (2022). https://www.nippon-foundation.or.jp/en/news/articles/2022/20220118-66716.html (Accessed 11 April 2022).

Thomson v Weems (1884) 9 App Cas 671.

UK Insurance Act (2015). Sections. 3.3, S. 3.4, S.3.5. https://www.legislation.gov.uk/ukpga/2015/4/contents/enacted (Accessed 2 February 2022).

Veal, R. (2017). Unmanned ships on the IMO work agenda. *Shipping & Trade Law, 17*(5), 1–4.

Veal, R. (2021). The IMO MASS Regulatory Scoping Exercise: What Have We Learned? *Lloyd's Shipping & Trade Law, 21*(5), 1–5.

Veal, R., and Tsimplis, M. (2017). The Integration of Unmanned Ships Into the Lex Maritima. *Lloyd's Maritime & Commercial Law Quarterly, 2*, 303–335.

Veal, R., Tsimplis, M., and Serdy, A. (2019). The Legal Status and Operation of Unmanned Maritime Vehicles. *Ocean Development and International Law, 50*(1), 23–48.

Veal, R., Tsimplis, M., Serdy, A., Ntovas, A., and Quinn, S. (2016). *Liability for Operations in Unmanned Maritime Vehicles with Differing Levels of Autonomy*. European Defence Agency.

PART VII

Selected National & Regional Developments

CHAPTER 17

Selected Industry Issues Regarding Autonomous Vessels: The Canadian Perspective

Maria Katsivela

1 Introduction

Canada is a maritime nation with the longest shoreline in the world (Statistics Canada, 2016) bordering three oceans: the Atlantic, the Pacific, and the Arctic. As a ship-owning country (in 2021 it was ranked 30th in the world) Canada's marine shipping transports about 20% of Canadian exports and imports by dollar value (Expert Panel on the Social and Economic Value of Marine Shipping to Canada, 2017 in what follows) (UNCTAD, 2021). Canada also has in place marine (cargo) shipping across the entire country. Without marine shipping, essential goods would be much more expensive on Vancouver Island, on the island of

M. Katsivela (✉)
Programme de Common Law en Français, Faculty of Law,
University of Ottawa, Ottawa, ON, Canada
e-mail: mkatsive@uottawa.ca

© The Author(s), under exclusive license to Springer Nature Switzerland AG 2023

T. M. Johansson et al. (eds.), *Autonomous Vessels in Maritime Affairs*, Studies in National Governance and Emerging Technologies,
https://doi.org/10.1007/978-3-031-24740-8_17

Newfoundland, and in Northern Canada. Some goods would not be available at all since some communities in the Canadian Arctic are almost entirely dependent on marine shipping for the import of essential goods. In this way, marine shipping remains tightly woven into the Canadian economy and culture.

The objective of the present study is to spear through Maritime Autonomous Surface Ships (MASS) from a Canadian context. More specifically, the author seeks to describe the extent to which Canada has adopted autonomous vessels and outlined selected issues that arise in that respect. Furthermore, the author will comment on a niche MASS-companion development, i.e., smart ports in Canada that will be invited to accommodate service-related activities pertaining to those vessels.

2 The Emergence of Autonomous Vessels in Canada and Selected Issues Surrounding Them

Autonomous ships in Canada are an emerging reality. As is the case with different parts of the world (Mayflower in the United Kingdom, Yara Birkeland in Norway), Canada is developing autonomous vessels and generic services. The following table (Table 1) provides a cursory overview of progress in this field in different parts of Canada:

Anticipating an increasing interest in autonomous vessels in Canada and worldwide, in mid-2019, Transport Canada launched the Canadian Forum for Maritime Autonomous Surface Ships (CFMASS) (NRC, 2019 in what follows for the subcommittees) to ensure that Canada, and its maritime stakeholders, were prepared to seize the opportunity to partake in the global race towards MASS deployment. Realizing this requires new technology and innovation as well as a coordinated response, the Forum aimed at bringing together a network of stakeholders to help guide the development of MASS technology in Canada for the benefit of Canadians. Initially, three subcommittees were created; one to focus on innovation and technology; one to identify, monitor, and support the required domestic and international policy, legislative/regulatory requirements; and one to explore international and domestic collaborations to determine how MASS can be a part of Canada's smart logistical networks and have a competitive advantage in the area of MASS globally.

There was increasing momentum until March 2020 when all attention turned to the pandemic causing a shift in federal mandate. To keep the momentum going on the innovation front with a goal to

Table 1 Autonomous vessels or related initiatives in Canada

Company/organization	*Region*	*Objective behind deployment—types of vessels/vehicles/systems*	*Remarks*
Open Ocean Robotics (Open Ocean Robotics, 2021)	West Coast	Collecting data (for example, detecting and monitoring oil spills, measuring changes in the ocean due to climate change, helping ships plot fuel efficient routes) and surveillance	A remote operator oversees these vessels with sensory feed providing situational awareness (Colin Angus, 2021). The vessels (remotely controlled or partially autonomous) of Open Ocean Robotics are registered with Transport Canada but are subject to an exemption since they do not comply with conventional COLREGs regulations (Colin Angus, 2021) This raises the issue of whether autonomous vessels are able to respect applicable rules such as the COLREGs. Although MASS is subject to existing maritime rules in Canada, exemptions from COLREGs may apply in certain cases. The development of rules to govern MASS at the International Maritime Organization (IMO) level will provide guidance as to how COLREGs and other conventions will apply to MASS. Canada is a very active participant in this field at the IMO level

(continued)

Table 1 (continued)

Company/organization	*Region*	*Objective behind deployment—types of vessels/vehicles/systems*	*Remarks*
Robert Allan Ltd. (RAL)	West coast	Ship handling and firefighting	RAL has conceived a series of autonomous tug designs, the so-called RAmora with the latest design being the RAmora 2400 (Vince den Hertog et al. 2016 in what follows). These are remotely operated (by a human operator) tugs, with high levels of automation. Such vessels reduce human error and the exposure of a human crew to the dangers of the sea especially in the context of firefighting. Even though there are no RAmora tugs built or in service yet, RAL is confident that, in time, the acceptance of this new types of vessels by the industry coupled with further developing rules governing autonomous vessels will allow this project to materialize As with the previous initiative, this industry endeavor raises the need to further develop regulation to govern MASS. This is currently taking place at the international level (IMO) where, as previously noted, Canada is a very active participant. This initiative also underlines the need for a higher level of acceptance of autonomous vessels by the marine industry in Canada. Designing firms, however, seem to anticipate a change of attitude in the future and are getting ready to serve the shipping industry

Company/organization	*Region*	*Objective behind deployment—types of vessels/vehicles/systems*	*Remarks*
International Submarine Engineering Ltd (ISE)	Canada/World	ISE: autonomous and remotely operated (underwater) robotic vehicles and terrestrial robotics (ISE, 2021)	
Cellula Robotics	Canada/World	Autonomous underwater vehicles (Cellula Robotics, 2020)	
Ocean Networks Canada (ONC)	West Coast (University of Victoria)	Underwater smart ocean observing systems (ONC, 2021)	

(continued)

Table 1 (continued)

Company/organization	*Region*	*Objective behind deployment—types of vessels/vehicles/systems*	*Remarks*
Intelligent Maritime Corridors (IMC) International Council (IC)	Canada/World	The IMC promotes a high-profile ecosystem, a neutral and independent world arena of collaboration and co-development around the new «intelligent maritime corridor» concept based on new disruptive technologies, blue economy principles, and sustainable development goals (IMC, 2021)	An example of an IMC project that is crucial for the competitiveness of Canada is the historical international St-Lawrence and Great Lakes maritime system counting 10 federated States and being 3000 km long (Denis Provençal & Donald Roussel, 2021 in what follows). Over the next decades, this corridor will be going through significant physical and technological changes advocated by this non-governmental forum and a community of like-minded industries, public and multidisciplinary academic partners that will set up a new international maritime transport system (IMTS) architecture. The coordination and advancement of policies and regulations with new codes and standards will support numerous business disruptive solutions, favoring an optimal environment for the next generation of intelligent ports, navigation systems and vessels supporting the global supply chain efficiency and resilience. According to the IMC, in the future, autonomous vessels assisted via remote operation centers and deployed on ocean and inland waters under its necessary expertise are going to be one of the masterpieces signifying a profound change in energy transition. As such, the IMC will play a role in the fight against climate change and the protection of biodiversity of lake, river and ocean ecosystems As with previous initiatives, this initiative anticipates an increased use of MASS in Canada and internationally in the future and raises the issue of whether the necessary systems and services are present in the country to service them providing solutions in this direction

Company/organization	*Region*	*Objective behind deployment—types of vessels/vehicles/systems*	*Remarks*
Shipping companies: Algoma Central Corporation, Canada Steamship Lines	Canada	Use of elements of autonomy and advanced information technologies to improve for example, navigational safety, navigation and vessel performance (CISMART, 2020)	
Government: Royal Canadian Navy (RCN)	Canada	RCN uses remotely controlled and semi-remotely controlled vessels, most often during gunnery exercises (Belanger, 2021)	RCN does not currently use, to our knowledge, fully autonomous vessels although the RCN and Defense Research and Development Canada (DRDC) has undertaken research considering different applications of such technology in a military context (Belanger, 2021; Government of Canada, 2016; Hunt, 2021)
Canadian Hydrographic Service (CHS)	Canada	CHS uses autonomous vessels to improve bathymetric, hydrographic and nautical data (CISMART, 2020)	Four fully electric catamarans (2.5 m long) are used all over Canada for shallow water survey mapping. CHS has also engaged in contracts involving XOCEAN (private company) to use their uncrewed surface vessels for hydrographic surveys (Éric Lebel & Graham Bondt, 2021)
University of Dalhousie Faculty of Engineering Microtransat Autonomous Sailboat student team	East Coast	The team is designing and building a sustainable, small-scale, fully autonomous sailboat (Dalhousie, 2021)	The autonomous sailboat Nautono will hopefully be launched in 2022 (Farr, 2021)

Source Adapted from (a) (Open Ocean Robotics, 2021); (b) Colin Angus (2021); (c) ISE (2021); (d) Cellula Robotics (2020); (e) ONC (2021), (f) IMC (2021); (g) CISMART (2020); (h) Belanger (2021); (i) Government of Canada (2016); (j) Hunt (2021); (k) Éric Lebe & Graham Bondt (2021); (l) Dalhousie (2021); and (m) Farr (2021)

position Canadian industry for the post-pandemic economic recovery, the Test/Research and Development subcommittee, chaired by Canada's National Research Council (NRC) Ocean Program Director, Marie-Chantal Ross, remained active with the objective of developing a technology roadmap, fostering innovation projects, and linking the research community across Canada with industry (Marie-Chantal Ross, 2021 in what follows). In both her roles as Program Director and CFMASS subcommittee Chair, Ms. Ross is adopting a proactive approach to the emerging technological reality in Canada and worldwide by collaborating with industrial, academic, and government stakeholders (such as ports, marine industry, and industry associations, governmental authorities, pilotage authorities, and academic institutions). The main focus is to develop living labs (aka test areas) for MASS across Canada allowing for efficient, smart, and environmentally friendly shipping solutions with a view to develop integrated ship to port operations for MASS, create remote control centers in Canada along with decision support tools for navigation in harsh and ice-infested waters, and position Canada as a leader in enabling MASS. Some of NRC's active collaborations in this area are with Queens, Memorial, and York Universities as well as CIDCO.

The mentioned initiatives constitute tangible proof that autonomous vessels are, indeed, an emerging reality in Canada. Some sectors of the Canadian marine industry are developing or using autonomous vessels more than others. Issues frequently present with respect to the described initiatives are the need to further develop rules governing MASS, the absence of widespread use of these vessels by the domestic marine industry, and the need to develop support mechanisms (for example test areas) for their operation in Canada, as highlighted previously.

Considering MASS as an emerging reality, following consultation with the Canadian Marine Advisory Council in April 2021, Transport Canada adopted, in 2022, a policy regarding the oversight of small marine autonomous surface ships ("MASS") (Transport Canada, 2022) to facilitate the operation of MASS within Canadian waters. The policy applies to MASS that is not more than 12 m in length (length as defined by the *Small Vessels Regulations* (SOR/2010–91), or not more than 15 Gross Tonnage with degrees of autonomy three (remotely controlled ship without seafarers on board) and four (fully autonomous ship capable of decision-making and determining actions by itself) (article 3.1). The policy requires the Authorized Representative (AR) of the MASS to apply to the Marine Technical Review Board (MTRB) for approval before operation. Elements to be considered and provided when applying to the MTRB are listed in the policy. This policy also requires the AR of the MASS to prepare a risk assessment, with proposed mitigating measures, to ensure that the safety of navigation during the MASS operation provides a level of safety at least equivalent to a regularly crewed vessel. The policy would be among the first domestic policies in the world to directly address the facilitation of operating small autonomous ships with no crew on board (Chris Given, 2021). For the rest and as previously noted, Canada subjects MASS to its existing maritime regulations and actively participates at the IMO level to develop rules that will apply to MASS.

Overall, frequently recurring issues in relation to the above initiatives include, especially, the need to develop regulation governing MASS—an effort currently taking place at the IMO level and in which Canada is actively participating apart from developing domestic regulation on small MASS; the absence of a widespread use of these vessels by the domestic marine industry, and the need to develop support mechanisms in anticipating their increased use in the future.

3 Smart Ports: The Canadian Case

When a vessel reaches a (Canadian) port, stevedores and marine terminal operators arrange to load and unload the ships. Other companies provide supplies to vessels and local shipyards or conduct repairs to vessels, trucks, cargo handling equipment etc. In each port, there are warehouses and distribution centers where cargo can be stored and processed. There are also government agencies providing safety and health inspections and procedures.

All of the above services are a part of everyday ports' operations in Canada and worldwide. According to the Canada Marine Act (S.C. 1998, c. 10), Canada's national port system consists of 17 Port Authorities (Canada Port Authorities [CPA]). Canada Port Authorities handle more than 60% of the overall marine commercial tonnage (Transport Canada, 2019 in what follows). In fact, in 2016, they handled 5.7 million twenty-foot equivalent unit (TEUs)—a growth of 35% over the last 10 years.

The importance of Canadian ports should also be examined in light of the recent COVID-19 pandemic. Throughout this challenging time, Canada Port Authorities (CPAs) continued operations, moving cargo, employing people, and supporting communities in a sustainable, safe, and innovative manner, all with remarkably little disruption (Association of Canadian Port Authorities, 2021 in what follows). In a recent submission of the Association of Canadian Port Authorities to the federal government of Canada in advance of the 2021 federal budget, the Association stated that as managers of data as much as they are movers of cargo, Canada's ports are part of a global logistics movement to apply new (digital) technologies such as blockchain, artificial intelligence, and internet of things to move cargo and people in a greener, safer, and more efficient manner.

The mentioned digitalization of the Canadian ports makes reference to the presence of smart ports in Canada. A smart port is a port that uses automation and innovative technologies including Artificial Intelligence (AI), Big Data, Internet of Things (IoT), and Blockchain to improve its performance (Port Technology, 2021). Artificial intelligence has been defined as "*... the theory and development of computer systems able to perform tasks that traditionally have required human intelligence*" *(Ilias* Kapsis, 2020 *in what follows)*. AI offers a broad range of tools including machine learning techniques; robotics dealing with the design and operation of programmable machines; and algorithms and automated decision-making systems (ADMS), which uses the knowledge learned from the analysis of big data to predict human and machine behavior and to put together autonomous responses.

The Internet of Things (IoT) is a system comprised of interrelated computing devices, mechanical and digital machines, objects, animals, or people that are provided with unique identifiers and the ability to transfer data over a network without requiring human-to-human or human-to-computer interaction (IoT for all, 2021 in what follows). In more simple terms, IoT is about extending the power of the internet beyond computers and smartphones to a whole range of other things, processes, and environments. The Internet of Things (IoT) is at the epicenter of the Digital Transformation Revolution that is changing the shape of businesses, enterprises, and people's lives.

Big data is data that contains greater variety, arriving in increasing volumes and with more velocity (Oracle, 2021 in what follows). This is also known as the three "V"s. Put simply, big data is larger, more complex data sets, especially from new data sources. These data sets are so voluminous that traditional data processing software is unable to manage them. That being said, these massive volumes of data can be used to address business problems that could not be tackled before. For example, big data allows big businesses to anticipate customer demand and have a clearer view of customer satisfaction, get insights to improve decisions about financial and planning considerations, predict mechanical failures, and even teach machines instead of programming them by developing, due to big data, train machine learning models that machines can use.

Blockchain is a digital database or the technology used to create such a database containing information (such as records of financial transactions) that can be simultaneously used and shared within a large decentralized, publicly accessible network (Merriam Webster Dictionary, 2021).

Practical examples of smart port applications branch out from four strands of need (Marine Insights, 2021 in what follows). Firstly, increasing connectivity and communication among all port stakeholders (terminals, port, users, rail, road transport, port administration and port authority, customs, shipping lines, cargo handling) by using, for example, sensors and feedback systems installed on equipment, quays, berths, bridges recording and transmitting real-time data of operations, and health of the systems. Such smart port technologies deploying data volumes have successfully demonstrated the streamlining and optimization of both maritime and intermodal traffic (from port/terminal to points of delivery and distribution and vice-versa). These have assuaged congestion, idle times, revenue losses and depreciation, pollution, and even accidents. Secondly, using a wide range of technologies (greater wireless networking at ultra-modern 4G and 5G speeds, RF Long-Range Data communication, advanced protocols) for better performance, enhanced accuracy, seamless management, and lesser downtime. Thirdly, assimilating data used at every level of port operation and regarding all stakeholders. In this respect, the creation of port data centers dedicated to storage, distribution, processing, and managing all real-time and recorded data allow room for improvement and traffic efficiency. Fourthly, allowing robotics, computerized algorithms for workflow, and computer-aided management of freight (for example, cranage and cargo loading/unloading/transportation systems) with a view to easing the inefficiencies of conventional methods.

Different Canadian ports have embraced, to a different extent, the concept of smart ports. In the section that follows the author seeks to comment on some of the smart port operations at the port of Vancouver, the port of Montreal, and the port of Halifax, three major Canadian ports.

The *port of Vancouver* (PV) (British Columbia) is Canada's largest port. The following smart port initiatives are present at the port of Vancouver (port of Vancouver, 2021, in what follows).

1. The *eHub app*: The app provides real-time insight into the PV operations, including container and cruise terminal status, port roadway and South Shore rail activities, and vessels in port. The app features: (a) real-time data collected from port authority-installed GPS transponder units on drayage trucks; (b) interactive maps for terminals and facilities, major railways, and vessels in port; (c) live monitoring from the port operations centre and partner agencies;
2. GPS dashboard: Container truck GPS data provides wait times at port terminals allowing truckers to monitor traffic at the port at all times. Webcams located at different places in the terminal allow live video feeds from around the port;
3. Noise monitoring: Since 2013, the PV has worked with partners and vendors to deploy and maintain a series of permanent noise monitoring port terminals. Eleven noise monitoring locations at the port stream data to the port's *noise monitoring web portal* where anyone can view real-time noise data, as well as live atmospheric data such as temperature, pressure, wind and humidity. Users can also explore how noise level trends change over time for a selected location;
4. Supply chain performance: The PV Supply Chain Strategy is a multi-year, port stakeholder-supported series of initiatives developed to achieve sustainable growth in all cargo sectors by coordinating development of the most reliable and consistent supply chain including rail, road and maritime transport in North America. The goals of the program are to: (a) lead and influence new operating practices; (b) measure and monitor service performance; and (c) drive investment and participation in the network. In this regard, the West Coast Supply Chain Visibility Program aims to create a comprehensive system of records for data related to goods movement and provide insights to unlock the full economic potential of the Pacific Gateway. This program develops and implements a series of operational planning and optimization tools tailored to participating industry members. These tools will support actions to increase capacity and operating efficiencies across the supply chain. At the same time, rail, trucking and vessel metrics are used to monitor the movement of

cargo in the different modes of transport increasing visibility of the intermodal supply chain and allowing seamless operations;

5. Container Tracking: In 2018 and in partnership with Deloitte, the Vancouver Fraser Port Authority introduced a blockchain application to add visibility and transparency into the container examination process. This helped optimize ground operations and expedite container inspection by more effectively tracking movement of shipping containers subject to examination. It also reduced costs and improved user and port client experience (Forbes, 2021).

The PV has commented on the advent of autonomous vessels (port of Vancouver, 2018, in what follows). It admits that these could gain more traction in the vessel industry as time goes by. However, for the time being, numerous practical and regulatory hurdles stand in the way of the widespread application of autonomous vessels.

The *port of Montréal* (PM) in the province of Québec (East coast of Canada) is a river port that has embraced the concept of smart ports (Daniel Olivier, 2020 in what follows). The PM is the second largest port in Canada and the fifth largest port in the east coast of North America. According to Daniel Olivier, Business Intelligence and Innovation Director of the Port of Montreal, the aim of the PM is to become one of the world's leading AI port hubs.

Some of the smart solutions at the PM (Daniel Olivier, 2020):

1. The trucking portal: since 2016, the PM has put into effect an open portal for the trucking community in order for truckers to access real time congestion at the port (port of Montreal, 2021a, 2021b). By using this portal, truckers can access congestion data at the port, real time transaction times and also view predictive analytics of how long transaction times will be in the next 12 hours. This solution which is aimed at reducing the congestion at the port and protect the environment is based on AI machine learning;
2. Fast-trucking cargo in times of health crisis: following the COVID-19 pandemic AI was used at the PM to fast-track containers that contained much needed cargo used by front line workers (Port of Montreal (Health), 2021). In this way, 4 days before the arrival of a ship to the PM the captain of the ship gives to the PM all the data on the cargo of the ship. An algorithm then scans all the

cargo to look for key words or codes and identify the content of the containers before the ship arrives. When the ship arrives at the port and the containers are unloaded, the ones containing critical cargo are fast tracked, reducing wait times (dwell time of critical cargo at the port in the context of COVID-19 is reduced to less than 12 hours), accelerating in this way delivery of the cargo to front line workers; and

3. Managing traffic at the port (Daniel Olivier, 2020): AI is currently used at the PM to count passengers and vehicles present at the port. This is done with the view to manage the offer and demand of vehicles (for example, taxis) and avoid line ups for crews and passengers. The risk of traffic and the ensuing adverse environmental effects created by congestion and line-ups is therefore reduced.

Apart from these local initiatives, the PM is part of international collaboration projects regarding smart ports. Here are some of them:

1. The ePIcenter project (2020) (ePIcente, 2020). This project is led by the Port of Antwerp (Belgium) in collaboration with 36 partners representing leading ports (including the PM), forwarders, cargo owners, logistics providers, knowledge institutes and technology firms. The project is funded by the European Horizon 2020 programme and aims at enabling seamless transport of goods, focusing especially on the technological and operational opportunities that smart port technologies and autonomous (electric) vehicles provide. ePIcenter has a truly global scope, with a number of large-scale demonstrators on main shipping routes from Europe to Canada and the US, as well as new trade routes such as the Northern Sea Route and the new Silk Road routes. Technology innovators and environmental experts will collaborate to develop new solutions which increase the efficiency and sustainability of global supply chains;
2. TradeLens (TradeLens, 2018): this initiative, led by Maersk and IBM and to which the PM, *Canada Border and Services Agency* (CBSA) and a lot of shipping lines and stakeholders participate, aims to bring the shipping industry into the digital age through a secure interface exclusively dedicated to freight transport. Underpinned by blockchain technology, TradeLens is a platform open to the entire

ecosystem that participates in the global supply chain. It will allow more effective collaborations and secure sharing of data (such as shipment information along the supply chain) on a common platform. This will lead to streamlining the multiple exchanges in the shipping industry reducing inefficiencies in the supply chain; and

3. ChainPORT (PM 2021a, 2021b): Initiated by the Hamburg Port Authority and the Port of Los Angeles, chainPORT is a cross-national partnership among the world's leading ports. This project goes beyond bilateral partnerships. It aims to bring together port authorities, their partners and customers to share experience and create common strategies (such as increase interconnectivity, adopt cyber-resilience standards) for present and future issues.

It is evident, therefore, that the PM has embraced the idea of smart ports and is increasingly active in this field. Regarding MASS, all five leading Canadian container ports (PM included) are currently collaborating with the NRC regarding the role of ports within a national MASS roadmap (Daniel Olivier, 2021).

Another major port of Canada is the *Port of Halifax* (PoH) (Dolphin Delivery, 2021). The world's largest shipping lines call on the PoH, connecting the port to more than 150 countries (Halifax Port Authority, 2021). Over 1,300 vessels were welcomed into the PoH in 2020 (Halifax Port Authority, 2021). The PoH prides itself on being a data-driven, full-service port that can accommodate the largest containerized cargo vessels calling on the East Coast of North America (Halifax Port Authority, 2021). Its port operation center contains a great number of smart port services including (Halifax Port Authority, 2021):

- Vessel Forecast Summary;
- Container Tracking;
- Halifax Truck Fluidity;
- Import Rail Dwell;
- Ocean Transit Times; and
- Terminal Gates Metrics.

In 2020, the total impact of the PoH on the Province of Nova Scotia was over $3.6 billion in economic output with the direct portion being

$2.3 billion (Halifax Port Authority, 2021 in what follows). This level of activity generates over 18, 775 jobs.

According to the PoH communications manager "when it comes to active projects, we are considering ways in which we can better utilize all our existing assets and infrastructure to benefit Canadians. Being collaborative, future focused and sustainable are among our guiding principles. Through our recently called innovation space called 'The PIER' at the Seaport, where PIER is short for Port Innovation, Engagement and Research, we are working collaboratively with partners to tackle the big challenges facing the transportation and supply chain industries that no one company can solve on their own" (Lane Farguson, Halifax Port Authority, 2021).

The digitalization of the mentioned ports is a step forward towards accommodating MASS in the future. As SINTEF and TCOMS have noted, it is timely to pursue a fully integrated ship-port approach towards this complex system-of-systems (smart ports—MASS) (SINTEF, 2020 in what follows). This is necessary in order for ports to fully harness the benefits of smart and autonomous vessel developments. It requires a continuous improvement of automation and autonomy in ship-related operations in port (e.g., bunkering and re-supply services), to complement ongoing shore-side advancements in areas such as cargo handling. Similarly, smart capabilities will be required to enable the remote or autonomous operations of tugs including the mooring and berthing of cargo vessels. Extending the integration between the port and ships, as well as further improving transport efficiency (both in terms of monetary and spatial resources) will require the operationalization of Just-in-Time vessel arrivals and more intelligent coordination and management of vessel traffic from a fleet management perspective. Leveraging the increased connectivity and data availability, smarter approaches for verifying the compliance of foreign-flagged vessels to international conventions (i.e., Port State Control) can be implemented.

Overall, the digitalization of Canadian ports to accommodate autonomous vessels is the way forward. This becomes evident when looking at the emergence of autonomous vessels and related operations in Canada as well as the adoption of regulation to govern them. Focusing on the digitalization of smart ports as well as further developing operations to accommodate autonomous vessels are important considerations to take into account at the domestic (Canadian) level with respect to MASS.

4 Conclusions

We are living in an era of a digital revolution which is invading modern societies one sector at a time: health care, retail, cars, finances, media, and entertainment are some of the sectors touched by this new trend. Shipping constitutes no exception as autonomous vessels make their appearance internationally and in Canadian context. This emerging reality in Canada has taken the form of coast-to-coast public or private sector initiatives materializing in the development of autonomous surface or underwater vessels, forums promoting discussion on autonomous vessels or projects servicing such vessels. Common issues underlying this emerging reality are the need for more widespread acceptance by the marine industry in Canada and the need to further develop rules, operations, and services to accommodate MASS. Recently, a policy was adopted in Canada to facilitate the operation of small MASS alongside international (IMO) initiatives undertaken to regulate some common legal concerns relating to autonomous vessels. At the same time, smart port initiatives are presently surfacing in Canada. Modern ports strive to digitalize their processes and services seeking more efficient operations and environmentally friendly solutions not only at the port level but also for door-to-door processes. Although smart ports do not currently service autonomous vessels in Canada, their further development in this direction seems imperative as MASS is gaining attention and importance year-by-year domestically and worldwide.

Acknowledgements The author is deeply thankful to all the professionals who helped in the realization of this study.

References

Angus, C. (2021). Interview with Colin Angus, Co-Founder of Open Ocean Robotics.

Association of Canadian Port Authorities. (2021). Leveraging the Resilience of Ports to Rebuild the Canadian economy (2021) https://acpa-aapc.ca/wp-content/uploads/2021/02/ACPA-2021-Federal-Budget-Submission_EN.pdf

Belanger, F. (2021). Interview with Lieutenant (Navy) François Belanger, Legal Officer (J.D. Candidate, 2023) and ex-Naval Warfare Officer, Royal Canadian Navy.

Cellula Robotics. (2020). https://www.cellula.com/

CISMART. (2020). Development of Canadian Asset Map and Assessment of Global Competitiveness in the Area of Autonomous Surface Ships. http://cismart.ca/wp-content/uploads/2020/11/CISMaRT-Report-to-ISED-on-Autonomous-Surface-Ships-Final-Posted-Online-2020.pdf
CMLA. (2020). Maritime Labour and Immigration Committee Report. http://www.canadianmaritimelaw.com/2020/06/updates-in-maritime-labour-and.html
Dalhousie. (2021). MicroTransat Autonomous Sailboat. https://www.dal.ca/faculty/engineering/electrical/about/student-societies/microtransat-autonomous-sailboat.html
Dolphin Delivery. (2021). The Five Largest Major Ports in Canada. https://dolphindelivery.ca/the-5-largest-major-ports-in-canada/
Lebel, É., & Bondt, G. (2021). Interview with Éric Lebel and Graham Bondt, CHS.
Farguson, L. (2021). Interview with Lane Farguson, Manager, Media Relations & Communications of the Port of Halifax.
Farr, J. (2021). Interview with Jade Farr, Project Manager, Dalhousie Microtransat Autonomous Sailboat Team.
Forbes. (2021). Vancouver Fraser Port Authority Improves Supply Chain Visibility With Computer Vision-Based Container Tracking. https://www.forbes.com/sites/amazonwebservices/2021/10/26/vancouver-fraser-port-authority-improves-supply-chain-visibility-with-computer-vision-based-container-tracking/?sh=23a988a35366
Given, C. (2021). The SIU remains Very Active on all Matters. *The Canadian Sailor*. https://seafarers.ca/wp-content/uploads/2021/08/LeMARIN_June-2021_WEB.pdf
Government of Canada. (2016). Enhancing the Navy's Protection Against Modern Threats. Defence Research and Development Canada. http://www.drdc-rddc.gc.ca/en/dynamic-article.page?doc=enhancing-the-navy-s-protection-against-modern-threats/ilnc82yb
Halifax Port Authority. (2021). Port of Halifax. https://www.portofhalifax.ca/
Hertog, V. D., Oscar, L., & Stapleton, R. (2016). *Revolutionary RAmora Brings Teleoperated Capability to Ship-Handling Tugs*. Presentation. ITS, Boston.
Hunt, J. (2021). Victory at Sea: Unmanned Surface Vessels and the Distribution of Future RCN Capabilities. Master of Defence Studies. Canadian Forces College. https://www.cfc.forces.gc.ca/259/290/23/286/HuntJ.pdf
IMC. (2021). Alliance and Synergy for Intelligent Maritime Corridors. A Proposal as Part of the Development of the Quebec Research and Innovation Strategy 2022. Conseil International CMI—IMC International Council.
IoT for All. (2022). What is the Internet of Things, or IoT? A Simple Explanation. https://www.iotforall.com/what-is-internet-of-things
ISE (International Submarine Engineering Ltd). (2021). https://ise.bc.ca/

Kapsis, I. (2020). Artificial Intelligence in Financial Services: Systemic Implications and Regulatory Responses. *Banking and Financial Services Policy Report: A Journal on Trends in Regulation and Supervision, 39*(4), 1–21, 3.

Katsivela, M. (2022). *Autonomous Vessels: Regulatory and Ethical Concerns*. Éditions Thémis.

Marine Insights. (2021). What are Smart Port Technologies. https://www.marineinsight.com/tech/what-are-smart-port-technologies/

Merriam Webster Dictionary. (2021). Blockchain. https://www.merriam-webster.com/dictionary/blockchain

MSC. (2018). IMO Doc MSC 100/WP.8, para. 3.

NRC (National Research Council of Canada). (2019). Workshop Presentation. The Canadian Forum for Maritime Autonomous Surface Ships (MASS): Sub-Committee on Test/Research and Development. http://cismart.ca/wp-content/uploads/2019/12/CFMASS-SubCom-TRD-v3-Fraser-Winsor.pdf

Olivier, D. (2021). Interview with Daniel Olivier, Director, Business Intelligence and Innovation at Port of Montreal.

Olivier, D. (2020). Panel session. Innovative Technologies Leading the Way in Smart Piers. *Smart Ports TV*. https://www.smartports.tv/a/panel-session-innovative-technologies-leading-the-way-in-smart-piers

ONC. (2021). Ocean Networks Canada. https://www.oceannetworks.ca/innovation-centre/smart-ocean-systems/ocean-observing-systems

Open Ocean Robotics. (2021). Open Ocean Robotics. https://openoceanrobotics.com/

Oracle. (2021). What is Big Data. https://www.oracle.com/ca-en/big-data/what-is-big-data/

Port of Montreal. (2021a). Portail du camionage. https://www.portmtlcamions.com/en/

Port of Montreal. (2021b). Health. Artificial Intelligence at the Service of the Port Operations in this Time of Health Crisis. https://www.port-montreal.com/en/the-port-of-montreal/news/news/artificial-intelligence

Port of Montreal. (2020). ePIcenter Project Kicks Off. https://www.port-montreal.com/en/the-port-of-montreal/news/news/press-release/epicenter-press-release

Port of Montreal. (2018). The Port of Montreal joins Maersk IDM platform. *Tradelens*. https://www.port-montreal.com/en/the-port-of-montreal/news/news/press-release/tradelens

Port of Vancouver. (2021). Port Dashboard. https://www.portvancouver.com/port-dashboard/

Port of Vancouver. (2018). Roberts Bank Terminal 2. Container Vessel Call Forecast Study. https://www.ceaa-acee.gc.ca/050/documents/p80054/126252E.pdf

Port Technology. (2021). What is a Smart Port. https://www.porttechnology.org/news/what-is-a-smart-port/
Provençal, D., & Roussel, D. (2021). Interview of the author with Denis Provençal and Donald Roussel cofounders of IMC.
Ross, M.-C. (2021). Interview with Marie-Chantal Ross, Program Director of the National Research Council of Canada Ocean Program.
SINTEF. (2020). R&D Roadmap for Smart & Autonomous Sea Transport Systems. https://www.sintef.no/contentassets/1005d8bd6f854f0aabb2ead2a207a1fc/rd-road-map-smart-autonomous-shipping.pdf
Statistics Canada. (2016). International Perspective. https://www150.statcan.gc.ca/n1/pub/11-402-x/2012000/chap/geo/geo01-eng.htm
The Council of Canadian Academies. (2017). Expert Panel on the Social and Economic Value of Marine Shipping to Canada. The Value of Commercial Marine Shipping to Canada. https://cca-reports.ca/wp-content/uploads/2018/08/ValueMarineShipping_fullreport_EN.pdf
The Maritime Executive. (2021). Autonomous Vessels are Becoming a Commercial Reality. https://www.maritime-executive.com/editorials/autonomous-vessels-are-becoming-a-commercial-reality
Transport Canada. (2019). Backgrounder on Canada's Port System. https://tc.canada.ca/en/marine/backgrounder-canada-s-port-system
Transport Canada. (2022). Oversight of Small MASS. https://tc.canada.ca/en/marine-transportation/marine-safety-management-system-tp-13585-e-tier-i-policies/tier-i-policy-oversight-small-maritime-autonomous-surface-ships-mass
UNCTAD (United Nations Conference on Trade and Development). (2021). *Review of Maritime Transport*, 36. https://unctad.org/system/files/official-document/rmt2021_en_0.pdf

CHAPTER 18

The Societal Impacts of Autonomous Ships: The Norwegian Perspective

Ørnulf Jan Rødseth, Dag Atle Nesheim, Agathe Rialland, and Even Ambros Holte

1 Introduction

Autonomous ships have generated significant interest in researchers for a decade marked by the first large concept study, the EU-financed Maritime Unmanned Navigation through Intelligence in Networks (MUNIN) project (Rødseth & Burmeister, 2012). Despite slower developments than initially expected, there are still high expectations and correspondingly

Ø. J. Rødseth (✉) · D. A. Nesheim · A. Rialland · E. A. Holte
SINTEF Ocean, Trondheim, Norway
e-mail: OrnulfJan.Rodseth@sintef.no

D. A. Nesheim
e-mail: DagAtle.Nesheim@sintef.no

A. Rialland
e-mail: Agathe.Rialland@sintef.no

E. A. Holte
e-mail: even.holte@sintef.no

© The Author(s) 2023

T. M. Johansson et al. (eds.), *Autonomous Vessels in Maritime Affairs*, Studies in National Governance and Emerging Technologies,
https://doi.org/10.1007/978-3-031-24740-8_18

high investments in ship autonomy around the world. Design projects examined in our research are the container ship "Yara Birkeland", the ASKO cargo ferries, the inland waterway vessel Seafar, and the container ship "Zhi Fei" (CNS, 2021; Kongsberg, 2020; Seafar, 2022; Yara, 2018). In addition, several large research projects are ongoing worldwide, e.g., the EU projects AUTOSHIP (2022) and AEGIS (2022), the Korean Autonomous Surface Ship project, and the Norwegian SFI AutoShip (KASS, 2022; NTNU, 2022). Figures published by these projects add up to research investments of close to 200 million Euros.

The definition of "an autonomous ship" is still debated with opinions ranging from decision support on conventional ships to fully uncrewed and automatic operations. In this chapter, we will only assess "constrained autonomy" which is defined as uncrewed operation with limited but relatively advanced automation onboard and supported in complex situations by operators in a remote-control center (RCC) (Rødseth, 2021). The focus is on uncrewed cargo transport, but autonomous passenger transport will also be investigated, where it is anticipated that there will be safety personnel onboard to assist passengers in normal operations as well as in emergencies while nautical operations, e.g., sailing and berthing, will be handled by constrained autonomy.

Section 2 details both actual and proposed use cases for autonomous ships in Norway with a brief qualitative description of expected societal effects also detailing what attributes of autonomous ship operations contribute to these effects. The concept of "societal impact" can be many-faceted, but in this chapter societal impact is specifically based on a selection of 8 of the 17 sustainable development goals (SDG) (detailed in Sect. 3). In Sect. 3 the SDGs will also be linked to concrete societal effects and to the autonomous ship attributes discussed in Sect. 2. Measuring societal impact depends on the delimitation of the system being assessed and therefore it can be complex and difficult to accurately measure with concrete key performance indicators (KPI). Section 4 will explore these issues in some detail and look at where quantitative KPIs can be used; and just as importantly where they are less useful. This section also describes some KPIs that have been developed in the writers' research projects. Section 5 summarizes the chapter and provides some conclusions.

2 Autonomous Shipping—The Norwegian Perspective

The general societal impacts are more context-dependent than environmental impacts alone. Thus, most of this chapter's analysis of societal benefits will be limited to Norway. Below is a set of key characteristics for Norway that are contextually significant for an assessment of societal impacts of autonomous shipping.

- High education, high costs: Norway has a highly educated workforce with high gender equality and high wages—only 10% of the workforce earning less than EUR 3000 per month and the average being EUR 5000 (SSB, 2022). Note: more than 50% of Norwegian seafarers are officers;
- Large and advanced maritime industry: The Norwegian maritime industry accounts for about 3% of gross domestic product and 29% of exports. It is a high-end industry, mainly focusing on various types of specialized ships (MTIF, 2020); and
- Long coast, sparse population: Norway has around 5.4 million people mostly spread along a long coast. The boundary to international waters is around 2600 km but the physical length is more than 25,000 km if the coast around major islands and fjords are counted. Sea transport is thus a critical part of the infrastructure in Norway (MTIF, 2020).

2.1 *Some Relevant Attributes of Autonomous Ships*

Smaller ships can be more cost-effective with autonomy than without. This is due to reduced crew cost and removal of accommodation. These benefits will be larger as ship sizes decrease (Gribkovskaia et al., 2019). Thus, autonomy is a promising innovation when considering new transport systems, based on many smaller ships, rather than larger ships which have been the predominate "economy of scale" trend. The main attributes of autonomous ships that make them an attractive option to solve certain specific societal problems are briefly described below. They are also included as the bottom row of Fig. 1.

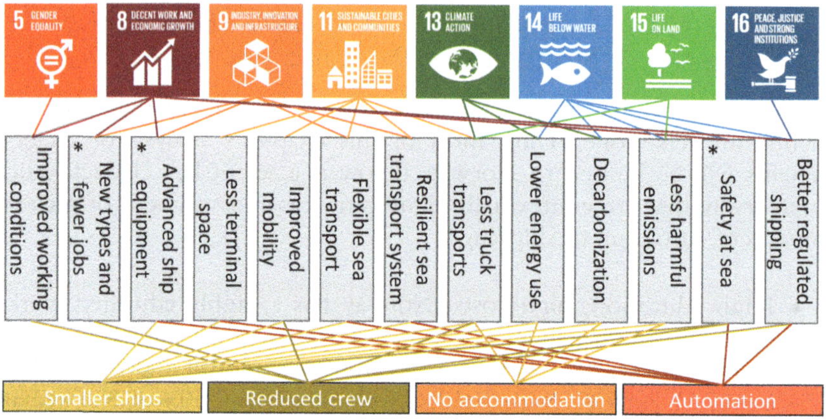

Fig. 1 Mapping between SDG, main societal effects, and autonomy attributes (*Source* Authors)

- Smaller ships give benefits in themselves in being more flexible, lower cost, and requiring less infrastructure than larger ships. On shorter voyages they are also suitable for battery operation;
- Reduced crew costs due to automation controlling the ship during most operations and only using RCC crew in more complex cases. It is likely that it will be possible to get below one crew per ship controlled when the RCC is designed to operate several ships (Kretschmann et al., 2017). This reduces operational costs, again more for smaller ships than larger ones;
- Removing crew accommodation reduces construction costs and eliminates energy consumption from the accommodation section. It also increases the cargo carrying capacity or reduces ship sizes. On the other hand, autonomous ships have additional costs related to new sensor systems and automation, but the authors believe it is likely that this is more than offset by the cost reductions; and
- Automation of the ship and its interfaces to the port, including cargo handling, makes it possible to operate around the clock without additional costs for, e.g., shore crew working at non-conventional times. This will be important for smaller ports where it may not be possible to always have a crew available. This is also an enabler for city center terminals with minimal real estate use and very fast turn-around for ship calls.

2.2 Some Norwegian Examples

2.2.1 Yara Birkeland and ASKO—Reducing the Impact of Truck Transport

Yara Birkeland (Yara, 2018) and the ASKO ferries are very different ship concepts, but one main societal effect quoted by both projects is reducing the negative impact of truck transport (Kongsberg, 2020). The ASKO ferries (two being built initially) are roll-on roll-off (RORO) ferries with a capacity of 16 EU standard trailers without tractor units. Yara Birkeland is a crane-operated ship with a capacity of 120 20-foot containers. The ships are electric powered with batteries and are completely emission free. Cargo handling will be fully automated and can in principle take place around the clock. For the ASKO project specifically, resilience is also an important factor. The main transport road today goes through the Oslo-fjord tunnel. The tunnel is frequently closed, requiring a longer detour with significant delays and increased environmental impact, which the ferries will help mitigate.

2.2.2 Passenger and Car Transport in Rural areas—The Need for On-Demand Operations

Norway is a country with a sparse population where many live along the coast. Many small communities are on islands or separated by deep fjords. Passenger and car ferries play an important role where bridges or tunnels cannot be built or are too expensive. To keep operational costs at a reasonable level, these ferries will normally not operate during the night. Autonomy may make it cost-effective to have a small safety crew onboard also during night operations. For very small populations, e.g., less than 100 persons on an island, one may even consider training the residents to operate safety equipment themselves. This may make it possible to offer around the clock, with fully uncrewed, and on-demand services. Some projects are now developing concepts for such operations in Norway. In Finland, the operation of an autonomous ferry was demonstrated in 2018 (FinFerries, 2018).

2.2.3 Cargo Transport in Urban and Rural Areas—Low Real-Estate Impact

Urban areas have high real estate costs and low tolerance for, e.g., noise from port areas. This means that port areas are in many cases being moved out of the city. This often also brings increased truck transport from the new port areas to the city. Smaller and highly automated ships offer an option to serve city centers with minimal requirements to infrastructure and demand for high-value real estate for cargo storage. This requires that cargo immediately be moved from the landing site to its destination. This could be based on palletized cargo or RORO solutions for containers or similar concepts (AEGIS, 2022).

2.2.4 *Passenger Transport in Inner-City Areas—Flexible and Low Cost*

Many cities have internal waterways in the form of rivers and canals. Normally, these are passed with bridges, but bridges are expensive and may also hinder waterway traffic. In the same way, as described in Sect. 2.2.2, ferries without a crew or with only a safety operator can be a good substitute for a bridge, possibly offering 24-hour services without excessive operational costs (Hyke, 2022; Zeabuz, 2022).

3 Societal Impacts and How to Measure It

3.1 *Defining Societal Impact*

In 2015, the United Nations defined the 17 sustainable development goals (SDG) to be a "blueprint to achieve a better and more sustainable future for all" (UN, 2022). Sea transport is relevant for most of these goals (Alamoush et al., 2021), but in the context of automation and autonomy, we have selected eight of them, as illustrated in the top row of Fig. 1.

The second row of boxes shows the more concrete societal effects that we have been investigating in our projects and how they are linked to the SDGs. These will be further discussed in Sect. 4. The third and final row shows the four attributes of autonomous ships that are considered the main contributors to the effects in row 2. These were discussed in Sect. 2.2.

3.2 *Measuring Societal Impact*

Key performance indicators (KPIs) are quantifiable, measurable indicators of performance. They allow for statistical analysis, qualitative snapshots, historical trends, and benchmarks between comparable concepts. At first glance, they seem very well suited toward assessing the impact of autonomous shipping. Unfortunately, when assessing the societal benefits from autonomous shipping, we need to consider the nature and complexity of societal impact.

"While environmental objectives and criteria can be based on science, a social taxonomy has to be based on international authoritative standards of topical relevance [...]" (EU, 2022).

This statement sums up two key aspects related to societal impact: It is difficult to quantify, and it is more susceptible to context. Trying to create a generic set of societal KPIs which are quantifiable and universally relevant, carries the risk of focusing on what is possible to quantify rather than what is relevant to express.

Recognizing these challenges, the results from two EU H2020 projects for autonomous ships conducting cargo transport operations, the AEGIS (2022) and AUTOSHIP (2022) are presented below. In addition, KPIs relevant within the context of passenger transport are also included (project Smarter Transport) (Smartere Transport, 2018).

The KPIs listed in Tables 1, 2, and 3 were developed as tools for assessing autonomous-ships and transport systems at the conceptual stage and to exemplify how quantitative societal impact assessments can be done. Each of the KPIs listed is mapped to the UN's sustainable development goals from Fig. 15. Note that KPIs related to GHG emissions (SDG 13) are not included in the tables as these are extensively discussed in other papers (e.g. Lindstad et al., 2021).

Tables 1, 2 and 3 have been assembled by the authors based on internal and non-published reports from the respective projects.

4 Main Societal Effects of Autonomous Shipping

In the following, each of the societal effects indicated in the middle row of Fig. 1 is discussed in detail. Most effects are generally positive, but those that may have negative effects are marked with a star in the upper left corner in Fig. 1. In cases where the Norwegian perspective is specifically relevant for the analysis, a brief discussion of why is included.

4.1 Improved Working Conditions

Autonomy and automation are often applied to tasks that are "3D": Dirty, Dangerous, or Dull. One can question which onboard jobs fall into the 3D category, but it has been shown that working on a ship is much more

Table 1 Societal KPIs from AEGIS (2022)

KPI name	*KPI description*	*SDG*
Accident rate	Number of incidents resulting in damage or injury	SDG8
Fatality rate	Number of occurrences of death by accident	SDG8
Fire incidents	Number of incidents involving smoke, heat and flames causing damage	SDG8, SDG11
Crime	All actions which constitute an offence and is punishable by Law	SDG16
Labour conditions	Quality of working environment	SDG8
Employment	Influence on the occupational rate	SDG8
Income	Influence on earnings	SDG8
Worker commuting time	Total journey employees take from home to work and back again	SDG8, SDG11
Training	Time invested in teaching an employee a particular working Skill	SDG5, SDG8 SDG16
Acoustic emissions	Amount of noise emitted by AEGIS vessels to society	SDG8, SDG15
Traffic	Amount of goods transported in ports/terminals	SDG11
Citizen complaints	Total number of societies protests against some of the AEGIS proposals' activities	SDG11
Area used for port operations	Total amount of surface needed to operate AEGIS proposals successfully	SDG11

Source Authors

dangerous than working in similar jobs on land. This is mainly due to work-related accidents onboard (Roberts et al., 2014). Thus, removing crew from the ship should improve occupational safety for the workers.

Shifting crew from ship to shore provides the potential for more standard working hours in the RCC rather than exhausting shifts on board (Jepsen et al., 2015). Shore-based work and more ordered working conditions may also encourage more women to seek maritime jobs (Kim et al., 2019).

At the height of the recent Covid-19 pandemic, an estimated 400,000 seafarers were stranded on vessels around the world with extended time on board, and often with no opportunity to go ashore during port stays (Lucas et al., 2021). In addition, the pandemic led to a lack of sufficient

Table 2 Societal KPIs from AUTOSHIP (2022)

KPI name	*KPI description*	*SDG*
Reduction in tonne-km transported on road	The reduction in tonne-km transported on road is found by calculating the distance a truck would have to drive to transport the goods between the same two points as if the ship is transporting the goods (D_{truck}), and multiplying with the total transported weight (M)	SDG11, SDG15
Reduction in truck transport km	Reduction in truck-km is estimated by first calculating how many trucks would be needed if the autonomous ship is not performing the freight n_{truck}. Then calculating how far each truck would need to drive D_{truck} and finally the total reduced truck transport distance	SDG11, SDG15
Number of hours of tasks at dangerous areas removed	Removing people from manual tasks such as cargo handling, mooring and deck operations, improves safety by reducing the risk of personnel injury from moving equipment. n is the number of locations visited in the time period for measuring number of reduced manual tasks, $t_{\text{task}}(j)$ is the duration of the task at location j	SDG8

Source Authors

healthcare onboard and restricted access to onshore healthcare. While this type of crisis hopefully is rare, it shows how vulnerable ship crews can be to external international disruptions.

4.2 New Types of Jobs and Fewer Jobs

So far, the effects of autonomy on the employment of Norwegian seafarers are positive, as both ASKO and Yara replace trucks with new ships operated from an RCC by licenced ship officers. However, automation will likely reduce the number of jobs, but also likely have more effect on lower qualified workers than on the higher. Shipping has already seen

Table 3 Societal KPIs from Smartere Transport (2018), assembled by authors

KPI name	*KPI description*	*SDG*
Transport cost for passenger, expressed as ***generalized travel cost***	Estimated travel time- and cost, expressed by the sum of the monetary and non-monetary costs of a journey for a specific transport operation	SDG11
Total travel time	Total travel time consist of travel time in rush hours between starting point and end destination. Calculated from time spent getting to starting point for commuting service, actual waiting time at bus stop/ quay, potential waiting time divided by the factor of two, and time spent on the actual commuting service	SDG11
Service regularity	Number of delayed departures/trips per annum, expressed in % of all scheduled trips Number of cancelled departures/trips per annum, expressed in % of all scheduled trips	SDG11
Passenger comfort	Noise level in passenger area, measured in dB (decibel)	SDG11

Source Authors

a dramatic reduction in crew sizes from the 1970s when computerized automation systems were introduced on ships. It is to be expected that this trend will continue, although not at the same speed. One limiting factor is port operations where the most demanding tasks still require ship crews (Kooij & Hekkenberg, 2021). More ship maintenance work in port or dry dock is expected, which may also increase the number of jobs in this part of the maritime sector. Therefore, it is difficult to estimate the actual impact on future jobs that autonomy will bring. As noted initially, it is also to be expected that many smaller autonomous ships both in short sea and inland waterways will replace truck transport (AEGIS, 2022) which most likely will reduce the total number of transport jobs. For Norwegian policymakers, this may be less of a problem as much of the truck transport is by foreign drivers and trucks, either doing cabotage or being employed by foreign customers.

The reduction of jobs may also have geographic differences. As the RCC will be on land, the owner of the ship may prefer to have it under the same jurisdiction as the ship. This may also become a requirement from the ship's flag state authority. As the qualification of the operators most likely will be at least on the level of today's officers, the savings in using convenience flags and foreign ratings will be lower. Thus, one may see that owners will flag home their ships as well as the RCC crew. For some countries, like Norway, this may increase the number of jobs in the maritime sector, particularly when seen together with cargo being transferred from truck to ship. However, there is little doubt that it will have a negative impact on countries that traditionally provide many ratings to the world fleet.

The jobs will also be substantially different. While today's concepts for RCC operations focus on remote control from a "virtual bridge", this will not be feasible in the longer perspective. More autonomy onboard will create an environment where one operator supervises several ships and relies on automation to control those ships which are not immediately under attention (Porathe, 2014). This will require dramatically new workstation designs and job profiles. On the other hand, it is also likely that basic maritime skills will be necessary, and that it is primarily a question of supplementing current officer training with new skills to operate advanced automation systems (Rødseth, 2021). In Norway, such courses are already under development for RCC operators (USN, 2021).

4.3 Advanced Ship Equipment

The higher degree of automation will require much more advanced ship and RCC equipment than what is the norm today. New sensors and anti-collision decision support, as well as continuous connectivity to land will be required. This will likely give benefits to the high-end ship equipment industry, such as the Norwegian. However, this may also reduce the market share or prices for some other countries' industries, therefore there may be a drawback for the latter.

4.4 Less Terminal Space

Areas close to the shoreline are now seen as among the most valuable, especially in urban areas. Public demand for moving ports and terminals from city centers is ever-increasing. This will increase last-mile truck transport as cargo now will be landed farther from the city. Autonomy may make it possible to use several smaller ships rather than the large ships used today. By automating cargo handling, e.g., in combination with RORO solutions as in ASKO (Kongsberg, 2020), very little land-based infrastructure will be required. If this is combined with just-in-time arrival and departure of cargo, one can set up waterborne transport solutions directly into city centers or to small rural quays with minimal requirements on terminal infrastructure. This could emerge as an attractive alternative to truck transport. The introduction of autonomous ships may also have an impact on more conventional port operations. As the demand for intermodal connections is expected to increase, including smaller autonomous ships and barges for hinterland and last-mile transport, cargo can be expected to spend less time at the terminal and thus reduce the need for terminal storage area.

4.5 *Improved Mobility*

As discussed in Sects. 2.2.2 and 2.2.4, autonomous ships and passenger ferries carry the potential of revitalizing mobility in both urban and rural areas. This can help to answer the increased demand for new transport solutions, while minimizing environmental impact through zero-emission propulsion technologies. With operations without crew or only safety personnel onboard, a significant cost element in short-distance transport at sea is removed. This allows realization of new and high-frequency services as viable alternatives to high-cost investments in land-based transport infrastructure. In addition, with the opportunity to provide around-the-clock services to the public, such solutions can easily be connected to other modes of public transport and thereby support more sustainable living and commuting services. Likewise, as discussed in Sect. 2.2.3, the same mechanism may be used in sparsely populated areas to provide, e.g., on-demand car and passenger ferry services. In addition, many small autonomous ferries can reduce waiting times on higher traffic fjord crossings and may prove a good alternative to bridges or tunnels.

4.6 *Flexible Sea Transport*

Autonomy may make it cost-effective to use many smaller ships instead of fewer and larger ships. This concept can also be used for large seagoing ships on intercontinental voyages. Smaller ships, e.g., 2000 to 4000 TEU capacity, will put less pressure on the ports and their hinterland transport and may significantly reduce investments in cargo handling equipment

(Van Es, 2019). Ships can use smaller ports and cargo can be moved closer to the final destination and reduce transhipments and overall transport costs. The viability of this concept is supported by an investigation by McKinsey (Glave & Saxon, 2015) that reports that at calls in a certain European port, an 18,000 TEU ship on average only moves around 2 500 containers during the port call (Glave & Saxon, 2015).

4.7 *Resilient Sea Transport Systems*

A larger fleet of smaller ships can also increase transport system resilience as smaller ships are easier to operate, occupy a smaller space in narrow passages, and are less dependent on large and complex ports and terminals. The 2021 Ever Given incident in the Suez Canal is a prime example of one of the risks associated with large ships in narrow passages. Similar risks are also applicable to short-sea shipping and inland waterways. Additionally, uncrewed ships are minimally impacted by quarantine or other restrictions related to persons either onboard the ship or in the terminals. This may make it easier to operate in adverse circumstances such as during the COVID-19 pandemic.

4.8 *Less Truck Transports*

The traditional advantages of road transport versus ships are frequency, flexibility, and customization (door-to-door) via small batch sizes. Increasing vessel size or reducing operational speeds are two well-known principles for reducing fuel consumption and cost per transported unit on ships. However, this may further increase the disadvantages relative to truck transport: frequency and flexibility. An economic analysis by Akbar et al. (2021) of a hub-and-spoke shipping network composed of conventional mother ships and autonomous daughter ships performing cargo transhipment at specific ports, shows that autonomous ships can contribute to considerable cost savings—11% on average of operating costs savings, and up to 20% cost reduction when introducing an autonomous mother ship to the network. A similar study of a liner shipping network serving 13 ports along the Norwegian coastline using autonomous ships estimated a cost reduction of 13% compared to conventional ships (Msakni et al., 2020). Thus, autonomous vessels, conveying operational cost savings combined with an innovative hub and spoke system, can serve as a game changer to make waterborne transport much more competitive compared to trucks (Lindstad, 2020).

The estimated benefit of shifting cargo from road to sea and rail, based on the removal of all Norwegian road shipments longer than 300 km, is about 0.48 mill MT CO2 eq. over the period 2021–2030 (Miljødirektoratet, 2020). The Yara Birkeland autonomous ship transport alone is estimated to reduce diesel-powered truck haulage by 40,000 journeys a year (Kongsberg, 2020). In addition to GHG emission reductions, we foresee few accidents, less congestion, less noise, and less dust and particulate matter emissions.

4.9 *Lower Energy Consumption*

In theory, shipping can fully decarbonize through electro-fuels produced using renewable energy. However, the use of electro-fuels require about 2.5 times more energy than conventional fuels on a well-to-wake perspective. This makes them inevitably costly, and heavily dependent on a large ramp-up of renewable electricity (Lindstad et al., 2021). Improving energy efficiency and reducing abatement cost is therefore key to the viable adoption of electro-fuels. Uncrewed and autonomous ships can reduce energy use through the removal of accommodation and other spaces for human occupation. Based on a study of a 230-m long bulk carrier from the MUNIN project, Kretschmann et al. (2017) have estimated an overall 6% energy saving from removing the deckhouse and hotel system. For small vessels, engaged in a shorter distance and high-frequency services, batteries can provide the most energy-efficient power source. From well to wake, the energy intensity of an electric battery is about 1.5, compared to 2.4 for conventional fuels (Lindstad et al., 2021). Finally, uncrewed operation can enable new and more energy-efficient hull designs, as some constraints related to crew comfort and safety onboard may be reduced or removed. This could also include designs for more efficient cargo handling or adaptions to, e.g., wind propulsion.

4.10 *Decarbonization*

As discussed in Sect. 4.9, the least energy-intense solution and most mature technology for zero-emission ship propulsion is electric batteries. While this option is limited for larger ocean-going vessels, it is highly compatible with smaller vessels in short-range and high-frequency shuttle systems. Autonomy, enabling the cost-effective deployment of smaller vessels, represents a real opportunity to expand the electrification of nearshore shipping activity, and a direct contribution to reducing both GHG emissions and other harmful air emissions, as demonstrated by the Yara Birkeland and the ASKO ferries (Yara, 2018; Kongsberg, 2020).

Additional solutions for reducing a ship's carbon intensity may also be developed from autonomy. First, considering conventional combustion systems, the reduced energy needs of smaller ships, without compromising the carrying capacity for vessels of a certain size, allow for the drop-in of more expensive but zero-emissions electro-fuels; second, considering novel fuel systems, the freed space onboard can enable the implementation of alternative fuels requiring larger and heavier tank systems such as green ammonia or green hydrogen, without compromising the shipload capacity; third, assuming full autonomous control of the machinery system, the available space could in theory be considered for an onboard carbon-capture system (CCShip, 2021; Feenstra et al., 2019).

4.11 Less Harmful Emissions

Decarbonization often means the use of electric energy from batteries or from fuel cells as discussed in Sects. 4.9 and 4.10. In many cases, and always for batteries, this will totally remove emissions to air from ship transport (excluding the production process of the batteries themselves). This includes particulate matter, NOx, SOx, or any other exhaust-associated emissions. This can have significant positive effects on life on land and under sea, particularly in short sea or inland waterways transport and has been used, as such, to justify both the Yara and ASKO projects' advances of autonomous shipping.

4.12 Safety at Sea

As discussed in Sect. 4.1, an uncrewed ship, by definition, eliminates onboard human injuries and fatalities while at sea. Automating cargo operations will also remove safety risks associated with port operations.

Regarding human errors resulting in safety incidents at sea, Galieriková (2019) states that studies of maritime accidents identify human error as the primary contributing cause for up to 70% of accidents. Many of these incidents are attributable to fatigue, badly designed systems, or faulty safety management procedures. While autonomous ships still will have a crew in the RCC, it can reasonably be expected that many of the contributing factors to today's incident scenarios, will be removed. Normal work schedules can be used, eliminating some of the fatigue problems, while design requirements, procedures, and equipment standards are expected to be stricter than on today's ships. Thus, it is reasonable to expect that the operators' contributions to marine accidents will be heavily reduced (de Vos et al., 2021).

Conversely, human intervention can play a major role in reducing the consequences of incidents, though it is difficult to clearly quantify these effects even on conventional vessels. Wróbel et al. (2017) concludes that the net effect may be negative for uncrewed ships. The design of the autonomous ships and what roles the RCC operators are assigned will have an impact here. What is even more difficult to assess is the number of safety incidents which were worsened through human intervention.

4.13 Better Regulated Shipping

Ships sailing under flags of convenience are sometimes a challenge in today's shipping industry. One of the main reasons for owners choosing this option is to reduce costs, but it can also be to minimize technical requirements and regulation of crew working conditions (ITF, 2022). The authors assess it unlikely that autonomous ships will be under a convenience flag both for cost reasons (see Sect. 4.1) and because the high complexity of such ships requires more competent flag state authorities for the necessary risk and reliability analysis.

Autonomous ships will also be digitalized throughout, and all information about the ship and its operations can be recorded in the RCC. This may enable flag and coastal state authorities to oversee normal operations and more detailed investigate incidents. This should also improve operators' compliance with flag, coast, and port state requirements. One can also expect that insurers will scrutinize how ships are operated and the relationship the operator has to authorities' requirements.

5 Conclusions

In this chapter, our focus has been on "constrained autonomy", i.e., relatively advanced automation on an uncrewed ship which is supported by RCC personnel in more complex situations. Other levels of autonomy may have a different societal impact, but we foresee such differences as a matter of degree rather than on the "types" of impact.

The societal impact created by autonomous shipping is foreseen as largely positive, especially from a Norwegian perspective where no significant negative impacts have been found. Some aspects of societal benefits are very context-dependent, such as the effect on the job market, while others are more generic, such as reduced emissions. Overall, we see a clear link between UN's Sustainable Development Goals and the main attributes of autonomous shipping, although the quantification of these relationships is difficult to define. Currently, several initiatives are developing KPIs for assessing societal impact but we foresee there will always be a need for qualitative assessments in addition to KPIs.

Some of the societal benefits from autonomous ships are what we may call indirect, as autonomous ships in some cases can be seen as an enabler of other measures. This is particularly true in the case of reduced GHG emissions from shipping where the main effect of autonomy is related to the possibility to run on alternative and low-carbon fuels and not autonomous operation per se. Nevertheless, we see this indirect contribution from autonomous shipping as vital for the achievement of the International Maritime Organization (IMO)2030 and IMO2050 goals.

Acknowledgements The work presented in this text has received funding from the European Union's Horizon 2020 research and innovation programme under grant agreement No. 815012 (AUTOSHIP) and grant agreement No. 859992 (AEGIS).

References

AEGIS. (2022). Advanced, Efficient and Green Intermodal Systems, EU Project. https://aegis.autonomous-ship.org/

Akbar, A., Aasen, A. K., Msakni, M. K., Fagerholt, K., Lindstad, E., & Meisel, F. (2021). An Economic Analysis of Introducing Autonomous Ships in a Short-Sea Liner Shipping Network. *International Transactions in Operational Research, 28*(4), 1740–1764.

Alamoush, A. S., Ballini, F., & Dalaklis, D. (2021). Port Sustainable Supply Chain Management Framework: Contributing to the United Nations' Sustainable Development Goals. *Maritime Technology and Research, 3*(2), 137–161.

AUTOSHIP. (2022), *Autonomous Shipping Initiative for European Waters.* https://www.autoship-project.eu/

CCShip. (2021). CCShip—Deploying Carbon Capture and Storage for Ships to Enable Maritime CO_2 Emission Mitigation. Research Project Lead by SINTEF Energy. Funded by the Research Council of Norway. https://prosjektbanken.forskningsradet.no/project/FORISS/320260

CNS. (2021). China's First Autonomous Container Ship Put on Sea Trial. *China News Service.* http://www.ecns.cn/news/cns-wire/2021-09-16/detail-ihaqyxhs7013953.shtml

de Vos, J., Hekkenberg, R. G., & Banda, O. A. V. (2021). The Impact of Autonomous Ships on Safety at Sea–A Statistical Analysis. *Reliability Engineering & System Safety, 210*, 107558.

EU. (2022). EU Platform on Sustainable Finance. Final Report on Social Taxonomy. https://ec.europa.eu/info/sites/default/files/business_economy_euro/banking_and_finance/documents/280222-sustainable-finance-platform-finance-report-social-taxonomy.pdf

Feenstra, M., Monteiro, J., van den Akker, J. T., Abu-Zahra, M. R., Gilling, E., & Goetheer, E. (2019). Ship-Based Carbon Capture Onboard of Diesel or LNG-Fuelled Ships. *International Journal of Greenhouse Gas Control, 85*, 1–10.

FinFerries. (2018). Finferries' Falco World's First Fully Autonomous Ferry. https://www.finferries.fi/en/news/press-releases/finferries-falco-worlds-first-fully-autonomous-ferry.html

Galieriková, A. (2019). The Human Factor and Maritime Safety. *Transportation Research Procedia, 40*, 1319–1326.

Glave T. & Saxon S. (2015). *How to Rethink Pricing at Container Terminals* (Report). McKinsey & Company, Travel, Transport & Logistics.

Gribkovskaia, V., Borgen, H., Holte, E. A., Lindstad, E., & Nordahl, H. (2019). Autonomous Ships for Coastal and Short-Sea Shipping. In *SNAME Maritime Convention*. OnePetro.

Hyke. (2022). https://hydroliftsmartcityferries.com/

ITF (International Transport Workers' Federation). (2022). Flags of Convenience. https://www.itfglobal.org/en/sector/seafarers/flags-of-convenience

Jepsen, J. R., Zhao, Z., & van Leeuwen, W. M. (2015). Seafarer Fatigue: A Review of Risk Factors, Consequences for Seafarers' Health and Safety and Options for Mitigation. *International Maritime Health, 66*(2), 106–117.

KASS. (2022). Korean Autonomous Surface Ship Project. https://kassproject.org/en/main.php

Kim, T. E., Sharma, A., Gausdal, A. H., & Chae, C. J. (2019). Impact of Automation Technology on Gender Parity in Maritime Industry. *WMU Journal of Maritime Affairs, 18*(4), 579–593.

Kongsberg. (2020). Crossing Into New Territory. *The Full Picture Magazine*. https://www.kongsberg.com/maritime/the-full-picture-magazine/2020/12/asko/

Kooij, C., & Hekkenberg, R. (2021). The Effect of Autonomous Systems on the Crew Size of Ships–A Case Study. *Maritime Policy & Management, 48*(6), 860–876.

Kretschmann, L., Burmeister, H. C., & Jahn, C. (2017). Analyzing the Economic Benefit of Unmanned Autonomous Ships: An Exploratory Cost-Comparison Between an Autonomous and a Conventional Bulk Carrier. *Research in Transportation Business & Management, 25*, 76–86.

Lindstad, E. (2020). From Road to Sea With Autonomous Ships. *Presentation at OCEAN Week 2018*. https://nfas.autonomous-ship.org/wp-content/uploads/2020/09/11_lindstad.pdf

Lindstad, E., Lagemann, B., Rialland, A., Gamlem, G. M., & Valland, A. (2021). Reduction of Maritime GHG Emissions and the Potential Role of E-Fuels. *Transportation Research Part d: Transport and Environment, 101*, 103075.

Lucas, D., Jego, C., Jensen, O. C., Loddé, B., Pougnet, R., Dewitte, J. D., Sauvage, T., & Jegaden, D. (2021). Seafarers' Mental Health in the COVID-19 Era: Lost at Sea? *International Maritime Health, 72*(2), 138–141. https://doi.org/10.5603/IMH.2021.0023

Miljødirektoratet. (2020). Klimakur 2030—TILTAK OG MIDLER MOT 2030, M-1625. www.miljodirektoratet.no/klimakur

Msakni, M. K., Akbar, A., Aasen, A. K., Fagerholt, K., Meisel, F., & Lindstad, E. (2020). Can Autonomous Ships Help Short-Sea Shipping Become More Cost-Efficient? In *Operations Research Proceedings 2019* (pp. 389–395). Springer.

MTIF. (2020). Norwegian Ministry of Trade, Industry, and Fisheries: Meld. St. 10 (2020–2021), Grønnere og smartere—morgendagens maritime næring (In Norwegian). Report to Parliament: Greener and Smarter—Tomorrow's Maritime Industry.

NTNU. (2022). Centre for Research-based Innovation (SFI) AutoShip. https://www.ntnu.edu/sfi-autoship

Porathe, T. (2014). Remote Monitoring and Control of Unmanned Vessels–The MUNIN Shore Control Centre. In *Proceedings of the 13th International Conference on Computer Applications and Information Technology in the Maritime Industries (COMPIT '14)* (pp. 460–467).

Roberts, S. E., Nielsen, D., Kotłowski, A., & Jaremin, B. (2014). Fatal Accidents and Injuries Among Merchant Seafarers Worldwide. *Occupational Medicine, 64*(4), 259–266.

Rødseth, Ø. J. (2021). Constrained Autonomy for a Better Human–Automation Interface. In *Sensemaking in Safety Critical and Complex Situations* (pp. 235–247). CRC Press.

Rødseth, Ø. J., & Burmeister, H. C. (2012). Developments Toward the Unmanned Ship. *Proceedings of International Symposium Information on Ships–ISIS, 201*, 30–31.

Seafar. (2022). Seafar Remote Navigation. https://seafar.eu/

Smartere Transport. (2018). Develop a Future Oriented System for Water-borne Passenger Transport in City Areas With Seamless Connectivity to Other Transport Modes and Which Increases Share of Public Transport (In Norwegian). https://www.regjeringen.no/contentassets/827bdf0cac9243dcafd5fa5c12be5456/smartere-transport-i-more-og-romsdal.pdf

SSB. (2022). Statistics Norway. Labour Market and Earnings. https://www.ssb.no/en/arbeid-og-lonn

UN. (2022). Sustainable Development Goals. https://www.un.org/sustainabledevelopment/sustainable-development-goals/

USN. (2021). University of South-Eastern Norway, *Først i verden med ny maritim utdanning*. https://www.usn.no/aktuelt/nyhetsarkiv/forst-i-verden-med-ny-maritim-utdanning

Van Es, T. E. (2019). *Reducing Container Barge in-Port Times: A Simulation Study*. Master thesis, Delft University of Technology, Delft.

Wróbel, K., Montewka, J., & Kujala, P. (2017). Towards the Assessment of Potential Impact of Unmanned Vessels on Maritime Transportation Safety. *Reliability Engineering & System Safety, 165*, 155–169.

Yara. (2018). The First Ever Zero Emission Autonomous Ship. https://www.yara.com/knowledge-grows/game-changer-for-the-environment/

Zeabuz. (2022). https://www.zeabuz.com/

Open Access This chapter is licensed under the terms of the Creative Commons Attribution 4.0 International License (http://creativecommons.org/licenses/by/4.0/), which permits use, sharing, adaptation, distribution and reproduction in any medium or format, as long as you give appropriate credit to the original author(s) and the source, provide a link to the Creative Commons license and indicate if changes were made.

The images or other third party material in this chapter are included in the chapter's Creative Commons license, unless indicated otherwise in a credit line to the material. If material is not included in the chapter's Creative Commons license and your intended use is not permitted by statutory regulation or exceeds the permitted use, you will need to obtain permission directly from the copyright holder.

CHAPTER 19

US Perspectives on Regulating Maritime Autonomy

Annie Brett

1 Introduction

The rapid development of autonomous vessels is forcing regulators around the world to grapple with questions of how to incorporate autonomous vessels into existing regulatory frameworks (Ringbom, 2019). Unmanned vessels create significant conflicts with existing maritime laws, both at the national and international levels (Savitz et al., 2020). The maritime community will need to make considerable changes to current regulations in addition to creating new regulations aimed specifically at governing new uses and consequences of autonomous vessels.

The scope of this regulatory task should not be underestimated: not only do autonomous vessels require substantive changes to legal regimes that have not been updated in decades but the speed of technological

A. Brett (✉)
University of Florida Levin College of Law, Gainesville, FL, USA
e-mail: Brett@law.ufl.edu

© The Author(s), under exclusive license to Springer Nature Switzerland AG 2023

T. M. Johansson et al. (eds.), *Autonomous Vessels in Maritime Affairs*, Studies in National Governance and Emerging Technologies,
https://doi.org/10.1007/978-3-031-24740-8_19

innovation means that these changes must be made rapidly to ensure that autonomous vessels are not operating completely outside of maritime law. This places pressure on regulatory agencies and requires tradeoffs between the speed at which regulations are enacted and the completeness of these regulations. If regulators act quickly, they risk implementing regulation that has been less thoroughly developed or fails to fully anticipate the suite of potential uses and consequences of autonomy. If regulators choose to act slowly and wait until more complete information on autonomy is available, they risk autonomous vessels operating without comprehensive regulation in the interim or private industry and other nations acting first to create conflicting regulations that could become de facto standards.

The United States of America (US) is one of the countries grappling with the question of how to strike this balance and effectively regulate autonomous vessels. While much of the US legal response to autonomous vessels should reflect approved International Maritime Organization (IMO) policies once these are developed, in the absence of concrete international standards, the US, like other maritime nations, is proceeding with its own approach to creating a regulatory framework for autonomous vessels. The US response to autonomous vessels has its own nuances and taken as a case study, highlights overarching challenges with regulating autonomous vessels that can provide insight globally. Ultimately, these national frameworks will likely be completed before the IMO has finalized policies for Maritime Autonomous Surface Ships (MASS), giving the US and other nations that develop their own regulatory systems significant opportunities to serve as models for international frameworks to govern autonomous vessels. The US has been an important participant in international discussions around regulating autonomous vessels and understanding how the US is approaching autonomous vessel regulation at a national level provides insight into how it may approach international negotiations.

This chapter discusses the evolution of maritime autonomy governance in the US, looking to several contemporary examples from other autonomous industries, including airspace and space activities, to understand the US approach to governing autonomous maritime vessels. It evaluates the areas that have received less focus in the US process and recommends further attention be paid to these issues when establishing regulatory frameworks for autonomous vessels in the future.

2 Understanding the US Regulatory Landscape

2.1 US Regulation of Autonomy

The US approach to regulating autonomous systems of all kinds, from aerial drones to self-driving cars to autonomous vessels, reflects the realities and constraints of the US legal system. In general, US lawmakers and regulators have been slow to react to technological advances with new legislation and rules (Mandel, 2009). This is not a unique phenomenon to the US, with many slow-moving regulatory systems around the world struggling to adapt to rapidly changing technologies.

In the US, autonomous technologies so far have not required major new federal legislation from Congress, but instead rely on a complex suite of new implementing rules from federal executive agencies, often in combination with state or local legislation (McNeal, 2014). Developing and implementing these regulations takes years and the consequences of getting regulation wrong are high. Lock-in and political barriers to amending existing regulation often leave little room to adapt regulation over time (Biber, 2013). Laws and policies that are enacted must therefore be flexible enough that they can accommodate rapidly evolving technologies while still being specific enough that they place needed guardrails on the operation of emerging technologies (Ritter & Mayer, 2018).

While regulation of emerging technologies needs time to be developed in a nuanced enough way to be effective, there are also serious consequences to acting too slowly. The US has experienced some of these consequences and lags behind other major developing countries in regulating many Fourth Industrial Revolution technologies. In the world of big data, for instance, the European Union (EU) passed the landmark General Data Protection Regulation in 2016 (Jones & Kaminski, 2021). As of 2022, the US has not only failed to create any equivalent federal data protection legislation but has nothing in the pipeline that suggests that this may be developed soon (Magnuson, 2021). The result of a lack of overarching regulation governing data in the US is a patchwork landscape that is economically costly, leads to widespread violations of fundamental rights, and fails to provide needed regulatory guidance for the future (Devins et al., 2017; Lerman, 2013). The US so far has been willing to accept these consequences as preferable to regulating too quickly and creating ineffective laws.

The US approach to autonomy reflects this overall cautious approach to regulating emerging technologies. The US government has recognized the importance of Artificial Intelligence to the US economy, including autonomous vessels, with numerous Executive Orders and government plans reiterating the need to create clear regulation that incentivizes innovation and prevents adverse outcomes from the deployment of autonomy in the US (Executive Order, 2019). While regulation of autonomous vessels is still in the early stages, the government is further along when it comes to several other use cases of autonomy. Aerial drones, for instance, were some of the earliest examples of actively deployed autonomy in the US and provide a roadmap for how the US may approach regulation of other types of autonomy, including vessels.

Aerial drones were the subject of significant public concern in the US when they first became commercially available, with the potential for privacy violations spurring relatively fast regulatory action (Takahashi, 2012). The Federal Aviation Administration lead the development of a regulatory framework for unmanned aerial systems, ultimately carrying out an extensive rulemaking process specifically for aerial drones (14 CFR). Regulating aerial drones bears many similarities to how vessels may be regulated, from the mobile nature of aerial vehicles through jurisdictions to the broad authority of the FAA to regulate aircraft activities. Despite their different operational environments, aerial drones implicate many of the same regulatory questions as autonomous vessels under US law, from the liability and safety issues created by collisions to the conflicts with existing national and international regulations that may arise. Similar to the FAA's authority over aerial drones, overarching jurisdiction is given to the Coast Guard to regulate vessels, allowing a nationwide approach to regulation that may mirror the FAA's approach to aerial drones. The United States Coast Guard (USCG), due to their own adoption and use of aerial drones to help carry out USCG missions, worked closely with the FAA during their rulemaking process and should be aware of and able to draw on this approach when they craft their own regulatory responses to autonomous vessels.

2.2 US Regulation of Vessels

The USCG is the main regulatory entity overseeing vessel activity in the US. The USCG has wide-ranging authority to carry out eleven missions: Ports, Waterways & Coastal Security; Drug Interdiction; Aids to Navigation; Search & Rescue (SAR); Living Marine Resources; Marine Safety; Defense Readiness (National Security and Military Preparedness);

Migrant Interdiction; Maritime Environmental Protection; Polar, Ice and Alaska Operations; Law Enforcement (NASEM, 2020). The broad sweep of these missions generally gives the USCG considerable latitude to regulate in areas related to their operational needs.

When it comes to the regulation of vessels, USCG has wide authority to create and implement measures intended to ensure safety at sea, enforce environmental provisions, and prevent illegal maritime activity including ensuring that international standards such as International Regulations for Preventing Collisions at Sea, 1972 are implemented and enforced on US vessels. Existing regulations are extensive, dictating the minutiae of how vessels in the US are required to be operated. The advent of autonomous vessels creates challenges in many of the USCG's mission areas and will require significant updates to existing rules and regulations (Allen, 2018). The USCG's authority over vessels and maritime commerce is established by a complex suite of laws that enable the USCG to carry out its eleven missions, many of which are relevant to autonomous vessel use. This chapter does not aim to give a full accounting of this legal authority and the challenges posed by autonomous vessels, work which other maritime stakeholders have already carried out (NASEM, 2020).

The USCG is not the only US federal agency dealing with vessels and maritime operations: other government agencies have responsibilities that overlap with the USCG. The National Oceanic and Atmospheric Administration deals with environmental issues and consumptive uses of marine natural resources. The Department of Transportation has authority over transportation issues, including some related to vessel operations. State and local authorities have significant roles in determining policies for how vessels are used in and around coastal infrastructure such as ports. Long-standing relationships and memorandum of understandings (MOUs) allow the USCG to work closely with these other agencies to ensure coordination in the approach to new issues, however, the US regulatory system remains by and large fragmented between agencies and the approach to autonomous vessels will ultimately be led by the US Coast Guard.

3 US Regulatory Approaches to Autonomous Vessels

The US recognizes the importance of autonomous vessels to the future of the maritime industry and is in the early stages of developing a regulatory framework for autonomous vessels. As in other jurisdictions, existing regulations will need to be adapted to accommodate manning changes and new rules may be needed to fully address the issues posed by maritime autonomy. To date, Congress has not indicated that it plans to enact federal legislation to address autonomous vessels, nor are there clear signals that such legislation is needed. Instead, the regulation of autonomous vessels will likely be left to federal agencies under their existing regulatory authorities. As the agency tasked with regulating vessels and other maritime activities, the US Coast Guard will lead the development and promulgation of regulations aimed at autonomous vessels.

Autonomous vessels are currently used in the US both by government entities and private companies. Leading development and deployment of autonomous vessels is the US Navy, which has been investing in integrating autonomous systems in their operations for over two decades (US Navy, 2004). The Navy is distinct from other autonomous vessel users in the US both for the sheer volume of resources devoted to developing autonomous systems and for the size of the autonomous vessels they are deploying. Unlike other government and private sector actors in the US who primarily use very small, unmanned platforms, the Navy has already completed several trials of relatively large autonomous vessels. The USCG also recognizes the powerful operational advantages of using autonomous vessels and seeks to incorporate autonomous vessels into various parts of USCG missions (Savitz et al., 2020). Unlike the Navy, resource constraints prevent the USCG from playing a significant role in funding research or developing autonomous technologies themselves, instead they seek to be a "fast follower" in adopting autonomous platforms as they become commercially available (NASEM, 2020).

The National Oceanic and Atmospheric Administration (NOAA) is also an early adopter of autonomous vessels. NOAA mainly uses these vessels to obtain scientific information and has been instrumental in incentivizing the development of relatively low-cost, passively powered autonomous observation platforms that are able to be deployed for months at a time and collect data at ocean basin scales (Roemmich et al., 2009). These platforms already play a critical role in supplementing baseline oceanographic data and providing insight about areas that costly and temporally limited research vessels are unable to reach (Roemmich et al.,

2004). Many of the autonomous vessels they use are small enough that they may not ultimately be considered vessels.

Beyond government agencies, the private sector is also looking to autonomous vessels. Private autonomous vessel use in the US is not as advanced as in some other countries, though numerous research & development (R&D) efforts are underway to apply autonomous systems in all areas of maritime operations. One of the most notable emerging uses of autonomous vessels in the US is by the private space industry. Commercial space tourism ventures are adopting autonomous vessels as a mechanism for retrieving rockets after they splash down on their return. This is a critical phase of space operations but there is no clear regulatory regime that governs how these vessels should operate. In lieu of established regulatory oversight, companies are developing agreements on an ad hoc basis with the USCG and other government agencies as needed to allow operations to continue (Marine Exchange, 2020). This ad hoc regime is one that is difficult for all involved participants: the space industry wants additional certainty to understand the legal constraints governing this area of operation, while the USCG is concerned that these arrangements may lead to larger safety issues down the road if these agreements do not fully cover all potential impacts of autonomous vessels, for instance, the safety issues caused by the increased presence of recreational boaters interested in witnessing space vessel retrieval. On both sides, parties realize that the lengthy meetings and collaborations between local government, federal government, and private sector actors required to develop these operating agreements are too time and resource intensive to continue to be feasible as commercial space operations continue to grow. This reflects a tension felt throughout the maritime sector, where private companies are increasingly noting the need for regulatory certainty in order to support investments in autonomous technologies.

Commercial use of autonomous vessels prompted the first steps toward regulatory action by the US Coast Guard in 2020. The rulemaking process for federal agencies in the US is proscribed by the Administrative Procedure Act and entails a multi-step process that allows for public input and iterative refinement of rules before they are finalized. The first stage in this process is often a request for information (RFI) that alerts the public to the fact that an agency is considering regulatory action in a certain area and solicits information from relevant stakeholders to guide the agency as they develop new rules. The next step is to use this information to develop a draft rule, issued under a Notice of Proposed Rulemaking. The public can comment on this draft rule before the agency takes this feedback into account and finalizes the proposed rule and it is enacted in the Code of Federal Regulations.

The USCG is in the early stages of this rulemaking process with regard to autonomous vessels. In August 2020, the Coast Guard issued an initial Request for Information on the "Integration of Automated and Autonomous Commercial Vessels and Vessel Technologies into the Maritime Transportation System (US Coast Guard, 2020)". The Coast Guard's focus in this RFI is informative in understanding the areas the USCG is most likely to focus on for autonomous vessel regulation moving forward. Responses to the RFI in turn highlight areas that industry members and other stakeholders feel are most relevant for the USCG to address as they regulate autonomous vessels.

3.1 Conflicts with Existing Regulation

The primary concern of the USCG, and the many stakeholders submitting responses to the RFI, was the potential conflict between existing USCG regulation and the operation of autonomous vessels. The question of what is a vessel is central to many of these conversations in the US, as it has been in the international discussions led by the IMO (McLaughlin, 2011). The USCG has not weighed in formally on this matter, leaving US stakeholders and academics to continue to speculate about what the defining characteristics of a vessel are (Allen, 2018; Vallejo, 2015). Many comments to the USCG's RFI were addressed to this specific question, with users of smaller autonomous vessels, like NOAA that uses small, passively powered autonomous platforms to collect scientific data, arguing that not all types of autonomous platforms should be considered vessels (NOAA, 2020; Saildrone, 2020). The question of whether autonomous vessels should legally be considered vessels must be addressed to provide regulatory certainty for the maritime industry.

Beyond the threshold question of what constitutes a vessel, many of the issues raised by autonomy that were articulated in the USCG RFI focused on safety and reflect international conversations around harmonizing COLREGs with unmanned vessels (Henderson, 2006; Ringbom, 2019). As US commentators pointed out, several of the USCG's regulations enacting COLREGs set out specific duties for vessels that rely on the assumption that ships are manned and that may be unable to be fulfilled on autonomous vessels (Allen, 2020). These conflicts have been discussed extensively in other jurisdictions and current US discussions reflect these broader concerns (NASEM, 2020). These concrete, legal barriers to autonomous vessel deployment have driven much of the conversation about regulatory structures for autonomous vessels. However, focusing only on these superficially obvious conflicts runs the risk of missing the forest for the trees and undermining the creation of an effective regulatory framework.

3.2 Other Barriers to Autonomous Vessel Deployment

Legal barriers are not the only barriers that must be overcome to allow autonomous vessel deployment. Regulation must also consider the role of informal policy or logistical barriers that may prevent the wide-scale deployment of autonomous vessels. The USCG RFI focused specifically on issues around testing, training, and port infrastructure when considering these other barriers.

Currently, one of the most important stages of autonomous vessel development is testing. In these relatively early stages of autonomy, ensuring that both the public and private sectors can test new technologies safely and economically is critical for fostering innovation in the maritime sector. The US has not yet made as much progress in this area as other countries that have set aside specific areas for testing autonomous vessels. Many stakeholders responding to the RFI noted the importance of developing testing procedures and providing separate, safe areas for testing autonomous vessels without concerns of harming existing marine traffic. The CG has not formally indicated how they plan to move forward in this area, but this will likely be an outcome of the final rulemaking process on autonomous vessels. This is an area where the action is needed quickly, with companies already looking for opportunities to test autonomous technologies safely. This pressure may lead to action outside of the rulemaking process to create ad hoc mechanisms to improve the testing of autonomous platforms.

Another potential barrier to autonomous vessel operation in the US is around ports. These are bottlenecks for existing maritime activities, with many uses crowded together in ways that amplify safety and security risks from autonomous vessels. Ports are jurisdictionally complicated areas, with the USCG working with local port authorities to control and manage traffic, enhancing the difficulty of introducing autonomous vessels into these areas. Several local port authorities responded to the USCG's RFI, stressing the consequences of malfunctioning vessels in and around major ports. Autonomous vessels may exacerbate what are already complex and accident-prone systems. Regulation in these areas must protect existing port functions and navigate the already complex relationships between different authorities and stakeholders. In addition to local port authorities, for example, pilots often also hold significant political power in regard to operations in their local ports. These players must be fully informed and supportive of any USCG approach to regulating autonomous vessel activities near ports.

The last major barrier identified by the USCG and echoed by many of the comments to the RFI, was the need to create a workforce with adequate training in the use of new technologies while at the same time ensuring that existing maritime expertise is maintained (Transportation Trades Division, 2020). Training programs will be essential for educating mariners on emerging forms of autonomy, both for new entrants to the profession as well as continuing education or reskilling programs for those already working on vessels in the US (GMATEK, 2020). The difficulty of implementing an effective training pipeline was highlighted by commenters. The maritime workforce is already challenged in many ways, having diminished rapidly in recent decades (American Bureau of Shipping (AFL-CIO, 2020). There are concerns that autonomy will result in widespread job loss. While many seamen have seen this happen in professions they work closely with, like a longshoreman, it is unclear whether the advent of autonomy will result in a net gain or loss of jobs in the maritime profession. Regardless, the USCG must have a nuanced approach to understanding the workforce consequences of autonomy and supporting the maritime profession in the future.

3.3 *Threats to and from Autonomous Vessels*

Mitigating threats to and from autonomous vessels is top of mind for both the USCG and maritime stakeholders. Understanding and quantifying the risks posed by autonomous vessels and to autonomous vessels are inherently limited due to the lack of historical data on these issues. The difficulty in assessing risk is compounded by uncertainty around how existing maritime liability and other regulatory risk-allocating measures will apply to unmanned vessels. In lieu of quantifiable data, stakeholders are turning to a holistic analysis of maritime operations to understand where the largest threats raised by autonomous vessels are likely to be found.

The general safety risks of autonomous vessels continue to be a large part of the discussion of how these vessels are regulated. In the early days of their development and deployment, there have been significant concerns about how these vessels will be able to interact with other vessels and human activities and how to design autonomous vessels so they are resistant to piracy and other illegal activity. Regulatory adjustments to COLREGs, 1972 and other maritime safety regimes will form an important part of ensuring appropriate safety measures are in place, as will policies put in place by marine classification societies and insurers. For instance, these groups will help to determine what happens when autonomous vessels become disabled due to heavy weather or other circumstances. Breakage is a routine part of vessel operations, ensuring that autonomous vessels are developed with the redundancy necessary to ensure that they can continue to function with limited or no manned repair services available will likely be driven initially by classification and insurance standards. Regardless of the quality of the safety provisions that are put in place, some accidents will nonetheless happen. Understanding how liability and response regimes will apply when dealing with autonomous vessels is a critical area for USCG and other regulatory bodies to address. Beyond physical safety issues, the cybersecurity threats to autonomous vessels were also an important concern for those responding to the USCG's initial RFI due to the lack of crew on board able to respond and override any vessel interference (Mileski, 2018).

4 Conclusions

With the RFI complete and information from maritime stakeholders in hand, the next steps for the USCG will be to create a draft Rule to regulate autonomous vessels in the US. The Coast Guard's RFI and approach to regulating autonomous vessels picked up on many of the essential questions facing autonomous vessel operation and regulation. However, there were a number of important areas that were not as fully considered during this early-stage discussion. Recognizing and addressing these areas is necessary as the USCG and other regulatory bodies move forward with designing governance systems for autonomous vessels.

One theme continually emphasized by stakeholders responding to the USCG RFI was the importance of regulatory certainty in supporting investment in autonomous vessels (American Waterways Operators, 2020). This is a lesson that has also been central to early efforts to regulate space and aerial drone activities. Private companies are less willing to spend significant amounts of money on the R&D needed to develop and deploy autonomous vessels while the future regulatory regime for autonomous vessels remains highly uncertain. Some think that any final regulation that the USCG creates is better than remaining in an uncertain limbo state for years while the pros and cons of smaller issues are debated. In any case, the economic potential for autonomous vessels is significant and eventually likely to make up a significant segment of maritime commerce. Firms that are early movers may have some advantage and regulation ultimately should be established in such a way that not only enables but incentivizes investment in autonomous technology development.

While most of the discussion around autonomous vessels is focused on current use cases and how autonomy will first be adopted by the maritime sector, there are also entirely new uses that regulating agencies must consider. Autonomy will eventually be used for many, if not all, of the purposes existing vessels are used for, but they will also be deployed in new ways. Space activities are one of the most obvious of these new uses, but others from deep-sea mining robots to autonomous devices picking up trash in ocean basins will provide additional stress on existing regulatory regimes that by and large do not contemplate these types of uses. Perhaps the most difficult piece of creating regulation for autonomous vessels will be to try and understand what these emergent uses will look like and to create regulation that is flexible enough to accommodate them as they arise. This is an issue that many other agencies that deal with the regulation of emerging technologies have grappled with, and the USCG approach should look to these other uses cases for lessons learned to improve autonomous vessel regulation.

The USCG's RFI framing reflects the IMO's MASS scoping exercise in considering primarily the autonomy as applied to large commercial vessels. The initial USCG RFI was limited specifically to gathering information about the use of autonomy on commercial vessels. While not explicit in the call for information, most responses dealt with the deployment of autonomy on large cargo vessels specifically. Far fewer entities considered the implications of autonomous fishing vessels, towboats, or other types of commercial vessels. This focus certainly makes sense, given that efforts to commercialize autonomy are currently centered on ocean-going cargo vessels. However, regulatory regimes will need to take into account the myriad of other commercial uses that autonomy will eventually be adapted to. The US recognizes that its regulation of autonomous vessels will ultimately have to harmonize with the IMO's international determinations, processes which the US is actively watching and participating in.

Beyond other commercial uses, it will also be important to understand the impacts of non-commercial use of autonomy in the maritime sector. Regulating these uses separately was an essential feature of the Federal Aviation Administration (FAA) effective response to aerial drones. In the maritime space, scientists are already some of the leading users of autonomous vessels, using these platforms to collect scientific data across large scales. These scientific uses differ meaningfully from the commercial uses contemplated by the USCG's current rulemaking process, most importantly in the size, speed, and potential risk presented by the autonomous vessels. Likewise, while recreational versions of autonomous vessels are not being sold commercially yet, several types of autonomous vessels are being developed and it is only a matter of time before these and other models come to market. Unlike large MASS, scientific and recreational autonomous vessels tend to be considerably smaller, often passively powered, and only capable of moving at speeds of a couple of knots (Saildrone, 2020). These vessels likely will need to be regulated differently than other types of vessels, considerations that the US process has not significantly addressed to date. The FAA's approach with aerial drones separated out certain types of small, non-commercial drones for a more relaxed permitting regime. The USCG could follow this lead, using the existing understanding of what legally comprises a vessel in combination with risk analysis methods to determine thresholds for vessel size, speed, or use under which autonomous platforms may not be considered vessels and could be exempt from more stringent COLREGs requirements. Smaller unmanned platforms that do not meet the legal definition of a vessel will need their own regulatory oversight, though it may be more relaxed in response to the relatively smaller risks posed by these vessels.

Defense and law enforcement uses of autonomous vessels are also on the rise. The advantages of being able to deploy vessels that are unmanned are myriad, allowing vessels to be smaller, lengthening potential deployment times, and decreasing the risk if vessels are disabled or destroyed (US Navy, 2004). Many are thinking about the military uses for autonomous vessels, with many of the world's navies leading technological development of autonomous platforms. In the US, autonomous vessels are also likely to be used heavily by the USCG and other law enforcement agencies to augment existing surveillance infrastructure and increase maritime law enforcement abilities (NASEM, 2020). These new uses will have to comply with legal constraints in the US, for instance through the Fourth Amendment's prohibitions on unreasonable searches and seizures. Additional intervention may ultimately be needed from Congress if it seems that the USCG is overstepping its legal authority in use of autonomous vessels for surveillance or other law enforcement purposes.

The environmental impacts of autonomous vessels and these new uses also must be considered. While there is insufficient research currently available to effectively quantify these impacts, regulatory efforts still should attempt to understand likely environmental outcomes and provide mitigation mechanisms as needed. For example, addressing what should happen to disabled or abandoned autonomous vessels at sea is essential to ensure that these vessels are not merely left drifting the world's oceans, breaking down over time and increasing marine pollution (Hardy & Barlow, 2008; Washington State Department of Ecology Spills Prevention, 2020).

The US regulatory process has also been primarily focused on maritime stakeholder perspectives on the advent of autonomous vessels. This is a fitting focus, but it is one that should not be so primary that other agencies and stakeholders that have information on the impacts of autonomy in non-maritime sectors are overlooked. Other industries, for instance, aviation, are in some ways ahead of the maritime industry in making the transition to autonomy. Likewise, much of the academic research on the impacts of autonomy is taking place outside of the maritime industry. Incorporating lessons learned from these outside sources will be critical in crafting the best possible regulatory structures for autonomous vessels. Current US, and international, discussions have primarily been focused on resolving very maritime-specific issues raised by autonomous vessels, for instance in adjusting the manning requirements articulated in COLREGs. This narrow view is limited. Effective regulatory regimes will depend on having a broad understanding that reaches beyond the niche field of maritime cargo operations. Moving forward, the USCG and other regulatory bodies internationally should actively work to bring in experts from other fields to provide outside perspectives that can help to guide future legal regimes.

References

AFL-CIO Transportation Trades Department. (2020). Comment on Request for Information on Integration of Automated and Autonomous Commercial Vessels and Vessel Technologies into the Maritime Transportation System 85 FR 48548 (October 13, 2020). Available at: https://www.regulations.gov/comment/USCG-2019-0698-0036

Allen, C. (2020). Comment on Request for Information on Integration of Automated and Autonomous Commercial Vessels and Vessel Technologies into the Maritime Transportation System. *Federal Register, 85*, 48548. Available at: https://www.regulations.gov/comment/USCG-2019-0698-0004. Accessed 3 May 2022.

Allen, C. H. (2018). Determining the Legal Status of Unmanned Maritime Vehicles: Formalism vs Functionalism. *Journal of Maritime Law and Commerce, 49*(4), 477.

American Waterways Operators. (2020). Comment on Request for Information on Integration of Automated and Autonomous Commercial Vessels and Vessel Technologies into the Maritime Transportation System. *Federal Register, 85*, 48548. Available at: https://www.regulations.gov/comment/USCG-2019-0698-0024. Accessed 5 May 2022.

Biber, E. (2013). Adaptive Management and the Future of Environmental Law. *Akron Law Review, 46*, 933.

Devins, C., Felin, T., Kauffman, S., & Koppl, R. (2017). The Law and Big Data. *Cornell Journal of Law and Public Policy, 27*(2), 357–413.

Executive Order No. 13,859 (2019). Maintaining American Leadership in Artificial Intelligence.

GMATEK. (2020). Comment on Request for Information on Integration of Automated and Autonomous Commercial Vessels and Vessel Technologies into the Maritime Transportation System. *Federal Register, 85*, 48548. Available at: https://www.regulations.gov/comment/USCG-2019-0698-0019. Accessed 9 May 2022.

Hardy, T., & Barlow, G. (2008). *Unmanned Underwater Vehicle (UUV) Deployment and Retrieval Considerations for Submarines*. International Naval Engineering Conference and Exhibition 2008.

Henderson, C. A. H. (2006). Murky Waters: The Legal Status of Unmanned Undersea Vehicles. *Naval Law Review, 53*, 55.

Jones, M., & Kaminski, M. E. (2021). An American's Guide to the GDPR. *Denver Law Review, 98*, 93–128. Available at: https://ssrn.com/abstract=3620198. Accessed 15 June 2022.

Lerman, J. (2013). Big Data and Its Exclusions. *Stanford Law Review Online, 1*(2011), 55–63.

Magnuson, W. (2021). A Unified Theory of Data. *Harvard Journal on Legislation, 58*, 23.

Mandel, G. N. (2009). Regulating Emerging Technologies. *Law, Innovation and Technology, 1*(1), 75–88.

Marine Exchange of Southern California and Vessel Traffic Service of Los Angeles and Long Beach. (2020). Comment on Request for Information on Integration of Automated and Autonomous Commercial Vessels and Vessel Technologies into the Maritime Transportation System. *Federal Register, 85*, 48548. Available at: https://www.regulations.gov/comment/USCG-2019-0698-0032. Accessed 17 May 2022.

McLaughlin, R. (2011). Unmanned Naval Vehicles at Sea: USVz, UUVs, and the Adequacy of the Law. *Journal of Law Information and Science, 21*, 100. https://doi.org/10.1525/sp.2007.54.1.23

McNeal, G. S. (2014). Drones and Aerial Surveillance: Considerations for legislators. *Brookings Institution: The Robots Are Coming: The Project on Civilian Robotics*. Available at: https://www.brookings.edu/research/drones-and-aerial-surveillance-considerations-for-legislatures/. Accessed 7 June 2022.

Mileski, J. (2018). Cyberattacks on Ships: A Wicked Problem Approach. *Maritime Business Review, 3*(414), 414–417.

NASEM. (2020). *Leveraging Unmanned Systems for Coast Guard Missions*. In Leveraging Unmanned Systems for Coast Guard Missions.

NOAA (2020). Comment on Request for Information on Integration of Automated and Autonomous Commercial Vessels and Vessel Technologies into the Maritime Transportation System. *Federal Register, 85*, 48548. Available at: https://www.regulations.gov/comment/USCG-2019-0698-0027. Accessed 5 May 2022.

Ringbom, H. (2019). Regulating Autonomous Ships—Concepts, Challenges and Precedents. *Ocean Development and International Law, 50*, 1.

Ritter, J., & Mayer, A. (2018). Regulating Data as Property: A New Construct for Moving Forward. *Duke Law & Technology Review, 16*, 220–277. Available at: http://ec.europa.eu/justice/data-protection/international. Accessed 4 June 2022.

Roemmich, D., Johnson, G. C., Riser, S., Davis, R., Gilson, J., Owens, W. B., Garzoli, S. L., Schmid, C., & Ignaszewski, M. (2009). The Argo Program: Observing the Global Ocean with Profiling Floats. *Oceanography, 22*(2), 34–43.

Roemmich, D., Riser, S., Davis, R., & Desaubies, Y. (2004). Autonomous Profiling Floats: Workhorse for Broad-Scale Ocean Observations. *Marine Technology Society Journal, 38*(2), 21–29.

SAILDRONE. (2020). Comment on Request for Information on Integration of Automated and Autonomous Commercial Vessels and Vessel Technologies into the Maritime Transportation System. *Federal Register, 85*, 48548. Available at: https://www.regulations.gov/comment/USCG-2019-0698-0035. Accessed 25 May 2022.

Savitz, S., Davenport, A. C., & Ziegler, M. D. (2020). *The Marine Transportation System, Autonomous Technology, and Implications for the U.S. Coast Guard*. Rand Corporation.

Takahashi, T. T. (2012). Drones and Privacy. *Columbia Science & Technology Law Review, 14*(1), 72.

Transportation Trades Division AFL-CIO. (2020). Comment on Request for Information on Integration of Automated and Autonomous Commercial Vessels and Vessel Technologies into the Maritime Transportation System. *Federal Register, 85*, 48548. Available at: https://www.regulations.gov/comment/USCG-2019-0698-0036. Accessed 22 May 2022.

US Coast Guard. (2020). Request for Information: Integration of Automated and Autonomous Commercial Vessels and Vessel Technologies into the Maritime Transportation System.

US Navy. (2004). *The Navy Unmanned Undersea Vehicle (UUV) Master Plan*. Department of the Navy, Tech. Rep., 127. Available at: https://www.hsdl.org/?view&did=708654. Accessed 13 June 2022.

Vallejo, D. A. G. (2015). Electric Currents: Programming Legal Status into Autonomous Unmanned Maritime Vehicles. *Case Western Reserve Journal of International Law, 47*, 405.

Washington State Department of Ecology Spills Prevention, Preparedness, and Response Program. (2020). Comment on Request for Information on Integration of Automated and Autonomous Commercial Vessels and Vessel Technologies into the Maritime Transportation System. *Federal Register, 85*, 48548. Available at: https://www.regulations.gov/comment/USCG-2019-0698-0037. Accessed 27 May 2022.

PART VIII

Tying the Threads

CHAPTER 20

Autonomous Ships: Where Is It Going from Here?

Paul Topping

1 Introduction

When the topic of autonomous ships comes up, many think of images drawn from science fiction. Completely crewless ships moving goods to and from automated ports that move cargo by robots on and off autonomous trains and trucks, that in turn voyage to automated distribution centers, and so on. Right now, that is more science fiction than reality, but many companies and organizations are working towards some form of that reality.

Much of the work on autonomous ships is more focused on the automation of critical tasks instead. In the near term, most work aims to reduce the load on crews; relieving them of long repetitive labor or manual tracking of data. Gradually, in the future, we may see more automation leading to a degree of autonomy of ships.

P. Topping (✉)
Chamber of Marine Commerce, Ottawa, Canada
e-mail: ptopping@cmc-ccm.com

© The Author(s), under exclusive license to Springer Nature Switzerland AG 2023

T. M. Johansson et al. (eds.), *Autonomous Vessels in Maritime Affairs*, Studies in National Governance and Emerging Technologies,
https://doi.org/10.1007/978-3-031-24740-8_20

This book is the first of two volumes examining autonomy from a vessel perspective. In other words, its focus has been on the ship-side and has examined a dizzying range of complex technological, societal, and legal issues from experts in their fields that contribute to the development of marine autonomous ships systems. This chapter seeks to sum up and tie things together. Like most things in life, each of the issues discussed does not exist on their own alone in a bubble, but often depend on many other things and impact them (for good or for bad).

2 Technological Issues

The following elements briefly explore key components that need to be developed to attain a fully autonomous ship that can load, navigate from one port to the next, unload and manage navigational challenges and port challenges along the way. This book explored the relationships around the world that can lead to greater opportunities to share data and skills needed to innovate in the marine space in general as countries progress along technological readiness levels.

2.1 *Simplifying Vessel Design*

Fully autonomous ships would require a simplified vessel design while adopting sophisticated technology. A crewless vessel would not need accommodation blocks, climate control for humans, galleys, showers, toilets, and the waste management systems that go with them. However, even crewless vessels would need humans to go on board at some point, such as for repairs and maintenance or, as discussed further on, if a vessel is required to be a platform for a rescue effort.

Given the number of parameters that need to be monitored in a ship using conventional internal combustion engines, an emerging direction has been to design autonomous ships to be fully electric. Such a design would remove the need for a lot of complex machinery, fuel management systems, and engine management systems. While this dovetails with greenhouse gas reduction objectives, there is no current electric energy technology commercially available that is capable of powering transoceanic voyages. Most fully autonomous vessels currently in service are small fully electric vessels on very short runs with almost no navigation hazards. In other words, most are small ferries.

2.2 Sensors

The technological issues for automating tasks and autonomy are very broad both for implementing automation and autonomy. The first level of challenge is having sensors that provide sufficient data to control systems to have situational awareness—distance, mass, winds, energy applied, and other conditions that impact the task being automated. Basically, the systems need to be able to "see, hear and feel" as humans would carry out their intended task.

Technologies to "see" include active systems that project energy and sense reflected energy such as radar, lidar, lasers, and infrared. Other systems are passive such as infrared and thermal sensors. Global positioning systems can tell where a ship is with a few meters in some places, but for a ship to navigate in confined waters or in congested waters with multiple vessels (including recreational boats), more immediate situational awareness is needed. The ship needs to "see" the navigation threats around it, such as small recreational vessel traffic or large debris. Automotive technology, such as adaptive cruise control and blind spot alarms, have been successful, but such approaches to assist navigation are only being to be explored in the marine sector.

The need to "hear" stems from traditional alarms and horns from other ships, or shore, or within the ship itself to convey immediate warnings. These now can be managed in other ways; electronic messages would be more precise, but such technology is not yet in place uniformly for machine reading. Much of this issue over time may be replaced by future standards for ship-to-ship automated communications to provide positional information (a possible extension of Automatic Identification System (AIS)) and intentions for navigating closer quarters.

Technologies to "feel" the workings of the ship already exist in many types of sensors onboard from fuel levels, machinery temperatures, and motor operation, vibration sensors, with much integration happening into more centralized control systems onboard. Current sensor and network technologies largely address this and continue to improve the speed and bandwidth of information managed.

New ships have multiple sensors throughout their mechanical spaces that also communicate with shore side (service firms or the ship owner). This has created an environment aboard the newest ships where they now have vast amounts of data to manage—driven by the frequency sensors measure and report. Interoperability will be the key issue. Providers of many technologies often prefer to "own the customer" and make various parts uniquely proprietary—such as the sensors on an engine to only work with the controllers supplied by its manufacturer. One can have all the sensors needed for all ships' functions and the fastest networks to transmit their data onboard and to remote control sites, but if all the data is in different code, or different structures, even the best AI controllers could see compounding errors.

2.3 Controls

The next level is a control system to integrate all combined inputs of sensors under its charge and react as needed to ensure safe and smooth operation. For full-ship autonomy, a control system is needed that integrates and oversees all the other control systems across a ship: from engines, fuel or power, cargo conditions, navigation, communications, and cargo operations control. A key challenge is how the AI needed to operate a ship would manage multiple inputs and likely multiple conflicting sensor inputs.

Ultimately, this gives rise to a need for AI to develop some kind of situational awareness and then a degree of intelligence to analyse the combined inputs and determine actions. Even a remotely operated ship, would need a degree of autonomy to manage itself. Maintaining cargo conditions or responding to an engine fault would be examples, where it would be preferable for the ship to have autonomy to respond quickly rather than through remote control centers, which could be susceptible to communication delays and failures.

This gives rise to decision algorithms and more advanced artificial intelligence. It also gives rise to a need for communication. Finally, "who is in charge?" will be one of the biggest questions in designing control systems and impacting decisions on adopting automation and autonomous ships. This is discussed below in societal issues and legal issues.

A ship does not operate entirely on its own. It voyages under traffic control regimes and various authorities can direct it to slow down, change course, or stop, from governments, ports, waterways, and ship owners themselves. As ships pass by each other or to navigate in traffic, radio communications between ships and between ships and shore are key to avoiding collisions. So how can a fully autonomous ship communicate?

Auto-generated messages can be useful to a degree, but current technology lacks the means to describe all possible situations that a live crew can handle. However, some machine-to-machine communications can provide important information in a clear format to authorities or other ships—if their technologies talk to each other. How would an autonomous ship communicate to a crewed ship it needs to pass? AI generated natural language messages—audio or written, hold promise, but are not near operational use yet. Similarly, AI natural language recognition systems still have shortfalls—especially for languages, dialects, idiom, and accents that differ between such a system's creators and the people it seeks to communicate with.

2.4 Security

Security issues are another key operational concern. This involves both cybersecurity and physical security. In addition to risks by hackers in remote locations, various people still need to board ships, so, even ships' data systems that are "air gapped" (operate with no internet connection) are vulnerable. Cybersecurity incidents on existing systems range from inconveniences to major incidents and have touched the marine sector. Threats originate from small hackers to organized criminal operatives, to hostile state actors with various goals from intelligence collecting, to minor disruptions, and to creating major impacts. An autonomous ship would present a significant target for any of these threat actors.

As more automation is brought online, security plans and measures will need to be updated. At a recent seminar discussing trends in security issues related to ransomware, hijacking control systems, along with other types of hacking and cyber warfare, one expert observed that gone are the days where one designs a system solely for its needs and assumes all interactions will be benign. Yet at the same time, autonomous ships will need interoperability of their systems—which can multiply vulnerabilities—and need to ensure security measures do not hinder that interoperability of a ship's systems.

Security issues should be one of the fundamental design considerations in any technology and should be part of the workflows by ship owners and builders on projects to automate ships. Without such an approach in mind, new systems will be developed with vulnerabilities inherently "baked in". Many might see the risk as low for their trade or profile of their company, but bad actors seeking to damage a target country or industry see a low-profile company or organization as an easier target. So, imagine what may happen if a single vessel's engine controllers are hijacked by a bad actor who makes the vessel randomly accelerate when inside a major port. Now imagine that is a small fully autonomous passenger ferry. Damages could be catastrophic for the ship owner, the port, and wider society for a comparatively low cost to the bad actor. The point is anyone can be a target so all of us need to act in a collective way to work with governments to ensure security standards are effective and cost-efficient and manage the threats we face.

3 Technological Progress

In terms of automation, we are seeing progress in reducing administrative load onboard ships. Deployment of sensors and auto data recording systems eliminates the need for manually reporting or entering data into logs. This supports meeting monitoring requirements under environmental regulations (e.g. quantity, types, and locations of discharges and emissions) tracking shifts of personnel (e.g. for required experience for certification or managing hours of work and rest) and other issues.

Automation can also be used in repetitive high-risk tasks, beginning with things as simple as motorizing lifting appliances and evolving to more sophisticated tasks. Robots are taking on inspection roles in hazardous environments such as inside tanks (low oxygen, toxic gases) or underwater hull structures, with some carrying out minor reports. Navies and organizations involved with salvage and rescue are also developing autonomous and automated vessels.

On navigation applications, we now see automated plotting of optimal routes that integrate weather forecasts, currents, and bathymetric data. As well, there are auto-docking systems are being tested that can guide a ship approaching docks or entering locks. In 2021, a US domestic shipping firm successfully trialed an autopilot system for a challenging narrow waterway with several sharp turns (RAND Logistics and Wärtsilä, 2021).

We also see is progress in cargo loading and unloading. A Canadian firm recently developed a new diesel-electric propelled self-unloading bulk carrier with a new generation of cargo handling system that eliminated the need for shifting the vessel during loading (CSL, 2022).

The technological progress so far supports all the elements for developing a large fully autonomous vessel. As reported in Chapter 3 of this volume, the US Navy successfully completed a trial of a 59-meter unmanned surface vessel making an autonomous voyage from Mobile, Alabama, to Port Hueneme, California. Of the 4700 nautical mile voyage,

97% was in autonomous mode, with crew needed for transiting the Panama Canal. In California, it participated in exercises with crewed vessels operating 98% of that time in autonomous mode and maintained compliance with the International Maritime Organization (IMO) Collision Regulations.

While we are progressing on the technology side, more work is needed on the associated societal issues.

4 Societal Issues

Both ship automation and autonomous ships can bring substantive change that will raise societal questions.

The first one is "do we trust it?". As we see cases of accidents and fatalities reported in autonomous vehicles in cities, society has been growing wary of autonomous transport in general. Automation of onboard ships' systems is generally accepted as it is less public facing. As many early autonomous vessels have been short-run passenger and vehicle ferries, "do we trust it?" can be a question not only of public acceptance but also essential for the commercial viability of some vessels. Key approaches to addressing these concerns are the fact that autonomous vessels and automated onboard systems continue to be regulated and that they have to date operated safely.

Yet the industry needs to pay attention to public concern, as despite data showing increasing automation in new vehicles such as blind spot warning and radar cruise control are reducing accidents, a few accidents profiled in a national news cycle can quickly change many perceptions. As well, while human error can be reduced by replacing humans with machines, the machines were built by humans, so human error is not eliminated, and some amount of error is "baked in". That "baked in" error is also present in all external systems to which the ship needs to navigate safely; from depth soundings to GPS to weather forecasts. What is hoped for is that error is less than the current rates (and experience so far seems to suggest this is the case).

Given automated systems may replace humans, the next question for many from a wider societal view is, "are robots replacing more jobs?". This applies to both ship automation and autonomous ships. Much of the current industry focus is more on shipboard automation which would aim to reduce workloads of crew. Surveys of labor show that seafarers are worried about automation, but see benefits for systems that save time (e.g., dishwashing systems for galley) or enhance safety (docking assistance, inspection robotics). (Chris Given, SIU Canada, Presentation on MASS, May 26). As well, there is currently an overall shortage of officers in the marine sector in many parts of the world (ICS, 2022; ICS & BIMCO, 2021).

In recent years, many traditional industries saw the emergence of disruptive competitors; retail saw online shopping, taxis saw ride-hailing apps, and hotels saw room-sharing applications. It may be possible that a future disruptive investor will create a fleet of fully autonomous ships, but as noted above the state of the technology is not yet there. Yet, disruptive investors may see opportunity in such assumptions and push the development of the technology others see as impossible, even if it takes years. That's what they do.

Another key theme of questions is how autonomous ships will interact with the marine environment and humans. This brings the next question of "How will they interact with humans?" This involves many scenarios from how an autonomous ship would interact with a crewed ship, or shoreside personnel in traffic management as discussed above, and leads to other questions of an autonomous cargo ships be used as vessels of opportunity in search and rescue.

On land, many early autonomous vehicles were only allowed to operate in designated areas or special lanes with implanted sensors to guide them, which of course limited their use. In the marine mode, international ships voyage across waters of multiple jurisdictions, such external dependencies on new types of advanced navigational aids would create issues in countries that are unable to provide them—which would impact shipowners, the customers, and the countries themselves. Hence, autonomous ships so far and those being planned are designed to work without such aids, but to function under existing navigation technologies, namely, GPS and electronic charting.

Questions on how autonomous ships would play with their surrounding environments lead to coastal states' concerns. The nature of global commerce is ships are registered in one country (its flag state) but often trade elsewhere (coastal states). As such, while the flag state is the primary regulator of the ship, the ship operates across many coastal states. As ships get more automated and evolved into autonomous vessels, compatibility challenges between autonomous vessels and coastal states may emerge from an infrastructure and regulatory standpoint.

These concerns have been around for conventional vessels for centuries and are the primary reason the regulation of global maritime shipping is coordinated by the United Nations' IMO. Historically, global standards from IMO allow for a uniform and predictable regulatory environment across the many jurisdictions that a ship may pass through. However, when a public concern arises over some aspect of ships and their operations, coastal states have been known to impose their own rules locally on international shipping. When multiple states act this way, a patchwork of regulations emerges and thus it is important for IMO to get these issues right, which is discussed below.

Autonomous ships can provide the benefit of being able to operate in a high-hazard environment without putting humans in danger. This may involve military use (supply, combat, or routine patrols), delivery of aid in major storms, or salvage of a vessel in rough seas or with hazardous cargo. Military use could involve delivering supplies in a war zone, where it could function as any other civilian ship but without a crew, but it could also mean an autonomous ship functioning like a drone as an active combatant. Given the complexity of decisions in these cases which may carry substantial costs, such as who to rescue or not, who to fire on, and when to cease salvage operations, many of these roles are envisioned with human control.

As new designs of autonomous and automated vessels emerge, new applications will follow, wherever automation makes a desired task possible. One interesting example is a three meter fully autonomous vessel that tows a hydrophone to provide a low-cost means to survey waters for the presence of whales for both researchers studying them and shipowners hoping to avoid collisions with them.

In the end, most questions on autonomous ships need to balance private and public interests, which leads to the first question "can we trust it?" and into legal issues.

5 Legal Issues

What has been discussed so far are both the technical and sociological issues; namely our capacity to develop autonomous ships and how we would then interact with them. Related to this is the law, which for maritime shipping is mainly developed at IMO and implemented by its member states.

5.1 Global Rules

The current global legal framework for both how ships are built and how they operate is all based on conventional ship designs (with internal combustion engines) that are crewed and under the control of a Ship's Master and ship owners or operators. To make autonomous vessels work under this legal regime will likely require substantial changes, which is why IMO is reviewing key rules to see how marine autonomous ship systems fit within its rules and how they should be adapted.

Current rules on the minimum size of a crew would no longer apply for a fully autonomous ship—though it is not hard to see in these early phases a direction to retain some degree of crew of oversight. Another aspect is many rules for ship operations require the master, or some other responsible person, to take responsibility for the vessel (IMO, 2022). IMO also administers compensation and liability rules—which set out compulsory insurance and processes to resolve who pays and how much after an accident. This in turn guides the marine insurance industry in its policies ship owners depend on to manage risk. Liability can include a wide range of damages, loss of the ship, environmental damage, lost or damaged cargoes, and salvage issues. As with earlier changes to online commerce from traditional commerce, the basic structure of liability between parties will likely remain, but some of the specific parties may change. For example, the responsibilities of a ship's Master could be shifted to a remote controller (who may likely retain the Master and Captains qualifications and titles).

As well, ships and their captains have obligations under international law to go to the assistance of vessels in distress and to aid people in distress at sea (IMO et al., 2015). This issue has recently come into stark light with recent tragic refugee migrations by the sea in the English Channel and the Mediterranean Sea. How could this translate to an autonomous vessel solely designed to move cargo with no accommodations, food, sanitary facilities, and means to meet needs? This is an area where there will be likely some give and take between ship design and rules as autonomous ships evolve.

IMO is currently reviewing its framework of regulations from the viewpoint of both automated and autonomous vessels with them to develop a Code on Marine Autonomous Ship Systems (IMO, 2022). Conventional vessels that are highly automated have been shown to have higher compliance rates with rules on keeping records and reporting. Fully autonomous vessels lacking a crew and a master would not fit in IMO current framework. Most fully autonomous vessels are usually of a small enough size that IMO rules do not apply and the large US navy vessels mentioned earlier, being government vessels, are also excluded from IMO rules.

While IMO rules may not fit fully autonomous vessels, and substantial changes are needed, many rules would remain in place. These include rules that govern how a ship is built, how some cargoes need to be managed, how ships are to operate in ship traffic, and standard means of communication. An un-crewed ship would still have an owner or operator who would be responsible for its conduct and for liabilities.

5.2 *National and Local Rules*

Many countries also impose national rules; notably pilotage. Pilotage concerns the practice of specialized navigators, called pilots, who have expertise in navigating local waters. International ship owners rely on pilots to guide their ships safety through inland waters and ultimately to berth. Many governments set requirements for a ship voyaging in specific waters to have a pilot on board.

How could such a requirement be met by crewless autonomous ship? While many see this as a barrier to completely crewless ships, others see this as an opportunity for the use of remote pilotage not unlike remote control.

Other national and local rules concern issues such as speed limits on local waters or avoidance of protected areas, these requirements will need to be communicated to an autonomous ship by its owner or operator.

6 So, Where Is this Going from Here?

While some 1000 autonomous or automated ships are operating worldwide, few are large commercial cargo carriers. This is still in the nascent stages but is growing. The major factor driving these issues that has not yet been mentioned in this chapter is cost. All the technologies involved are in experimental phases and come with very high cost and shipowners currently face extremely high costs for new regulations.

Since 2020, all shipowners had to shift their fuel from traditional heavy fuel oil to fuel oils that meet a sulfur cap of 0.50% and represents a 40% cost premium over traditional fuel. While some 4000 ships (4%–8% of the global fleet) opted for scrubbers to meet emissions standards, this also comes with extra capital costs and operating costs. The cost premium is compounded with the increasing cost of fuel since early 2022 and with much higher costs of future low and zero-carbon fuels (some up twice the price as conventional fuels).

By 2024–2025, most ship owners will need to have fitted systems to treat their ballast water to remove organisms so that they are not released to become invasive species. This would be at a cost range of about $1 million to $10 million per vessel depending on the vessel size and complexity to fit the system.

By 2030, ship owners are expected to meet a requirement to reduce GHG emissions by 40% from 2008 baseline levels, on the way to what many countries expect to be net zero emissions by 2050. To meet such a target both for 2030 and 2050 require shipowners to adopt new fuels and propulsion technology, the costs of which would likely dwarf the previously discussed costs above. As well, future market-based measures will also bring a cost on ship owners.

These costs are on top of the normal operating costs of any vessel, from fuel, maintenance, and crew salaries, to port fees, pilotage fees, insurance, and other fees. Unless a proposal for a fully autonomous vessel is able to show a reasonable return on investment within a short-term period, ship owners are unlikely to be supportive given the cost pressures they face. For shipowners with suitable ships, smaller ones on short commercially stable routes, more automation and autonomy may offer cost savings either on a new build or the conversion of an existing ship.

Proposals for *automating* current ships face considerably less cost and can offer considerable cost savings. Work testing navigational assist and auto-docking systems on large-scale vessels has been underway for at least the last two years. Some are testing systems in challenging waterways to set the bar high (RAND Logistics and Wärtsilä, 2021).

Many new systems to automate onboard tasks do not require a complete retrofit of the ship. They also can make the lives of the crew on board a lot easier by eliminating repetitive mundane tasks, and reducing the risks to the crew by taking measurements remotely in high-hazard areas.

In the near term, ship automation will provide the experience needed to grow towards autonomy.

One final observation may be that we are in a similar period of technological change as the advent of the automobile replaced horse-drawn carriages in many parts of the world. In the earliest days of that change about a century ago, many local authorities made the owner of a "horseless carriage" pay for a man to walk in front of it with a red flag to warn people going about in the community of its presence. Much of this was a reaction to the change itself as it impacted the way people worked and moved about that had been done for centuries. It was a shock for many to see people able to go to places further away and in less time. It was also frightening to some as societies realized how the world would change from that technological step.

Certainly, the review at IMO and the work of smart ports and robotics is taking more of a rational viewpoint to examine the very reasonable regulatory questions to facilitate this change. Work is certainly underway as well in standards issuing organizations, such as the International Organization for Standardization (ISO)s, both to examine risks and standardized responses. As we move forward in time, one wonders if people in the later future may see some of today's industry and regulatory responses as either prudent approaches or another kind of rule to carry a red flag.

References

CSL. (2022). *CSL's New Purpose-Designed Diesel-Electric Self-Unloading Ship Begins Service for Windsor Salt*. Available at: https://www.cslships.com/en/media-center/news-events/csls-new-purpose-designed-diesel-electric-self-unloading-ship-begins; https://mvnukumi.com. Accessed 14 May 2022.

International Chamber of Shipping. (2022). *The Perfect Storm: The Impact of COVID-19 on Shipping, Seafarers and Maritime Labour Markets*. Available at: https://www.ics-shipping.org/publication/the-perfect-storm-the-impact-of-covid-19-on-shipping-seafarers-and-maritime-labour-markets/. Accessed 16 June 2022.

International Chamber of Shipping and Baltic and International Maritime Council. (2021). *BIMCO/ICS Seafarer Workforce Report 2021*. International Chamber of Shipping and BIMCO. Available at: https://www.ics-shipping.org/press-release/new-bimco-ics-seafarer-workforce-report-warns-of-serious-potential-officer-shortage/. Accessed 16 June 2022.

International Maritime Organization. (2022). *In Focus: Autonomous Shipping*. Available at: https://www.imo.org/en/MediaCentre/HotTopics/Pages/Autonomous-shipping.aspx. Accessed 13 May 2022.

International Maritime Organization, United Nations High Commissioner for Refugees, and International Chamber of Shipping. (2015). *Rescue at Sea—A Guide to Principles and Practice as Applied to Refugees and Migrants*. Available at: https://wwwcdn.imo.org/localresources/en/OurWork/Safety/Documents/UNHCR-Rescue_at_Sea-Guide-ENG-screen.pdf. Accessed 13 May 2022.

RAND Logistics and Wärtsilä. (2021). *Sailing Straight and True on Crooked River*. https://www.wartsila.com/voyage/insights/article/sailing-straight-and-true-on-crooked-river?utm_source=google&utm_medium=search-paid&utm_term=auts&utm_content=cta-link&utm_campaign=2021-WV-Search-Article-Crooked-river&gclid=EAIaIQobChMI4_qgpo7d9wIVlseGCh2fwQPaEAAYASAAEgIQj_D_BwE. Accessed 13 May 2022.

The manufacturer's authorised representative in the EU is Springer Nature Customer Service Centre GmbH, Europaplatz 3, 69115 Heidelberg, Germany. If you have any concerns regarding our products, please contact ProductSafety@springernature.com

Printed and bound by CPI Group (UK) Ltd, Croydon, CR0 4YY
30/09/2026
02225228-0005